Procopius

Title: Procopius

Author:

This is an exact replica of a book published in 1896. The book reprint was manually improved by a team of professionals, as opposed to automatic/OCR processes used by some companies. However, the book may still have imperfections such as missing pages, poor pictures, errant marks, etc. that were a part of the original text. We appreciate your understanding of the imperfections which can not be improved, and hope you will enjoy reading this book.

THE ATHENIAN SOCIETY'S
PUBLICATIONS

II

250 Copies of this work have been privately printed on ordinary paper solely for distribution amongst the Members of the Athenian Society. None of these copies are for sale.

5 Special Copies have also been privately printed on Japanese Vellum. None of these copies are for sale.

The Council of the Society pledge themselves never to reprint nor to re-issue in any form.

This Copy is No. 24

PROCOPIUS

LITERALLY AND COMPLETELY TRANSLATED FROM THE GREEK FOR THE FIRST TIME

ATHENS: PRIVATELY PRINTED FOR THE ATHENIAN SOCIETY: MDCCCXCVI

PREFACE

PROCOPIUS, the most important of the Byzantine historians, was born at Caesarea in Palestine towards the beginning of the sixth century of the Christian era. After having for some time practised as a "Rhetorician," that is, advocate or jurist, in his native land, he seems to have migrated early to Byzantium or Constantinople. There he gave lessons in elocution, and acted as counsel in several law-cases. His talents soon attracted attention, and he was promoted to official duties in the service of the State. He was commissioned to accompany the famous Belisarius during his command of the army in the East, in the capacity of Counsellor or Assessor: it is not easy to define exactly the meaning of the Greek term, and the functions it embraced. The term "Judge-Advocate" has been suggested,[1] a legal adviser who had a measure

[1] By Mr. Hodgkin, "Italy and her Invaders," vol. iii., p. 638.

b

PREFACE

of judicial as well as administrative power. From his vivid description of the early years of Justinian's reign, we may conclude that he spent some considerable time at the Byzantine court before setting out for the East, at any rate, until the year 532, when Belisarius returned to the capital: he would thus have been an eye-witness of the " Nika " sedition, which, had it not been for the courage and firmness displayed by Theodora, would probably have resulted in the flight of Justinian, and a change of dynasty.

In 533 he accompanied Belisarius on his expedition to Africa. On the way, he was intrusted with an important mission to Sicily. He appears to have returned to Byzantium with Belisarius in 535. He is heard of again, in 536, as charged with another mission in the neighbourhood of Rome, which shows that, at the end of 535, he had accompanied Belisarius, who had been despatched to Italy and Sicily to conquer the territory in the occupation of the Goths. This expedition terminated successfully by the surrender of Vitiges and his captivity at Byzantium in 540.

As the reward of his services, Justinian

PREFACE

bestowed upon him the title of "Illustrious" (*Illustris*), given to the highest class of public officials, raised him to the rank of a Senator, and, finally, appointed him Praefect of Byzantium in 562. He does not, however, seem to have been altogether satisfied: he complains of having been ill-paid for his labours; for several years he was even without employment. This is all that is known of his life. He died shortly before or after the end of the reign of Justinian (565), when he would have been over sixty years of age.

His career seems to have been as satisfactory as could be reasonably expected, all things being taken into consideration; but the violent hatred displayed by him against Justinian in the "Anecdota" or "Secret History"—if the work be really his[1]—appears to show that he must have had some real or imaginary grounds of complaint; but history throws no light upon these incidents of his political career.

Another question which has been much discussed by the commentators is: "What were the religious opinions of Procopius?"

---

[1] The best modern authorities are agreed that he was really the author.

viii   PREFACE

His own writings do not decide the question ;
he seems to shew a leaning towards heathenism
and Christianity alternately.   The truth seems
to be that, being of a sceptical turn of mind,
he was indifferent ; but that, living under an
orthodox Emperor, he affected the forms and
language of Christianity.   Had he been an
open and avowed adherent of Paganism, he
would scarcely have been admitted to the
Senate or appointed to the important official
position of Praefect of Byzantium. His description of the plague of 543, which is
exceedingly minute in its details, has given
rise to the idea that he was a physician, but
there is no proof of this.   The same thing
might have been with equal justice said of
Thucydides; or we might assert that Procopius
was an architect, on the strength of his having
written the " Buildings."

Procopius, holding a position in a period of
transition between classical Greek and Byzantine literature, is the first and most talented of
Byzantine historians.   His writings are charac-
terized by an energetic combination of the Attic
models of the affected, but often picturesque
style employed by the Byzantine writers.
Although he is not free from errors of taste,
he expresses his ideas with great vigour, and

PREFACE

his thoughts are often worthy of a better age. The information which he has given us is exceedingly valuable. He had ample opportunities of observation, and his works present us with the best picture of the reign of Justinian, so important in Greco-Roman annals.

His chief work is the "Histories," in eight books: two on the Persian wars (408-553), two on the Vandal wars (395-545), and four[1] on the Gothic wars, bringing down the narrative to the beginning of 559. The whole work is very interesting; the descriptions are excellent: in the matter of ethnographical details, Procopius may be said to be without a rival among ancient historians.

He shews equal descriptive talent in his work on the "Buildings" of Justinian, a curious and useful work, but spoiled by excessive adulation of the Emperor. Gibbon is of opinion that it was written with the object of conciliating Justinian, who had been dissatisfied with the too independent judgment of the "Histories." If this be the case, we can understand why the historian avenged himself in the "Secret History,"

[1] Or, rather, three, the fourth being only a kind of supplement.

which is a veritable *chronique scandaleuse* of the Byzantine Court from 549-562. Justinian and Theodora, Belisarius and his wife Antonina, are painted in the blackest colours. Belisarius, who is treated with the least severity, is nevertheless represented as weak and avaricious, capable of any meanness in order to retain the favour of the Court and his military commands, which afforded him the opportunity of amassing enormous wealth. As for Antonina and Theodora, the revelations of the "Secret History" exhibit a mixture of crime and debauchery not less hideous than that displayed by Messalina. Justinian is represented as a monstrous tyrant, at once cunning and stupid, "like an ass," in the the words of the historian, and as the wickedest man that ever lived. The author declares that he and his wife are spirits or demons, who have assumed the form of human beings in order to inflict the greatest possible evils upon mankind. These accusations seem to be founded sometimes upon fact, sometimes upon vague rumours and blind gossip. Generally speaking, the author of the "Secret History" seems sincere, but at the same time he shows a narrowness by confounding all Justinian's acts in one sweeping censure, and

PREFACE   xi

in attributing to him the most incredible re-
finements of political perversity. Critics have
asked the question whether the author of such
a work can be Procopius of Caesarea, the im-
partial historian of the wars. Direct proofs of
authenticity are wanting, since the most ancient
authors who attribute it to him—Suidas and
Nicephorus Callistus—lived centuries later.[1]
But it is easy to understand that a work of
this kind could not be acknowledged by its
author, or published during the lifetime of
Justinian. In later times, it circulated privately, until the lapse of time had rendered
the Byzantine Court indifferent to the hideous

[1] As internal evidence in favour of the identity of
the author of the " Secret History," and the " Wars "
and " Buildings," the few following points, amongst
many, may be noticed. The reference in the preface to
the " History of the Wars," that the author was born at
Caesarea, is more closely defined by the statement in
the " Secret History " that he was from Caesarea in
Palestine; in both works an account of the relations of
Justinian to the Church is promised, but the promise is
not fulfilled. The " Secret History " refers to the
extravagant " building " mania of the Emperor. In all
three works we meet with a constant recurrence of the
same ideas, the same outspoken language, greatly em-
bittered in the " Secret History," the same fanatical
pragmatism, the same association of luck, destiny, and
divinity, of guilt and expiation, the same superstition in
the forms of demonology, belief in dreams and miracles,
and lastly the same commonplaces, expressions, and
isolated words.

picture of the vices of a previous age. The work is evidently that of a contemporary of Justinian; it can only have been written by a functionary familiar with the ins and outs of Court intrigue, who had private grievances of his own to avenge. It is true that it sheds little lustre upon the character of Procopius, since it exhibits him as defaming the character of the masters whom he had formerly served and flattered. But this kind of inconsistency is not uncommon in writers of memoirs, who often revenge themselves posthumously by blackening the reputation of their former masters. Although the author writes under the influence of the most violent resentment, there seems no reason to doubt that, although details may be exaggerated, the work on the whole gives a faithful picture of the Byzantine Court of the period.

The following sketch of the " Character and Histories of Procopius " from Gibbon,[1] although modern authorities have taken exception to it in certain points, will be read with interest: " The events of Justinian's reign, which excite our curious attention by their number, variety, and importance, are

[1] " Decline and Fall," chap. xl.

PREFACE

xiii

diligently related by the secretary of Belisarius, a rhetorician, whom eloquence had promoted to the rank of senator and praefect of Constantinople. According to the vicissitudes of courage or servitude, of favour or disgrace, Procopius successively composed the *history*, the *panegyric*, and the *satire* of his own times. The eight books of the Persian, Vandalic, and Gothic wars, which are continued in the five books of Agathias, deserve our esteem as a laborious and successful imitation of the Attic, or at least of the Asiatic, writers of ancient Greece. His facts are collected from the personal experience and free conversations of a soldier, a statesman, and a traveller; his style continually aspires, and often attains, to the merit of strength and elegance; his reflections, more especially in the speeches which he too frequently inserts, contain a rich fund of political knowledge ; and the historian, excited by the generous ambition of pleasing and instructing posterity, appears to disdain the prejudices of the people and the flattery of courts. The writings of Procopius were read and applauded by his contemporaries; but, although he respectfully laid them at the foot of the throne, the pride of Justinian must have been wounded by the

praise of an hero who perpetually eclipses the glory of his inactive sovereign. The conscious dignity of independence was subdued by the hopes and fears of a slave, and the secretary of Belisarius laboured for pardon and reward in the six books of imperial *edifices*.[1] He had dexterously chosen a subject of apparent splendour, in which he could loudly celebrate the genius, the magnificence, and the piety of a prince, who, both as a conqueror and legislator, had surpassed the puerile virtues of Cyrus and Themistocles. Disappointment might urge the flatterer to secret revenge, and the first glance of favour might again tempt him to suspend and suppress a libel, in which the Roman Cyrus is degraded into an odious and contemptible tyrant, in which both the Emperor and his consort Theodora are seriously represented as two demons, who had assumed a human form for the destruction of mankind. Such base inconsistency must doubtless sully the reputation and detract from the credit of Procopius; yet, after the venom of his malignity has been suffered to exhale, the residue of the 'Anecdotes,' even the most disgraceful facts, some of which had been tenderly hinted

[1] The Ædificia, or "Buildings," of Justinian.

PREFACE   XV

in his public history, are established by their
internal evidence, òr the authentic monuments
of the times."[1] It remains to add that in
some passages, owing to imperfections in the
text or the involved nature of the sentences,
it is difficult to feel sure as to the meaning.
In these the translator can only hope to have
given a rendering which harmonises with the
context and is generally intelligible, even if
the Greek does not seem to have been strictly
followed.

For a clear and succinct account of the
reign of Justinian, the four chapters in Gibbon
(xl.-xliv.), which are generally admitted to be
the most successful in his great work, should
be read.

[1] The article on *Procopius* in the "Encyclopædia
Britannica" (9th edition) by Professor Bryce should
also be consulted.

CONTENTS

INTRODUCTION

PAGE

Arrangement of the work—The manner in which it has
been drawn up—The causes of events omitted in
previous writings—The duty of the historian towards
posterity—Lessons necessary to tyrants—Semiramis,
Sardanapalus, and Nero—Facts relating to Belisarius,
Justinian, and Theodora 1

CHAPTER I

Birth and character of Antonina—Her marriage with
Belisarius—Her adulterous amours—Services rendered
by her to the Empress Theodora—Her passion for the
Thracian Theodosius—Adoption of the latter—The
lovers surprised by Belisarius—His weakness—Revela-
tion made by the slave Macedonia—Flight of Theodosius
—Vengeance of Antonina upon Macedonia, and upon
Constantine, who had spoken insultingly of her—Theodosius refuses to return to her until the departure of
her son Photius—Retirement of Photius—Demands of
Theodosius—His return—Infatuation of Belisarius—His
return to Byzantium—Theodosius enters a cloister at
Ephesus—Despair of Antonina—She causes him to be
recalled—His resistance—His secret return . . . 5

CHAPTER II

Departure of Belisarius, accompanied by the "consular"
Photius, for the war against Chosroes, King of Persia

CONTENTS

PAGE

— Antonina remains at Byzantium — Her intrigues
against Photius—The latter denounces her adulterous
intimacy with Theodosius—Indignation of Belisarius—
His agreement with Photius—His vengeance postponed
—Entry of the Roman army into Persia—Downfall of
John the Cappadocian—Antonina's perjuries—She sets
out for the army—Theodosius sent back to Ephesus—
Capture of Sisauranum—Arrival of Antonina—Retire-
ment of Belisarius—Arethas and the Saracens—Colchis
or Lazica invaded by Chosroes—Capture of Petra—
Reverse sustained by Chosroes—The Huns defeated by
Valerian—Insurrectionist movement amongst the Per-
sians—Letter of Theodora to Zabarganes—Return of
Chosroes to Persia 13

CHAPTER III

Arrest of Antonina—Hesitation of Belisarius—Photius repairs to Ephesus, and extorts from Calligonus a con-
fession of his mistress's secrets—Theodosius, having
taken refuge in a temple, is given up by Andreas the
Bishop—Intervention of Theodora—Photius removes
Theodosius, and puts him away in Cilicia—The latter
and Calligonus set free—The Empress hands over
Antonina's enemies to her—Her vengeance—Punishment of the senator Theodosius—Forced reconciliation
between Belisarius and his wife—Arrest of Photius: his
firmness under torture—Calligonus restored to Antonina
—Theodosius restored to her arms—The Empress's
favours—She promises him a high military command
—His death from dysentery—Long imprisonment of
Photius—Sacred asylums violated—Weakness displayed
by the priests—Deliverance of Photius, who enters a
convent at Jerusalem — Perjury of Belisarius — His
punishment—Failure of the third expedition against
Chosroes—Capture of Callinikus—Roman prisoners—
Belisarius accused of treachery and cowardice . . 23

CONTENTS xix

CHAPTER IV

Illness of Justinian—Resolutions of the army consequent
upon his supposed death—Peter and John the Glutton
denounce Belisarius and Buzes—The latter put away
and tortured—Disgrace of Belisarius—He is superseded
by Martin in the command of the army of the East—
His treasures carried away by Theodora—His friendship
for Antonina—His letter to Belisarius—Submission of
the latter to his wife—Division of his fortune—Betrothal
of Joannina, his daughter, to Anastasius, grandson of
Theodora—Belisarius appointed Count of the Royal
Stable and again commander of the army in Italy—
Comparison of the two expeditions 31

CHAPTER V

Conduct of Belisarius in Italy—His greed—Defection of
Herodianus—Loss of Spoletum—Success of Totila and
his Goths—Rupture with John—Betrothal of the latter
to Justina, daughter of Germanus—Recall of Belisarius
—Perusia taken by the Goths—The marriage between
Joannina and Anastasius consummated by a trick on the
part of the dying Empress—Return of Antonina, who
separates the young pair—Belisarius despised for his
weakness—Sergius causes the loss of the Roman army
in Africa — Murder of Pegasius by Solomon — The
vengeance of Heaven 41

CHAPTER VI

History of Justin and his two brothers, poor Illyrian hus-
bandmen—Their enrolment in the army—Their admission into the Palace Guards, in the reign of Leo—
Justin condemned to death, during the reign of
Anastasius, by the General John Kyrtus, for some
breach of discipline—His escape by divine intervention
—He becomes praefect of the Praetorian guards—In
spite of his ignorance, he is proclaimed Emperor—The

way in which he was assisted to sign imperial documents—The Empress Lupicina-Euphemia—Justinian, the nephew of Justin, the real master of the Empire—His cruelty, his avarice, his inconsistency in regard to the laws—He oppresses Italy, Africa, and the rest of the Empire—Amantius condemned, to avenge an outrage upon the bishop John—Perjury towards Vitalianus 50

CHAPTER VII

Byzantium divided between two factions : the Blues and the Greens—Justinian puts himself at the head of the former—The Empire entirely upset by the quarrels between these factions—The Blues dress their hair after the manner of the Huns—Their general attire—Their excesses—Behaviour of the Greens—Corruption of the morals of young men—Murder committed with impunity—Inaction on the part of the authorities—Acts of violence committed upon both sexes—A woman throws herself into the sea to save her virtue—Culpability of Justinian—His partiality for the oppressors, upon whom he bestows favours and dignities . . 56

CHAPTER VIII

Calamities in the provinces—Justinian's apathy—Waste of the public money during his reign—Useless presents of money made to the Huns—Extravagance in buildings on the sea-shore—Attack upon the fortunes of private individuals—Description of Justinian's personal appearance—His resemblance to Domitian—Domitian's wife—Alterations in established institutions . . 65

CHAPTER IX

The bear-keeper Acacius, Theodora's father—His widow loses her place in the amphitheatre of the Greens and takes another in that of the Blues—Her daughters—The beginning of Theodora's career—Her precocious

CONTENTS

xxi

PAGE

immorality—Her accomplishments—Her debaucheries—Her intercourse with Hecebolus, governor of Pentapolis—Her return from the East—Justinian, enamoured of her, wishes to marry her—Assassination of Hypatius—The Praefect Theodotus Colocynthius—Punishment of malefactors—His exile and death . . 73

CHAPTER X

The Empress Euphemia—Her opposition to the marriage of Justinian and Theodora—Justin repeals the law prohibiting the marriage of a patrician with a stage-performer—Justinian and Theodora colleagues on the throne—Death of Justin—Effect of the marriage—Adulation of the senate, clergy, people, and army—General feeling of discouragement—Personal advantages of Theodora—Pretended antagonism between her and Justinian—Theodora deceives the Christians and the factions—Consolidation of despotism . . 84

CHAPTER XI

Legislative innovations—Avarice and cruelty of Justinian—Barbarian invasions provoked—Exorbitant subsidies to the chiefs of the Huns and Chosroes King of Persia, followed by disturbances and violation of truce—Saracens, Slavs, Antes, and other barbarous peoples—Desolation of the provinces—Religious persecutions and confiscation of Church property—Montanists, Sabbatians, Arians, and Samaritans—Pretended conversions—Manicheans and Polytheists—Caesarea, the author's birthplace—Revolt of the peasants under Julian—Hellenism—Law against paederasty—Persecution of astrologers—Continuous emigration . . . 91

CHAPTER XII

Downfall and death of Zeno, grandson of Anthemius, Emperor of the West—Robbery of Tatian, Demosthenes,

xxii CONTENTS

PAGE

the wealthy Hilara, Dionysus of Libanus and John
of Edessa—Forged wills—Theodora and Justinian evil
spirits, not simple human beings—Justinian the putative
son of Sabbatius—His mother's intimate relations with
a spirit—The adventure of a monk—Justinian's temperate manner of living—His fondness for women—
Theodora's intercourse with a spirit—Reputation of
Macedonia during Justin's time—Her prediction to
Theodora—Dream of her marriage with the Prince
of the Demons 100

CHAPTER XIII

Justinian's qualities—His accessibility—His partiality for
the clergy—His gifts to the churches—His passion for
blood and money, shared by him with Theodora—
Flattery of Tribonianus — Justinian's fickleness and
ill-faith—Venality of justice—Corruption of officials—
Justinian's fasting and temperate mode of life . . 109

CHAPTER XIV

Abolition of various old customs—The attributes of the
quaestor and imperial secretaries—The senate a mere
cipher—Corruption of the "Referendaries"—Guilty
conduct of Zeno, the Cilician 116

CHAPTER XV

Cruelty of Theodora—Her voluptuous life—Her ambition
—Her character and Justinian's compared—Her harsh-
ness towards persons of rank—Their servility—Pretended mildness of Justinian—Theodora's eagerness for
vengeance—Her partiality—The insult offered by her
to a patrician—Her stay at Heraeum, on the sea-shore 122

CHAPTER XVI

Assassination of Amalasunta, Queen of the Goths, by Peter,
Theodora's agent—The secretary, Priscus, obliged to

CONTENTS xxiii

PAGE

enter a cloister—Justinian's hypocrisy—Disgrace of
Areobindus, Theodora's lover—Her way of getting rid
of persons of rank—Punishment of Basianus—False
accusation against Diogenes, a member of the municipal
council—Suborning of witnesses—Theodora's courage . 130

CHAPTER XVII

Murder of Callinicus, governor of Cilicia—His property
confiscated by Justinian—Theodora's severe measures
against prostitutes—She compels two girls of noble
birth to marry—Her frequent abortions—Disappear-
ance of her natural son, John—Corrupt morals of the
ladies of the capital—Theodora disposes of ecclesiastical
dignities—Takes upon herself the general superintend-
ence of marriages—Adventure of Saturninus—Persecution of John of Cappadocia 138

CHAPTER XVIII

Justinian, a devil in the form of a man, causes the destruction of millions of men — His policy towards the
Vandals, Goths, and other barbarians—Chosroes and
the Persians—Invasion of the Huns, Saracens, and
others—Justinian's theological studies—Religious persecution—Divine anger—Inundations, earthquakes, and
the plague 149

CHAPTER XIX

A dream relating to Justinian's avarice—The vast treasures
of Anastasius squandered by Justinian—He makes himself master of the fortunes of private individuals by
false accusations, and squanders them in presents of
money to the barbarians, who plunder the Empire—
Fulfilment of the dream 159

xxiv CONTENTS

PAGE

CHAPTER XX

Justinian impoverishes private individuals by "monopolies"
—Two new magistrates appointed at Constantinople—
A Praetor of the People to judge cases of robbery—
Legislation in regard to paederasty and female morality
—Establishment of an inquisition against heretics—
Condemnations and confiscations—Degradation of the
quaestorship in the hands of Junilus and Constantine
—Their venality 164

CHAPTER XXI

The impost called "Aerikon"—Exactions authorised by
Justinian — The property of John the Cappadocian
confiscated—The farming of the taxes entrusted to
salaried commissioners — Increased spoliation — Oath
taken against venality — Increasing corruption of
officials—The Thracians and Illyrians at first check
the depredations of the Huns, Goths, and other barbarians, and then, in turn, take to plundering themselves 171

CHAPTER XXII

John of Cappadocia replaced by Theodotus, and Theodotus
by Peter Barsyames, the Syrian, an old usurer—His
greed—He suppresses the gratuities to the soldiers--
Traffic in every kind of employment—Speculation in
wheat—Scarcity of provisions at Byzantium—Discon-
tent — Barsyames upheld by Theodora and his own
sorceries—His connection with the Manicheans—Their
influence over Justinian—Barsyames supersedes John
of Palestine as treasury minister—He abolishes the
assistance rendered to the unfortunate 179

CHAPTER XXIII

Ruin of private properties—Abolition of the remission of
arrears of taxes, even in the case of cities taken by

CONTENTS   XXV

PAGE

the barbarians—The imposts called Synōnē, Epibolē,
and Diagraphē—Soldiers billeted in private houses   . 188

CHAPTER XXIV

Oppression of the soldiers by the Logothetes—Division of
the soldiers into three classes—Their promotion sus-
pended—Their pay diverted to other purposes—The
diminishing army — Praetorian soldiers disbanded —
Alexander the Logothete in Italy — The general's
aides-de-camp — The frontier garrisons abandoned —
Palace guards, Scholares, and supernumeraries —
Armenians—Peter, the Master of Offices, the murderer
of Amalasunta—Palace officials, Domestics, and Protectors—Suppression of the quinquennial gratuity—
The imperial officers and dignitaries   195

CHAPTER XXV

Unjust treatment of merchants, mariners, and artisans—
The straits of the Bosphorus and the Hellespont
burdened with custom-house dues — Enormous dues
levied by Addens in the port of Byzantium—Change
in the silver coinage: its depreciation—Monopoly of
the silk trade—Ruin of Berytus and Tyre—Malversa-
tions of Peter Barsyames and his successors—Tyranny
of Theodora and avarice of Justinian   202

CHAPTER XXVI

Destruction of city decorations and ornaments—Advocates
deprived of their fees by the institution of arbitrators
—Physicians and professors deprived of their pensions
—Public spectacles discontinued—The consulship suppressed—Scarcity of corn and water at Byzantium,
Rome, and Alexandria—Generosity of Theodoric, the
conqueror of Italy—Greed of Alexander Forficula—

CONTENTS

Disbanding of the garrison of Thermopylae—Spoliation of Athens and other Greek cities—Hephaestus
and Diocletian 210

CHAPTER XXVII

Conduct of Justinian and Theodora in regard to the clergy
and council of Chalcedon—Arsenius the Samaritan per-
secutes the Christians of Scythopolis with impunity—
Paul, archbishop of Alexandria, has the deacon Psoes
put to death—Rhodon, the governor, by his orders,
tortures him : but he is dismissed, and then put to
death, together with Arsenius, through the influence of
Theodora—Liberius, the new governor, and Pelagius,
legate of Pope Vigilius at Alexandria, depose Paul,
who buys back the favour of Justinian—Resistance of
Vigilius—Faustinus, governor of Palestine, denounced
by the Christians as a Samaritan—His condemnation
by the Senate—The sentence annulled by Justinian—
Outrages upon the Christians 221

CHAPTER XXVIII

Laws changed for money considerations—Affair of the
church of Emesa — Priscus the forger — A hundred
years' prescription granted to the churches—Mission
of Longinus—Persecution of the Jews at the Passover
—Justinian's intolerance 228

CHAPTER XXIX

Justinian's hypocrisy—Letters sent to both Liberius and
John Laxarion, confirming them as governors of Egypt
—Intervention of Pelagius and Eudaemon—Murder of
John—Liberius acquitted by the Senate—Fine inflicted
by Justinian—Confiscation of the inheritances of Eudaemon, Euphratas, and Irenaeus—New law as to the
inheritances of municipal councillors—Spoliation of

CONTENTS

xxvii

PAGE

the daughter of Anatolia and Ascalon, the widow of
Mamilianus—Affair of Tarsus—Malthanes and the Blues
of Cilicia — Unpunished assassinations — Justinian's
corruptness—Leo the Referendary 232

Chapter XXX

The "posts" and "spies"—Rapidity of the imperial couriers
—Their chief routes—Superiority of the Persians—Reverses of the Romans in Lazica at the hands of Chosroes
—The army commissariat—Spoliation of the lawyer
Evangelius—Justinian's sarcasm—He and Theodora required their feet to be kissed by those who had audience
of them—Their titles of "master" and "mistress"—
The palace crowded by applicants for audiences—The
death of Justinian alone will show how the vast wealth
of the Empire has been spent 240

THE SECRET HISTORY

OF THE

COURT OF JUSTINIAN

ΠΡΟΚΟΠΙΟΥ ΑΝΕΚΔΟΤΑ

ΠΡΟΟΙΜΙΟΝ.

α'. Ὅσα μὲν οὖν Ῥωμαίων τῷ γένει ἔν τε πολέμοις ἄχρι δεῦρο ξυνηνέχθη γενέσθαι, τῇδέ μοι δεδιήγηται, ᾗπερ δυνατὸν ἐγεγόνει, τῶν πράξεων τὰς δηλώσεις ἁπάσας, ἐπὶ καιρῶν τε καὶ χωρίων ἐπιτηδείων ἁρμοσαμένῳ· τὰ δὲ ἐνθένδε, οὐκ ἔτι μοι τρόπῳ τῷ εἰρημένῳ ξυγκείσεται, ἐπεὶ ἐνταῦθα γεγράψεται πάντα, ὁπόσα δὴ τετύχηκε γενέσθαι πανταχόθι τῆς Ῥωμαίων ἀρχῆς. αἴτιον δέ, ὅτι δὴ οὐχ οἷόν τε ἦν, περιόντων ἔτι τῶν αὐτὰ εἰργασμένων, ὅτῳ δεῖ ἀναγράφεσθαι τρόπῳ. οὔτε γὰρ διαλαθεῖν πλήθη κατασκόπων οἷόν τε ἦν, οὔτε φωραθέντα μὴ ἀπολωλέναι θανάτῳ οἰκτίστῳ·

THE

SECRET HISTORY

OF THE

COURT OF JUSTINIAN

INTRODUCTION

I HAVE thus described the fortunes of the Romans in their wars up to the present day, as far as possible assigning the description of events to their proper times and places. What follows will not be arranged with the same exactness, but everything shall be written down as it took place throughout the whole extent of the Roman empire. My reason for this is, that it would not have been expedient for me to describe these events fully while those who were their authors were still alive; for, had I done so, I could neither have escaped the notice of the multitude of spies, nor, had I been detected, could I

2 ΠΡΟΚΟΠΙΟΥ ΑΝΕΚΔΟΤΑ

οὐδὲ γὰρ ἐπὶ τῶν συγγενῶν, τοῖς γε οἰκειοτά-
τοις τὸ θαρρεῖν εἶχον· ἀλλὰ καὶ πολλῶν, τῶν
ἐν τοῖς ἔμπροσθεν λόγοις εἰρημένων, ἀπο-
κρύψασθαι τὰς αἰτίας ἠναγκάσθην.

β΄. Τὰ τότε δ' οὖν τέως ἄρρητα μείναντα,
καὶ τῶν ἔμπροσθεν δεδηλωμένων, ἐνταῦθά μοι
τοῦ λόγου τὰς αἰτίας σημῆναι δεήσει. Ἀλλά
μοι εἰς ἀγώνισιν ἑτέραν ἰόντι, χαλεπήν τινα
καὶ δεινῶς ἄμαχον, τῶν Ἰουστινιανῷ τε καὶ
Θεοδώρᾳ βεβιωμένων, βαμβαίνειν τε καὶ ἀνα-
ποδίζειν, ἐπὶ πλεῖστον ἐκεῖνο διαριθμουμένῳ
ξυμβαίνει, ὅτι δή μοι ταῦτα ἐν τῷ παρόντι
γεγράψεται, τὰ μήτε πιστὰ, μήτε εἰκότα
φανησόμενα τοῖς ὄπισθεν γενησομένοις, ἄλλως
τε ὁπηνίκα ἐπὶ μέγα ῥεύσας ὁ χρόνος, παλαιο-
τέραν τὴν ἀκοὴν ἀπεργάσεται· δέδοικα, μὴ
καὶ μυθολογίας ἀποίσομαι δόξαν, κἀν τοῖς
τραγῳδοδιδασκάλοις τετάξομαι.

γ΄. Ἐκείνῳ μέντοι τὸ θαρρεῖν ἔχων, οὐκ
ἀποδειλιάσω τὸν ὄγκον τοῦ ἔργου, ὥς μοι οὐκ
ἀμαρτύρητος ὁ λόγος ἐστίν. οἱ γὰρ νῦν ἄν-

COURT OF JUSTINIAN

have avoided a most horrible death; for
I could not even have relied upon my
nearest relatives with confidence. Indeed,
I have been forced to conceal the real
causes of many of the events recounted in
my former books. It will now be my duty,
in this part of my history, to tell what
has hitherto remained untold, and to
state the real motives and origin of the
actions which I have already recounted.
But, when undertaking this new task,
how painful and hard will it be, to be
obliged to falter and contradict myself as
to what I have said about the lives of
Justinian and Theodora: and particularly
so, when I reflect that what I am about
to write will not appear to future genera-
tions either credible or probable, especially
when a long lapse of years shall have
made them old stories; for which reason
I fear that I may be looked upon as
a romancer, and reckoned among play-
wrights. However, I shall have the
courage not to shrink from this important work, because my story will not lack
witnesses; for the men of to-day, who

ΠΡΟΚΟΠΙΟΥ ΑΝΕΚΔΟΤΑ

θρωποι, δαημονέστατοι μάρτυρες τῶν πράξεων
ὄντες, ἀξιόχρεῳ παράπομποι ἐς τὸν ἔπειτα
χρόνον τῆς ὑπὲρ αὐτῶν πίστεως ἔσονται. καίτοι με καὶ ἄλλο τι ἐς λόγον τόνδε ὀργῶντα,
πολλάκις ἐπὶ πλεῖστον ἀνεχαίτισε χρόνον.

δ΄. Ἐδόξασα γὰρ, τοῖς ἐς τὸ ἔπειτα γενησομένοις ἀξύμφορον ἔσεσθαι τοῦτό γε, ἐπεὶ
τῶν ἔργων τὰ πονηρότατα μάλιστα ξυνοίσει
ἄγνωστα χρόνῳ τῷ ὑστέρῳ εἶναι, ἢ τοῖς
τυράννοις ἐς ἀκοὴν ἥκοντα, ζηλωτὰ γίνεσθαι.
τῶν γὰρ κρατούντων ἀεὶ τοῖς πλείστοις εὔ-
πορος ὑπὸ ἀμαθίας, ἡ ἐς τῶν προγεγενημένων
τὰ κακὰ μίμησις, καὶ πρὸς τὰ ἡμαρτημένα
τοῖς παλαιοτέροις ῥᾷόν τε καὶ ἀπονώτερον, ἐς
ἀεὶ τρέπονται.

ε΄. Ἀλλά με ὕστερον, ἐς τῶνδε τῶν ἔργων
τὴν ἱστορίαν τοῦτο ἤνεγκεν, ὅτι δὴ τοῖς ἐς τὸ
ἔπειτα τυραννήσουσιν ἔνδηλον ἔσται, ὡς
μάλιστα μὲν, καὶ τὴν τίσιν αὐτοὺς τῶν
ἁμαρτανομένων περιελθεῖν οὐκ ἀπεικὸς εἴη,
ὅπερ καὶ τοῖσδε τοῖς ἀνθρώποις ξυνηνέχθη
παθεῖν· ἔπειτα δὲ καὶ ἀνάγραπτοι αὐτῶν αἱ
πράξεις, καὶ οἱ τρόποι ἐς ἀεὶ ἔσονται, ἀπ᾽

COURT OF JUSTINIAN

are the best informed witnesses of these facts, will hand on trustworthy testimony of their truth to posterity. Yet, when I was about to undertake this work, another objection often presented itself to my mind, and for a long time held me in suspense.

I doubted whether it would be right to hand down these events to posterity; for the wickedest actions had better remain unknown to future times than come to the ears of tyrants, and be imitated by them. For most rulers are easily led by lack of knowledge into imitating the evil deeds of their predecessors, and find it their easiest plan to walk in the evil ways of their forefathers.

Later, however, I was urged to record these matters, by the reflection that those who hereafter may wish to play the tyrant will clearly see, in the first place, that it is probable that retribution will fall upon them for the evil that they may do, seeing that this was what befell these people; and, secondly, that their actions and habits of life will be pub-

ΠΡΟΚΟΠΟΥ ΑΝΕΚΔΟΤΑ

αὐτοῦ τε ἴσως ὀκνηρότερον παρανομήσουσιν.

θ'. Τίς γὰρ ἂν τὸν Σεμιράμιδος ἀκό-
λαστον βίον, ἢ τὴν Σαρδαναπάλλου καὶ
Νέρωνος μανίαν, τῶν ἐπιγενομένων ἀνθρώπων
ἔγνω, εἰ μὴ τοῖς τότε γεγραφόσι τὰ μνημεῖα
ταῦτ' ἐλέλειπτο; ἄλλως τε καὶ τοῖς τὰ ὅμοια
πεισομένοις, ἂν οὕτω τύχοι, πρὸς τῶν τυράννων
οὐκ ἀκερδὴς αὕτη παντάπασιν ἡ ἀκοὴ ἔσται·
παραμυθεῖσθαι γὰρ οἱ δυστυχοῦντες εἰώθασι,
τῷ μὴ μόνοις σφίσι τὰ δεινὰ ξυμπεσεῖν.

ζ'. Διά τοι ταῦτα πρῶτα μὲν, ὅσα
Βελισαρίῳ μοχθηρὰ εἴργασται, ἐρῶν ἔρχομαι·
ὕστερον δὲ καὶ ὅσα Ἰουστινιανῷ καὶ Θεοδώρᾳ
μοχθηρὰ εἴργασται, ἐγὼ δηλώσω.

COURT OF JUSTINIAN

lished abroad for all time, and therefore they will perhaps be less ready to transgress. Who, among posterity, would have known of the licentious life of Semiramis, or of the madness of Sardanapalus or Nero, if no memorials of them had been left to us by contemporary writers? The description of such things, too, will not be entirely without value to such as hereafter may be so treated by tyrants; for unhappy people are wont to console themselves by the thought that they are not the only persons who have so suffered.

For these reasons, I shall first give a description of the evil wrought by Belisarius, and afterwards I shall describe the misdeeds of Justinian and Theodora.

ΚΕΦΑΛΑΙΟΝ Α΄.

α΄. Ἦν τῷ Βελισαρίῳ γυνὴ, ἧς δὴ ἐν τοῖς ἔμπροσθεν λόγοις ἐμνήσθην, πάππου μὲν καὶ πατρὸς ἡνιόχων, ἔν τε Βυζαντίῳ καὶ Θεσσαλονίκῃ τὸ ἔργον τοῦτο ἐνδειξαμένων, μητρὸς δὲ τῶν τινος ἐν θυμέλῃ πεπορνευμένων. αὕτη τὰ πρότερα μάχλον τινὰ βιώσασα βίον, καὶ τὸν τρόπον ἐξερρωγυῖα, φαρμακεῦσί τε πατρῴοις πολλὰ ὡμιληκυῖα, καὶ τὴν μάθησιν τῶν οἱ ἀναγκαίων ποιησαμένη, ἐγγυητὴ ὕστερον Βελισαρίῳ γυνὴ γέγονε, μήτηρ ἤδη παίδων γενομένη πολλῶν.

β΄. Εὐθὺς μὲν οὖν ἠξίου μοιχεύτρια τὸ ἐξ ἀρχῆς εἶναι, ξυγκαλύπτειν μέντοι τοὔργον τοῦτο ἐν σπουδῇ εἶχεν, ἐγκαταδυομένη τοῖς οἰκείοις ἐπιτηδεύμασιν, οὐδέ τι πρὸς τοῦ ξυνοικοῦντος δειμαίνουσα δέος, (οὔτε γὰρ αἰδὼ

CHAPTER I

THE wife of Belisarius, whom I have spoken of in my previous writings, was the daughter and grand-daughter of chariot-drivers, men who had practised their art in the circus at Byzantium and at Thessalonica. Her mother was one of the prostitutes of the theatre. She herself at first lived a lewd life, giving herself up to unbridled debauchery; besides this, she devoted herself to the study of the drugs which had long been used in her family, and learned the properties of those which were essential for carrying out her plans. At last she was betrothed and married to Belisarius, although she had already borne many children.

She formed adulterous connections as soon as she was married, but took pains to conceal the fact, by making use of familiar artifices, not out of any respect for her husband (for she never felt any

τινα ἔργου ὁτουοῦν ἔλαβε πώποτε, καὶ τὸν
ἄνδρα μαγγανείαις πολλαῖς κατείληφεν), ἀλλὰ
τὴν ἐκ τῆς βασιλίδος ὑποπτεύουσα τίσιν.
λίαν γὰρ ἐς αὐτὴν ἡ Θεοδώρα ἠγριαίνετό τε,
καὶ ἐσεσήρει. ἐπεὶ δὲ αὐτὴν ἐν τοῖς οἱ
ἀναγκαιοτάτοις ὑπουργήσασα χειροήθη πεποίηται, πρῶτα μὲν Σιλβέριον διαχρησαμένη
τρόπῳ, ᾧπερ ἐν τοῖς ὄπισθεν λόγοις εἰρήσεται, ὕστερον δὲ Ἰωάννην κατεργασαμένη
τὸν Καππαδόκην, ὥσπερ μοι ἐν τοῖς ἔμπροσθεν λόγοις ἐρρήθη, ἐνταῦθα δὴ ἀδεέστερόν
τε, καὶ οὐκ ἔτι ἀποκρυπτομένη, ἅπαντα
ἐξαμαρτάνειν οὐδαμῇ ἀπηξίου.

γ'. Ἦν δέ τις νεανίας ἐκ Θράκης ἐν τῇ
Βελισαρίου οἰκίᾳ, Θεοδόσιος τοὔνομα, δόξης
γεγονὼς ἐκ πατέρων Εὐνομιανῶν καλουμένων·
τοῦτον, ἡνίκα ἐς Λιβύην ἀποπλεῖν ἔμελλεν,
ἔλουσε μὲν ὁ Βελισάριος τὸ θεῖον λουτρὸν,
καὶ χερσὶν ἀνελόμενος ἐνθένδε οἰκείαις, εἰσ-
ποιητὸν ἐποιήσατο ξὺν τῇ γυναικὶ παῖδα·
ᾗπερ εἰσποιεῖσθαι Χριστιανοῖς νόμος· καὶ
ἀπ' αὐτοῦ ἡ Ἀντωνίνα τὸν Θεοδόσιον, ἅτε
παῖδα ὄντα ἱερῷ λόγῳ, ἠγάπα τε ὡς τὸ εἰκὸς,

COURT OF JUSTINIAN 6

shame at any crime whatever, and hood-
winked him by enchantments), but because
she dreaded the vengeance of the Empress;
for Theodora was very bitter against her,
and had already shown her teeth. But,
after she had made Theodora her humble
friend by helping her when in the greatest
difficulties, first of all by making away
with Silverius, as shall be told hereafter, and afterwards by ruining John of
Cappadocia, as I have already described,
she became less timid, and, scorning all
concealment, shrank from no kind of
wickedness.

There was a Thracian youth, named
Theodosius, in the household of Belisarius,
who by descent was of the Eunomian
faith. On the eve of his departure for
Libya, Belisarius held the youth over the
font, received him into his arms after
baptism, and thenceforth made him a
member of his household, with the consent
of his wife, according to the Christian
rite of adoption. Antonina therefore received Theodosius as a son consecrated
by religion, and in consequence loved

κἀν τοῖς μάλιστα ἐπιμελομένη, ὑφ' αὑτὴν
εἶχεν· εἶθ' ὕστερον αὐτοῦ ἐρασθεῖσα ἐκτόπως,
ἐν τῷ διάπλῳ τούτῳ, καὶ κατακορὴς γεγονυῖα
τῷ πάθει, ἀπεσείσατο μὲν θείων τε καὶ
ἀνθρωπίνων πραγμάτων δέος τε καὶ αἰδῶ
ξύμπασαν· ἐμίγνυτο δὲ αὐτῷ τὰ μὲν πρῶτα
ἐν παραβύστῳ, τελευτῶσα δὲ, καὶ οἰκετῶν
καὶ θεραπαινίδων παρόντων. κάτοχος γὰρ ἤδη
τῷ πόθῳ τούτῳ γεγενημένη, καὶ διαφανῶς
ἐρωτόληπτος οὖσα, οὐδὲν ἔτι τοῦ ἔργου κώ-
λυμα ἔβλεπε.

δ'. Καί ποτε ὁ Βελισάριος ἐπ' αὐτο-
φώρῳ τὴν πρᾶξιν λαβὼν ἐν Καρχηδόνι,
ἐξηπάτητο πρὸς τῆς γυναικὸς ἑκών γε εἶναι.
ὁ μὲν γὰρ ἄμφω ἐν δωματίῳ καταγείῳ
εὑρὼν ἐμεμήνει· ἡ δὲ οὔτε ἀποδειλιά-
σασα, οὔτε καταδυσαμένη τῷ ἔργῳ τούτῳ,
"Ἐνταῦθα, ἔφη, τῶν λαφύρων τὰ τιμιώτατα
σὺν τῷ νεανίᾳ κρύψουσα ἦλθον, ὡς μὴ ἐς
βασιλέα ἔκπυστα γένηται." Ἡ μὲν οὖν ταῦτα
σκηπτομένη εἶπεν· ὁ δὲ ἀναπεισθῆναι δόξας

COURT OF JUSTINIAN

him, paid him especial attention, and
obtained complete dominion over him.
Afterwards, during this voyage, she became madly enamoured of him, and, being
beside herself with passion, cast away
all fear of everything human or divine,
together with all traces of modesty, and
enjoyed him at first in secret, afterwards
even in the presence of her servants
and handmaidens; for she was by this
time so mad with lust, that she disregarded everything that stood in the
way of her passion.

Once, when they were at Carthage,
Belisarius caught her in the act, but permitted himself to be deceived by his wife.
He found them both together in an underground chamber, and was furiously enraged at the sight; but she showed no
sign of fear or a desire to avoid him, and
said, "I came to this place with this
youth, to hide the most precious part of
our plunder, that the Emperor might not
come to know of it." This she said by
way of an excuse, and he, pretending to
be convinced, let it pass, although he saw

8 ΠΡΟΚΟΠΙΟΥ ΑΝΕΚΔΟΤΑ

ἀφῆκε, καίπερ τῷ Θεοδοσίῳ ἐκλελυμένον τὸν ἱμάντα ὁρῶν, τὸν ἀμφὶ τὰ αἰδοῖα τὰς ἀναξυρίδας ξυνδέοντα. ἔρωτι γὰρ τῆς ἀνθρώπου ἀναγκασθεὶς, ἐβούλετό οἱ τὴν τῶν οἰκείων ὀφθαλμῶν θέαν ὡς ἥκιστα ἀληθίζεσθαι.

ε΄. Τῆς δὲ μαχλοσύνης ἀεὶ προϊούσης ἐς κακὸν ἄφατον, οἱ μὲν ἄλλοι θεώμενοι τὰ πραττόμενα, ἐν σιωπῇ εἶχον· δούλη δέ τις, Μακεδονία ὄνομα, ἐν Συρακούσαις, ἡνίκα Σικελίας ἐκράτησε Βελισάριος, ὅρκοις δεινοτάτοις τὸν δεσπότην καταλαβοῦσα, μὴ ποτε αὐτὴν τῇ κεκτημένῃ καταπροήσεσθαι, πάντα αὐτῷ λόγον ἐξήνεγκε, δύο παιδάρια πρὸς μαρτυρίαν παρασχομένη, οἷς δὴ τὰ ἀμφὶ τὸν κοιτῶνα ὑπηρετεῖν ἐπιμελὲς ἦν.

ς΄. Ταῦτα μαθὼν Βελισάριος, τῶν οἱ ἑπομένων τινὶ τὸν Θεοδόσιον ἐκέλευσε διαχειρίσασθαι. ὁ δὲ προμαθὼν εἰς Ἔφεσον φεύγει. τῶν γὰρ ἑπομένων οἱ πλεῖστοι, τῷ ἀβεβαίῳ τῆς τοῦ ἀνθρώπου γνώμης ἠγμένοι, ἀρέσκειν τὴν γυναῖκα μᾶλλον ἐν σπουδῇ εἶχον, ἢ τῷ ἀνδρὶ δοκεῖν εὐνοϊκῶς ἔχειν, οἵ γε καὶ τὰ σφίσιν ἐπικείμενα τότε ἀμφ'

COURT OF JUSTINIAN 8

that the belt which held Theodosius's drawers over his private parts was undone; for he was so overpowered by his love for the creature that he preferred not to believe his own eyes. However, Antonina's debauchery went on from bad to worse, till it reached a shameful pitch. All who beheld it were silent, except one slave woman, named Macedonia, who, when Belisarius was at Syracuse after the conquest of Sicily, first made her master swear the most solemn oaths that he never would betray her to her mistress, and then told him the whole story, bringing as her witnesses two boys who attended on Antonina's bed-chamber.

When Belisarius heard this, he told some of his guards to make away with Theodosius, but the latter, being warned in time, fled to Ephesus: for the greater part of Belisarius's followers, influenced by the natural weakness of his character, were at more pains to please his wife than to show their devotion to him; and this was why they disclosed to her the orders they had received concerning

ΠΡΟΚΟΠΙΟΥ ΑΝΕΚΔΟΤΑ

αὐτῷ προύδοσαν. Κωνσταντῖνος δὲ, Βελισάριον ὁρῶν περιώδυνον γεγονότα τοῖς ξυμπεσοῦσι, τά τε ἄλλα ξυνήλγει, καὶ τοῦτο ἐπεῖπεν, ὡς· "Ἔγωγε θᾶσσον ἂν τὴν γυναῖκα ἢ τὸν νεανίαν κατειργασάμην." Ὅπερ Ἀντωνίνα μαθοῦσα, κεκρυμμένως αὐτῷ ἐχαλέπαινεν, ὅπως ἔγκοτα ἐνδείξηται τὸ εἰς αὐτὸν ἔχθος. ἦν γὰρ σκορπιώδης τε, καὶ ὀργὴν σκοτεινή.

ζ. Οὐ πολλῷ δὲ ὕστερον, ἢ μαγγανεύσασα, ἢ θωπεύσασα, πείθει τὸν ἄνδρα, ὡς οὐχ ὑγιὲς τὸ κατηγόρημα τὸ ταύτης γένοιτο· καὶ ὃς Θεοδόσιον μὲν μελλήσει οὐδεμιᾷ μετεπέμψατο· Μακεδονίαν δὲ καὶ τὰ παιδία τῇ γυναικὶ ἐκδοῦναι ὑπέστη. οὓς δὴ ἅπαντας πρῶτα τὰς γλώττας, ὥσπερ λέγουσιν, ἀποτεμοῦσα, εἶτα κατὰ βραχὺ κρεουργήσασα, καὶ θυλακίοις ἐμβεβλημένη, ἐς τὴν θάλατταν ὀκνήσει οὐδεμιᾷ ἔρριψε, τῶν τινος οἰκετῶν Εὐγενίου ὄνομα ὑπουργήσαντός οἱ ἐς ἅπαν τὸ ἄγος· ᾧ δὴ καὶ τὸ ἐς Σιλβέριον εἴργασται μίασμα.

COURT OF JUSTINIAN

Theodosius. When Constantine saw Belisarius's sorrow at what had befallen him, he sympathized with him, but was so imprudent as to add: "For my own part, I would have killed the woman rather than the youth."

This having been reported to Antonina, she conceived a secret hatred for him, until she could make him feel the weight of her resentment; for she was like a scorpion, and knew how to hide her venom.

Not long afterwards, either by enchantments or by caresses, she persuaded her husband that the accusation brought against her was false; whereupon, without any hesitation, he sent for Theodosius, and promised to deliver up to his wife Macedonia and the boys, which he afterwards did. It is said that she first cut out their tongues, and then ordered them to be hewn in pieces, put into sacks and thrown into the sea. In this bloody deed she was assisted by one of her slaves named Eugenius, who had also been one of those who perpetrated the outrage on Silverius.

η΄. Καὶ Κωνσταντῖνον δὲ οὐ πολλῷ ὕστερον, Βελισάριος τῇ γυναικὶ ἀναπεισθεὶς κτείνει. Τὰ γὰρ ἀμφὶ τῷ Πραισιδίῳ καὶ τοῖς ξιφιδίοις τηνικάδε ξυνηνέχθη γενέσθαι, ἅπερ μοι ἐν τοῖς ἔμπροσθεν λόγοις δεδήλωται. Μέλλοντος γὰρ τοῦ ἀνθρώπου ἀφίεσθαι, οὐ πρότερον ἀνῆκεν ἡ Ἀντωνίνα, ἕως αὐτὸν τοῦ λόγου ἐτίσατο, οὗπερ ἐγὼ ἀρτίως ἐμνήσθην. Καὶ ἀπ' αὐτοῦ ἔχθος μέγα περιεβάλλετο ὁ Βελισάριος, ἔκ τε βασιλέως, καὶ τῶν ἐν Ῥωμαίοις λογίμων ἁπάντων.

θ΄. Ταῦτα μὲν οὖν τῇδε κεχώρηκε. Θεοδόσιος δὲ οὐκ ἔφη ἐς Ἰταλίαν ἀφίξεσθαι οἷός τε εἶναι, ἵνα δὴ τότε διατριβὴν εἶχον Βελισάριός τε καὶ Ἀντωνίνα, ἢν μὴ Φώτιος ἐκποδὼν γένηται. Ὁ γὰρ Φώτιος πρόχειρος μὲν φύσει ἐς τὸ δάκνεσθαι ἦν· ἤν τις αὐτοῦ παρ' ὁτῳοῦν δύνηται μᾶλλον· ἐν μέντοι τοῖς ἀμφὶ Θεοδοσίῳ, καὶ δικαίως ἀποπνίγεσθαί οἱ ξυνέβαινεν· ὅτι δὴ αὐτὸς μὲν, καίπερ υἱὸς ὢν, ἐν οὐδενὶ ἐγίγνετο λόγῳ· ὁ δὲ δυνάμει τε πολλῇ ἐχρῆτο, καὶ χρήματα μεγάλα περιεβάλλετο. Λέγουσι γὰρ αὐτὸν ἐκ Καρχηδόνος τε καὶ Ῥαβέννης, ἐς ἑκατὸν κεντηνάρια, ἐξ

COURT OF JUSTINIAN

Shortly afterwards, Belisarius was persuaded by his wife to kill Constantine. What I have already recounted about Praesidius and his daggers belongs to this period. Belisarius would have let him go, but Antonina would not rest until she had exacted vengeance for the words which I have just repeated. This murder stirred up a great hatred against Belisarius on the part of the Emperor and of the chief nobles of the Empire.

Such was the course of events. Meanwhile, Theodosius refused to return to Italy, where Belisarius and Antonina were then staying, unless Photius were sent out of the way; for Photius was naturally disposed to show his spite against anyone who supplanted him in another's good graces; but he was quite right in feeling jealous of Theodosius, because he himself, although Antonina's son, was quite neglected, whereas the other was exceedingly powerful and had amassed great riches. They say that he had taken treasure amounting to a hundred centenars of gold [about £400,000] from the treasure-houses of the two cities

ΠΡΟΚΟΠΙΟΥ ΑΝΕΚΔΟΤΑ

ἀμφοῖν παλατίοιν συλήσαντα ἔχειν. ἐπεὶ καὶ μόνῳ κατ᾽ ἐξουσίαν διαχειρίσαι ταῦτα ξυνέβη.

ι΄. Ἡ δὲ Ἀντωνίνα, ἐπεὶ τὴν Θεοδοσίου γνώμην ἔμαθεν, οὐ πρότερον ἀνῆκεν, ἐνεδρεύουσά τε τὸν παῖδα, καὶ φονίοις τισὶν ἐπιβουλαῖς αὐτὸν μετιοῦσα, ἕως καταπράξασθαι ἴσχυσεν αὐτὸν μὲν ἐνθάδε ἀπαλλαγέντα ἐς Βυζάντιον ὁδῷ ἰέναι, οὐκέτι φέρειν τὰς ἐνέδρας οἷόν τε ὄντα· τὸν δὲ Θεοδόσιον ἐς τὴν Ἰταλίαν παρ᾽ αὐτὴν ἥκειν. Οὗ δὴ, κατακόρως τῆς τε τοῦ ἐρωμένου διατριβῆς, καὶ τῆς τοῦ ἀνδρὸς εὐηθείας ἀποναμένη, χρόνῳ ὕστερον ξὺν ἀμφοῖν ἐς Βυζάντιον ἧκεν. Ἔνθα δὴ Θεοδόσιον ἐδεδίσσετο τὸ συνειδέναι, καὶ ἔστρεφεν αὐτοῦ τὴν διάνοιαν. Λήσειν γὰρ ἐς τὸ παντελὲς, οὐδαμῇ ᾤετο· ἐπεὶ τὴν γυναῖκα ἑώρα, οὐκέτι τὸ πάθος ἐγκρυφιάζειν οἵαν τε οὖσαν, οὐδὲ κεκρυμμένως ἐξερρωγέναι, ἀλλὰ διαρρήδην μοιχαλίδα, εἶναί τε καὶ ὀνομάζεσθαι ὡς ἥκιστα ἀπαξιοῦσαν.

ια΄. Διὸ δὴ αὖθις ἐς τὴν Ἔφεσον ἀφι-

COURT OF JUSTINIAN

of Carthage and Ravenna, since he had obtained sole and absolute control of the management of them.

When Antonina heard this determination of Theodosius, she never ceased to lay traps for her son and to concoct unnatural plots against him, until she made him see that he must leave her and retire to Byzantium; for he could no longer endure the designs against his life. At the same time she made Theodosius return to Italy, where she enjoyed to the full the society of her lover, thanks to the easy good-nature of her husband. Later on, she returned to Byzantium in company with both of them. It was there that Theodosius became alarmed lest their intimacy should become known, and was greatly embarrassed, not knowing what to do. That it could remain undetected to the end he felt was impossible, for he saw that the woman was no longer able to conceal her passion, and indulge it in secret, but was an open and avowed adulteress, and did not blush to be called so.

For this reason he returned to

κόμενος, καὶ ἀποθριξάμενος ᾗπερ εἴθισται, ἐνέγραψεν εἰς τοὺς Μοναχοὺς καλουμένους αὐτόν. Τότε δὴ κατ' ἄκρας ἐμάνη, καὶ τὴν ἐσθῆτα ξὺν τῇ διαίτῃ ἐς τρόπον μεταβαλοῦσα τὸν πένθιμον, περιῄει συχνὰ κατὰ τὴν οἰκίαν κωκύουσα, ὀλολυγῇ τε κεχρημένη, ὠλοφύρετο οὐκ ἀπολελειμμένου τἀνδρὸς, ὁποῖον αὐτῇ ἀγαθὸν ὠλώλει, ὡς πιστὸν, ὡς εὔχαριν, ὡς εὐνοϊκὸν, ὡς δραστήριον. Τελευτῶσα δὲ, καὶ τὸν ἄνδρα ἐς ταύτας δὴ ἐπαγαγομένη τὰς ὀλοφύρσεις, ἐκάθισεν. Ἔκαμε γοῦν ὁ ταλαίπωρος, τὸν ποθεινὸν ἀνακαλῶν Θεοδόσιον· ὕστερον καὶ ἐς βασιλέα ἐλθὼν, αὐτόν τε καὶ τὴν βασιλίδα ἱκετεύων, ἀνέπεισε Θεοδόσιον μεταπέμψασθαι, ἅτε ἀναγκαῖον αὐτῷ κατὰ τὴν οἰκίαν ὄντα τε καὶ ἐσόμενον.

ιβʹ. Ἀλλὰ Θεοδόσιος ἀπεῖπε μηδαμῇ ἐνθένδε ἰέναι, ὡς ἀσφαλέστατα ἐμπεδώσειν ἰσχυρισάμενος τὸ τῶν μοναχῶν ἐπιτήδευμα. Ἦν δὲ ἄρα ὁ λόγος κατάπλαστος, ὅπως ἐπειδὰν τάχιστα Βελισάριος ἐκ Βυζαντίου ἀποδημοίη, αὐτὸς παρὰ τὴν Ἀντωνίναν ἀφίκηται λάθρα· ὅπερ οὖν καὶ ἐγένετο.

COURT OF JUSTINIAN 12

Ephesus, and after having submitted to the tonsure, joined the monastic order. At this Antonina entirely lost her reason, showed her distress by putting on mourning and by her general behaviour, and roamed about the house, wailing and lamenting (even in the presence of her husband) the good friend she had lost—so faithful, so pleasant, so tender a companion, so prompt in action. At last she even won over her husband, who began to utter the same lamentations. The poor fool kept calling for the return of his well-beloved Theodosius, and afterwards went to the Emperor and besought him and the Empress, till he prevailed upon them to send for Theodosius, as a man whose services always had been and always would be indispensable in the household. Theodosius, however, refused to obey, declaring that it was his fixed determination to remain in the cloister and embrace the monastic life. But this language was by no means sincere, for it was his intention, as soon as Belisarius left the country, to rejoin Antonina by stealth at Byzantium, as, in fact, he did.

ΚΕΦΑΛΑΙΟΝ Β'.

α΄. Αὐτίκα Βελισάριος μὲν, ὡς Χοσρόῃ πολεμήσων, ξὺν τῷ Φωτίῳ ἐστέλλετο· Ἀντωνίνα δὲ αὐτοῦ ἔμεινεν, οὐκ εἰωθὸς αὐτῇ πρότερον τοῦτό γε. Τοῦ γὰρ μὴ κατὰ μόνας τὸν ἄνθρωπον καθιστάμενον ἐν αὐτῷ τε γενέσθαι, καὶ τῶν ἐκείνης μαγγανευμάτων ὀλιγωροῦντα, φρονῆσαί τι ἀμφ' αὑτῇ τῶν δεόντων, πανταχόσε τῆς γῆς ξὺν αὐτῷ στέλλεσθαι ἐπιμελές οἱ ἐγένετο. Ὅπως δὲ καὶ αὖθις Θεοδοσίῳ παρὰ Ἀντωνίναν ἐσιτητὰ εἴη, Φώτιον ἐκποδών οἱ γενέσθαι ἐν βουλῇ ἐποιεῖτο. Πείθει τοίνυν τῶν Βελισαρίῳ ἑπομένων τινὰς, ἐρεσχελεῖν τε αὐτὸν ἐς ἀεὶ, καὶ προπηλακίζειν, οὐδένα ἀνιέντας καιρόν· αὐτή τε γὰρ, γράφουσα ἐς ἡμέραν σχεδόν τι ἑκάστην, διέβαλλέ τε διηνεκὲς, καὶ ἐπὶ τῷ παιδὶ πάντα ἐκίνει. Οἷς δὴ ὁ νεανίας ἀναγκασθεὶς, διαβόλως ἔγνω τῇ

CHAPTER II

SHORTLY afterwards Belisarius was sent by the Emperor to conduct the war against Chosroes, and Photius accompanied him. Antonina remained behind, contrary to her usual custom; for, before this, she had always desired to accompany her husband on all his travels wherever he went, for fear that, when he was by himself, he might return to his senses, and, despising her enchantments, form a true estimate of her character. But now, in order that Theodosius might have free access to her, Antonina began to intrigue in order to get Photius out of her way. She induced some of Belisarius's suite to lose no opportunity of provoking and insulting him, while she herself wrote letters almost every day, in which she continually slandered her son and set every one against him. Driven to bay, the young man was forced to accuse his mother, and,

ΠΡΟΚΟΠΙΟΥ ΑΝΕΚΔΟΤΑ

μητρὶ χρῆσθαι· ἥκοντά τέ τινα ἐκ Βυζαντίου, ὃς δὴ ἀπήγγελε Θεοδόσιον λάθρα ξὺν 'Αντωνίνῃ διατριβὴν ἔχειν, παρὰ Βελισάριον εὐθὺς εἰσάγει, φράζειν ἐπιστείλας τὸν πάντα λόγον.

β΄. Ἅπερ ἐπεὶ ὁ Βελισάριος ἔγνω, ὀξὺ θυμωθεὶς ὑπερφυῶς, παρὰ τοῦ Φωτίου πόδας ἐπὶ στόμα πίπτει, καὶ αὐτοῦ ἐδεῖτο τιμωρεῖν αὐτῷ, πάσχοντι ὑφ' ὧν ἥκιστα χρῆν ἀνόσια ἔργα, "Ὦ παῖ" λέγων "γλυ-"κύτατε· πατέρα μὲν τὸν σὸν, ὅστις ποτὲ "ἦν, οὐδαμῆ οἶσθα, ἐπεί σε ὑπὸ τιτθοῦ τρε-"φόμενον ἔτι καταλιπὼν, ξυνεμετρήσατο τὸν "ἑαυτοῦ βίον· οὐ μὴν οὐδέ του τῶν αὐτοῦ "ὤνησαι· ἦν γὰρ τὰ ἐς τὴν οὐσίαν οὐ "λίαν εὐδαίμων. Ὑπ' ἐμοὶ δὲ, καίπερ ὄντι "πατρῴῳ, τραφεὶς, τήν τε ἡλικίαν τηλικόσδε "[ἣ], ὡς σὸν εἶναι ἀμύνειν ἀδικουμένῳ μοι "ἐς τὰ μάλιστα, ἔς τε ὑπάτων ἀξίωμα "ἥκεις, καὶ πλούτου περιβέβλησαι τοσόνδε "χρῆμα, ὥστε πατήρ τε καὶ μήτηρ, καὶ τὸ "ξυγγενὲς ἅπαν, ἔγωγε καλοίμην ἂν, ὦ "γενναῖε, καὶ εἴην δικαίως. Οὐχ αἵματι

COURT OF JUSTINIAN

when a witness arrived from Byzantium
who told him of Theodosius's secret com-
merce with Antonina, Photius led him
straightway into the presence of Belisarius
and ordered him to reveal the whole story.

When Belisarius learned this, he flew
into a furious rage, fell at Photius's feet,
and besought him to avenge him for the
cruel wrongs which he had received at
the hands of those who should have been
the last to treat him in such a manner.
" My dearest boy," he exclaimed, " you
have never known your father, whoever
he may have been, for he ended his life
while you were still in your nurse's arms;
his property has been of little or no assistance to you, for he was by no means
wealthy.   Bred under my care, though I
was but your stepfather, you have now
reached an age when you are capable
of assisting me to avenge the wrongs
from which I suffer.   I have raised you
to the consulship, and have heaped riches
upon you, so that I may justly be regarded by you as your father, your
mother, and your whole family; for it is

ΠΡΟΚΟΠΙΟΥ ΑΝΕΚΔΟΤΑ

" γὰρ, ἀλλὰ τοῖς ἔργοις εἰώθασι δῆτα σταθ-
" μᾶσθαι, τὴν ἐς ἀλλήλους στοργὴν, ἄνθρωποι.
" Ὥρα σοι τοίνυν, μὴ περιιδεῖν ἐμὲ μὲν,
" πρὸς τῇ τῆς οἰκίας διαφθορᾷ, καὶ χρη-
" μάτων ἐστερημένον πλῆθος τοσούτων· τὴν
" δὲ μητέρα τὴν σὴν αἶσχος ἀναδουμένην,
" οὕτω δὴ μέγα πρὸς πάντων ἀνθρώπων.
" Ἐνθυμοῦ τε, ὡς αἱ τῶν γυναικῶν ἁμαρτάδες,
" οὐκ ἐπὶ τοὺς ἄνδρας ἵενται μόνον, ἀλλὰ
" καὶ παίδων ἅπτονται μᾶλλον, οὕς γε καὶ
" δόξαν τινὰ φέρεσθαι ἐκ τοῦ ἐπὶ πλεῖστον
" συμβήσεται, ὡς φύσει τὸν τρόπον ταῖς γει-
" ναμέναις ἐοίκασιν. Οὕτωσί τε λογίζου
" περὶ ἐμοῦ, ὡς ἐγὼ τὴν γυναῖκα τὴν
" ἐμαυτοῦ πάνυ μὲν φιλῶ· καὶ ἥν μοι
" τίσασθαι τὸν διαφθορέα τῆς οἰκίας ἐξῆν,
" οὐδὲν αὐτὴν ἐργάσομαι φαῦλον· περιόντος
" δὲ Θεοδοσίου, ταύτῃ τὸ ἔγκλημα ἐπιχω-
" ρεῖν οὐκ ἂν δυναίμην."

γ΄. Ταῦτα ἀκούσας ὁ Φώτιος, ὑπηρετή-
σειν μὲν ὡμολόγει ἐς ἅπαντα· δεδιέναι δὲ

COURT OF JUSTINIAN

not by the ties of blood but by deeds
that men are accustomed to measure
their attachment to each other. The
hour has now come when you must not
remain an indifferent spectator of the
ruin of my house and of the loss with
which I am threatened, of so large a
sum of money, nor of the immeasurable
shame which your mother has incurred
in the sight of all men. Remember that
the sins of women reflect disgrace not
only on their husbands, but also upon
their children, whose honour suffers all
the more because of their natural like-
ness to their mothers.

"Be well assured that, for my own
part, I love my wife with all my heart;
and should it be granted to me to punish
the dishonourer of my house, I will do
her no hurt; but, as long as Theodosius
remains alive, I cannot condone her mis-
conduct."

On hearing these words Photius replied that he would do all that he could
to aid his stepfather, but, at the same
time, he feared that he himself might

μή τι λάβοι ἐνθένδε κακόν· τὸ θαρσεῖν ἐπὶ
τῷ ἀβεβαίῳ τῆς Βελισαρίου γνώμης τά γε
ἐς τὴν γυναῖκα οὐ σφόδρα ἔχων· ἄλλα τε γὰρ
αὐτὸν πολλὰ, καὶ τὸ Μακεδονίας δυσωπεῖν
πάθος. Διὸ δὴ, ἄμφω ἄπαντας ἀλλήλοις
ὠμοσάτην, ὅσοι δὴ ἐν Χριστιανοῖς δεινότατοι
ὅρκοι εἰσί τε καὶ ὀνομάζονται, μήποτε ἀλλή-
λων καταπροήσεσθαι, ἄχρι τῶν ἐς τὸν ὄλεθρον
φερόντων κινδύνων.

δ΄. Ἐν μὲν οὖν τῷ παρόντι, τῷ ἔργῳ
ἐγχειρεῖν ἔδοξε σφίσιν ἀξύμφορον εἶναι·
ὁπηνίκα δὲ Ἀντωνίνα ἐκ Βυζαντίου ἀφίκηται,
ἐς δὲ τὴν Ἔφεσον Θεοδόσιος ἴοι, τηνικάδε
τοῦ χρόνου Φώτιον, ἐν τῇ Ἐφέσῳ γενόμενον,
Θεοδόσιόν τε καὶ τὰ χρήματα, οὐδενὶ πόνῳ
χειρώσασθαι.—Τότε μὲν οὖν, αὐτοί τε τὴν
ἐσβολὴν παντὶ τῷ στρατῷ ἐς τὴν Περσίδα
πεποίηνται χώραν· ἀμφί τε Ἰωάννῃ τῷ
Καππαδόκῃ ἐν Βυζαντίῳ ξυνηνέχθη γενέσθαι,
ἅπερ μοι ἐν τοῖς ἔμπροσθεν λόγοις δεδήλωται.
Ἔνθα δὴ τοῦτό μοι τῷ δέει σεσιώπηται

COURT OF JUSTINIAN 16

come to some harm by so doing; for he was unable to feel any confidence in Belisarius, because of his weakness of character, especially where his wife was concerned. He dreaded the fate of Macedonia, and of many other victims. For this reason he insisted that Belisarius should swear fidelity to him by the most sacred oaths known to Christians, and they bound themselves never to abandon each other, even at the cost of their lives.

For the present, they both agreed that it would be unwise to make any attempt; and they resolved to wait until Antonina had left Byzantium to join them, and Theodosius had returned to Ephesus, which would give Photius the opportunity of going thither and easily disposing of both Theodosius and his fortune. They had just invaded the Persian territory with all their forces, and during this time the ruin of John of Cappadocia was accomplished at Byzantium, as I have told in the former books of my history. I have there only been silent, through fear, on

μόνον, ὅτι γε οὐκ εἰκῆ τόν γε Ἰωάννην καὶ τὴν αὐτοῦ παῖδα ἡ Ἀντωνίνα ἐξηπατήκει, ἀλλ᾽ ὅρκων αὐτοὺς πλήθει, τῶνπερ οὐδὲν φοβερώτερον ἔν γε Χριστιανοῖς εἶναι δοκεῖ, πιστωσαμένη, μηδεμιᾷ δολερᾷ γνώμῃ ἐς αὐτοὺς χρῆσθαι.

ε΄. Ταῦτά τε διαπεπραγμένη, καὶ πολλῷ ἔτι μᾶλλον ἐπὶ τῇ τῆς βασιλίδος θαρροῦσα φιλίᾳ, Θεοδόσιον μὲν ἐς Ἔφεσον στέλλει, αὐτὴ δὲ μηδὲν ὑποτοπάζουσα ἐναντίωμα, ἐπὶ τὴν ἕω κομίζεται. Ἄρτι δὲ Βελισαρίῳ τὸ Σισαυράνων φρούριον ἑλόντι, ὁδῷ ἰοῦσα πρός του ἀναγγέλλεται. Καὶ ὃς, τἆλλα πάντα ἐν οὐδενὶ λόγῳ πεποιημένος, ὀπίσω ὑπῆγε τὸ στράτευμα. Ξυνηνέχθη γὰρ, ἧπέρ μοι τὰ πρότερα δεδιήγηται, καὶ ἕτερα ἄττα ἐν τῷ στρατοπέδῳ γενέσθαι, ἅπερ αὐτὸν ἐς τὴν ἀναχώρησιν ὥρμα. Τοῦτο μέντοι πολλῷ ἔτι θᾶσσον ἐνταῦθα ἀνῆγεν. Ἀλλ᾽ ὅπερ τοῦδε τοῦ λόγου ἀρχόμενος εἶπον, οὔ μοι ἀκίνδυνον τηνικάδε τοῦ χρόνου ἔδοξεν εἶναι, τὰς αἰτίας τῶν πεπραγμένων ἁπάσας εἰπεῖν.

ς΄. Ἔγκλημά τε ἀπ᾽ αὐτοῦ ἐγένετο Βελισαρίῳ πρὸς πάντων Ῥωμαίων· ὅτι δὴ τῆς πολιτείας τὰ καιριώτατα αὐτὸς, περὶ ἐλάσσονος πραγμάτων τῶν κατὰ τὴν οἰκίαν,

COURT OF JUSTINIAN   17

one point, that it was not by mere hazard
that Antonina succeeded in deceiving John
and his daughter, but by numerous oaths,
sworn on all that Christians deem most
holy, she made them believe that she intended to do them no harm.

After this, having risen greatly in
favour with the Empress, she sent Theodosius to Ephesus, and herself, foreseeing
no trouble, set out for the East.

Belisarius had just captured the fortress of Sisauranum, when he was told
of his wife's arrival; whereupon he
immediately ordered his army to turn
back, disregarding the interests of the
Empire for the sake of his private feelings.
Certain matters had indeed happened, as
I have already set forth, which made a
retreat advisable, but his wife's presence
hastened it considerably. But, as I said
at the beginning, I did not then think
it safe to describe the real motives of
men's actions.

Belisarius was reproached by all the
Romans for having sacrificed the interests
of his country to his domestic affairs.

πεποίηται. Ἀρχὴν μὲν γὰρ τῷ τῆς γυναικὸς πάθει ἐχόμενος, ὡς ἀπωτάτω γενέσθαι γῆς τῆς Ῥωμαίων οὐδαμῆ ἤθελεν, ὅπως, ἐπειδὰν τάχιστα πύθηται τὴν γυναῖκα ἐκ Βυζαντίου ἥκειν, ἀναστρέψας, αὐτίκα δὴ μάλα καταλαβεῖν τε, καὶ τίσασθαι οἷός τε εἴη.

ζ. Διὸ δὴ τοὺς μὲν ἀμφὶ Ἀρέθαν Τίγριν ποταμὸν διαβαίνειν ἐκέλευσεν οἵ γε οὐδὲν ὅ τι καὶ λόγου ἄξιον διαπεπραγμένοι, ἐπ᾿ οἴκου ἀπεκομίσθησαν· αὐτὸς δὲ οὐδὲ ὥρας ὁδῷ ἀπολελεῖφθαι ὁρῶν τῶν Ῥωμαίων ἐν σπουδῇ εἶχε. Φρούριον γὰρ τὸ Σισαυράνων, διὰ μὲν πόλεως Νισίβιδος ἰόντι, (οὐ) πλέον ὁδῷ ἡμέρας εὐζώνῳ ἀνδρὶ τῶν Ῥωμαϊκῶν ὁρίων διέχει. Ἑτέρωθι δὲ τούτου δὴ τοῦ μέτρου, ξυμβαίνει τὸ μεταξὺ εἶναι. Καίτοι, εἰ παντὶ τῷ στρατῷ Τίγριν ποταμὸν διαβῆναι κατ᾿ ἀρχὰς ἤθελεν, οἶμαι ἂν αὐτὸν ξύμπαντα λῃίσασθαι τὰ ἐπὶ Ἀσσυρίας χωρία· καὶ μέχρις ἐς Κτησιφῶντα πόλιν, οὐδενὸς τὸ παράπαν ἀντιστατοῦντος σφίσιν, ἀφῖχθαι· καὶ τούς τε Ἀντιοχέων αἰχμαλώτους, ὅσοι τε

COURT OF JUSTINIAN 18

The reason was that, in his first transport of passion against his wife, he could not bring himself to go far away from Roman territory; for he felt that the nearer he was, the easier it would be for him to take vengeance upon Theodosius, as soon as he heard of the arrival of Antonina.

He therefore ordered Arethas and his people to cross the river Tigris, and they returned home, without having performed anything worthy of record, while he himself took care not to retire more than an hour's journey from the Roman frontier. The fortress of Sisauranum, indeed, for an active man, is not more than a day's journey from the frontier by way of Nisibis, and only half that distance if one goes by another route. But had he chosen to cross the river Tigris at first with all his host, I have no doubt that he would have been able to carry off all the riches of Assyria, and extend his conquests as far as the city of Ctesiphon, without meeting with any opposition. He might even have secured the release of the Antiochians, and all

Ῥωμαίων ἄλλοι ἐνταῦθα ὄντες ἐτύγχανον, διασωσάμενον ἐπανήκειν ἐς τὰ πάτρια ἤθη.

η΄. Ἔπειτα δὲ καὶ Χοσρόῃ αἰτιώτατος γέγονεν, ἀδεέστερον ἐπ᾽ οἴκου ἀποκομίζεσθαι ἐκ τῆς Κολχίδος. Ὅντινα δὲ τρόπον τετύχηκε, τοῦτο αὐτίκα δηλώσαιμι. Ἡνίκα Χοσρόης ὁ Καβάδου, εἰς γῆν ἐμβαλὼν τὴν Κολχίδα, τά τε ἄλλα διεπράξατο, ἅπερ μοι ἔμπροσθεν δεδιήγηται, καὶ Πέτραν εἷλε, πολλοὺς τοῦ Μήδων στρατοῦ διεφθάρθαι ξυνέβη, τῷ τε πολέμῳ καὶ ταῖς δυσχωρίαις. Δύσοδός τε γάρ, ὥσπερ μοι εἴρηται, ἡ Λαζικὴ ἐστι καὶ ὅλως κρημνώδης. Καὶ μὴν καὶ λοιμοῦ ἐπιπεσόντος σφίσι, τὸ πλεῖστον τοῦ στρατοῦ ἀπολωλέναι ξυνέπεσε· πολλοὺς δὲ αὐτῶν καὶ τῶν ἀναγκαίων τῇ ἀπορίᾳ διεφθάρθαι ξυνέβη. Ἐν τούτῳ δὲ καί τινες ἐκ γῆς τῆς Περσίδος ἐνταῦθα ἐπιχωριάζοντες, ἤγγελλον, ὡς Ναβέδην μὲν Βελισάριος ἀμφὶ πόλιν Νίσιβιν μάχῃ νικήσας, πρόσω χωροίη· πολιορκίᾳ δὲ τὸ Σισαυράνων ἑλὼν φρούριον, Βλησχάμην τε καὶ Περσῶν ἱππεῖς ὀκτακο-

COURT OF JUSTINIAN

the other Romans who were there in captivity, before returning home.

Furthermore, he was chiefly to blame for the extreme ease with which Chosroes led his army home from Colchis. I will now relate how this came to pass. When Chosroes, the son of Cabades, invaded Colchis, with the result which I have recounted elsewhere, and took Petra, the Medes nevertheless sustained severe losses, both in battle and owing to the difficulties of the country; for, as I have said already, Lazica is a country almost inaccessible, owing to its rocks and precipices. They had at the same time been attacked by pestilence, which carried off the greater part of the troops, and many died from want of food and necessaries. It was at this crisis of affairs that certain men from Persia came into that country, bringing the news that Belisarius had beaten Nabedes in a battle near the city of Nisibis, and was pressing forward; that he had taken the fortress of Sisauranum, and had made prisoners of Bleschames and eight hundred Persian

σίους δορυαλώτους πεποίηται, στράτευμα δὲ
ἄλλο Ῥωμαίων ξύν γε Ἀρέθᾳ, τῷ Σαρακηνῶν
ἄρχοντι, πέμψειεν, ὅπερ διαβὰν ποταμὸν
Τίγριν, ξύμπαντα λεηλατήσει τὰ ἐκείνῃ
χωρία, πρότερον ἀδῄωτα ὄντα.

θ. Ἐτύγχανε δὲ καὶ στράτευμα Οὔννων,
ἐπὶ Ἀρμενίους, τοὺς Ῥωμαίων κατηκόους, ὁ
Χοσρόης στείλας, ὅπως, τῇ ἐς αὐτοὺς ἀσχολίᾳ,
μηδεμία τοῖς ταύτῃ Ῥωμαίοις τῶν ἐν Λαζικῇ
πρασσομένων αἴσθησις γένηται. Τούτους τε
τοὺς βαρβάρους ἀπήγγελλον ἕτεροι, Βαλε-
ριανῷ καὶ Ῥωμαίοις ὑπαντιάσασιν ἐς χεῖρας
ἐλθόντας, παρὰ πολὺ αὐτῶν ἡσσηθέντας τῇ
μάχῃ, ἐκ τοῦ ἐπὶ πλεῖστον ἀπολωλέναι.
Ἅπερ οἱ Πέρσαι ἀκούσαντες, καὶ κακοπαθείᾳ
μὲν τῇ ἐν Λαζοῖς κεκακωμένοι, δεδιότες δὲ
μή τινι ἐν τῇ ἀπορίᾳ ἐντυχόντες πολεμίων
στρατῷ, ἐν κρημνοῖς καὶ χωρίοις λοχμώ-
δεσιν, ἅπαντες οὐδενὶ κόσμῳ διαφθαρεῖεν,
περιδεεῖς ἀμφί τε παισὶ καὶ γυναιξὶ καὶ τῇ
πατρίδι γεγενημένοι, εἴ τι καθαρὸν ἦν ἐν τῷ
Μήδων στρατῷ, Χοσρόῃ ἐλοιδοροῦντο, ἐπικαλοῦντες, ὡς ἔς τε τοὺς ὅρκους ἠσεβηκὼς, καὶ
τὰ κοινὰ νόμιμα πάντων ἀνθρώπων ἐσβάλοι

COURT OF JUSTINIAN 20

lancers; that another corps of Romans
under Arethas, the chief of the Saracens,
had been detached to cross the Tigris,
and ravage the land to the east of that
river, which up to that time had remained free from invasion.

It happened also that the army of
Huns, whom Chosroes had sent into
Roman Armenia, in order, by this diver-
sion, to prevent the Romans from hinder-
ing his expedition against the Lazi, had
fallen in with and been defeated by
Valerian, at the head of a Roman army,
and almost annihilated. When this news
was brought to the Persians, having
been reduced to desperate straits by
their ill success at Lazica, they feared
that, if an army should cut them off in
their critical position, they might all die
of hunger amidst the crags and precipices
of that inaccessible country. They feared,
too, for their children, their wives and
their country; and all the flower of
Chosroes' army railed bitterly at him for
having broken his plighted word and
violated the common law of nations, by

ΠΡΟΚΟΠΙΟΥ ΑΝΕΚΔΟΤΑ

μὲν, ἐν σπονδαῖς, ἐς Ῥωμαίων τὴν γῆν οὐδενὶ προσῆκον· ἀδικοίη δὲ πολιτείαν ἀρχαίαν τε καὶ ἀξιωτάτην πασῶν μάλιστα, ἧς τῷ πολέμῳ περιεῖναι οὐκ ἂν δύναιτο. Ἔμελλον δὲ νεωτέροις ἐγχειρεῖν πράγμασιν. Οἷς δὴ ὁ Χοσρόης ξυνταραχθεὶς, εὕρετο τοῦ κακοῦ ἴασιν τήνδε. Γράμματα γὰρ αὐτοῖς ἀνελέξατο, ἅπερ ἔναγχος ἡ βασιλὶς τῷ Ζαβεργάνῃ ἐτύγχανε γράψασα.

ί. Ἐδήλου δὲ ἡ γραφὴ τάδε· "Ὅπως " σε, ὦ Ζαβεργάνη, διὰ σπουδῆς ἔχω, " εὔνουν σε οἰομένη τοῖς ἡμετέροις πράγμα- " σιν εἶναι, οἶσθα ἐπὶ πρεσβείᾳ οὐ πολλῷ " πρότερον ἐς ἡμᾶς ἀφιγμένος. Οὐκοῦν " [πράττοις] ἂν εἰκό[τα τῇ] δόξῃ, ἣν ἐπὶ " σοὶ ἔχω, εἴ γε βασιλέα Χοσρόην εἰρην[αῖα] " πείθοις ἐς πολιτείαν τὴν ἡμετέραν βούλεσθαι. " Οὕτω γάρ σοι ἀγαθὰ μεγάλα πρὸς ἀνδρὸς " ἀναδέχομαι τοὐμοῦ ἔσεσθαι· ὅς γε οὐδὲν " ἂν ὅ τι καὶ ἄνευ γνώμης τῆς ἐμῆς πράξειεν." Ταῦτα ὁ Χοσρόης ἀναλεξάμενος, ὀνειδίσας τε Περσῶν τοῖς λογίοις εἰ πολιτείαν οἴονται

COURT OF JUSTINIAN

invading a Roman State in a most un-
warrantable manner, in time of peace, and
for having insulted an ancient and most
powerful State which he would not be
able to conquer in war. The soldiers
were on the point of breaking out into
revolt, had not Chosroes, alarmed at the
state of affairs, discovered a remedy for
it. He read to them a letter which the
Empress had just written to Zaberganes,
in the following terms:

" You must know, O Zaberganes, since
you were ambassador at our Court not
long ago, that we are well disposed towards you, and that we do not doubt that
you have our interests at heart. You
will easily realise the good opinion which
I have formed of you, if you will persuade
King Chosroes to maintain peaceful relations with our empire. I promise you,
in that case, the fullest recompense on
the part of my husband, who never does
anything without my advice."

When Chosroes had read this, he re-
proachfully asked the spokesmen of the
Persians whether they thought that that

ΠΡΟΚΟΠΙΟΥ ΑΝΕΚΔΟΤΑ

εἶναι, ἣν γυνὴ διοικεῖται, τὴν τῶν ἀνδρῶν ὁρμὴν ἀναστέλλειν ἔσχεν. Ἀλλὰ καὶ ὡς ξὺν δέει πολλῷ ἐνθένδε ἀπῄει, τοὺς ἀμφὶ Βελισάριον οἰόμενος σφίσιν ἐμποδὼν στήσεσθαι. Οὐδενὸς δέ οἱ τῶν πολεμίων ὑπαντιάσαντος, ἄσμενος ἐς γῆν τὴν οἰκείαν ἀπεκομίσθη.

COURT OF JUSTINIAN

was an Empire which was managed by a woman, and thus managed to quell their impetuosity; but, nevertheless, he retired from his position in alarm, expecting that his retreat would be cut off by Belisarius and his forces; but, as he found himself unopposed on his march, he gladly made his way home.

ΚΕΦΑΛΛΑΙΟΝ Γ'.

α'. Γενόμενος δὲ ὁ Βελισάριος ἐς γῆν τὴν Ῥωμαίων, εὑρίσκει τὴν γυναῖκα ἐκ Βυζαντίου ἀφικομένην. Καὶ αὐτὴν μὲν ἐν ἀτιμίᾳ ἐφύλασσε· πολλάκις τε διαχειρίσασθαι αὐτὴν ἐγχειρήσας, ἐμαλθακίσθη, ἐμοὶ μὲν δοκεῖ ἔρωτος ἡσσηθεὶς διαπύρου τινός. Φασὶ δὲ αὐτὸν καὶ μαγγανείαις πρὸς τῆς γυναικὸς καταλαμβανόμενον, ἐν τῷ παραυτίκα ἐκλύεσθαι.

β'. Φώτιος δὲ κάτοχος ἐς τὴν Ἔφεσον στέλλεται, τῶν τινὰ εὐνούχων Καλλίγονον ὄνομα, προαγωγὸν τῆς κεκτημένης ὄντα, δεσμεύσας τε καὶ ξὺν αὐτῷ ἔχων· ὅσπερ αὐτῷ αἰκιζόμενος ἐν τῇ ὁδῷ ταύτῃ, ἅπαντα ἐξήνεγκε τὰ ἀπόρρητα. Καὶ Θεοδόσιος μὲν προμαθὼν, ἐς τὸ ἱερὸν Ἰωάννου καταφεύγει τοῦ ἀποστόλου· ὅπερ ἐνταῦθα ἁγιώτατόν τε ἐπιεικῶς καὶ ἔντιμόν ἐστιν. Ἀνδρέας δὲ, ὁ τῆς Ἐφέσου ἀρχιερεὺς, χρήμασίν οἱ ἀνα-

CHAPTER III

WHEN Belisarius entered Roman territory, he found that his wife had arrived
from Byzantium. He kept her in custody
in disgrace, and was frequently minded to
put her to death, but had not the heart
to do so, being overpowered, I believe,
by the ardour of his love. Others, however, say that his mind and resolution
were destroyed by the enchantments which
his wife employed against him.

Meanwhile, Photius arrived in a state
of fury at Ephesus, having taken with
him in chains Calligonus, a eunuch and
pander of Antonina, whom, by frequently
flogging him during the journey, he
forced to tell all his mistress's secrets.
Theodosius, however, was warned in time,
and took sanctuary in the temple of
St. John the Apostle, which is revered
in that town as a most sacred spot ;
but Andrew, the bishop of Ephesus, was

πεισθεὶς, τὸν ἄνθρωπον ἐνεχείρισεν. Ἐν τούτῳ ἡ Θεοδώρα ἀμφὶ τῇ Ἀντωνίνῃ δειμαίνουσα, (ἠκηκόει γὰρ ὅσα δὴ αὐτῇ ξυνεπεπτώκει·) Βελισάριον ξὺν αὐτῇ ἐς Βυζάντιον μεταπέμπεται. Φώτιος δὲ ταῦτα ἀκούσας, Θεοδόσιον μὲν ἐς Κίλικας πέμπει, οὗ δὴ οἱ δορυφόροι τε καὶ ὑπασπισταὶ διαχειμάζοντες ἔτυχον, τοῖς παραπόμποις ἐπιστείλας, λαθραιότατα μὲν τὸν ἄνδρα τοῦτον διακομίζειν· ἐς Κίλικας δὲ ἀφικομένους (κεκρυμμένως) ἐς τὰ μάλιστα ἐν φυλακῇ ἔχειν, μηδενὶ αἴσθησιν παρεχομένους, ὅποι γῆς εἴη. Αὐτὸς δὲ, ξύν τε Καλλιγόνῳ καὶ τοῖς Θεοδοσίου χρήμασιν ἁδροῖς τισιν οὖσιν, ἐς Βυζάντιον ἦλθεν.

γʹ. Ἐνταῦθα ἡ βασιλὶς ἐπίδειξιν πεποίηται ἐς πάντας ἀνθρώπους, ὅτι δὴ χάριτας φονίους εἰδείη, μείζοσί τε καὶ μιαρωτέροις ἀμείβεσθαι δώροις. Ἀντωνίνα μὲν γὰρ, ἕνα οἱ ἔναγχος τὸν Καππαδόκην ἐχθρὸν ἐνεδρεύσασα, προύδωκεν· αὐτὴ δὲ, πλῆθος ἐκείνῃ ἐγχειρίσασα ἀνδρῶν, ἀνεγκλήτως ἀνῄρηκε.

COURT OF JUSTINIAN

bribed into delivering him up into the hands of Photius.

Meanwhile, Theodora was very anxious about Antonina, when she heard what had befallen her. She summoned both Belisarius and his wife to Byzantium: on hearing this, Photius sent Theodosius away to Cilicia, where his own spearmen were in winter quarters, giving orders to his escort to take the man thither as secretly as possible, and, when they arrived at Cilicia, to guard him with exceeding strictness, and not to let anyone know in what part of the world he was. He himself, with Calligonus and Theodosius's treasures, which were very considerable, repaired to Byzantium.

At that juncture, the Empress clearly proved to all that she knew how to recompense the murderous services which Antonina had rendered her, by even greater crimes committed to further her plans. Indeed, Antonina had only betrayed one man to her by her wiles, her enemy John of Cappadocia, but the Empress caused the death of a large number of innocent per-

ΠΡΟΚΟΠΙΟΥ ΑΝΕΚΔΟΤΑ

Τῶν γὰρ Βελισαρίῳ καὶ Φωτίῳ ἐπιτηδείων, τινῶν μὲν τὰ σώματα αἰκισαμένη· (καὶ τοῦτο μόνον ἐπικαλέσασα, ὅτι ἐς τὼ ἄνδρε τούτω εὐνοϊκῶς ἔχοιεν, οὕτω διέθετο· ὥστε αὐτοῖς ἐς ὅ τί ποτε ἡ τύχη ἐτελεύτα, οὔπω νῦν ἴσμεν·) ἄλλους δὲ φυγῇ ἐζημίωσε, ταὐτὸ τοῦτο ἐπενεγκοῦσα.

δ΄. Ἕνα μέντοι τῶν Φωτίῳ ἐς τὴν Ἔφεσον ἐπισπομένων, Θεοδόσιον ὄνομα, καίπερ ἐς ἀξίωμα βουλῆς ἥκοντα, τὴν οὐσίαν ἀφελομένη, ἐν δωματίῳ καταγείῳ τε καὶ ὅλως ζοφώδει, ἔστησεν ἐπὶ φάτνης τινός, βρόχον οἱ τοῦ τραχήλου ἀναψαμένη εἰς τοσόνδε βραχὺν, ὥστε αὐτῷ δὴ ἐντετάσθαι, καὶ χαλαρὸν μηδαμῇ εἶναι. Ἑστηκὼς ἀμέλει διηνεκὲς ἐπὶ ταύτης δὴ τῆς φάτνης, ὁ τάλας ἤσθιέ τε καὶ ὕπνον ᾑρεῖτο, καὶ τὰς ἄλλας ἤνυεν ἁπάσας τῆς φύσεως χρείας· ἄλλο τέ οἱ οὐδὲν ἐς τὸ τοῖς ὄνοις εἰκάζεσθαι, ὅ τι μὴ βρωμᾶσθαι, ἐλέλειπτο. Χρόνος δὲ τῷ ἀνθρώπῳ οὐχ ἧσσων ἢ μηνῶν τεσσάρων ἐν

COURT OF JUSTINIAN 25

sons, whom she sacrificed to the vengeance
of Antonina. The intimates of Belisarius
and Photius were some of them flogged,
although the only charge against them
was their friendship for these two persons; and no one, to the present day,
knows what afterwards became of them;
while she sent others into exile, who
were accused of the same crime—friendship for Photius and Belisarius. One
of those who accompanied Photius to
Ephesus, Theodosius by name, although
he had attained the rank of senator, was
deprived of all his property, and imprisoned by Theodora in an underground
dungeon, where she kept him fastened
to a kind of manger by a rope round his
neck, which was so short that it was
always quite tense and never slack. The
wretched man was always forced to
stand upright at this manger, and
there to eat and sleep, and do all his
other needs; there was no difference
between him and an ass, save that he
did not bray. No less than four months
were passed by him in this condition,

4—2

26 ΠΡΟΚΟΠΙΟΥ ΑΝΕΚΔΟΤΑ

ταύτῃ τῇ διαίτῃ ἐτρίβη, ἕως μελαγχολίας νόσῳ ἁλοὺς, μανείς τε ἐκτόπως, καὶ οὕτω δὴ ταύτης τῆς εἱρκτῆς ἀφεθεὶς, εἶτα ἀπέθανεν.

ε΄. Καὶ Βελισάριον οὔ τι ἑκούσιον Ἀντωνίνῃ τῇ γυναικὶ καταλλαγῆναι ἠνάγκασε. Φώτιον δὲ αἰκισμοῖς τε ἄλλοις ἀνδραποδώδεσι περιβαλοῦσα, καὶ ξάνασα κατά τε τοῦ νώτου καὶ τῶν ὤμων πολλὰς, ἐκλέγειν ἐκέλευεν, ὅποι ποτὲ γῆς Θεοδόσιός τε καὶ ὁ προαγωγὸς εἴη. Ὁ δὲ, καίπερ ὑπὸ τῆς βασάνου κατατεινόμενος, τὰ ὀμωμοσμένα ἐμπεδοῦν ἔγνω, ἀνὴρ νοσώδης μὲν καὶ ἀνειμένος γεγονὼς πρότερον· ἐς δὲ τὴν ἀμφὶ τὸ σῶμα θεραπείαν ἐσπουδακώς· ὕβρεώς τε γενόμενος ἢ ταλαιπωρίας τινὸς ἄπειρος. Οὐδὲν γοῦν αὐτὸς τῶν Βελισαρίου κεκρυμμένων ἐξεῖπεν.

ς΄. Ὕστερον μέντοι ἅπαντα, τὰ τέως ἀπόρρητα, ἐς φῶς ἐληλύθει. Καὶ Καλλίγονον μὲν ἤδ' ἐνταῦθα εὑροῦσα, τῇδε παρέδωκε· τὸν δὲ Θεοδόσιον μετακαλέσασα ἐς Βυζάντιον, ἐπειδὴ ἀφίκετο, εὐθὺς μὲν κρύπτει

COURT OF JUSTINIAN   26

until he was seized with melancholy and
became violently mad, upon which he
was released from his prison and soon
afterwards died.

As for Belisarius, she forced him
against his will to become reconciled
to his wife Antonina. Photius, by her
orders, was tortured like a slave, and
was beaten with rods upon the back and
shoulders, and ordered to disclose where
Theodosius and the pander eunuch were.
But he, although cruelly tortured, kept
the oath which he had sworn inviolate;
and although he was naturally weak and
delicate, and had always been forced to
take care of his health, and had never
had any experience of ill-treatment or
discomfort of any kind, yet he never
revealed any of Belisarius's secrets.

But afterwards all that had hitherto
been kept secret came to light. Theodora
discovered the whereabouts of Calligonus,
and restored him to Antonina. She also
found where Theodosius was, and had
him conveyed to Byzantium, and, on his
arrival, concealed him straightway in the

27 ΠΡΟΚΟΠΙΟΥ ΑΝΕΚΔΟΤΑ

ἐν παλατίῳ· τῇ δὲ ὑστεραίᾳ μεταπεμψαμένη Ἀντωνίναν, "Ὦ φιλτάτη πατρικία," ἔφη, "μάργαρον ἐς χεῖρας τὰς ἐμὰς τῇ προτεραίᾳ "ἐμπέπτωκεν, οἷον οὐδείς ποτ' ἀνθρώπων "εἶδεν. Καί σοι βουλομένῃ οὐκ ἂν φθονή- "σαιμι τοῦ θεάματος τούτου, ἀλλ' ἐπιδείξω." Καὶ ἡ μὲν, οὐ ξυνιεῖσα τοῦ πρασσομένου, τὸ μάργαρόν οἱ ἐπιδεῖξαι πολλὰ ἐλιπάρει. Ἡ δὲ, τὸν Θεοδόσιον ἐξ οἰκιδίου τῶν τινος εὐνούχων ἐξαγαγοῦσα, ἐπέδειξεν. Ἀντωνίνα δὲ, τὰ μὲν πρῶτα περιχαρὴς ἄγαν γεγονυῖα ὑφ' ἡδονῆς, ἀχανὴς ἔμεινε· χάριτάς τέ οἱ δεδρακέναι ὡμολόγει πολλὰς, σώτειράν τε καὶ εὐεργέτιν ἀποκαλοῦσα, καὶ δέσποιναν ὄντως. Τοῦτον δὲ τὸν Θεοδόσιον ἡ βασιλὶς κατασχοῦσα ἐν παλατίῳ, τρυφῆς τε καὶ τῆς ἄλλης εὐπαθείας ἠξίου· στρατηγόν τε ἠπείλησε Ῥωμαίοις αὐτὸν οὐκ εἰς μακρὰν καταστήσεσθαι. Ἀλλά τις προτερήσασα δίκη, νόσῳ ἁλόντα δυσεντερίας, ἐξ ἀνθρώπων αὐτὸν ἀφανίζει.

ζ. Ἦν δὲ οἰκίδια τῇ Θεοδώρᾳ, ἀπόκρυφα μὲν καὶ ὅλως λεληθότα, ζοφώδη τε καὶ

COURT OF JUSTINIAN

palace. On the morrow she sent for Antonina, and said to her, "Dearest lady, a pearl fell into my hands yesterday, so beautiful that I think no one has ever seen its like. If you would like to see it, I will not grudge you the sight of it, but will gladly show it to you."

Antonina, who did not understand what was going on, begged eagerly to be shown the pearl, whereupon Theodora led Theodosius by the hand out of the chamber of one of her eunuchs and displayed him to her. Antonina was at first speechless through excess of joy, and when she had recovered herself, warmly protested her gratitude to Theodora, whom she called her saviour, her benefactress, and truly her mistress. Theodora kept Theodosius in her palace, treated him with every luxury, and even boasted that, before long, she would appoint him generalissimo of the Roman armies. But divine justice, which carried him off through dysentery, prevented this.

Theodora had at her disposal secret and absolutely secluded dungeons, so

άγείτονα, ἔνθα δὴ οὔτε νυκτὸς οὔτε ἡμέρας δήλωσις γίνεται. Ἐνταῦθα τὸν Φώτιον ἐπὶ χρόνου μῆκος καθείρξασα ἐτήρει. Ὅθεν δὴ αὐτῷ ξυνέβη τις τύχη, οὐχ ἅπαξ μόνον, ἀλλὰ καὶ δὶς διαφυγόντα ἀπαλλαγῆναι. Καὶ τὰ μὲν πρῶτα, καταφυγὼν εἰς τὸν ναὸν τῆς Θεοτόκου, ὃς παρὰ Βυζαντίοις ἁγιώτατός ἐστί τε καὶ ὠνομάσθη, παρὰ τὴν ἱερὰν τράπεζαν ἱκέτης καθῆστο. Ἐντεῦθέν τε αὐτὸν ἀναστήσασα, βίᾳ τῇ πάσῃ, καθεῖρξεν αὖθις. Τὸ δὲ δὴ δεύτερον, ἐς τῆς Σοφίας τὸ ἱερὸν ἥκων, ἐς αὐτήν που τὴν θειαν δεξαμενὴν ἐξαπιναίως ἐκάθισεν· ἥνπερ μάλιστα πάντων νενομίκασι Χριστιανοὶ σέβειν. Ἀλλὰ κἀνθένδεν ἐφέλκειν αὐτὸν ἡ γυνὴ ἴσχυσεν. Χωρίον γὰρ ἀβέβηλον πώποτε ἀνέφαπτον αὐτῇ οὐδὲν γέγονεν· ἀλλ' αὐτῇ βιάζεσθαι τὰ ἱερὰ ξύμπαντα, οὐδὲν πρᾶγμα ἐδόκει εἶναι. Καὶ ξὺν τῷ δήμῳ, οἱ τῶν Χριστιανῶν ἱερεῖς καταπεπληγμένοι τῷ δέει, ἐξίσταντο· καὶ ἐνεχώρουν αὐτῇ ἅπαντα. Τριῶν μὲν οὖν αὐτῷ ἐνιαυτῶν χρόνος ἐν ταύτῃ τῇ διαίτῃ ἐτρίβη·

COURT OF JUSTINIAN   28

solitary and so dark that it was impossible to distinguish between night and day. In one of these she kept Photius imprisoned for a long time. He managed, however, to escape, not only once, but twice. The first time he took sanctuary in the Church of the Mother of God, which is one of the most sacred and famous churches in Byzantium, wherein he sat as a suppliant at the holy table; but she ordered him to be removed by main force and again imprisoned. The second time he fled to the Church of St. Sophia, and suddenly took refuge in the holy font, which is held in reverence by Christians above all other places; but the woman was able to drag him even from thence, for to her no place ever was sacred or unassailable; and she thought nothing of violating the holiest of sanctuaries. The Christian priests and people were struck with horror at her impiety, but nevertheless yielded and submitted to her in everything.

Photius had lived in this condition for nearly three years, when the prophet

ὕστερον δὲ, ὁ προφήτης αὐτῷ Ζαχαρίας ἐπιστὰς ὄναρ, ὅρκοις, φασὶν, ἐκέλευε φεύγειν· συλλήψεσθαί οἱ ἐν τῷ ἔργῳ τῷδε ὁμολογήσας. Ταύτῃ τε τῇ ὄψει ἀναπεισθεὶς, ἀνέστη τε ἐνθένδε, καὶ διαλαθὼν, εἰς τὰ Ἱεροσόλυμα ἦλθε· μυρίων μὲν αὐτὸν διερευνωμένων ἀνθρώπων, οὐδενὸς δὲ τὸν νεανίαν, καίπερ ἐντυχόντα, ὁρῶντος. Οὗ δὴ ἀποθριξάμενός τε, καὶ τῶν Μοναχῶν καλουμένων τὸ σχῆμα περιβαλλόμενος, τὴν ἐκ Θεοδώρας κόλασιν διαφυγεῖν ἔσχε.

η΄. Βελισάριος δὲ, τὰ ὀμωμοσμένα ἠλογηκὼς, τιμωρεῖν τε οὐδαμῇ τούτῳ ἐλόμενος πάσχοντι, ὥσπερ ἐρρήθη, ἀνόσια ἔργα. Ἐς πάντα οἱ λοιπὸν τὰ ἐπιτηδεύματα πολέμια, τὰ πρὸς τοῦ Θεοῦ, ὡς τὸ εἰκὸς, εὗρεν· εὐθὺς γὰρ ἐπί τε Μήδους καὶ Χοσρόην σταλεὶς, τὸ τρίτον ἐσβαλόντας ἐς Ῥωμαίων τὴν γῆν, κακότητα ὦφλε. Καίτοι ἐδόκει τι λόγου ἄξιον διαπεπρᾶχθαι, τὸν πόλεμον ἐνθένδε ἀποσεισάμενος. Ἀλλ᾿ ἐπεὶ Χοσρόης Εὐφράτην διαβὰς ποταμὸν, Καλλίνικον πόλιν

COURT OF JUSTINIAN

Zacharias appeared to him in a dream, commanded him to escape, and promised his assistance. Relying upon this vision, he rose, escaped from his prison, and made his way to Jerusalem in disguise; though tens of thousands must have seen the youth, yet none recognised him. There he shaved off all his hair, assumed the monastic habit, and in this manner escaped the tortures which Theodora would have inflicted upon him.

Belisarius took no account of the oaths which he had sworn, and made no effort to avenge Photius's sufferings, in spite of the solemn vows which he had made to do so. Hereafter, probably by God's will, all his warlike enterprises failed. Some time afterwards he was dispatched against the Medes and Chosroes, who had for the third time invaded the Roman Empire, and fell under suspicion of treachery, although he was considered to have performed a notable achievement in driving the enemy away from the frontier; but when Chosroes, after crossing the Euphrates, took the populous

ΠΡΟΚΟΠΙΟΥ ΑΝΕΚΔΟΤΑ

πολυάνθρωπον οὐδενὸς ἀμυνομένου εἷλε, μυριάδας ἠνδραπόδισε ᾽Ρωμαίων πολλάς· Βελισάριος δὲ, [ὃς] οὐδὲ ὅσον ἐπισπέσθαι τοῖς πολεμίοις ἐν σπουδῇ ἔσχε, δόξαν ἀπήνεγκεν ὡς δυοῖν θάτερον, ἢ ἐθελοκακήσας, ἢ ἀποδειλιάσας, αὐτοῦ ἔμεινεν.

COURT OF JUSTINIAN

city of Callinikus without a blow, and made slaves of tens of thousands of Romans, Belisarius remained quiet, and never so much as offered to attack the enemy, whereby he incurred the reproach of either treachery or cowardice.

ΚΕΦΑΛΑΙΟΝ Δ'.

α'. Ὑπὸ τοῦτον τὸν χρόνον, καί τι ἕτερον αὐτῷ ἐπιπεσεῖν ξυνηνέχθη τοιόνδε. Ὁ μὲν λοιμὸς, οὗπερ ἐν τοῖς ἔμπροσθεν λόγοις ἐμνήσθην, ἐπενέμετο τοὺς ἐν Βυζαντίῳ ἀνθρώπους. Βασιλεῖ δὲ Ἰουστινιανῷ χαλεπώτατα νοσῆσαι ξυνέβη, ὥστε καὶ ἐλέγετο ὅτι ἀπολώλει. Τοῦτον δὲ τὸν λόγον παραγαγοῦσα ἡ φήμη, διεκόμισεν ἄχρι ἐς τὸ Ῥωμαίων στρατόπεδον. Ἐνταῦθα ἔλεγον τῶν ἀρχόντων τινὲς, ὡς, ἢν βασιλέα Ῥωμαῖοι ἕτερόν τινα ἐν Βυζαντίῳ καταστήσωνται σφίσιν, οὐ μήποτε αὐτοὶ ἐπιτρέψωσιν. Ὀλίγῳ δὲ ὕστερον βασιλεῖ μὲν ῥαΐσαι ξυνέβη, τοῖς δὲ τῶν Ῥωμαίων στρατοῦ ἄρχουσι διαβόλοις ἐπ' ἀλλήλοις γενέσθαι. Πέτρος τε γὰρ ὁ στρατηγὸς, καὶ Ἰωάννης, ὅνπερ ἐπίκλησιν Φαγᾶν ἐκάλουν, Βελισαρίου τε καὶ Βούζου ἐκεῖνα λεγόντων, ἰσχυρίζοντο ἀκηκοέναι, ἅπερ μοι ἀρτίως δεδήλωται.

β'. Ταῦτά γε ἡ βασιλὶς Θεοδώρα,

CHAPTER IV

ABOUT this time Belisarius underwent another disgrace. The people of Byzantium were ravaged by the pestilence of which I have already spoken. The Emperor Justinian was attacked by it so severely that it was reported that he had died. Rumour spread these tidings abroad till they reached the Roman camp, whereupon some of the chief officers said that, if the Romans set up any other emperor in Byzantium, they would not acknowledge him. Shortly after this, the Emperor recovered from his malady, whereupon the chiefs of the army accused one another of having used this language. The General Peter, and John, surnamed "The Glutton," declared that Belisarius and Buzes had used the words which I have just quoted. The Empress Theodora, thinking that these

32 ΠΡΟΚΟΠΙΟΥ ΑΝΕΚΔΟΤΑ

ἐπικαλέσασα ἐφ' ἑαυτῇ, τοῖς ἀνθρώποις εἰρῆσθαι, μεστὴ (θυμοῦ) ἐγεγόνει. Ἅπαντας οὖν εὐθὺς μετακαλέσασα ἐς Βυζάντιον, ζήτησίν τε τοῦ λόγου τούτου ποιησαμένη, τὸν Βούζην μετεπέμψατο εἰς τὴν γυναικωνῖτιν ἐξαπιναίως, ὥς τι αὐτῷ κοινολογησομένη τῶν ἄγαν σπουδαίων. Ἦν δέ τι οἴκημα ἐν παλατίῳ κατάγειον, ἀσφαλές τε καὶ λαβυρινθῶδες, καὶ οἷον ταρτάρῳ εἰκάζεσθαι, ἵνα δὴ τοὺς προσκεκρουκότας, ὡς τὰ πολλὰ καθείρξασα, ἐντηρῇ. Καὶ ὁ Βούζης οὖν ἐς τὸ βάραθρον τοῦτο ἐμβέβληται· ἐνταῦθά τε ἀνήρ, ἐξ ὑπάτων γενόμενος, ἄγνωστος ἀεὶ τοῦ παρόντος καιροῦ ἔμεινεν. Οὔτε γὰρ αὐτός, ἐν σκότῳ καθήμενος, διαγινώσκειν οἷός τε ἐγεγόνει, πότερον ἡμέρα ἢ νύκτωρ εἴη, οὔτε ἄλλῳ τῳ ἐντυχεῖν εἶχεν. Ἄνθρωπος γάρ, ὅσπερ οἱ ἐς ἡμέραν ἑκάστην τὰ σιτία ἐρρίπτει, ὥσπερ τι θηρίον θηρίῳ ἄφωνος ἀφώνῳ ὡμίλει. Καὶ πᾶσι μὲν τετελευτηκέναι εὐθὺς ἔδοξε· λόγον μέντοι ἢ μνήμην ποιεῖσθαι αὐτοῦ οὐδεὶς [ἐτόλμα]. Ἐνιαυτοῖν δὲ δυοῖν ὕστερον πρὸς μησὶ τέσσαρσιν οἰκτισαμένη, τὸν ἄνδρα ἀφῆκε. Καὶ ὃς ὥσπερ ἀναβεβιωκὼς ἅπασιν ὤφθη. Ξυνέβη τε τῷ ἀνθρώπῳ ἐνθένδε ἀεὶ

COURT OF JUSTINIAN

words applied to herself, was greatly enraged. She straightway summoned all the commanders to Byzantium to make an inquiry into the matter, and suddenly sent for Buzes to come into her private apartments, on the pretext of discussing important matters of business with him. There was in the palace an underground building, which was securely fastened, and as complicated as a labyrinth, and which might be compared to the nether world, wherein she kept imprisoned most of those who had offended her. Into this pit she cast Buzes; and although he was of a consular family, nothing was known for certain concerning him; as he sat in the darkness, he could not tell day from night; nor could he ask, for he who flung him his daily food never spoke, but acted like one dumb beast with another. All thought him dead, but none dared to mention him or allude to him. Two years and four months afterwards, Theodora relented and released him, and he appeared in the world like one raised from the dead; but ever afterwards he

ἀμβλυώττειν τε, καὶ τὸ ἄλλο σῶμα νοσώδει εἶναι. Τὰ μὲν οὖν ἀμφὶ τῷ Βούζῃ τῇδε ἐχώρησε.

γ΄. Βελισάριον δὲ βασιλεὺς, καίπερ οὐδενὸς τῶν κατηγορουμένων ἁλόντα, ἐγκειμένης τῆς βασιλίδος, παραλύσας ἧς εἶχεν ἀρχῆς, Μαρτῖνον ἀντ' αὐτοῦ τῆς ἑῴας στρατηγὸν κατεστήσατο· τούς τε Βελισαρίου δορυφόρους τε καὶ ὑπασπιστὰς, καὶ τῶν οἰκετῶν εἴ τι ἐν πολέμῳ δόκιμον ἦν, τῶν τε ἀρχόντων, καὶ τῶν ἐν παλατίῳ εὐνούχων τισὶν, ἐπέστειλε διαδάσασθαι. Οἱ δὲ κλήρους ἐπ' ἐκείνοις ἐμβεβλημένοι, αὐτοῖς ὅπλοις ἅπαντας ἐν σφίσιν αὐτοῖς διενείμαντο, ὥσπερ κατατυχεῖν ἑκάστῳ συνέβη. Καὶ τῶν φίλων δὲ, καὶ ἄλλως αὐτῷ τὰ πρότερα ὑπουργηκότων πολλοῖς, ἀπεῖπον παρὰ Βελισαρίῳ μηκέτι ἰέναι. Καὶ περιήρχετο πικρὸν θέαμα, καὶ ἄπιστος ὄψις, Βελισάριος ἰδιώτης ἐν Βυζαντίῳ, σχεδόν τι μόνος, σύννους ἀεὶ καὶ σκυθρωπὸς, καὶ τὸν ἐξ ἐπιβουλῆς ὀρρωδῶν θάνατον.

COURT OF JUSTINIAN

was short-sighted and diseased in body. Such was the fate of Buzes.

Belisarius, although none of the charges brought against him could be proved, was removed by the Emperor, at the instance of Theodora, from the command of the army in the East, which was given to Martinus. The command of the Dory-phori[1] and Hypaspitae[2] of Belisarius, and of those of his servants who had distinguished themselves in war, was by his orders divided amongst the generals and certain of the palace eunuchs. They cast lots for these soldiers, together with their arms, and divided them amongst themselves as the lot fell. As for his friends and the many people who had before served under him, Justinian forbade them to visit him. Thus was seen in the city a piteous spectacle which men could scarce believe to be real, that of Belisarius simply a private individual, almost alone, gloomy and thoughtful, ever dreading to be set upon and assassinated.

[1] Spearmen, lancers.
[2] Shield-bearers.

5—2

δ΄. Μαθοῦσα δὲ ἡ βασιλὶς, πολλά οἱ ἐπὶ τῆς ἕω χρήματα εἶναι, πέμψασα τῶν ἐν παλατίῳ εὐνούχων τινὰ, κεκόμισται πάντα. Ἐτύγχανε δὲ Ἀντωνίνα, ὥς μοι εἴρηται, τῷ μὲν ἀνδρὶ διάφορος γεγενημένη, τῇ δὲ βασιλίδι φιλτάτη καὶ ἀναγκαιοτάτη τυγχάνουσα ἐν τοῖς μάλιστα, ἅτε Ἰωάννην ἔναγχος κατεργασαμένη τὸν Καππαδόκην. Διὸ δὴ χαρίσασθαι ἡ βασιλὶς τῇ Ἀντωνίνῃ βουλευσαμένη, ἅπαντα ἔπραττεν, ὅπως ἐξαιτήσασθαί τε τὸν ἄνδρα ἡ γυνὴ, καὶ ἀπὸ ξυμφορῶν τηλικῶνδε ῥύσασθαι δόξειε· ταύτῃ τε οὐ μόνον τῷ ταλαιπώρῳ ἐς τὸ παντελὲς καταλλαγῆναι συμβήσεται, ἀλλὰ καὶ διαρρήδην αὐτὸν, ἅτε πρὸς αὐτῆς διασεσωσμένον, αἰχμάλωτον ἀναρπάσασθαι. Ἐγένετο δὲ ὧδε.

ε΄. Ἦλθε μέν ποτε Βελισάριος πρωῒ ἐς παλάτιον, ᾗπερ εἰώθει, ξὺν ἀνθρώποις οἰκτροῖς τε καὶ ὀλίγοις τισίν. Οὐκ εὐμενῶν δὲ πειρασάμενος βασιλέως τε καὶ τῆς βασιλίδος, ἀλλὰ καὶ περιυβρισμένος ἐνταῦθα, ὑπ' ἀνδρῶν μοχθηρῶν τε καὶ ἀγελαίων, οἴκαδε ἀμφὶ δείλην ὀψίαν ἀπιὼν ᾤχετο· συχνά τε περιστρεφόμενος ἐν τῇ ἀναχωρήσει ταύτῃ, καὶ πανταχόσε περισκοπούμενος, ὁπόθεν ποτὲ

COURT OF JUSTINIAN   34

When the Empress learned that he had amassed much treasure in the East, she sent one of the palace eunuchs to fetch it away to the Court. Antonina, as I have already said, was now at variance with her husband, and the nearest and dearest friend of the Empress, because she had just destroyed John of Cappadocia. To please Antonina, the Empress arranged everything in such a fashion that she appeared to have pleaded for her husband's pardon, and to have saved him from these great disasters; whereby the unhappy man not only became finally reconciled to her, but her absolute slave, as though he had been preserved by her from death. This was brought about as follows:

One day Belisarius came early to the palace as usual, accompanied by a small and miserable retinue. He was ungraciously received by the Emperor and Empress, and even insulted in their presence by low-born villains. He went home towards evening, often turning himself about, and looking in every direction

προσιόντας αὐτῷ τοὺς ἀπολλύντας ἴδοι. Ξὺν ταύτῃ τε τῇ ὀρρωδίᾳ, εἰς τὸ δωμάτιον ἀναβὰς, ἐπὶ τῆς στιβάδος καθῆστο μόνος· γενναῖον μὲν οὐδὲν ἐννοῶν, οὐδὲ ὅτι ἀνὴρ ἐγεγόνει, ἐν μνήμῃ ἔχων· ἱδρῶν δὲ ἀεὶ καὶ ἰλιγγιῶν, καὶ ξὺν τρόμῳ πολλῷ ἀπορούμενος· φόβοις τε ἀνδραποδώδεσι καὶ μερίμναις ἀποκναιόμενος φιλοψύχοις τε καὶ ὅλως ἀνάνδροις. Ἀντωνίνα δὲ, ἅτε οὔτε τὰ πρασσόμενα ὅλως ἐπισταμένη, οὔτε τι τῶν ἐσομένων καραδοκοῦσα, περιπάτους ἐνταῦθα ἐποιεῖτο συχνοὺς, ὀξυρεγμίαν σκηπτομένη· ἔτι γὰρ εἰς ἀλλήλους ὑπόπτως εἶχον. Μεταξὺ δέ τις ἐκ παλατίου, Κουαδρᾶτος ὄνομα, ἧκεν ἤδη δεδυκότος ἡλίου, τήν τε αὔλειον ὑπερβὰς, ἐξαπιναίως παρὰ τὴν ἀνδρωνίτιδα ἔστη θύραν, φάσκων πρὸς τῆς βασιλίδος ἐνταῦθα ἐστάλθαι. Ὅπερ ἐπεὶ Βελισάριος ἤκουσε, χεῖρας καὶ πόδας ἐπὶ στιβάδος ἑλκύσας, ὕπτιος ἔκειτο, πρὸς τὴν ἀναίρεσιν ἑτοιμότατος· οὕτως ἅπαν αὐτὸν τὸ ἀρρενωπὸν ἀπελελοίπει.

COURT OF JUSTINIAN 35

for those whom he expected to set upon
him. In this state of dread, he went
up to his chamber, and sat down alone
upon his couch, without a brave man's
spirit, and scarce remembering that he
had ever been a man, but bathed with
sweat, his head dizzy, trembling and despairing, racked by slavish fears and
utterly unmanly thoughts. Antonina, who
knew nothing of what was going on,
and was far from expecting what was
about to come to pass, kept walking
up and down the hall, on pretence of
suffering from heartburn; for they still
regarded each other with suspicion.
Meanwhile, an officer of the palace,
named Quadratus, came just after sunset,
passed through the court, and suddenly
appeared at the door of the men's apartments, saying that he brought a message
from the Empress.

Belisarius, on hearing him approach,
drew up his hands and feet on to the
bed, and lay on his back in the readiest
posture to receive the final stroke, so
completely had he lost his courage.

ΠΡΟΚΟΠΙΟΥ ΑΝΕΚΔΟΤΑ

ς΄. Οὕτω τοίνυν ὁ Κουαδρᾶτος παρ᾽ αὐτὸν εἰσελθών, γράμματά οἱ τῆς βασιλίδος ἐπέδειξεν. Ἐδήλου δὲ ἡ γραφὴ τάδε· "Ἃ "μὲν. εἰργάσω ἡμᾶς, ὦ βέλτιστε, οἶσθα. "Ἐγὼ δὲ τὰ πολλὰ ὀφείλουσα τῇ σῇ γυναικὶ, "ταύτῃ δὴ τὰ ἐγκλήματά σοι ἀφεῖναι ξύμπαντα "ἔγνωκα, ἐκείνῃ τὴν σὴν δωρουμένη ψυχὴν. "Τὸ μὲν οὖν ἔνθεν σοι τὸ θαρσεῖν ὑπέρ τε τῆς "σωτηρίας καὶ τῶν χρημάτων περίεστιν· "ὁποῖος δὲ σὺ πρὸς αὐτὴν ἔσῃ, διὰ τῶν "πραχθησομένων εἰσόμεθα." Ταῦτα ἐπεὶ Βελισάριος ἀνελέξατο, ἅμα μὲν ὑφ᾽ ἡδονῆς ἐπὶ μέγα ἀρθείς, ἅμα δὲ καὶ τῷ παρόντι ἐπίδειξιν ἐθέλων ποιεῖσθαι τῆς γνώμης, ἀναστὰς εὐθὺς παρὰ τοὺς γυναικὸς πόδας ἐπὶ στόμα πίπτει. Καὶ χειρὶ μὲν ἑκατέρᾳ περιλαβὼν αὐτῆς ἄμφω τὰς κνήμας, τὴν δὲ γλῶσσαν ἀεὶ τῶν ταρσῶν τῆς γυναικὸς μεταβιβάζων, τοῦ μὲν βίου καὶ τῆς σωτηρίας αἰτίαν ἐκάλει· ἀνδράποδον δὲ αὐτῆς τὸ ἐνθένδε πιστὸν ὡμολόγει, καὶ οὐκ ἀνὴρ ἔσεσθαι.

ζ΄. Καὶ τῶν χρημάτων δὲ ἡ βασιλὶς ἐς

COURT OF JUSTINIAN 36

Quadratus, before entering, showed him the Empress' letter. It ran as follows:

"You are not ignorant, my good sir, of all your offences against me; but I owe so much to your wife, that I have determined to pardon all your offences for her sake, and I make her a present of your life. For the future you may be of good cheer as regards your life and fortune: we shall know by your future conduct what sort of husband you will be to your wife!"

When Belisarius read this, he was greatly excited with joy, and, as he wished at the same time to give some present proof of his gratitude, he straightway rose, and fell on his face at his wife's feet. He embraced her legs with either hand, and kissed the woman's ankles and the soles of her feet, declaring that it was to her that he owed his life and safety, and that hereafter he would be her faithful slave, and no longer her husband.

The Empress divided Belisarius's fortune into two parts; she gave thirty

τριάκοντα χρυσοῦ κεντηνάρια τῷ βασιλεῖ δοῦσα, τἆλλα Βελισαρίῳ ἀπέδοτο. Τὰ μὲν οὖν ἀμφὶ Βελισαρίῳ τῷ στρατηγῷ τῇδε κεχωρήκει, ᾧπερ ἡ τύχη οὐ πολλῷ πρότερον Γελίμερά τε καὶ Οὐίττιγιν δορυαλώτους παρεδεδώκει. Ἐκ παλαιοῦ δὲ Ἰουστινιανόν τε καὶ Θεοδώραν πλοῦτος ὁ τοιούτου τοῦ ἀνδρὸς ἀκριβῶς ἔκνιζεν, ὑπέρογκός τε ὢν καὶ βασιλικῆς αὐλῆς ἄξιος. Ἔφασκόν τε, ὡς τῶν δημοσίων χρημάτων Γελίμερός τε καὶ Οὐιττίγιδος τὸ πλεῖστον ἀποκρυψάμενος λάθρα ἔτυχε, μοῖραν δὲ αὐτῶν βραχεῖάν τέ τινα καὶ οὐδαμῇ ἀξιόλογον βασιλεῖ ἔδωκε. Πόνους δὲ τοὺς τοῦ ἀνθρώπου, καὶ τῶν ἔξωθεν τὴν βλασφημίαν, διαριθμούμενοι, ἅμα δὲ καὶ σκῆψιν ἀξιόχρεων ἐπ᾽ αὐτῷ οὐδεμίαν κεκομισμένοι, ἡσυχῇ ἔμενον. Τότε δὲ ἡ βασιλὶς αὐτοῦ λαβομένη, κατωρρωδηκότος τε καὶ ἀποδειλιάσαντος, ὅλως πράξει μιᾷ διεπράξατο ξυμπάσης αὐτοῦ τῆς οὐσίας κυρία γενέσθαι.

η᾽. Ἐς κῆδος γὰρ ἀλλήλοις ξυνηλθέτην

COURT OF JUSTINIAN

centenars of gold to the Emperor, and allowed Belisarius to keep the rest. Such was the fortune of the General Belisarius, into whose hands Fate had not long before given Gelimer and Vitiges as prisoners of war. The man's wealth had for a long time excited the jealousy of Justinian and Theodora, who considered it too great, and fit only for a king. They declared that he had secretly embezzled most of the property of Gelimer and Vitiges, which belonged to the State, and that he had restored a small part alone, and one hardly worthy of an Emperor's acceptance. But, when they thought of what great things the man had done, and how they would raise unpopular clamour against themselves, especially as they had no ground whatever for accusing him of peculation, they desisted; but, on this occasion, the Empress, having surprised him at a time when he was quite unmanned by fear, managed at one stroke to become mistress of his entire fortune; for she straightway established a relationship

38 ΠΡΟΚΟΠΙΟΥ ΑΝΕΚΔΟΤΑ

εὐθὺς, Ἰωαννίνα τε ἡ Βελισαρίου θυγάτηρ, ἧσπερ μόνης ἐγεγόνει πατὴρ, Ἀναστασίῳ τῷ τῆς βασιλίδος θυγατριδῷ μνηστὴ γέγονε. Βελισάριος μὲν οὖν ἀρχήν τε ἀπολαβεῖν τὴν οἰκείαν ἠξίου, καὶ στρατηγὸς τῆς ἑῴας ἀποδειχθεὶς, πάλιν ἐπὶ Χοσρόην καὶ Μήδους ἐξηγήσεσθαι τῷ Ῥωμαίων στρατῷ. Ἀντωνίνα δὲ οὐδαμῶς εἴα· περιυβρίσθαι ἐν τοῖς ἐκείνῃ χωρίοις πρὸς αὐτοῦ ἔφασκεν, ἅπερ οὐκέτι τὸ λοιπὸν ὄψεσθαι.

θ. Διὸ δὴ Βελισάριος, ἄρχων τῶν βασιλικῶν καταστὰς ἱπποκόμων, ἐς τὴν Ἰταλίαν τὸ δεύτερον ἐστάλη, ὁμολογήσας βασιλεῖ, ὥς φασι, χρήματα μήποτε αὐτὸν ἐν τῷδε τῷ πολέμῳ αἰτήσειν, ἀλλὰ ξύμπασαν αὐτὸς τὴν τοῦ πολέμου παρασκευὴν χρήμασιν οἰκείοις ποιήσασθαι. Πάντες μὲν οὖν ὑπετόπαζον τά τε ἀμφὶ τῇ γυναικὶ ταύτῃ, ἧπερ ἐρρήθη, Βελισάριον διοικήσασθαι, καὶ βασιλεῖ ταῦτα ὁμολογῆσαι ἀμφὶ τῷ πολέμῳ, ἀπαλλαξείοντα τῆς ἐν Βυζαντίῳ διατριβῆς· ἐπειδάν τε τάχιστα τοῦ τῆς πόλεως περιβόλου ἐκτὸς γένηται, ἁρπάσασθαί τε αὐτίκα τὰ ὅπλα, καί

COURT OF JUSTINIAN

38

between them, betrothing Joannina, Belisarius's only daughter, to her grandson Anastasius.

Belisarius now asked to be restored to his command, and to be nominated general of the army of the East, in order to conduct the war against Chosroes and the Medes, but Antonina would not permit this; she declared that she had been insulted by her husband in those countries, and never wished to see them again.

For this reason Belisarius was appointed Constable,[1] and was sent for a second time into Italy, with the understanding, they say, with the Emperor, that he should not ask for any money to defray the cost of this war, but should pay all its expenses out of his own private purse. Everyone imagined that Belisarius made these arrangements with his wife and with the Emperor in order that he might get away from Byzantium, and, as soon as he was outside the city walls, straightway take up

[1] Or "Count," Master of the royal stables.

ΠΡΟΚΟΠΙΟΥ ΑΝΕΚΔΟΤΑ

τι γενναῖον καὶ ἀνδρὶ πρέπον, ἐπί τε τῇ γυναικὶ καὶ τοῖς βιασαμένοις φρονῆσαι. Αὐτὸς δὲ πάντα τὰ ξυμπεσόντα ἐν ἀλογίᾳ πεπεποιημένος, ὅρκων τε τῶν Φωτίῳ καὶ τοῖς ἄλλοις ἐπιτηδείοις ὀμωμοσμένων ἐν λήθῃ τε πολλῇ καὶ ὀλιγωρίᾳ γενόμενος, εἴπετο τῇ γυναικὶ, καταστὰς ἐκτόπως εἰς αὐτὴν ἐρωτόληπτος, καὶ ταῦτα ἑξήκοντα ἤδη γεγονυῖαν ἔτη.

ί. Ἐπειδὴ μέντοι ἐν Ἰταλίᾳ ἐγένετο, εἰς ἡμέραν ἑκάστην ἀπ' ἐναντίας αὐτῷ τὰ πράγματα ἐχώρει· ἐπεὶ οἱ διαρρήδην τὰ ἐκ θεοῦ πολέμια ἦν. Πρῶτον μέν γε, τὰ τῷ στρατηγῷ τούτῳ ἐν τοῖς ξυμπίπτουσιν ἐπί τε Θευδάτον καὶ Οὐίττιγιν βουλευόμενα, καίπερ οὐκ ἐπιτηδείως τοῖς πρασσομένοις δοκοῦντα ἔχειν, ἐς ξύμφορον ἐκ τοῦ ἐπὶ πλεῖστον ἐτελεύτα τέλος· ἐν δὲ τῷ ὑστέρῳ, δόξαν μὲν ἀπήνεγκεν, ὅτι δὴ τὰ βελτίω βεβούλευται· ἅτε καὶ τῶν κατὰ τὸν πόλεμον τόνδε πραγμάτων γεγονὼς ἔμπειρος, ἀλλ' ἐν τοῖς ἀποβαίνουσι κακοτυχοῦντι, τὰ πολλὰ ἐς ἀβουλίας δόκησιν αὐτῷ ἀπεκρίθη. Οὕτως ἄρα, οὐκ ἀνθρώπων βουλαῖς, ἀλλὰ τῇ ἐκ θεοῦ ῥοπῇ πρυτανεύεται τὰ ἀνθρώπεια· ὃ δὴ τύχην εἰώθασι καλεῖν

COURT OF JUSTINIAN 39

arms and do some brave and manly deed against his wife and his oppressors. But he made light of all that had passed, forgot the oaths which he had sworn to Photius and his other intimates, and followed his wife in a strange ecstasy of passion for her, though she was already sixty years of age.

When he arrived in Italy, things went wrong with him daily, for he had clearly incurred the enmity of heaven. In his former campaign against Theodatus and Vitiges, the tactics which he had adopted as general, though they were not thought to be suitable to the circumstances, yet, as a rule, turned out prosperously: in this second campaign, he gained the credit of having laid his plans better, as was to be expected from his greater experience in the art of war; but, as matters for the most part turned out ill, people began to have a poor opinion of him and his judgment. So true it is that human affairs are guided, not by men's counsel, but by the influence of heaven, which we commonly

ΠΡΟΚΟΠΙΟΥ ΑΝΕΚΔΟΤΑ

ἄνθρωποι· οὐκ εἰδότες ὅτου δὴ ἕνεκα ταύτῃ
πρόεισι τὰ ξυμβαίνοντα, ᾖπερ αὐτοῖς ἔνδηλα
γίνεται. Τῷ γὰρ ἀλόγῳ δοκοῦντι εἶναι φιλεῖ
τὸ τῆς τύχης ὄνομα προσχωρεῖν. Ἀλλὰ
ταῦτα μὲν, ὥς πη ἑκάστῳ φίλον, ταύτῃ
δοκείτω.

COURT OF JUSTINIAN 40

call fortune, because we see how events
happen, but know not the cause which de-
termines them. Therefore, to that which
seems to come to pass without reason
is given the name of " chance." But
this is a subject upon which everyone
must form his own opinion.

ΠΡΟΚΟΠΙΟΥ ΑΝΕΚΔΟΤΑ

ΚΕΦΑΛΑΙΟΝ Ε΄.

α΄. Βελισάριος δὲ τὸ δεύτερον ἐν Ἰταλίᾳ γενόμενος, αἴσχιστα ἐνθένδε ἀπήλλαξε· τῆς μὲν γὰρ γῆς ἐς πεντάετες ἐπιβῆναι οὐκ ἴσχυσεν, ὥσπερ μοι ἐν τοῖς ἔμπροσθεν λόγοις ἐρρήθη· ὅτι μὴ ἐνθάδε ὀχύρωμα ἦν· ναυτιλλόμενος δὲ πάντα τοῦτον τὸν χρόνον, τὰ ἐπιθαλάσσια [περιῄει]. Τωτίλας δὲ λυσσῶν ἦν αὐτὸν ἔξω τείχους λαβεῖν, οὐ μέντοι εὗρεν· ἐπεὶ ὀρρωδίᾳ πολλῇ αὐτός τε καὶ ξύμπας ὁ Ῥωμαίων στρατὸς εἴχετο. Διὸ δὴ οὔτε τῶν ἀπολωλότων τι ἀνεσώσατο, ἀλλὰ καὶ Ῥώμην προσαπώλεσε, καὶ τἆλλα ὡς εἰπεῖν ἅπαντα. Ἐγένετο δὲ φιλοχρήματος ἐν τούτῳ τῷ χρόνῳ πάντων μάλιστα, καὶ κέρδους αἰσχροῦ ἐπιμελητὴς ἀκριβέστατος, ἅτε οὐδὲν ἐκ βασιλέως κεκομισμένος, Ἰταλοὺς ἀμέλει σχεδὸν πάντας, οἵπερ ᾠκοῦντο ἐπὶ Ῥαβέννης καὶ Σικελίας, καὶ εἴ του ἄλλου κατατυχεῖν ἐν ἐξουσίᾳ ἔσχεν, ἐληΐσατο, οὐδενὶ κόσμῳ λογισμοὺς δῆθεν τῶν

CHAPTER V

AT the end of Belisarius's second expedition to Italy, he was obliged to retire in disgrace ; for, as I have told already, he was unable for a space of five years to effect a landing on the continent, because he had no stronghold there, but spent the whole time in hovering off the coast. Totila was very eager to meet him in the open field, but never found an opportunity, for both the Roman general and all the army were afraid to fight. For this reason he recovered nothing of all that had been lost, but even lost Rome as well, and pretty nearly everything else. During this time he became exceedingly avaricious and greedy for ignoble gain. Because he had received no funds from the Emperor, he plundered all the Italian peoples of Ravenna and Sicily, and the rest of Italy without mercy, by way of exacting vengeance for irregularities in their past lives. Thus he fell upon

ΠΡΟΚΟΠΙΟΥ ΑΝΕΚΔΟΤΑ

βεβιωμένων καταπραττόμενος. Οὕτω γοῦν, καὶ Ἡρωδιανὸν μετιὼν χρήματα ᾔτει, ἅπαντα τῷ ἀνθρώπῳ ἐπανασείων. Οἷς δὴ ἐκεῖνος ἀχθόμενος, ἀπετάξατο μὲν τῷ Ῥωμαίων στρατῷ, αὑτὸν δὲ εὐθὺς, ξύν τε τοῖς ἑπομένοις καὶ τῷ [Σπολετίῳ], Τωτίλᾳ καὶ Γότθοις ἐνέδωκεν.

β΄. Ὅπως δὲ αὐτῷ τε καὶ Ἰωάννῃ, τῷ Βιταλιανοῦ ἀδελφιδῷ, διχοστατῆσαι συνέβη, ὅπερ τὰ Ῥωμαίων πράγματα μάλιστα ἔσφηλεν, αὐτίκα δηλώσω. Ἐς τοῦτο ἀπεχθείας Γερμανῷ ἡ βασιλὶς ἦλθεν, ἐπιδηλότατόν τε ἅπασι τὸ ἔχθος ἐποίει, ὥστε αὐτῷ κηδεύειν, καίπερ βασιλέως ἀνεψιῷ ὄντι, ἐτόλμα οὐδείς· ἄνυμφοί τε αὐτῷ οἱ παῖδες γεγόνασι, μέχρις αὐτὴ ἐβίου. Ἥ τε θυγάτηρ αὐτῷ Ἰουστίνα, ἐπὶ ὀκτωκαίδεκα ἔτη ἡβήσασα, ἔτι ἀνυμέναιος ἦν. Διά τοι τοῦτο, ἡνίκα Ἰωάννης, πρὸς Βελισαρίου σταλεὶς, ἀφίκετο ἐς Βυζάντιον, ἐς λόγους αὐτῷ καταστῆναι ὁ Γερμανὸς, ἀμφὶ τῇ κηδείᾳ ἠνάγκαστο, καὶ ταῦτα λίαν ἀπὸ τῆς ἀξίας τῆς αὑτοῦ ὄντι. Ἐπεί τε τὸ πρᾶγμα ἤρεσκεν

COURT OF JUSTINIAN 42

Herodianus, and asked him for money
with the most dreadful threats; whereupon he, in his rage, threw off his
allegiance to Rome and went over with
his troops to Totila and the Goths,
and handed over to them the town of
Spoletum.

I will now tell how Belisarius fell out
with John, the nephew of Vitalianus, a
matter which was exceedingly prejudicial
to the interests of Rome. The Empress
was so violently incensed against Germanus, and showed her dislike of him
so plainly, that no one dared to connect
himself with him by marriage, although
he was the Emperor's nephew, and his
children remained unmarried as long as
she lived, while his daughter Justina
was also without a husband at the age
of eighteen. For this reason, when John
was sent by Belisarius on a mission to
Byzantium, Germanus was forced to
enter upon negotiations with him with
a view to marriage with his daughter,
although such an alliance was far be-
neath him. When both had settled the

ἄμφω, ὅρκοις ἀλλήλους ἔγνωσαν δεινοτάτοις καταλαβεῖν, ἦ μὴν τὸ κῆδος ἐπιτελέσειν δυνάμει τῇ πάσῃ· ἐπεὶ αὐτοῖν ἑκάτερος τὸ θαρσεῖν ἐπὶ θατέρῳ ὡς ἥκιστα εἶχεν· ὁ μὲν τῷ ξυνειδέναι, ὅτι δὴ τῶν ὑπὲρ τὴν ἀξίαν ὀρέγοιτο, ὁ δὲ κηδεστοῦ ἀπορούμενος.

γ'. Ἡ δὲ, οὐκ ἔχουσα τίς γένηται, διὰ πάσης ὁδοῦ ἰοῦσα, ἑκάτερον μετιέναι μηχανῇ πάσῃ οὐκ ἀπηξίου, ὅπως ἂν τὰ πραττόμενα μηχανῇ τῇ πάσῃ διακωλύοι. Ἐπεὶ δὲ αὐτοῖν καίπερ πολλὰ δεδιξαμένη ἀναπείθειν οὐδέτερον ἔσχε, διαρρήδην ἀπολεῖν τὸν Ἰωάννην ἠπείλησε. Καὶ ἀπ' αὐτοῦ, Ἰωάννης αὖθις ἐς Ἰταλίαν σταλεὶς, οὐδαμῇ ξυμμῖξαι Βελισαρίῳ ἐτόλμησε, τὴν ἐξ Ἀντωνίνης ἐπιβουλὴν δείσας, ἕως Ἀντωνίνα ἐς Βυζάντιον ἦλθε. Τήν τε γὰρ βασιλίδα ταύτῃ ἐπιστεῖλαι τὸν αὐτοῦ φόνον, οὐκ ἄπο τοῦ εἰκότος ἄν τις ὑπώπτευσε· καὶ τὸν Ἀντωνίνης σταθμωμένῳ τρόπον ἅπαντά τε Βελισάριον ἐνδιδόναι τῇ γυναικὶ ἐπισταμένῳ, δέος ἐγίνετο μέγα, καὶ τὸν [Ἰωάννην] ἐσῄει.

δ'. Τοῦτο γοῦν Ῥωμαίοις τὰ πράγματα, καὶ πρότερον ἐπὶ θατέρου σκέλους

COURT OF JUSTINIAN 43

matter to their satisfaction, they bound each other by the most solemn oaths to use their best endeavours to bring about this alliance; for neither of them trusted the other, as John knew that he was seeking an alliance above his station, and Germanus despaired of finding another husband for his daughter. The Empress was beside herself at this, and endeavoured to thwart them in every possible way; but as her threats had no effect upon either, she openly threatened to put John to death. After this, John was ordered to return to Italy, and, fearing Antonina's designs upon him, held no further communication with Belisarius until her departure for Byzantium; for he had good reason to suspect that the Empress had sent instructions to Antonina to have him murdered; and when he considered the character of Antonina and Belisarius's infatuation for his wife, which made him yield to her in everything, he was greatly alarmed.

From this time forth the power of Rome, which had long been unstable,

44 ΠΡΟΚΟΠΙΟΥ ΑΝΕΚΔΟΤΑ

ἑστῶτα, προσουδίζει χαμαί. Βελισαρίῳ μὲν
οὖν ὁ Γοτθικὸς πόλεμος τῇδε ἐχώρησεν.
᾽Απογνοὺς δὲ, βασιλέως ἐδεῖτο, ὅπως οἱ ἐξῇ
ἐνθένδε ὅτι τάχιστα ἀπαλλαγῆναι. Καὶ
ἐπεὶ ἐνδεχόμενον βασιλέα τὴν δέησιν ἔγνω,
ἄσμενος εὐθὺς ἀπιὼν ᾤχετο, χαίρειν πολλὰ
τῷ τε Ῥωμαίων στρατῷ καὶ ᾽Ιταλοῖς φράσας·
καὶ τὰ μὲν πλεῖστα ὑποχείρια τοῖς πολεμίοις
ἀπολιπών· Περυσίαν δὲ πικρότατα πολιορκίᾳ
πιεζομένην, ἥπερ, ἔτι αὐτοῦ ὁδῷ ἰέντος, κατ᾽
ἄκρας ἀλοῦσα, ἐς πᾶσαν κακοῦ ἰδέαν ἦλθεν,
ᾗπέρ μοι πρότερον δεδιήγηται.

ε´. Ξυνηνέχθη δὲ, καὶ κατὰ τὴν οἰκίαν,
τύχης ἐναντίωμα ξυμπεσεῖν τοιόνδε. Θεοδώρα
ἡ βασιλὶς, τῆς Βελισαρίου παιδὸς ἐξεργάζεσ-
θαι τὴν ἐγγύην ἐπειγομένη τῷ θυγατριδῷ,
συχνὰ γράφουσα, τοὺς γειναμένους τὴν κόρην
ἠνώχλει. Οἱ δὲ τὸ κῆδος ἀναδυόμενοι, ἀπετί-
θεντο μὲν ἐς παρουσίαν τὴν σφετέραν τὸν
γάμον· μεταπεμπομένης δὲ αὐτοὺς ἐς Βυζάν-

COURT OF JUSTINIAN 44

utterly fell to the ground for want of capable support. Such were the fortunes of Belisarius in the Gothic war. After this, despairing of success, he begged the Emperor to allow him to leave Italy with all speed. When he heard that his prayer had been granted, he joyfully retired, bidding a long farewell to the Roman army and the Italians. He left the greater part of Italy in the enemy's power and Perusia in the last agonies of a terrible siege : while he was on his road home, it was taken, and endured all the miseries of a city taken by assault, as I have already related. In addition to his ill-success abroad, he also had to submit to a domestic misfortune, which came about as follows :—The Empress Theodora was eager to bring about the marriage of her grandson, Anastasius, with Belisarius's daughter, and wearied her parents with frequent letters on the subject ; but they, not being desirous of contracting this alliance, put off the marriage until they could appear in person at Byzantium, and when the Em-

τιον τῆς βασιλίδος, ἀδύνατοι εἶναι ἀπαλλάσσεσθαι τανῦν ἐξ Ἰταλίας ἐσκήπτοντο. Ἡ δὲ γλιχομένη μὲν κύριον τὸν θυγατριδοῦν τοῦ Βελισαρίου καταστήσεσθαι πλούτου, ᾔδει γὰρ ἐπίκληρον ἐσομένην τὴν παῖδα, οὐκ ὄντος Βελισαρίῳ ἑτέρου του γόνου, ἐπὶ μέντοι τῇ Ἀντωνίνης γνώμῃ θαρσεῖν οὐδαμῇ ἔχουσα· δειμαίνουσά τε, μὴ μετὰ τὴν τοῦ βίου καταστροφὴν οὐ φανεῖσα πιστὴ ἐς τὸν αὑτῆς οἶκον, καίπερ αὐτῆς οὕτω φιλανθρώπου ἐν τοῖς ἀναγκαιοτάτοις τυχοῦσα, διασπάσηται τὰ ξυγκείμενα, ἐργάζεται ἀνόσιον ἔργον.

ϛʹ. Τῷ γὰρ μειρακίῳ τὴν παιδίσκην ξυνοικίζει, οὐδενὶ νόμῳ. Φασὶ δὲ ὡς καὶ πλησιάσαι οὔτι ἑκουσίαν ἠνάγκασε κρύβδην· οὕτω τε διαπεπαρθενευμένῃ, τὸν ὑμέναιον τῇ κόρῃ ξυστῆναι, τοῦ μὴ βασιλέα τὰ πρασσόμενα διακωλῦσαι. Τοῦ μέντοι ἔργου ἐξειργασμένου, ἔρωτι ἀλλήλοιν διαπύρῳ τινὶ, ὅ τε Ἀναστάσιος καὶ ἡ παῖς εἴχοντο· καὶ χρόνος σφίσιν οὐχ ἧσσων ἢ ὀκτὼ μηνῶν, ἐν ταύτῃ διαίτῃ ἐτρίβη. Ἡνίκα δὲ Ἀντωνίνα

COURT OF JUSTINIAN 45

press sent for them, made the excuse that they could not leave Italy. But she persisted in her determination to make her grandson master of Belisarius's fortune, for she knew that the girl would be his heiress, as he had no other children. She did not, however, trust Antonina's character, and feared lest, after her own death, Antonina might prove unfaithful to her house, although she had found her so helpful in emergencies, and might break the compact. These considerations prompted her to a most abominable act. She made the boy and girl live together without any marriage ceremony, in violation of the laws. It is said that the girl was unwilling to cohabit with him, and that the Empress had her secretly forced to do so, that the marriage might be consummated by the dishonour of the bride, and so the Emperor might not be able to oppose it. After this had taken place, Anastasius and the girl fell passionately in love with each other, and lived together in this manner for eight months.

τῆς βασιλίδος ἀπογενομένης ἐς Βυζάντιον
ἦλθεν, ἐπελάθετο μὲν ἐθελουσία ὧν ἐκείνη
ἔναγχος ἐς αὐτὴν εἴργαστο· ὡς ἥκιστα δὲ
ὑπολογισαμένη, ὡς ἢν τῳ ἑτέρῳ ἡ παῖς αὐτῇ
ξυνοικίζοιτο, πεπορνευμένη τὰ πρότερα ἔσται,
τὸν Θεοδώρας ἔκγονον κηδεστὴν ἀτιμάζει, τήν
τε παῖδα ὡς μάλιστα ἀκουσίαν, βιασαμένη,
ἀνδρὸς τοῦ ἐρωμένου ἀπέστησε.

ζ. Μεγάλην τε ἀγνωμοσύνης ἐκ τοῦ
ἔργου τούτου ἀπηνέγκατο δόξαν εἰς πάντας
ἀνθρώπους· ἥκοντά τε οὐδενὶ πόνῳ ἀναπείθει
τὸν ἄνδρα, τοῦ ἄγους αὐτῇ μεταλαχεῖν τοῦδε·
ὥστε διαρρήδην τηνικάδε ὁ τοῦ ἀνθρώπου τρόπος ἐλήλεγκται. Καίτοι διομοσάμενος Φωτίῳ
τε καὶ τῶν ἐπιτηδείων τισὶ πρότερον, καὶ τὰ
ὀμωμοσμένα οὐδαμῇ ἐμπεδώσας, συγγνώμης
ἐτύγχανε πρὸς πάντων ἀνθρώπων. Αἴτιον
γὰρ τοῦ ἀπίστου τἀνδρὸς οὐ τὴν γυναικοκρά-
τειαν, ἀλλὰ τὸ ἐκ τῆς βασιλίδος ὑπώπτευον
εἶναι. Ἐπεὶ δὲ Θεοδώρας ἀπογενομένης, ὥσπερ
μοι εἴρηται, οὔτε Φωτίου οὔτε ἄλλου του
τῶν οἱ ἀναγκαίων λόγος γεγένητο· ἀλλ' αὐτῷ

COURT OF JUSTINIAN 46

Immediately after the Empress's death, Antonina came to Byzantium. She found it easy to ignore the outrage which Theodora had committed upon her, and, without considering that, if she united the girl to another, she would be no better than a harlot, she drove away Theodora's grandson with insults, and forcibly separated her daughter from the man whom she loved.

This action caused her to be regarded as one of the most heartless women upon earth, but nevertheless the mother obtained, without any difficulty, Belisarius's approval of her conduct, on his return home. Thus did this man's true character reveal itself. Although he had sworn a solemn oath to Photius and to several of his intimates and broken it, yet all men readily forgave him, because they suspected that the reason of his faithlessness was not the dominion of his wife over him, but his fear of Theodora; but now that Theodora was dead, as I have told you, he thought nothing about Photius or any of his intimates, but en-

ΠΡΟΚΟΠΙΟΥ ΑΝΕΚΔΟΤΑ

δέσποινα μὲν ἡ γυνὴ ἐφαίνετο οὖσα· κύριος δὲ Καλλίγονος ὁ προαγωγὸς ἦν· τότε δὴ ἀπογνόντες αὐτοῦ ἅπαντες, ἐχλεύαζόν τε διαθρυλλοῦντες, καὶ ἅτε ἄνοιαν ὀφλισκάνοντι ἐλοιδοροῦντο. Τὰ μὲν οὖν ἡμαρτημένα Βελισαρίῳ ἀπαρακαλύπτως εἰπεῖν ταύτῃ πῃ ἔχει.

η΄. Τὰ δὲ Σεργίῳ, τῷ Βάκχου παιδὶ, ἐπὶ Λιβύης ἡμαρτημένα, διαρκῶς μὲν ἐν λόγοις μοι τοῖς ἐπιτηδείοις δεδήλωται· ὃς δὴ αἰτιώτατος γέγονε Ῥωμαίοις ἐνταῦθα διαφθαρῆναι τὰ πράγματα, τά τε πρὸς Λευάθας αὐτῷ πρὸς τῶν εὐαγγελίων ὀμωμοσμένα ἐν ἀλογίᾳ πεποιημένος· καὶ τοὺς ὀγδοήκοντα πρέσβεις οὐδενὶ λόγῳ διαχρησάμενος· τοσοῦτον δέ μοι τανῦν ἐντιθέναι τῷ λόγῳ δεήσει, ὡς οὔτε νῷ δολερῷ οἱ ἄνδρες οὗτοι παρὰ Σέργιον ἦλθον, οὔτε τινὰ σκῆψιν ὁ Σέργιος ὑποψίας περὶ αὐτοὺς εἶχεν, ἀλλὰ διώμοτος ἐπὶ θοίνην καλέσας, τοὺς ἄνδρας διεχρήσατο οὐδενὶ κόσμῳ.

θ΄. Ἀφ' οὗ δὴ Σολόμωνι, καὶ τῷ Ῥωμαίων στρατῷ, καὶ Λίβυσι πᾶσι, διεφθάρθαι ξυνέβη.

COURT OF JUSTINIAN   47

tirely submitted to the sway of his wife,
and her pander Calligonus. Then at last
all men ceased to believe in him, scorned
and flouted him, and railed at him for
an idiot. Such were the offences of Belisarius, about which I have been obliged
to speak freely in this place.

In its proper place, I have said
enough about the shortcomings of Sergius, the son of Bacchus, in Libya. I
have told how he was the chief cause
of the ruin of the Roman power in that
country, how he broke the oath which
he swore to the Levathae on the Gospels,
and how he, without excuse, put to
death the eighty ambassadors. I need
only add in this place, that these men
did not come to Sergius with any
treacherous intent, and that Sergius had
not the slightest reason for suspecting
them, but having invited them to a
banquet and taken an oath not to harm
them, he cruelly butchered them.

Solomon, the Roman army, and all
the Libyans were lost owing to this
crime ; for, in consequence of what he

ΠΡΟΚΟΠΙΟΥ ΑΝΕΚΔΟΤΑ

Δι' αὐτὸν γὰρ, ἄλλως τε καὶ Σολόμωνος τετελευτηκότος, ὥσπερ μοι εἴρηται, οὔτε τις ἄρχων, οὔτε τις στρατιώτης, ἐς πολέμου κίνδυνον ἰέναι ἠξίου. Μάλιστα δὲ πάντων Ἰωάννης, ὁ Σισιννιόλου, τῷ ἐς αὐτὸν ἔχθει ἀπόμαχος ἦν, ἕως Ἀρεόβινδος ἐς Λιβύην ἀφίκετο. Ἦν γὰρ ὁ Σέργιος μαλθακὸς μὲν καὶ ἀπόλεμος· τὸ δὲ ἦθος καὶ τὴν ἡλικίαν κομιδῇ νέος, φθόνῳ τε καὶ ἀλαζονείᾳ ἐς ὑπερβολὴν ἐχόμενος ἐς πάντας ἀνθρώπους, τεθρυμμένος τε τὴν δίαιταν καὶ τὰς γνάθους φυσῶν. Ἀλλ' ἐπεὶ τῆς Ἀντωνίνης, τῆς Βελισαρίου γυναικὸς, ἐγγόνης ἐτύγχανε μνηστὴρ γεγονὼς, τίσιν τινὰ ἐς αὐτὸν ἡ βασιλὶς ἐξενεγκεῖν ἢ παραλύειν τῆς ἀρχῆς οὐδαμῇ ἤθελε, καίπερ ἐνδελεχέστατα διαφθειρομένην Λιβύην ὁρῶσα, ἐπεὶ καὶ Σολόμωνα, τὸν Σεργίου ἀδελφὸν, τοῦ Πηγασίου φόνου, αὐτή τε καὶ βασιλεὺς, ἀθῷον ἀφῆκεν. Ὅ τι δὲ τοῦτ' ἔστιν, αὐτίκα δηλώσω.

ί. Ἐπειδὴ ὁ Πηγάσιος τὸν Σολόμωνα πρὸς τῶν Λευαθῶν ὠνήσατο, καὶ οἱ βάρβαροι ἐπ' οἴκου ἀπεκομίσθησαν, ὁ μὲν Σολόμων, ξύν τε Πηγασίῳ τῷ ἐωνημένῳ, καὶ στρα-

COURT OF JUSTINIAN   48

had done, especially after Solomon's
death, no officer or soldier would expose
himself to the dangers of war. John, the
son of Sisinniolus, was especially averse
to taking the field, out of the hatred
which he bore to Sergius, until Areobindus arrived in Libya.

Sergius was effeminate and unwarlike,
very young both in years and in mind,
excessively jealous and insolent to all
men, luxurious in his habits, and inflated
with pride. However, after he had become the accepted husband of the niece
of Antonina, Belisarius's wife, the Empress
would not permit him to be punished in
any way or removed from his office,
although she saw distinctly that the state
of affairs in Libya threatened its utter
ruin; and she even induced the Emperor
to pardon Solomon, Sergius's brother, for
the murder of Pegasius. How this came
to pass I will now explain.

After Pegasius had ransomed Solomon
from captivity among the Levathae, and
the barbarians had returned home, Solomon and Pegasius, who had ransomed

ΠΡΟΚΟΠΙΟΥ ΑΝΕΚΔΟΤΑ

τιώταις ὀλίγοις τισὶν, εἰς Καρχηδόνα ἐστέλλετο· ἐν δὲ τῇ ὁδῷ ταύτῃ λαβὼν ὁ Πηγάσιος ὅ τι δὴ ἀδικοῦντα Σολόμωνα χρῆναί οἱ ἔφασκεν ἐν μνήμῃ εἶναι, ὡς αὐτὸν ἔναγχος ἐκ τῶν πολεμίων ὁ θεὸς ῥύσαιτο. Ὁ δὲ χαλεπήνας, ὅτι δή οἱ ἅτε δορυαλώτῳ ὠνείδισε, τὸν Πηγάσιον εὐθὺς ἔκτεινε· ταῦτά τε σῶστρα τῷ ἀνθρώπῳ ἀπέδωκεν. Ἐπειδή τε ὁ Σολόμων ἐς Βυζάντιον ἦλθε, καθαρὸν αὐτὸν βασιλεὺς τοῦ φόνου ἐποίει, ἅτε προδότην ἀνελόντα τῆς Ῥωμαίων ἀρχῆς. Γράμματά τε αὐτῷ ἐδίδου, τὴν ὑπὲρ τούτων ἀσφάλειαν παρεχόμενος. Καὶ ὁ μὲν Σολόμων, οὕτω τὴν τίσιν διαφυγὼν, ἐπὶ τὴν ἑῴαν ἄσμενος (ᾔει), τήν τε πατρίδα καὶ γένος τὸ κατὰ τὴν οἰκίαν ὀψόμενος. Ἡ δὲ ἀπὸ τοῦ θεοῦ τίσις, ἐν ταύτῃ τῇ ὁδῷ καταλαβοῦσα, ἐξ ἀνθρώπων αὐτὸν ἀφανίζει. Τὰ μὲν οὖν ἀμφὶ Σολόμωνί τε καὶ Πηγασίῳ τῇδε ἐχώρησεν.

COURT OF JUSTINIAN 49

him, set out, accompanied by a few soldiers, to Carthage. On the way Pegasius reproached Solomon with the wrong he had done, and bade him remember that Heaven had only just rescued him from the enemy. Solomon, enraged at being taunted with his captivity, straightway slew Pegasius, and thus requited him for having ransomed him. But when Solomon reached Byzantium, the Emperor absolved him from the guilt of murder, on the pretext that he had slain a traitor to the Roman Empire, and gave him letters of acquittal. Solomon, having thus escaped all punishment for his crime, departed gladly for the East, to visit his own country and his family; but the vengeance of God fell upon him on the way, and removed him from amongst mankind. This is what happened in regard to Solomon and Pegasius.

7—2

ΠΡΟΚΟΠΙΟΥ ΑΝΕΚΔΟΤΑ

ΚΕΦΑΛΑΙΟΝ Ϛ'.

α'. Οἵτινες δὲ ἀνθρώπω Ἰουστινιανός τε καὶ Θεοδώρα ἤστην, τρόπῳ τε ὅτῳ διεσπάσαντο τὰ Ῥωμαίων πράγματα, ἐρῶν ἔρχομαι. Λέοντος ἐν Βυζαντίῳ τὴν αὐτοκράτορα ἀρχὴν ἔχοντος, γεωργοὶ νεανίαι τρεῖς, Ἰλλυριοὶ γένος, Ζίμαρχός τε καὶ Διτύβιστος, καὶ Ἰουστῖνος ὁ ἐκ Βεδεριανῆς, πράγμασιν ἐνδελεχέστατα τοῖς ἀπὸ τῆς πενίας οἴκοι μαχόμενοι, τούτων τε ἀπαλλαξείοντες, ἐπὶ τῷ στρατεύεσθαι ὥρμησαν. Καὶ πεζῇ βαδίζοντες ἐς Βυζάντιον ᾔεσαν, σισύρας ἐπὶ τῶν ὤμων αὐτοὶ φέροντες, ἐν αἷς δὴ ἄλλο οὐδὲν ὅτι μὴ διπύρους ἄρτους οἴκοθεν ἐμβεβλημένοι, ἀφίκοντο· ταχθέντας τε ἐν τοῖς στρατιωτικοῖς καταλόγοις βασιλεὺς αὐτοὺς ἐς τοῦ παλατίου τὴν φυλακὴν ἐπεξελέξατο. Κάλλιστοι γὰρ ἅπαντες τὰ σώματα ἦσαν.

β'. Χρόνῳ δὲ ὕστερον, Ἀναστασίῳ τὴν

CHAPTER VI

I NOW come to the description of the private life and character of Justinian and Theodora, and of the manner in which they rent the Roman Empire asunder.

At the time when Leo occupied the imperial throne, three young husband-men, of Illyrian birth, named Zimarchus, Ditybistus, and Justin of Bederiane, in order to escape from their utter poverty at home, determined to enlist in the army. They made their way to Byzantium on foot, with knapsacks of goat's-hair on their shoulders, containing nothing but a few biscuits which they had brought from home. On their arrival they were enrolled in the army, and chosen by the Emperor amongst the palace guards, being all three very handsome young men.

Afterwards, when Anastasius succeeded

ΠΡΟΚΟΠΙΟΥ ΑΝΕΚΔΟΤΑ

βασιλείαν παραλαβόντι, πόλεμος πρὸς τὸ Ἰσαύρων ἔθνος ὅπλα ἐπ᾽ αὐτὸν ἀραμένους (κατέστη)· στρατιάν τε λόγου ἀξίαν ἐπ᾽ αὐτοὺς ἔπεμψεν, ἧσπερ Ἰωάννης ἡγεῖτο, ἐπίκλησιν Κυρτός. Οὗτος Ἰωάννης τὸν Ἰουστῖνον, ἁμαρτάδος τινὸς ἕνεκα, ἐν δεσμωτηρίῳ καθεῖρξεν· ἡμέρᾳ τε τῇ ἐπιούσῃ ἐξ ἀνθρώπων αὐτὸν ἀφανιεῖν ἔμελλεν, εἰ μή τις μεταξὺ ἐπιγενομένη ὄψις ὀνείρου ἐκώλυσεν. Ἔφη γάρ οἱ ἐν ὀνείρῳ ὁ στρατηγός, ἐντυχεῖν τινα παμμεγέθη τε τὸ σῶμα, καὶ τἆλλα κρείσσω ἢ ἀνθρώπῳ εἰκάζεσθαι. Καὶ τὸν μὲν οἱ ἐπισκῆψαι μεθεῖναι τὸν ἄνδρα, ὅνπερ καθεῖρξας ἐκείνῃ τῇ ἡμέρᾳ ἐτύγχανεν· αὐτὸν δὲ, τοῦ ὕπνου ἐξαναστάντα, ἐν ἀλογίᾳ τὴν τοῦ ὀνείρου ὄψιν ποιήσασθαι. Ἐπιλαβούσης δὲ καὶ ἑτέρας νυκτὸς ἐδόκει μὲν ἐν τῷ ὀνείρῳ καὶ αὖθις τῶν λόγων ἀκούειν ὧνπερ ἠκηκόει τὸ πρότερον, ἐπιτελέσαι δὲ τὰ ἐπιτεταγμένα οὐδ᾽ ὣς βεβουλῆσθαι. Τρίτον τέ οἱ ἐπιστᾶσαν τὴν τοῦ ὀνείρου ὄψιν ἀπειλῆσαι μὲν τὰ ἀνήκεστα, ἢν μὴ τὰ ἐπηγγελμένα ποιοίη, ἐπειπεῖν τε ὡς αὐτοῦ τε τοῦ ἀνθρώπου καὶ τῆς ξυγγενείας χρέος οἱ μέγα ὀργισθησομένῳ ἐς χρόνον τὸν ὄπισθεν εἴη. Τότε μὲν οὖν οὕτως Ἰουστίνῳ περιεῖναι ξυνέβη.

COURT OF JUSTINIAN 51

to the throne, war broke out with the Isaurians who had rebelled against him. He sent a considerable army against them, under the command of John, surnamed " The Hunchback." This John arrested Justin for some offence and imprisoned him, and on the following day would have put him to death, had not a vision which he beheld in his sleep prevented him. He said that, in his dream, a man of great stature, and in every way more than human, bade him release the man whom he had that day cast into prison. When he awoke, he made light of this vision; and, although he saw again the same vision and heard the same words on the following night, not even then would he obey the command. But the vision appeared for the third time, and threatened him terribly if he did not do what he was commanded, and warned him that he would thereafter stand in great need of this man and his family when his wrath should fall upon him. Thus did Justin escape death.

ΠΡΟΚΟΠΙΟΥ ΑΝΕΚΔΟΤΑ

γ'. Προϊόντος δὲ τοῦ χρόνου, ἐς μέγα δυνάμεως οὗτος Ἰουστῖνος ἐχώρησεν. Ἄρχοντα γὰρ αὐτὸν Ἀναστάσιος Βασιλεὺς κατεστήσατο τῶν ἐν παλατίῳ φυλάκων. Ἐπειδή τε ὁ βασιλεὺς ἐξ ἀνθρώπων ἠφάνιστο, αὐτὸς τῇ τῆς ἀρχῆς δυνάμει τὴν βασιλείαν παρέλαβε, τυμβογέρων μὲν γεγονὼς ἤδη, ἀμάθητος δὲ γραμμάτων ἀπάντων, καὶ τὸ δὴ λεγόμενον ἀναλφάβητος ὤν· οὐ γεγονὸς ἐν Ῥωμαίοις πρότερον τοῦτό γε. Εἰθισμένου δὲ γράμματα οἰκεῖα τοῖς βιβλίοις ἐντιθέναι τὸν βασιλέα, ὅσα ἂν ἐπαγγέλλοντος αὐτοῦ γίνοιτο, αὐτὸς μέντοι οὔτε ἐπήγγελλεν, οὔτε τοῖς πρασσομένοις ξυνεπίστασθαι οἷός τε ἦν.

δ'. Ὃς δὲ παρεδρεύειν αὐτῷ ἔλαχεν ἀρχὴν τὴν τοῦ καλουμένου κοιαίστορος, Πρόκλος ὄνομα, αὐτὸς δὴ αὐτονόμῳ γνώμῃ ἅπαντα ἔπρασσεν. Ὅπως δὲ μαρτυρίαν τῆς βασιλέως χειρὸς ἔχοιεν, [οἷς] ἐπίκειται τὸ ἔργον τοῦτο, ἐπενοήθη τάδε. Ξύλῳ εἰργασμένῳ βραχεῖ ἐγκολάψαντες μορφήν τινα γραμμάτων τεττάρων, ἅπερ ἀναγνῶναι τῇ Λατίνων φωνῇ δύναται, γραφίδα τε βαφῇ βάψαντες, ᾗ βασιλεῖς γράφειν εἰώθασιν, ἐνεχειρίζοντο τῷ βασιλεῖ τούτῳ. Καὶ τὸ ξύλον, οὗπερ ἐμνήσθην, τῷ

COURT OF JUSTINIAN

As time went on, this Justin rose to great power. The Emperor Anastasius appointed him commander of the palace guard, and when that prince died, he, by the influence of his position, seized the throne. He was by this time an old man with one foot in the grave, so utterly ignorant of letters, that one may say that he did not know the alphabet —a thing which had never happened before amongst the Romans. It had been customary for the Emperor to sign the decrees which were issued by him with his own hand, whereas he neither made decrees, nor was capable of conducting affairs ; but Proclus, who acted as his quaestor and colleague, arranged every thing at his own pleasure. However, in order that the Emperor's signature might appear in public documents, his officers invented the following device. They had the shapes of four Latin letters cut in a thin piece of wood, and then, having dipped the pen in the imperial ink used by the Emperors in writing, they put it in the Emperor's hand, and laying the

ΠΡΟΚΟΠΙΟΥ ΑΝΕΚΔΟΤΑ

βιβλίῳ ἐνθέμενοι, λαβόμενοί τε τῆς βασιλέως χειρὸς, περιῆγον μὲν ξὺν τῇ γραφίδι ἐς τῶν τεττάρων γραμμάτων τὸν τύπον, ἐς πάσας τε τὰς τοῦ ξύλου αὐτὴν περιελίξαντες ἐντομὰς, οὕτω δὴ ἀπηλλάσσοντο, τοιαῦτα βασιλέως γράμματα φέροντες. Τὰ μὲν ἀμφὶ τῷ Ἰουστίνῳ ταύτῃ Ῥωμαίοις εἶχε.

ε΄. Γυναικὶ δὲ ὄνομα Λουππικίνῃ ξυνῴκει. Αὕτη δὲ δούλη τε καὶ βάρβαρος οὖσα, τοῦ πρόσθεν αὐτὴν ἐωνημένου παλλακὴ γέγονε. Καὶ αὐτὴ μὲν ξὺν Ἰουστίνῳ ἐπὶ βίου δυσμαῖς τὴν βασιλείαν ἔσχεν. Ἰουστῖνος μὲν οὖν οὔτε τι πονηρὸν τοὺς ὑπηκόους ἐργάζεσθαι οὔτε ἀγαθὸν ἴσχυεν. Εὐηθείᾳ γὰρ πολλῇ εἴχετο, ἄγλωττός τε παντάπασιν ὢν, καὶ ἀγροικιζόμενος μάλιστα.

ς΄. Ἀδελφιδοῦς δὲ αὐτῷ Ἰουστινιανὸς, νέος ὢν ἔτι, διῳκεῖτο τὴν ἀρχὴν ξύμπασαν, καὶ γέγονε Ῥωμαίοις ξυμφορῶν αἴτιος, οἵας τε καὶ ὅσας ἐς τὸν ἅπαντα αἰῶνα οὐδείς που πρότερον ἀκοῇ ἔλαβεν. Ἔς τε γὰρ ἀνθρώπων ἄδικον φόνον, καὶ χρημάτων ἁπαγὴν ἀλλοτρίων, ῥᾷστα ἐχώρει, καὶ οὐδὲν ἦν αὐτῷ μυριάδας πολλὰς ἀνθρώπων ἀφανισθῆναι, καίπερ αὐτῷ αἰτίαν οὐδεμίαν παρασχομένων. Καὶ φυλάσσειν μὲν τῶν καθεσταμένων οὐδὲν ἠξίου·

COURT OF JUSTINIAN   53

piece of wood on the paper to be signed,
they guided the Emperor's hand and pen
round the outline of the four letters,
making it follow all the convolutions cut
in the wood, and then retired with the
result as the Emperor's signature. This
was how the affairs of the Empire were
managed under Justin. His wife was
named Lupicina; she was a slave and a
barbarian, whom he had bought for his
mistress, and at the close of his life she
ascended the throne with him. Justin
was not strong enough to do his subjects
either good or harm; he was utterly
simple, a very poor speaker, and a complete boor. Justinian was his sister's
son, who, when quite a young man,
practically governed the State, and
brought more woe upon the Romans
than anyone we have ever heard of
before. He was ever ready to commit un-
righteous murders and rob men of their
estates, and thought nothing of making
away with tens of thousands of men
who had given him no cause for doing
so. He had no respect for established

54 ΠΡΟΚΟΠΙΟΥ ΑΝΕΚΔΟΤΑ

ἅπαντα δὲ νεοχμοῦν ἐς ἀεὶ ἤθελε, καὶ, τὸ
ξύμπαν εἰπεῖν, μέγιστος δὴ οὗτος διαφθορεὺς
τῶν εὖ καθεστώτων. Τὸν μὲν οὖν λοιμὸν,
ὅσπερ μοι ἐν τοῖς ἔμπροσθεν λόγοις ἐρρήθη,
καίπερ ἐπισκήψαντα εἰς τὴν γῆν ξύμπασαν,
διέφυγον ἄνθρωποι οὐχ ἥσσους ἢ ὅσοις διαφθαρῆναι τετύχηκεν, ἢ οὐδαμῆ τῇ νόσῳ ἁλόντες, ἢ
[ὑγιαζόμενοι,] ἐπειδὴ σφίσιν ἁλῶναι ξυνέβη.
Ἄνδρα δὲ τοῦτον διαφυγεῖν ἀνθρώπῳ γε
ὄντι τῶν πάντων Ῥωμαίων οὐδενὶ ξυνηνέχθη,
ἀλλ' ὥσπερ τι ἄλλο ἐξ οὐρανοῦ πάθος,
ὅλῳ τῷ γένει ἐπεισπεσὸν, ἀνέπαφον οὐδένα
παντελῶς εἴασε. Τοὺς μὲν γὰρ ἔκτεινεν
οὐδενὶ λόγῳ· τοὺς δὲ πενίᾳ μαχομένους ἀφεὶς,
ἀθλιωτέρους τῶν τετελευτηκότων εἰργάζετο,
εὐχομένους τὰ παρόντα σφίσι διαλῦσαι θανάτῳ
οἰκτίστῳ. Τινῶν μέντοι ξὺν τοῖς χρήμασι
καὶ τὰς ψυχὰς εἷλεν.

ζ΄. Ἐπεὶ δὲ οὐδὲν ἦν αὐτῷ μόνην καταλῦ-
σαι τὴν Ῥωμαίων ἀρχὴν, Λιβύης τε καὶ

COURT OF JUSTINIAN   54

institutions, but loved innovations in everything, and was, in short, the greatest destroyer of all the best of his country's institutions. As for the plague, of which I have made mention in the former books of my history, although it ravaged the whole earth, yet as many men escaped it as perished by it, some of them never taking the contagion, and others recovering from it. But no human being in all the Roman Empire could escape from this man, for he was like some second plague sent down from heaven to prey upon the whole human race, which left no man untouched. Some he slew without cause, others he reduced to a struggle with poverty, so that their case was more piteous than that of the dead, and they prayed daily to be relieved from their misery even by the most cruel death, while he robbed others of their lives and their property at the same time.

Not content with ruining the Roman Empire, he carried out the conquest of Italy and Africa, merely that he might

ΠΡΟΚΟΠΙΟΥ ΑΝΕΚΔΟΤΑ

Ἰταλίας οὐκ ἄλλου του ἕνεκα πεποιῆσθαι τὴν ἐπικράτησιν ἴσχυσεν ἢ ὥστε ξὺν τοῖς πρότερον ὑφ᾽ αὑτῷ οὖσι διολέσαι τοὺς ταύτῃ ἀνθρώπους. Οὔπω γοῦν δεκαταῖος εἰς τὴν δύναμιν γεγονὼς, Ἀμάντιον τῶν ἐν παλατίῳ εὐνούχων ἄρχοντα ξὺν ἑτέροις τισὶν ἐξ αἰτίας οὐδεμιᾶς ἔκτεινεν, ἄλλο οὐδὲν τῷ ἀνθρώπῳ ἐπενεγκὼν, πλήν γε δὴ ὅτι ἐς Ἰωάννην, τὸν τῆς πόλεως ἀρχιερέα, λόγον τινὰ προπετῆ εἴποι. Καὶ ἀπ᾽ αὐτοῦ φοβερώτατος γέγονεν ἀνθρώπων ἁπάντων.

η΄. Αὐτίκα δὲ καὶ Βιταλιανὸν τὸν τύραννον μετεπέμψατο, ᾧ δὴ τὰ πιστὰ πρότερον ὑπὲρ τῆς ἀσφαλείας παρέσχετο, διαλαχὼν αὐτῷ καὶ τῶν ἐν Χριστιανοῖς μυστηρίων. Ὀλίγῳ τε ὕστερον, ἐξ ὑποψίας αὐτῷ προσκεκρουκότα, ξὺν τοῖς ἐπιτηδείοις ἐν παλατίῳ λόγῳ οὐδενὶ διεχρήσατο, πίστεις οὕτω δεινοτάτας ἐμπεδῶσαι οὐδαμῆ ἀξιώσας.

COURT OF JUSTINIAN

treat them in the same way, and destroy the inhabitants, together with those who were already his subjects. He had not been in authority ten days before he put to death Amantius, the chief of the palace eunuchs, with several others. He had no complaint whatever against the man beyond that he had said something offensive about John the archbishop of the city. Owing to this, he became the most dreaded of all men in the world.

Immediately afterwards he sent for the usurper Vitalianus, to whom he had given the most solemn pledges for his safety, and had partaken of the Christian sacrament with him. Shortly afterwards, he conceived some suspicion of him, and made away with him and his companions in the palace, for no reason whatever, thus showing that he scorned to observe even the most solemn oaths.

ΚΕΦΑΛΑΙΟΝ Ζ'.

α'. Τοῦ δὲ δήμου ἐκ παλαιοῦ ἐς μοίρας δύο διεστηκότος, ὥσπερ μοι ἐν τοῖς ἔμπροσθεν λόγοις ἐρρήθη, μίαν αὐτὸς τὴν Βενέτων ἑταιρισάμενος, ἣ οἱ καὶ τὸ πρότερον κατεσπουδασμένη ἐτύγχανε, ξυγχεῖν τε καὶ συνταράξαι ἅπαντα ἴσχυσε. Καὶ ἀπ' αὐτοῦ ἐς γόνυ ἐλθεῖν Ῥωμαίοις τὴν πολιτείαν πεποίηκεν. Οὐχ ἅπαντες δὲ οἱ Βένετοι ἐπισπέσθαι τῇ τοῦδε ἀνδρὸς γνώμῃ ἔγνωσαν, ἀλλ' ὅσοι στασιῶται ὄντες ἐτύγχανον. Καὶ αὐτοὶ μέντοι, προϊόντος ἤδη τοῦ δεινοῦ, σωφρονέστατοι ἔδοξαν εἶναι ἀνθρώπων ἁπάντων. Ἐνδεεστέρως γὰρ ἢ κατὰ τὴν ἐξουσίαν ἡμάρτανον. Οὐ μὴν οὐδὲ τῶν Πρασίνων οἱ στασιῶται ἡσυχῇ ἔμενον· ἀλλὰ καὶ αὐτοὶ ἔπρασσον ἀεὶ τὰ ἐγκλήματα, ἐς ὅσον σφίσι δυνατὰ ἐγεγόνει,

CHAPTER VII

In the former part of my history I have explained how the people had long been divided into two factions. Justinian associated himself with one of these, the Blues, which had previously favoured him, and was thus enabled to upset everything and throw all into disorder. Thereby the Roman constitution was beaten to its knees. However, all the Blues did not agree to follow his views, but only those who were inclined to revolutionary measures. Yet, as the evil spread, these very men came to be regarded as the most moderate of mankind, for they used their opportunities of doing wrong less than they might have done. Nor did the revolutionists of the Green faction remain idle, but they also, as far as they were able, continually perpetrated all kinds of excesses, although in-

καίπερ κατὰ μόνας διηνεκὲς κολαζόμενοι. Ὅπερ αὐτοὺς ἐς τὸ θρασύνεσθαι πολλῷ ἔτι μᾶλλον ἐς ἀεὶ ἦγεν. Ἀδικούμενοι γὰρ εἰώθασιν ἐς ἀπόνοιαν τρέπεσθαι ἄνθρωποι.

β΄. Τότε οὖν, τοὺς Βενέτους αὐτοῦ ῥιπίζοντός τε καὶ διαφανῶς ἐρεθίζοντος, ἅπασα κατ' ἄκρας ἡ Ῥωμαίων ἀρχὴ ἐκινήθη, ὥσπερ σεισμοῦ ἢ κατακλυσμοῦ ἐπιπεσόντος, ἢ πόλεως ἑκάστης πρὸς τῶν πολεμίων ἁλούσης. Πάντα γὰρ ἐν ἅπασι ξυνεταράχθη, καὶ οὐδὲν ὑφ' ἑαυτοῦ τὸ λοιπὸν ἔμεινεν· ἀλλ' οἵ τε νόμοι, καὶ ὁ τῆς πολιτείας κόσμος, ξυγχύσεως ἐπιγενομένης, ἐς πᾶν τοὐναντίον ἐχώρησαν. Καὶ πρῶτα μὲν τοῖς στασιώταις τὰ ἐς τὴν κόμην ἐς νεώτερόν τινα μετεβέβλητο τρόπον. Ἀπεκείροντο γὰρ αὐτὴν, οὐδὲν ὁμοίως τοῖς ἄλλοις Ῥωμαίοις. Τοῦ μὲν γὰρ μύστακος καὶ τοῦ γενείου οὐδαμῇ ἥπτοντο· ἀλλ' αὐτοῖς κατακομᾶν ἐπὶ πλεῖστον, ὥσπερ οἱ Πέρσαι, ἐς ἀεὶ ἤθελον. Τῶν δὲ ἐν τῇ κεφαλῇ τριχῶν τὰ ἔμπροσθεν ἄχρι ἐς τοὺς κροτάφους ἀποτεμόμενοι, τὰ ὄπισθεν ἀποκρέμασθαι σφίσιν ἐπὶ μακρότατον λόγῳ οὐδενὶ εἴων, ὥσπερ οἱ Μασσαγέται. Διὸ δὴ καὶ Οὐννικὸν τὸ τοιοῦτον εἶδος ἐκάλουν.

COURT OF JUSTINIAN 57

dividuals of their number were continually being punished. This only made them bolder, for men, when they are treated harshly, usually become desperate.

At this time Justinian, by openly encouraging and provoking the Blue faction, shook the Roman Empire to its foundation, like an earthquake or a flood, or as though each city had been taken by the enemy. Everything was everywhere thrown into disorder; nothing was left alone. The laws and the whole fabric of the State were altogether upset, and became the very opposite of what they had been. First of all, the revolutionists altered the fashion of wearing the hair, for they cut it short, in a manner quite different to that of the rest of the Romans. They never touched the moustache and beard, but let them grow like the Persians: but they shaved the hair off the front part of their heads as far as the temples, and let it hang down long and in disorder behind, like the Massagetae. Wherefore they called this the Hunnic fashion of wearing the hair.

8—2

58 ΠΡΟΚΟΠΙΟΥ ΑΝΕΚΔΟΤΑ

γ΄. Ἔπειτα δὲ τὰ ἐς τὰ ἱμάτια εὐπάρυφοι ἠξίουν εἶναι ἅπαντες, κομπωδεστέραν ἢ κατὰ τὴν ἑκάστου ἀξίαν ἐνδιδυσκόμενοι τὴν ἐσθῆτα. Κτᾶσθαι γὰρ αὐτοῖς τὰ τοιαῦτα ἐξ οὐ προσηκόντων παρῆν. Τοῦ δὲ χιτῶνος τὸ ἀμφὶ τὼ χεῖρε μέρος ἐς τὸν καρπὸν ξυνῄει σφίσιν ἐν στενῷ μάλιστα. Τὰ δὲ ἐνθένδε ἄχρι ἐς ὦμον ἑκάτερον ἐς ἄφατόν τι εὔρους διεκέχυτο χρῆμα. Ὁσάκις τε ἡ χεὶρ αὐτοῖς σείοιτο, ἀναβοῶσιν ἐν τοῖς θεάτροις τε καὶ ἱπποδρομίοις, ἢ ἐγκελευομένοις, ᾗπερ εἰώθει, ἐς ὕψος αὐτοῖς τοῦτο τὸ μέρος ἀτεχνῶς ᾖρετο, αἴσθησιν παρεχόμενον τοῖς ἀνοήτοις, ὅτι δὴ αὐτοῖς οὕτω καλόν τε τὸ σῶμα καὶ ἁδρὸν εἴη ἂν, ὥστε δεῖν γε αὐτοῖς πρὸς τῶν τοιούτων ἱματίων καλύπτεσθαι· οὐκ ἐννοοῦσιν ὅτι δὴ αὐτοῖς τῷ τῆς ἐσθῆτος ἠραιωμένῳ τε καὶ κενῷ πολλῷ ἔτι μᾶλλον τὸ τοῦ σώματος ἐξίτηλον διελεγχθείη. Αἱ ἐπωμίδες δὲ καὶ ἀναξυρίδες, καὶ τῶν ὑποδημάτων τὰ πλεῖστα, ἐς τῶν Οὔννων τό τε ὄνομα καὶ τὸν τρόπον ἀπεκέκριτο σφίσιν.

δ΄. Ἐσιδηροφόρουν δὲ νύκτωρ μὲν τὰ πρῶτα ἐκ τοῦ ἐμφανοῦς ἅπαντες σχεδόν· ἐν δέ γε ἡμέρᾳ, ξιφίδια περὶ τὸν μηρὸν δίστομα ὑπὸ τῷ ἱματίῳ ἀποκρυψάμενοι· ξυνιστάμενοί τε

COURT OF JUSTINIAN   58

In the next place they all chose to wear richly-embroidered dresses, far finer than became their several stations in life, but they were able to pay for them out of their illicit gains. The sleeves of their tunics were made as tight as possible at the wrists, but from thence to the shoulder were of an astounding width, and whenever they moved their hands, in applauding in the theatre or the hippodrome, or encouraging the competitors, this part of the tunic was waved aloft, to convey to the ignorant the impression that they were so beautifully made and so strong that they were obliged to wear such robes as these to cover their muscles. They did not perceive that the empty width of their sleeves only made their bodies appear even more stunted than they were. The cloaks, drawers and shoes which they mostly affected were called after the Huns, and made in their fashion.

At first they almost all openly went about armed at night, but by day hid short two-edged swords upon their thighs under their cloaks. They gathered to-

ΠΡΟΚΟΠΙΟΥ ΑΝΕΚΔΟΤΑ

κατὰ συμμορίας, ἐπειδὰν συσκοτάζοι, ἐλωπο-
δύτουν τοὺς ἐπιεικεστέρους, ἔν τε ὅλῃ ἀγορᾷ
κὰν τοῖς στενωποῖς, ἀφαιρούμενοι τοὺς παραπεπτωκότας τά τε ἱμάτια ζώνας τε καὶ περόνας
χρυσᾶς, καὶ εἴ τι ἄλλο ἐν χερσὶν ἔχοιεν.
Τινὰς δὲ πρὸς τῇ ἁρπαγῇ καὶ κτείνειν ἠξίουν,
ὅπως μηδενὶ τὰ ξυμπεσόντα σφίσιν ἀναγγελλω-
σιν. Οἷς δὴ ἅπαντες, καὶ τῶν Βενέτων οἱ
μὴ στασιῶται μάλιστα ἤχθοντο. Ἐπεὶ δὲ
οὐδὲ αὐτοὶ ἀπαθεῖς ἔμενον, καὶ ἀπ᾽ αὐτοῦ
χαλκαῖς τὸ λοιπὸν ζώναις τε καὶ περόναις καὶ
ἱματίοις πολλῷ ἐλασσόνως ἢ κατὰ τὴν ἀξίαν
ὡς πλεῖστοι ἐχρῶντο, ὅπως δὴ μὴ τῷ φιλο-
κάλῳ ἀπόλωνται· καὶ οὔπω δεδυκότος ἡλίου,
εἰς τὰς οἰκίας ἀναχωροῦντες, ἐκρύπτοντο.
Μηκυνομένου δὲ τοῦ κακοῦ, καὶ οὐδεμιᾶς ἐπιστροφῆς ἐς τοὺς ἡμαρτηκότας πρὸς τῆς τῷ
δήμῳ ἐφεστώσης ἀρχῆς γινομένης, ἐπὶ μέγα τὸ
τῶν ἀνδρῶν θράσος ἐς ἀεί ἤρετο. Ἁμαρτία
γὰρ, παρρησίας ἀξιωθεῖσα, ἐπ᾽ ἄπειρον
φύρεσθαι πέφυκεν· ἐπεὶ καὶ κολαζόμενα τὰ
ἐγκλήματα φιλεῖ οὐκ ἐς τὸ παντελὲς ἀποκόπ-
τεσθαι. Φύσει γὰρ οἱ πλεῖστοι ἐς τὸ ἁμαρτάνειν εὐπετῶς τρέπονται. Τὰ μὲν οὖν τῶν
Βενέτων ἐφέρετο τῇδε.

COURT OF JUSTINIAN 59

gether in gangs as soon as it became
dusk, and robbed respectable people in
the market-place and in the narrow lanes,
knocking men down and taking their
cloaks, belts, gold buckles, and anything
else that they had in their hands. Some
they murdered as well as robbed, that
they might not tell others what had
befallen them. These acts roused the
indignation of all men, even the least
disaffected members of the Blue faction;
but as they began not to spare even these,
the greater part began to wear brazen
belts and buckles and much smaller cloaks
than became their station, lest their fine
clothes should be their death, and, before
the sun set, they went home and hid themselves. But the evil spread, and as the
authorities in charge of the people did
nothing to punish the criminals, these
men became very daring; for crime, when
encouraged to manifest itself openly,
always increases enormously, seeing that
even when punished it cannot be entirely
suppressed. Indeed, most men are naturally inclined to evil-doing. Such was the
behaviour of the Blues.

ΠΡΟΚΟΠΙΟΥ ΑΝΕΚΔΟΤΑ

ε'. Τῶν δὲ ἀντιστασιωτῶν οἱ μὲν εἰς τὴν ἐκείνων ἀπέκλινον μοῖραν, ἐπιθυμίᾳ τοῦ ξυναμαρτάνοντος δήμου δοῦναι τὴν δίκην· οἱ δὲ φυγῇ ἐχόμενοι, ἐς ἑτέρας τινὰς ἐλάνθανον χώρας· πολλοὶ δὲ καὶ αὐτοῦ καταλαμβανόμενοι, διεφθείροντο πρὸς τῶν ἐναντίων ἢ πρὸς τῆς ἀρχῆς κολαζόμενοι. Καὶ ἄλλοι δὲ νεανίαι πολλοὶ ἐς ταύτην δὴ τὴν ἑταιρείαν ξυνέρρεον, οὐδεπώποτε πρότερον περὶ ταῦτα ἐσπουδακότες, ἀλλὰ δυνάμεώς τε καὶ ὕβρεως ἐξουσίᾳ ἐνταῦθα ἠγμένοι. Οὐ γάρ ἐστιν οὐδὲν μίασμα ὑπὸ ἀνθρώπων ὠνομασμένον, ὅπερ οὐχ ἡμαρτήθη τε ἐν τούτῳ τῷ χρόνῳ, καὶ τιμωρίας ἐκτὸς ἔμεινε.

ϛ'. Πρῶτον μὲν οὖν, σφῶν τοὺς ἀντιστασιώτας διέφθειρον· προϊόντες δὲ καὶ τοὺς οὐδὲν προσκεκρουκότας αὐτοῖς διέφθειρον. Πολλοὶ δὲ καὶ χρήμασιν αὐτοὺς ἀναπείσαντες, ἀπεδείκνυον τοὺς σφετέρους ἐχθρούς, οὕσπερ ἐκεῖνοι διεχρῶντο εὐθύς· ὄνομα μὲν Πρασίνων αὐτοῖς ἐπενεγκόντες, ἀγνῶτας δὲ σφίσι παντάπασιν ὄντας. Καὶ ταῦτα οὐκ ἐν σκότῳ ἤδη ἢ ἐν παραβύστῳ ἐγένετο, ἀλλ' ἐν ἅπασι μὲν τῆς ἡμέρας καιροῖς· ἐν ἑκάστῳ δὲ τῆς πόλεως χώρῳ· ἀνδράσι τοῖς λογιμωτάτοις τῶν πρασσομένων, ἂν οὕτω τύχοι, ἐν ὀφθαλ-

COURT OF JUSTINIAN 60

As for the opposite faction, some of them joined the bands of their opponents, hoping thus to be able to avenge themselves upon the party which had ill-used them; some fled secretly to other lands, while many were caught on the spot and killed by their adversaries, or by order of the government. A number of young men also joined this party without having previously taken any interest in such matters, being attracted by the power and the licence which it gave them to do evil. Indeed, there was no sort of villany known amongst men which was not committed at this time unpunished.

In the beginning men put away their own opponents, but, as time went on, they murdered men who had done them no hurt. Many bribed the Blues to kill their personal enemies, whom they straightway slew, and declared that they were Greens, though they might never have seen them before. And these things were not done in the dark or by stealth, but at all hours of the day and in every part of the city, before the eyes, as it might be, of the

μοῖς ὄντων. Οὐδὲν γὰρ ἐπικαλύπτειν ἐδέοντο τὰ ἐγκλήματα, ἐπεί τοι αὐτοῖς οὐκ ἐπέκειτο κολάσεως δέος· ἀλλά τις προσῆν καὶ φιλοτιμίας ἀξίωσις, ἰσχύος τε καὶ ἀνδρείας ἐμποιουμένοις ἐπίδειξιν, ὅτι δὴ πληγῇ μιᾷ τῶν τινα παραπεπτωκότων γυμνὸν ἔκτεινον.

ζ'. Ἐλπίς τε οὐδενὶ τοῦ ἔτι βιώσεσθαι ἐν τῷ τῆς διαίτης σφαλερῷ ἔμενε. Πάντες γὰρ ἐγκεῖσθαι σφίσι τὸν θάνατον τῷ περιδεεῖς εἶναι ὑπώπτευον· καὶ οὐδὲ τόπος τις ὀχυρὸς, οὐδὲ καιρὸς ἐχέγγυός τινι ἐς τὴν σωτηρίαν ἔδοξεν εἶναι, ἐπεὶ κἂν τοῖς τῶν ἱερῶν τιμιωτάτοις, κἂν ταῖς πανηγύρεσι, λόγῳ οὐδενὶ διεφθείροντο. Πίστις τε οὐδεμία πρός τε τῶν φίλων καὶ τῶν ξυγγενῶν ἔτι ἐλέλειπτο. Πολλοὶ γὰρ καὶ τῇ τῶν οἰκειοτάτων ἐπιβουλῇ ἔθνησκον. Ζήτησις μέντοι οὐδεμία τῶν πεπραγμένων ἐγίνετο, ἀλλὰ τὰ πάθη ἀπροσδόκητα πᾶσιν ἔπιπτε, καὶ τοῖς πεπτωκόσιν οὐδεὶς ἤμυνε. Νόμου δέ τινος ἢ συμβολαίου δύναμίς τις ἐν τῷ βεβαίῳ τῆς τάξεως οὐκέτι ἐλέλειπτο, ἀλλ' ἐπὶ τὸ βιαιότερον ἅπαντα τετραμμένα ξυνεταράχθη· τυραννίδι τε ἦν πολιτεία ἐμφερὴς μάλιστα, οὐ καθεστώσῃ μέντοι γε, ἀλλὰ καθ' ἑκάστην τε ἀμειβομένῃ καὶ ἀεὶ ἀρχομένῃ.

COURT OF JUSTINIAN 61

chief men of the State; for they no longer needed to conceal their crimes, because they had no fear of punishment; but to kill an unarmed passer-by with one blow was a sort of claim to public esteem, and a means of proving one's strength and courage.

Life became so uncertain that people lost all expectation of security, for everyone continually had death before his eyes, and no place or time seemed to offer any hope of safety, seeing that men were slain indiscriminately in the holiest churches, and even during divine service. No one could trust friends or relations, for many were slain at the instance of their nearest of kin. No inquiry took place into such occurrences, but these blows fell unexpectedly upon everyone, and no one helped the fallen. Laws and contracts, which were considered confirmed, had no longer any force; everything was thrown into confusion and settled by violence. The government resembled a despotism, not a securely established one, but one which was changed almost daily, and was ever

ΠΡΟΚΟΠΙΟΥ ΑΝΕΚΔΟΤΑ

Τῶν τε ἀρχόντων αἱ γνῶμαι ὥσπερ ἐκπεπληγμέναις ἐῴκεσαν, ἑνὸς ἀνδρὸς φόβῳ δεδουλωμέναι τὸ φρόνημα, οἵ τε δικάζοντες τὰς ὑπὲρ τῶν ἀντιλεγομένων ποιούμενοι γνώμας τὰς ψήφους ἐδίδοσαν, οὐχ ᾗπερ αὐτοῖς ἐδόκει δίκαιά τε καὶ νόμιμα εἶναι, ἀλλ' ὥσπερ τῶν διαφερομένων ἑκάστῳ τὰ ἐκ τῶν στασιωτῶν δυσμενῆ τε καὶ φίλα ἐτύγχανεν ὄντα. Δικαστῇ [γὰρ] ὠλιγωρηκότι τῆς ἐκείνων προρρήσεως θάνατος ἡ ζημία ἐκέκριτο. Καὶ πολλοὶ μὲν δανεισταὶ τὰ γραμματεῖα τοῖς ὠφληκόσι ξὺν βίᾳ πολλῇ οὐδὲν τοῦ ὀφλήματος κεκομισμένοι ἀπέδοντο, πολλοὶ δὲ οὔτι ἑκούσιοι ἐλευθέρους τοὺς οἰκέτας ἀφῆκαν.

η'. Φασὶ δὲ καὶ γυναῖκάς τινας πολλὰ ὧν οὐκ ἐβούλοντο τοῖς αὐτῶν δούλοις ἀναγκασθῆναι. Ἤδη δὲ καὶ παῖδες οὐκ ἀφανῶν ἀνδρῶν, τούτοις δὴ τοῖς νεανίαις ἀναμιχθέντες, τοὺς πατέρας ἠνάγκαζον ἄλλα τε πολλὰ οὔτι ἐθελουσίους ποιεῖν, καὶ τὰ χρήματα σφίσι προΐεσθαι. Πολλοὶ δὲ καὶ ἀκούσιοι παῖδες τοῖς στασιώταις ἐς κοίτην ἀνοσίαν οὐκ ἀγνοούντων ἠναγκάσθησαν τῶν πατέρων ἐλθεῖν. Καὶ γυναιξὶ μέντοι ἀνδράσι ξυνοικούσαις, ταὐτὸν τοῦτο ξυνέθη παθεῖν.

COURT OF JUSTINIAN 62

beginning afresh. The minds of the
chief magistrates seemed stricken with
consternation, and their spirits cowed by
fear of one single man. The judges gave
sentence on disputed points not according
to what they thought to be lawful and
right, but according as each of the litigants
was a friend or an enemy of the ruling
faction; for any judge who disregarded
their instructions was punished with death.
Many creditors also were compelled by
main force to restore their bills to their
debtors without having received anything
of what was owing them, and many,
against their will, had to bestow freedom
upon their slaves.

It is said that some ladies were
forced to submit to the embraces of
their own slaves; and the sons of leading
men who had been mixed up with these
youths, forced their fathers to hand over
their property to them, and to do many
other things against their will. Many
boys, with their fathers' knowledge, were
forced to undergo dishonour at the hands
of the Blues, and women living with

ΠΡΟΚΟΠΙΟΥ ΑΝΕΚΔΟΤΑ

θ'. Καὶ λέγεται γυνὴ μὴ κόσμον περι-
βεβλημένη πολὺν, πλεῖν μὲν σὺν τῷ ἀνδρὶ ἐπὶ
τὸ προάστειον, τὸ ἐν τῇ ἀντιπέρας ἠπείρῳ·
ἐντυχόντων δὲ σφίσιν ἐν τῷ διάπλῳ τούτῳ
τῶν στασιωτῶν, καὶ τοῦ μὲν ἀνδρὸς αὐτὴν
ξὺν ἀπειλῇ ἀφαιρουμένων, ἐς δὲ ἄκατον τὴν
οἰκείαν ἐμβιβασάντων· ἐσελθεῖν μὲν ἐς τὴν
ἄκατον ξὺν τοῖς νεανίαις· ἐγκελευσαμένην τῷ
ἀνδρὶ λάθρα ἄλλα θαρσεῖν τε, καὶ μηδὲν ἐπ'
αὐτῇ δεδιέναι φαῦλον· "οὐ γάρ τοι ξυμβή-
σεσθαι, ἐς τὸ σῶμα αὐτῇ ὑβρισθῆναι·" ἔτι
δὲ τοῦ ἀνδρὸς ξὺν πένθει μεγάλῳ ἐς αὐτὴν
βλέποντος, ἐς τε τὴν θάλασσαν καθεῖναι τὸ
σῶμα, καὶ αὐτίκα μάλα ἐξ ἀνθρώπων ἀφανισθῆναι. Τοιαῦτα μὲν ἦν, τὰ τούτοις δὴ τότε
τοῖς στασιώταις ἐν Βυζαντίῳ τετολμημένα.

ι'. Ἧσσον δὲ ταῦτα τοὺς παραπεπτωκότας ἠνία, ἢ τὰ πρὸς Ἰουστινιανοῦ ἐς τὴν
πολιτείαν ἁμαρτηθέντα· ἐπεὶ τοῖς παρὰ τῶν
κακουργούντων πεπονθόσι τὰ χαλεπώτατα,
μέρος ἀφαιρεῖται τὸ πλεῖστον τῆς διατάξεως
ἐμβάσης ἀνίας, τὸ προσδοκᾶν ἀεὶ τὴν πρὸς
τῶν νόμων τε καὶ τῆς ἀρχῆς τίσιν. Ἐν γὰρ
τῷ πρὸς τὰ μέλλοντα εὐέλπιδες εἶναι ῥᾷον

COURT OF JUSTINIAN   63

their own husbands were forced to submit
to the like treatment.

We are told that a woman, who was
not over-well dressed, was sailing with
her husband in a boat towards the
suburb across the strait; they met on their
way some men of this faction, who took
her away from her husband with threats,
and placed her in their own boat. When
she entered the boat together with these
young men, she secretly told her husband
to take courage, and not to fear any evil
for her. " Never," said she, "will I permit myself to be outraged;" and while
her husband was gazing on her with the
greatest sorrow, she sprang into the sea,
and was never seen again. Such were
the outrages which the people of this
faction dared to commit in Byzantium.

Yet all this did not so much gall the
victims as Justinian's offences against the
State; for those who suffer most cruelly
from evil-doers are in great part consoled
by the expectation that the law and the
authorities will avenge them. If they have
any hope for the future, men bear their

τε καὶ ἀπονώτερον τὰ παρόντα σφίσι φέρουσιν ἄνθρωποι· βιαζόμενοι δὲ πρὸς τῆς τῇ πολιτείᾳ ἐφεστώσης ἀρχῆς, τοῖς τε ξυμπεσοῦσιν ἔτι μᾶλλον, ὡς τὸ εἰκὸς, περιαλγοῦσι, καὶ ἐς τὴν ἀπόγνωσιν τῷ ἀπροσδοκήτῳ τῆς τιμωρίας ἐς ἀεὶ τρέπονται. Ἡμάρτανε δὲ, οὐχ ὅτι μόνον προσποιεῖσθαι τοὺς κακουμένους ἥκιστα ἤθελεν, ἀλλ' ὅτι προστάτης τῶν στασιωτῶν ἐκ τοῦ ἐμφανοῦς καθίστασθαι οὐδαμῇ ἀπηξίου· χρήματά τε μεγάλα τοῖς νεανίαις τούτοις προΐετο, καὶ πολλοὺς μὲν ἀμφ' αὐτὸν εἶχε· τινὰς δὲ αὐτῶν ἔς τε τὰς ἀρχὰς καὶ τὰ ἄλλα ἀξιώματα καλεῖν ἐδικαίου.

COURT OF JUSTINIAN 64

present sufferings with a much lighter heart; but when they are outraged by the established government, they are naturally much more hurt by the evil which befalls them, and the improbability of redress drives them to despair. Justinian's fault was, not only that he turned a deaf ear to the complaints of the injured, but did not even disdain to behave himself as the avowed chief of this party; that he gave great sums of money to these youths, and kept many of them in his own retinue; that he even went so far as to appoint some of them to governments and other official posts.

ΚΕΦΑΛΑΙΟΝ Η'.

α'. Ταῦτα μὲν οὖν ἔν τε Βυζαντίῳ ἐπράττετο, καὶ πόλει ἑκάστῃ. Ὥσπερ γὰρ ἄλλο τι νόσημα, ἐνθένδε ἀρξάμενον τὸ κακὸν πανταχοῦ ἐπέσκηψε τῆς Ῥωμαίων ἀρχῆς. Βασιλεῖ δὲ τῶν πρασσομένων ἥκιστα ἔμελεν, ἐπεὶ οὐδέ τις αἴσθησις τῷ ἀνθρώπῳ ἐγένετο, καίπερ αὐτό[πτῃ] τῶν δρωμένων ἐν τοῖς ἱπποδρομίοις ἀεὶ γινομένῳ. Ἠλίθιός τε γὰρ ὑπερφυῶς ἦν, καὶ νωθεῖ ὄνῳ ἐμφερὴς μάλιστα, καὶ οἷος τῷ τὸν χαλινὸν ἕλκοντι ἕπεσθαι, συχνά οἱ σειομένων τῶν ὤτων. Ἰουστινιανὸς ταῦτά τε ἔπρασσε, καὶ ξύμπαντα τἆλλα ἐκύκα.

β'. Ὥσπερ ἐπειδὴ τάχιστα ἐπελάβετο τῆς τοῦ θείου ἀρχῆς, χρήματα μὲν τὰ δημόσια εὐθὺς καταναλοῦν κόσμῳ οὐδενὶ ἐν σπουδῇ εἶχεν, ἅτε αὐτῶν κύριος γεγονώς. Οὔννων γὰρ τοῖς ἀεὶ προστυγχάνουσι πλεῖστα ἐπὶ τῇ πολιτείᾳ προΐετο· ἐξ οὗ δὴ ἐφόδοις ἀπο-

CHAPTER VIII

THESE excesses took place not only in Byzantium, but in every city of the Empire: for these disorders were like bodily diseases, and spread from thence over the whole Roman Empire. But the Emperor cared not at all for what was going on, although he daily beheld what took place in the hippodrome, for he was exceedingly stupid, very much like a dull-witted ass, which follows whoever holds its bridle, shaking its ears the while. This behaviour on the part of Justinian ruined everything.

As soon as he found himself the head of his uncle's empire, he at once did his utmost to squander the public treasure over which he now had control. For he lavished wealth extravagantly upon the Huns who from time to time came across him; and, ever afterwards, the Roman

66 ΠΡΟΚΟΠΙΟΥ ΑΝΕΚΔΟΤΑ

κεῖσθαι συχναῖς ξυνέβαινε Ῥωμαίων τὴν γῆν. Ἀπογευσάμενοι γὰρ οἱ βάρβαροι οὗτοι Ῥωμαίου πλούτου, μεθίεσθαι οὐκέτι ἠνείχοντο τῆς ἐνταῦθα φερούσης ὁδοῦ. Πολλὰ δὲ ῥίπτειν καὶ ἐς θαλαττίους οἰκοδομίας τινὰς ἠξίου, βιαζόμενος τὸ τῶν κυμάτων ἐς ἀεὶ ῥόθιον. Ἐκ γὰρ τῆς ἠϊόνος ταῖς τῶν λίθων ἐπιβολαῖς ἐπίπροσθεν ἵει φιλονείκως ταῖς ἐκ τοῦ πόντου ἐπιρροαῖς, καὶ καθάπερ ἐξουσίᾳ πλούτου, πρὸς τὴν τῆς θαλάττης ἀντιφιλοτιμούμενος δύναμιν.

γ. Τάς τε τῶν Ῥωμαίων ἰδίας ἑκάστων οὐσίας ἐκ πάσης γῆς ἐς αὐτὸν ἤγειρε· τοῖς μὲν ὅ τι δὴ ἔγκλημα οὐχ ἁμαρτηθὲν ἐπικαλέσας· τῶν δὲ καὶ τὴν γνώμην, ἅτε αὐτὸν δεδωρημένων, τερατευσάμενος. Πολλοὶ δὲ φόνων τε καὶ ἄλλων ἐγκλημάτων τοιούτων ἁλόντες, εἶτα ἐξιστάμενοι αὐτῷ τῶν πάντων χρημάτων, διέφυγον ὧν ἥμαρτον μὴ δοῦναι τὴν δίκην· ἕτεροι δὲ χωρίων, οὐ δέον, τοῖς πέλας τινῶν, ἂν οὕτω τύχοι, ἀμφισβητοῦντες,

COURT OF JUSTINIAN   66

provinces were subjected to constant in-
cursions ; for these barbarians, having
once tasted our wealth, could not tear
themselves away from the road which
led to it. Justinian also threw away
great sums upon the construction of
large moles, as if he thought to restrain
the force of the never-resting waves.
He ran out stone breakwaters from the
beach far into the water to divert the
currents of the ocean, and, as it were,
to match his wealth against the power
of the sea.

As for the private fortunes of individual
Romans, he confiscated them for his own
use in all parts of the empire, either by
accusing their possessors of some crime
of which they were innocent, or by
distorting their words into a free gift
of their property to him. Many were
convicted on these charges of murder
and other crimes, and in order to escape
paying the penalty for them, gave him all
that they had. Some who were engaged
in making frivolous claims to land belonging to their neighbours, when they

ΠΡΟΚΟΠΙΟΥ ΑΝΕΚΔΟΤΑ

ἐπεὶ καταδιαιτήσασθαι τῶν ἀντιδίκων οὐδαμῆ εἶχον τοῦ νόμου σφίσιν ἀντιστατοῦντος· οἱ δὲ τούτοις δὴ τοῖς ἀντιλεγομένοις αὐτὸν δωρησάμενοι, ἀπηλλάσσοντο· αὐτοὶ μὲν χάριτι ἀζημίῳ κερδάναντες τὸ γνώριμοι γεγονέναι τῷ ἀνδρὶ τούτῳ· τρόπῳ δὲ παρανομωτάτῳ καταδικάσασθαι τῶν ἀντιδίκων ἰσχύσαντες.

δ'. Οὐκ ἄπο δὲ καιροῦ ἡγοῦμαι εἶναι, καὶ τὸ εἶδος τούτου δὴ τοῦ ἀνθρώπου σημῆναι. Τὸ μὲν οὖν σῶμα, οὔτε μακρὸς, οὔτε κολοβὸς ἄγαν, ἀλλὰ μέτριος ἦν· οὐ μέντοι ἰσχνὸς, ἀλλὰ κατὰ βραχὺ εὔσαρκος, τὴν δὲ δὴ ὄψιν στρογγύλος τε, καὶ οὐκ ἄμορφος· ἐπυρρία γὰρ, καὶ δυοῖν ἡμέραιν ἀπόσιτος ὤν. Ὅπως δὲ ἅπαν αὐτοῦ τὸ εἶδος συλλήβδην σημήνω, Δομετιανῷ, τῷ Οὐεσπασιανοῦ παιδὶ, ἐκ τοῦ ἐπὶ πλεῖστον ἐμφερέστερος ἦν· οὗπερ Ῥω-μαῖοι τῆς κακοτροπίας ἐς τοσόνδε ἀπώναντο, ὥστε οὐδὲ, κρεουργήσαντες ὅλον, ἐκλῦσαι τὴν ἐς αὐτὸν ὀργὴν ἔγνωσαν· ἀλλὰ δόγμα ἐγεγόνει τῆς συγκλήτου βουλῆς, μηδὲ ὄνομα τοῦ βα-σιλέως τούτου ἐν γράμμασιν εἶναι, μηδ' εἰκόνα ἡντιναοῦν αὐτοῦ διασώζεσθαι. Τό τε γοῦν ὄνομα τοῦτο, πανταχόσε ἐπὶ τῶν τῆς Ῥώμης γραμμάτων, καὶ εἴ που ἄλλῃ τοῦτο γεγράφθαι ξυνέβη ἐκκεκολαμμένον, ἰδεῖν με-

COURT OF JUSTINIAN 67

found that they had no chance of winning their cause, as the law was against them, would make him a present of the land in dispute, and so get out of the difficulty. Thus they gained his favour by a gift that cost them nothing, and got the better of their adversaries by the most illegal means.

It will not be out of place, I think, to describe his personal appearance. He was neither tall nor too short, but of a medium height, not thin, but inclined to be fat. His face was round and not ill-favoured, and showed colour, even after a two days' fast. In a word, he greatly resembled Domitian, Vespasian's son, more than anybody else. This was the Emperor whom the Romans detested so much that they could not slake their hatred for him, even when they had torn him to pieces, but a decree of the Senate was passed to remove his name from all documents, and that all statues of him should be destroyed; wherefore his name has been erased from every inscription at Rome and everywhere else, except where

ταξὺ τῶν ἄλλων πάρεστι μόνον· καί τις αὐτῷ εἰκὼν οὐδαμῆ φαίνεται οὖσα τῆς Ῥωμαίων ἀρχῆς, ὅτι μὴ χαλκῆ μία ἐξ αἰτίας τοιᾶσδε.

ε΄. Ἦν τῳ Δομετιανῷ γυνὴ ἐλευθέριος, καὶ ἄλλως κοσμία· καὶ οὐδὲ αὐτὴ κακόν τι οὐδένα εἰργάσατο πώποτε τῶν πάντων ἀνθρώπων· οὐδέ τις αὐτῇ τῶν τοῦ ἀνδρὸς πράξεων ἤρεσκε. Διόπερ αὐτὴν ἄγαν ἀγαπωμένην ἡ βουλὴ τότε μεταπεμψαμένη, αἰτεῖσθαι ὅ τι ἂν αὐτῇ βουλομένῃ εἴη, ἐκέλευεν. Ἡ δὲ τοῦτο μόνον ἱκέτευε, τό τε Δομετιανοῦ σῶμα λαβοῦσα θάψαι, καὶ μίαν αὐτῷ ἀναθεῖναι εἰκόνα χαλκῆν, ὅποι ἂν ἐθέλοι. Καὶ ἡ μὲν βουλὴ ξυνεχώρει ταῦτα· ἡ δὲ γυνὴ, τῆς ἀπανθρωπίας τῶν τὸν ἄνδρα κρεουργησάντων ἀπαλεῖψαι βουλομένη μνημεῖα τῷ ὄπισθεν χρόνῳ, ὑπενόει τάδε. Τὰ Δομετιανοῦ συλλεξαμένη κρέα, ξυνθεῖσά τε αὐτὰ ἐς τὸ ἀκριβὲς, καὶ ἐναρμοσαμένη ἐς ἄλληλα, κατέρραψε μὲν τὸ σῶμα ὅλον· τοῖς δὲ πλάσταις ἐνδειξαμένη ἐν εἰκόνι χαλκῇ τὸ πάθος ἀπομιμεῖσθαι τοῦτο ἐκέλευεν. Οἱ μὲν οὖν τεχνῖται τὴν εἰκόνα εὐθὺς ἐποίουν. Λαβοῦσα δὲ

COURT OF JUSTINIAN 68

it occurs in a list together with other emperors, and no statue of him is to be found in the Roman Empire, save one only, the history of which is as follows:

Domitian had married a lady of noble birth and admirable conduct, who never harmed anyone, and always disapproved of her husband's evil deeds. As she was so much beloved, the Senate sent for her, after the death of Domitian, and bade her ask whatever favour she pleased. All that she asked was to receive Domitian's body for burial, and permission to erect a bronze statue to him in whatever place she might choose. The Senate consented, and Domitian's wife, not wishing to leave to posterity a memorial of the brutality of those who had butchered her husband, adopted the following plan. She collected the pieces of his body, pieced them accurately together, joined them properly, and sewed the body together again. She then sent for the statuaries, and bade them reproduce this pitiable object in a brazen statue. The workmen straightway made the statue, and his wife, having received

ἡ γυνὴ ἔστησεν ἐπὶ τῆς εἰς τὸ Καπιτώλιον φερούσης ἀνόδου, ἐν δεξιᾷ ἐκ τῆς ἀγορᾶς ἐνταῦθα ἰόντι, εἰδός τε τὸ Δομετιανοῦ καὶ τὸ πάθος δηλοῦσαν, ἐς τόδε τοῦ χρόνου. Εἰκάσειεν ἄν τις τό τε ἄλλο Ἰουστινιανοῦ σῶμα, καὶ τὴν ὄψιν αὐτὴν, καὶ τὰ τοῦ προσώπου ἄπαντα ἤθη, ἐν ταυτῃ τῇ εἰκόνι διαφανῶς εἶναι.

ς'. Τὸ μὲν οὖν εἶδος τοιοῦτός τις ἦν· τὸν δὲ τρόπον ἐς μὲν τὸ ἀκριβὲς οὐκ ἂν φράσαιμι. Ἦν γὰρ οὗτος ἀνὴρ κακοῦργό τε καὶ εὐπαράγωγος, ὃν δὴ μωροκακόηθη καλοῦσιν· οὔτε αὐτὸς ἀληθιζόμενος τοῖς ἐντιγχάνουσιν, ἀλλὰ νῷ δολερῷ ἄπαντα ἐς ἀεὶ καὶ λέγων καὶ πράττων, καὶ τοῖς ἐξαπατᾶν ἐθέλουσιν ὑποκείμενος οὐδενὶ πόνῳ. Καί τις ἀήθης κρᾶσις ἐν αὐτῷ ἐπεφύκει, ἔκ τε ἀνοίας καὶ κακοτροπίας ξυγκεκραμένη. Καὶ τάχα τοῦτο ἦν, ὅπερ ἐν τοῖς ἄνω χρόνοις τῶν τις ἐκ τοῦ περιπάτου φιλοσόφων ἀπεφθέγξατο· ὡς καὶ τὰ ἐναντιώτατα ἐν ἀνθρώπου φύσει ξυμβαίνει εἶναι, ὥσπερ ἐν τῶν χρωμάτων τῇ μίξει. Γράφω μέντοι, ὧν μοι ἐφικέσθαι δυνατὸν γέγονεν.

ζ'. Ἦν τοίνυν ὁ βασιλεὺς οὗτος εἴρων, δολερὸς, κατάπλαστος, σκότιος ὀργὴν, διπλοῦς,

COURT OF JUSTINIAN

it from them, set it up in the street which leads up to the Capitol from the Forum, on the right hand side, where to this day one may see Domitian's statue, showing the marks of his tragic end. One may say that the whole of Justinian's person, his expression, and all his features can be traced in this statue.

Such was his portrait; but it would be exceedingly difficult to give an accurate estimate of his character; he was an evil-doer, and yet easily led by the nose, being, in common parlance, a fool as well as a knave. He never was truthful with anyone, but always spoke and acted cunningly, yet any who chose could easily outwit him. His character was a sorry mixture of folly and bad principles. One may say of him what one of the Peripatetic philosophers of old said long ago, that in men, as in the mixing of colours, the most opposite qualities combine. I will therefore only describe his disposition as far as I have been able to fathom it.

This prince was deceitful, fond of crooked ways, artificial, given to hiding

ἄνθρωπος δεινὸς, ὑποκρίνασθαι γνώμην τελεώ-
τατος, καὶ δάκρυα οὐχ ὑφ’ ἡδονῆς τινος ἢ
πάθους ἐκφέρων, ἀλλὰ τεχνάζων ἐπὶ καιροῦ
κατὰ τὸ τῆς χρείας παρὸν, ψευδόμενος ἐς
ἀεὶ, οὐκ εἰκῆ μέντοι, ἀλλὰ καὶ γράμματα,
καὶ ὅρκους δεινοτάτους ἐπὶ τοῖς ξυγκειμένοις
πεποιημένος, καὶ ταῦτα πρὸς τοὺς κατηκόους
τοὺς αὑτοῦ. Ἀνεχώρει δὲ τῶν τε ὡμολογη-
μένων καὶ ὀμωμοσμένων εὐθὺς, ὥσπερ τῶν
ἀνδραπόδων τὰ χείριστα, δέει τῶν ἐγκειμένων
σφίσι βασάνων, διώμοτα εἰς τὴν ὁμολογίαν
ἠγμένα. Φίλος ἀβέβαιος, ἐχθρὸς ἄσπονδος,
φόνων τε καὶ χρημάτων διάπυρος ἐραστὴς,
δύσερίς τε καὶ νεωτεροποιὸς, μάλιστα ἐς μὲν
τὰ κακὰ εὐπαράγωγος, ἐς δὲ τὰ ἀγαθὰ οὐδεμιᾷ ξυμβουλῇ ἥκων· ἐπινοῆσαι μὲν τὰ φαῦλα
καὶ ἐπιτελέσαι ὀξὺς, τῶν δὲ δὴ ἀγαθῶν καὶ
αὐτήν που τὴν ἀκοὴν ἁλμυρὰν εἶναι οἰόμενος.

η΄. Πῶς ἄν τις τῶν Ἰουστινιανοῦ τρό-
πων ἐφικέσθαι τῷ λόγῳ δυνατὸς εἴη ; ταῦτά
τε καὶ πολλὰ ἔτι μείζω κακὰ οὐ κατὰ ἄνθρωπον ἔχων ἐφαίνετο, ἀλλὰ πᾶσαν ἡ φύσις

COURT OF JUSTINIAN

his wrath, double-faced, and cruel, exceedingly clever in concealing his thoughts, and never moved to tears either by joy or grief, but capable of weeping if the occasion required it. He was always a liar, not merely on the spur of the moment; he drew up documents and swore the most solemn oaths to respect the covenants which he made with his subjects; then he would straightway break his plighted word and his oath, like the vilest of slaves, who perjure themselves and are only driven to confess through fear of torture. He was a faithless friend, an inexorable foe, and mad for murder and plunder; quarrelsome and revolutionary, easily led to do evil, never persuaded to act rightly, he was quick to contrive and carry out what was evil, but loathed even to hear of good actions.

How could any man fully describe Justinian's character? He had all these vices and other even greater ones, in larger proportion than any man; indeed, Nature seemed to have taken away all

ΠΡΟΚΟΠΙΟΥ ΑΝΕΚΔΟΤΑ

ἐδόκει τὴν κακοτροπίαν ἀφελομένη τοὺς ἄλλους ἀνθρώπους, ἐν τῇ τοῦδε τοῦ ἀνδρὸς καταθέσθαι ψυχῇ. Ἦν δὲ πρὸς τοῖς ἄλλοις ἐς μὲν τὰς διαβολὰς εὔκολος ἄγαν, ἐς δὲ τὰς τιμωρίας ὀξύς. Οὐ γάρ τι πώποτε διερευνησάμενος ἔκρινεν, ἀλλὰ ἀκούσας τοῦ διαβάλλοντος τὴν γνῶσιν εὐθὺς ἐξενεγκεῖν ἔγνω. Ἔγραφέ τε γράμματα οὐδεμιᾷ ὀκνήσει, χωρίων τε ἁλώσεις, καὶ πόλεων ἐμπρησμοὺς, καὶ ὅλων ἐθνῶν ἀνδραποδισμοὺς, ἐξ αἰτίας οὐδεμιᾶς ἔχοντα· ὥστε, εἴ τις ἄνωθεν ἅπαντα τὰ Ῥωμαίοις ξυνενεχθέντα σταθμώμενος ἀντισηκοῦν αὐτὰ τούτοις ἐθέλει, δοκεῖ μοι ἂν πλείω φόνον εὑρέσθαι ἀνθρώπων πρὸς τοῦ ἀνδρὸς τοῦδε ξυμβάντα, ἢ ἐν τῷ ἄλλῳ παντὶ αἰῶνι γεγενῆσθαι τετύχηκε.

θ. Τῶν δὲ ἄλλων χρημάτων ἐς μὲν τὴν ἀναίσθητον κτῆσιν ἀοκνότατος ἦν· οὐδὲ γὰρ οὐδὲ σκῆψιν ἠξίου τινὰ παραπέτασμα τοῦ δικαίου περιβεβλημένος, τῶν οὐ προσηκόντων ἐπιβατεύειν· γενομένων δὲ οἰκείων,

COURT OF JUSTINIAN   71

other men's vices and to have implanted
them all in this man's breast. Besides
all this, he was ever disposed to give ear
to accusations, and quick to punish. He
never tried a case before deciding it, but
as soon as he had heard the plaintiff
he straightway pronounced his judgment
upon it. He wrote decrees, without
the slightest hesitation, for the capture
of fortresses, the burning of cities, the
enslaving of whole races of men for no
crime whatever, so that, if anyone were
to reckon all the calamities of this
nature which have befallen the Roman
people before his time, and weigh them
against those which were brought about
by him, I imagine that it would be
found that this man was guilty of far
more bloodshed than any ruler of previous
times.

He had no hesitation in coolly appro-
priating people's property, and did not even
trouble himself to put forward any pretext or colourable legal ground for taking
another man's goods; and, when he had
got it, he was quite ready to squander it

72 ΠΡΟΚΟΠΙΟΥ ΑΝΕΚΔΟΤΑ

ἑτοιμότατος ἦν ἀλογίστῳ φιλοτιμίᾳ περιφρο-
νεῖν τε καὶ τοῖς βαρβάροις προίεσθαι οὐδενὶ
λόγῳ. Καὶ τὸ ξύμπαν εἰπεῖν, χρήματα οὔτε
αὐτὸς εἶχεν, οὔτε ἄλλων τινὰ ἔχειν τῶν
ἀπάντων εἴα· ὥσπερ οὐ φιλοχρηματίας ἡσσώμενος, ἀλλὰ φθόνῳ ἐς τοὺς ταῦτα κεκτημένους ἐχόμενος. Ἐξοικίσας οὖν ῥᾷστα τὸν
πλοῦτον ἐκ Ῥωμαίων τῆς γῆς, πενίας δημιουργὸς ἅπασι γέγονεν. Ἰουστινιανῷ μὲν
οὖν τὰ ἐς τὸν τρόπον, ὅσα γε ἡμᾶς δύνασθαι
φράσαι, τῇδέ πη εἶχεν.

COURT OF JUSTINIAN 72

in foolish munificence or to spend it in
unreasonable largesses to the barbarians.
In fine, he neither had any property
himself, nor would he suffer anyone else
of all his subjects to have any; so that
he did not seem to be so much governed
by avarice as by jealousy of those who
possessed wealth. He carelessly drove all
the wealth of the Romans out of the
country, and was the cause of general
impoverishment. Such was the character
of Justinian, as far as I am able to
describe it.

ΠΡΟΚΟΠΙΟΥ ΑΝΕΚΔΟΤΑ

ΚΕΦΑΛΑΙΟΝ Θ'.

α'. Έγημε δὲ γυναῖκα, ἣ ὅντινα τρόπον γενομένη τε καὶ τραφεῖσα, καὶ τῷδε τῷ ἀνθρώπῳ ἐς γάμον ξυναφθεῖσα, πρόρριζον Ῥωμαίοις τὴν πολιτείαν ἐξέτριψεν, ἐγὼ δηλώσω.

Ἀκάκιος ἦν τις ἐν Βυζαντίῳ, θηριοκόμος τῶν ἐν κυνηγεσίῳ θηρίων, μοίρας Πρασίνων, ὅνπερ Ἀρκτοτρόφον καλοῦσιν. Οὗτος ὁ ἀνὴρ, Ἀναστασίου τὴν αὐτοκράτορα ἀρχὴν ἔχοντος, ἐτελεύτησε νόσῳ, παίδων οἱ ἀπολελειμμένων τριῶν θήλεος γένους, Κομιτοῦς τε καὶ Θεοδώρας καὶ Ἀναστασίας· ὦν ἡ πρεσβυτάτη οὔπω ἑπταέτης γεγονυῖα ἐτύγχανεν. Ἡ δὲ γυνὴ ἐκπεσοῦσα ἑτέρῳ ἀνδρὶ ἐς κοίτην ἦλθεν, ὃς δὴ ξὺν αὐτῇ τῶν τε κατὰ τὴν οἰκίαν καὶ τοῦ ἔργου τούτου ἐπιμελήσεσθαι τὸ λοιπὸν ἔμελλεν. Ὁ δὲ τῶν Πρασίνων ὀρχηστὴς, Ἀστέριος ὄνομα, χρήμασι πρὸς ἑτέρου ἀναπεισθεὶς, τούτους μὲν τῆς τιμῆς ταύτης ἀπέστησε, τὸν δέ οἱ τὰ χρήματα δόντα ἐς αὐτὴν ἀντικατέστησεν οὐδενὶ πόνῳ. Τοῖς γὰρ ὀρχησταῖς τὰ τοιαῦτα ἐξῆν διοικεῖσθαι κατ' ἐξουσίαν ᾗ βούλοιντο.

CHAPTER IX

As for Justinian's wife, I shall now describe her birth, how she was brought up, how she married him, and how in conjunction with him she utterly ruined the Roman Empire.

There was one Acacius at Byzantium, of the Green faction, who was keeper of the wild beasts used in the amphitheatre, and was called the Bear-keeper. This man died of some malady during the reign of Anastasius, and left three daughters, Comito, Theodora and Anastasia, the eldest of whom was not yet seven years of age. His widow married her husband's successor in his house and profession; but the chief dancer of the Green faction, named Asterius, was easily bribed into taking away the office from this man and giving it to one who paid him for it: for the dancers had the

ΠΡΟΚΟΠΙΟΥ ΑΝΕΚΔΟΤΑ

β'. Ἐπεὶ δὲ τὸν δῆμον ξύμπαντα ἡ γυνὴ ἐν κυνηγεσίῳ ἀγηγερμένον εἶδε, στέμματα ταῖς παισὶν ἔν τε κεφαλῇ καὶ ἀμφοτέραις ταῖς χερσὶν ἐνθεμένη, ἐς τὴν ἱκετείαν ἐκάθισεν. Ἀλλ' οἱ Πράσινοι μὲν προσίεσθαι τὴν ἱκετείαν οὐδαμῇ ἔγνωσαν. Βένετοι δὲ αὐτὰς ἐπὶ ταύτης δὴ κατεστήσαντο τῆς τιμῆς· ἐπεὶ ὁ θηριοκόμος ἐτετελευτήκει καὶ αὐτοῖς ἔναγχος. Ἐπεὶ δὲ τὰ παιδία ταῦτα ἐς ἥβην ἦλθε, καθῆκεν αὐτὰ ἐπὶ τῆς ἐνταῦθα σκηνῆς αὐτίκα ἡ μήτηρ, ἐπεὶ εὐπρεπεῖς τὴν ὄψιν ἦσαν, οὐ μέντοι ὑπὸ χρόνον τὸν αὐτὸν ἁπάσας, ἀλλ' ὡς ἑκάστη ἔδοξέν οἱ ἐς τὸ ἔργον τοῦτο ὡραία εἶναι. Ἡ μὲν οὖν πρώτη Κομιτὼ ἤδη ἐν ταῖς καθ' αὑτὴν ἑταίραις λαμπρὰ ἐγεγόνει.

γ'. Θεοδώρα δὲ ἡ μετ' ἐκείνην, χιτωνίσκον χειριδωτὸν ἀμπεχομένη, δούλῳ παιδὶ πρέποντα, τά τε ἄλλα ὑπηρετοῦσα, εἴπετο, καὶ τὸ βάθρον ἐπὶ τῶν ὤμων ἀεὶ ἔφερεν, ἐφ' οὗπερ ἐκείνη ἐν τοῖς ξυλλόγοις καθῆσθαι εἰώθει. Τέως μὲν οὖν ἄωρος οὖσα, ἡ Θεοδώρα ἐς κοίτην ἀνδρὶ ξυνιέναι οὐδαμῇ εἶχεν·

COURT OF JUSTINIAN   74

power to manage these matters as they pleased.

When Theodora's mother saw the whole populace assembled in the amphitheatre to see the show of the wild beasts, she placed fillets on her daughters' heads and hands, and made them sit in the attitude of suppliants. The Greens regarded their appeal with indifference, but the Blues, who had lately lost their own bear-keeper, bestowed the office upon them. As the children grew up, their mother straightway sent them on the stage, for they were handsome girls. She did not send them on all at once, but as each one arrived at a fit age so to do. The eldest girl, Comito, had already become one of the most celebrated prostitutes of her time.

Theodora, the next eldest, was dressed in a little sleeved tunic, such as a slave-girl would wear, and waited on her sister, carrying on her shoulders the stool in which she was wont to sit in public. Theodora was still too young to have intercourse with a man after the

ΠΡΟΚΟΠΙΟΥ ΑΝΕΚΔΟΤΑ

οὐδὲ οἷα γυνὴ μίγνυσθαι· ἡ δὲ τοῖς κακοδαι-
μονοῦσιν ἀνδρίαν τινὰ μισητὴν ἀνεμίσγετο,
καὶ ταῦτα δούλοις, ὅσοι τοῖς κεκτημένοις
ἑπόμενοι ἐς τὸ θέατρον πάρεργον τῆς οὔσης
αὐτοῖς εὐκαιρίας τὸν ὄλεθρον τοῦτον εἰργά-
ζοντο· ἔν τε μαστρωπείῳ πολύν τινα χρόνον
ἐπὶ ταύτῃ δὴ τῇ παρὰ φύσιν ἐργασίᾳ τοῦ
σώματος διατριβὴν εἶχεν.

δ'. Ἐπειδὴ δὲ τάχιστα ἔς τε τὴν ἥβην
ἀφίκετο, καὶ ὡραία ἦν ἤδη, εἰς τὰς ἐπὶ
σκηνῆς καθῆκεν αὐτήν, ἑταίρα τε εὐθὺς ἐγεγόνει, οἵανπερ οἱ πάλαι ἄνθρωποι ἐκάλουν
Πεζήν. Οὐ γὰρ αὐλήτρια, οὐδὲ ψάλτρια ἦν·
οὐ μὴν οὐδὲ τὰ ἐς τὴν ὀρχήστραν αὐτῇ
ἤσκητο, ἀλλὰ τὴν ὥραν τοῖς ἀεὶ περιπίπ-
τουσιν ἀπεδίδοτο μόνον, ἐκ παντὸς ἐργαζομένη τοῦ σώματος. Εἶτα τοῖς μίμοις τὰ
ἐς τὸ θέατρον πάντα ὡμίλει· καὶ τῶν ἐνταῦθα
ἐπιτηδευμάτων μετεῖχεν αὐτοῖς, γελωτοποιοῖς
τισι βωμολοχίαις ὑπηρετοῦσα. Ἦν γὰρ
ἀστεία διαφερόντως, καὶ σκώπτρια· ἀπό-
βλεπτός τε ἐκ τοῦ ἔργου εὐθὺς ἐγεγόνει.
Οὐ γάρ τινος αἰδοῦς τῇ ἀνθρώπῳ μετῆν, ἢ
διατραπεῖσάν τις αὐτὴν πώποτε εἶδεν· ἀλλ'
ἐς ἀναισχύντους ὑπουργίας οὐδεμιᾷ ὀκνήσει
ἐχώρει.

COURT OF JUSTINIAN

manner of women, but she satisfied the unnatural passions of certain wretches, even the vilest slaves, who followed their masters to the theatre and amused their leisure by this infamy. She remained for some time also in a brothel, where she practised this hateful form of vice.

As soon, however, as she reached the age of puberty, as she was handsome, her mother sent her into the theatrical troupe, and she straightway became a simple harlot, as old-fashioned people called it; for she was neither a musician nor a dancer, but merely prostituted herself to everyone whom she met, giving up every part of her body to debauchery. She associated chiefly with the theatrical "pantomimes," and took part in their performances, playing in comic scenes, for she was exceedingly witty and amusing; so that she soon became well known by her acting. She had no shame whatever, and no one ever saw her put out of countenance, but she lent herself to scandalous purposes without the least hesitation.

ΠΡΟΚΟΠΙΟΥ ΑΝΕΚΔΟΤΑ

έ. Καὶ τοιαύτη τις ἦν, οἵα ῥαπιζομένη μέν τε καὶ κατὰ κόρρης πατασσομένη, χαριεντίζειν τε καὶ μέγιστα ἀνακαγχάζειν, ἀποδυσαμένη τε τά τε πρόσω καὶ τὰ ὀπίσω τοῖς ἐντυγχάνουσι γυμνὰ ἐπιδεῖξαι, ἃ τοῖς ἀνδράσι θέμις ἄδηλά τε καὶ ἀφανῆ εἶναι. Ἐς δὲ τοὺς ἐραστὰς ἐχλεύαζέ τε βλακεύουσα, καὶ νεωτέραις ἀεὶ τῶν μίξεων ἐνδιαθρυπτομένη ἐπιτεχνήσεσι, παραστήσασθαι τὰς τῶν ἀκολάστων ψυχὰς ἐς ἀεὶ ἴσχυεν· ἐπεὶ οὐδὲ πειρᾶσθαι πρός του τῶν ἐντυγχανόντων ἠξίου, ἀλλ' ἀνάπαλιν αὐτὴ γελοιάζουσά τε καὶ βωμολόχως ἰσχιάζουσα, τοὺς παραπεπτωκότας ἅπαντας, ἄλλως τε καὶ ἀγενείους ὄντας ἐπείρα.

ς'. Ἥσσων γάρ τις ἡδονῆς οὕτως ἁπάσης οὐδαμῆ γέγονεν, ἐπεὶ καὶ ἐς ξυναγώγιμον δεῖπνον πολλάκις ἐλθοῦσα ξὺν νεανίαις δέκα, ἢ τούτων πλείοσιν, ἰσχύϊ τε σώματος ἀκμάζουσι λίαν, καὶ τὸ λαγνεύειν πεποιημένοις ἔργον, ξυνεκοιτάζετο μὲν τὴν νύκτα ὅλην τοῖς συνδείπνοις ἅπασιν· ἐπειδὰν δὲ πρὸς τὸ ἔργον τοῦτο πάντες ἀπείποιεν, ἥδε παρὰ τοὺς ἐκείνων οἰκέτας ἰοῦσα, τριάκοντα ὄντας, ἂν οὕτω τύχοι, ξυνεδυάζετο μὲν τούτων ἑκάστῳ· κόρον δὲ οὐδὲ ὡς ταύτης μὲν τῆς μισητίας ἐλάμβανε. Καί ποτε ἐς τῶν τινος ἐπιφανῶν

COURT OF JUSTINIAN 76

She excelled in raising a laugh by being slapped on her puffed-out cheeks, and used to uncover herself so far as to show the spectators everything before and behind which decency forbids to be shown to men. She stimulated her lovers by lascivious jests, and continually invented new postures of coition, by which means she completely won the hearts of all libertines; for she did not wait to be solicited by anyone whom she met, but herself, with joke and gestures, invited everyone whom she fell in with, especially beardless boys.

She never succumbed to these transports; for she often went to a supper at which each one paid his share, with ten or more young men, in the full vigour of their age and practised in debauchery, and would pass the whole night with all of them. When they were all exhausted, she would go to their servants, thirty in number, it may be, and fornicate with each one of them; and yet not even so did she quench her lust. Once she went to the house of some great man, and

ΠΡΟΚΟΠΙΟΥ ΑΝΕΚΔΟΤΑ

οἰκίαν ἐλθοῦσα, μεταξὺ τοῦ πότου θεωμένων αὐτὴν, ὥς φασι, τῶν ξυμποτῶν ἀπάντων, ἐς τὸ προὖχον ἀναβᾶσα τῆς κλίνης, ἀμφὶ τὰ πρὸς ποδῶν ἀνασύρασά τε τὰ ἱμάται, οὐδενὶ κόσμῳ, ἐνταῦθα οὐκ ἀπηξίωσε τὴν ἀκολασίαν ἐνδείκνυσθαι. Ἡ δὲ κἀκ τῶν τριῶν τρυπημάτων ἐργαζομένη, ἐνεκάλει τῇ φύσει, δυσφορουμένη ὅτι δὴ μὴ καὶ τοὺς τιτθοὺς αὐτῇ εὐρύτερον ἢ νῦν εἰσι τρυπῴη, ὅπως καὶ ἄλλην ἐνταῦθα μίξιν ἐπιτεχνᾶσθαι δυνατὴ εἴη.

ζ΄. Καὶ συχνὰ μὲν ἐκύει· πάντα δὲ σχεδὸν τεχνάζουσα, ἐξαμβλίσκειν εὔθχυε. Πολλάκις δὲ κἀν τῷ θεάτρῳ ὑπὸ θεατῇ παντὶ τῷ δήμῳ ἀπεδύσατό τε καὶ γυμνὴ διὰ μέσον ἐγένετο, ἀμφὶ τὰ αἰδοῖα καὶ τοὺς βουβῶνας διάζωμα ἔχουσα μόνον, οὐχ ὅτι μέντοι ᾐσχύνετο καὶ ταῦτα τῷ δήμῳ δεικνύναι, ἀλλ' ὅτι ἐνταῦθα παντάπασι παριέναι οὐδενὶ ἔξεστιν, ὅτι μὴ τῷ ἀμφὶ τοὺς βουβῶνας μόνον διάζωμα ἔχοντι. Οὕτω μέντοι τοῦ σχήματος ἔχουσα, ἀναπεπτωκυῖά τε ἐν τῷ ἐδάφει, ὑπτία ἔκειτο. Θῆτες δέ τινες, οἷς δὴ τὸ ἔργον τόδε ἐνέκειτο, κριθὰς αὐτῇ ὕπερθεν τῶν αἰδοίων ἐρρίπτουν, ἃς δὴ οἱ χῆνες, οἳ ἐς τοῦτο παρεσκευασμένοι ἐτύγχανον, τοῖς στόμασιν ἐνθένδε κατὰ μίαν ἀνελόμενοι, ἤσθιον.

COURT OF JUSTINIAN

while the guests were drinking pulled up
her clothes on the edge of the couch and
did not blush to exhibit her wantonness
without reserve. Though she received
the male in three orifices she nevertheless
complained of Nature for not having made
the passage of her breasts wider, that she
might contrive a new form of coition
in that part of her person also.

She frequently became pregnant, but
as she employed all known remedies
without delay, she promptly procured
abortion. Often, even on the stage, she
stripped before the eyes of all the people,
and stood naked in their midst, wearing
only a girdle about her private parts and
groin; not because she had any modesty
about showing that also to the people,
but because no one was allowed to go on
the stage without a girdle about those
parts. In this attitude she would throw
herself down on the floor, and lie on her
back. Slaves, whose duty it was, would
then pour grains of barley upon her
girdle, which trained geese would then
pick up with their beaks one by one and

78 ΠΡΟΚΟΠΙΟΥ ΑΝΕΚΔΟΤΑ

Ἡ δὲ οὐχ ὅτι οὐκ ἐρυθριῶσα ἐξανίστατο, ἀλλὰ καὶ φιλοτιμουμένη ἐπὶ ταύτῃ δὴ τῇ πράξει ἐῴκει. Ἦν γὰρ οὐκ ἀναίσχυντος μόνον, ἀλλὰ καὶ ἀναισχυντοποιὸς πάντων μάλιστα. Πολλάκις δὲ καὶ ἀποδυσαμένη ξὺν τοῖς μίμοις ἐν μέσῳ εἱστήκει λορδουμένη τε καὶ τὰ ὀπίσω ἀποκοντῶσα, τοῖς τε διάπειραν αὐτῆς ἔχουσι, καὶ τοῖς οὔπω πεπλησιακόσι τὰ ἐκ παλαίστρας τῆς αὐτῇ εἰωθυίας βρενθυομένη.

η'. Οὕτω δὲ ἀκολάστως εἰς τὸ σῶμα τὸ αὐτῆς ὕβριζεν, ὥστε τὴν αἰδῶ οὐκ ἐν τῇ τῆς φύσεως χώρᾳ, κατὰ ταὐτὰ ταῖς ἄλλαις γυναιξίν, ἀλλὰ ἐν τῷ προσώπῳ ἔχειν ἐδόκει. Οἱ μὲν οὖν αὐτῇ πλησιάζοντες ἔνδηλοι εὐθὺς ἀπ' αὐτοῦ ἦσαν, ὅτι δὴ οὐ κατὰ τὸν νόμον τῆς φύσεως τὰς μίξεις ποιοῦνται· ὅσοι δὲ αὐτῇ ἐν ἀγορᾷ τῶν ἐπιεικεστέρων ἐντύχοιεν, ἀποκλινόμενοι σπουδῇ ὑπεχώρουν, μή του τῶν ἱματίων τῆς ἀνθρώπου ἀψάμενοι, μεταλαχεῖν τοῦ μιάσματος τούτου δόξειαν. Ἦν γὰρ τοῖς ὁρῶσιν ἄλλως τε καὶ ἀρχομένης ἡμέρας βλάσφημος οἰωνός. Ἐς μέντοι τὰς συνθεατρίας ἀγριώτατα εἰώθει ἐς ἀεὶ σκορπιαίνεσθαι· βασκανίᾳ γὰρ πολλῇ εἴχετο.

θ'. Ἐκηβόλῳ δὲ ὕστερον, Τυρίῳ ἀνδρὶ

COURT OF JUSTINIAN   78

eat. She did not blush or rise up, but appeared to glory in this performance; for she was not only without shame, but especially fond of encouraging others to be shameless, and often would strip naked in the midst of the actors, and swing herself backwards and forwards, explaining to those who had already enjoyed her and those who had not, the peculiar excellences of that exercise.

She proceeded to such extremities of abuse as to make her face become what most women's private parts are: wherefore her lovers became known at once by their unnatural tastes, and any respectable man who met her in the public streets turned away, and made haste to avoid her, lest his clothes should be soiled by contact with such an abandoned creature, for she was a bird of ill-omen, especially for those who saw her early in the day. As for her fellow-actresses, she always abused them most savagely, for she was exceedingly jealous.

Afterwards she accompanied Hecebolus, who had received the appointment

τὴν ἀρχὴν παραλαβόντι Πενταπόλεως, ἐς τὰ αἴσχιστα ὑπηρετήσουσα εἵπετο, ἀλλά τι τῷ ἀνθρώπῳ προσκεκρουκυῖα, ἐνθένδε ὅτι τάχιστα ἀπηλαύνετο· διὸ δὴ αὐτῇ ἀπορεῖσθαι τῶν ἀναγκαίων ξυνέπεσεν, ἅπερ τὸ λοιπὸν ἐπορίζετο τὴν ἐς σῶμα παρανομίαν, ᾗπερ εἴθιστο, ἐργαζομένη. Ἐς μὲν οὖν Ἀλεξάνδρειαν τὰ πρῶτα ἧκεν. Ἔπειτα δὲ πᾶσαν τὴν ἕω περιελθοῦσα, ἐς Βυζάντιον ἐπανῆκεν, ἐργασίᾳ χρωμένη ἐν πόλει ἑκάστῃ, ἥν γε ὀνομάζοντι, οἶμαι, ἀνθρώπῳ, οὐκ ἄν ποτε ἴλεως ὁ θεὸς εἴη· ὥσπερ οὐκ ἀνεχομένου τοῦ δαίμονος χῶρόν τινα τῆς Θεοδώρας ἀκολασίας ἀγνῶτα εἶναι. Οὕτω μὲν τετέχθαι τε τῇδε τῇ γυναικὶ καὶ τετράφθαι ξυνέβη, καὶ ὑπὲρ δημοσίους πολλὰς διαβοήτῳ γεγενῆσθαι ἐς πάντας ἀνθρώπους.

ί. Ἐπεὶ δὲ ἀφίκετο ἐς Βυζάντιον αὖθις, ἠράσθη αὐτῆς Ἰουστινιανὸς, ἔρωτα ἐξαίσιον οἷον· καὶ τὰ πρῶτα ἐπλησίαζεν ὡς ἐρωμένῃ, καίπερ αὐτὴν ἀναγαγὼν ἐς τὸ τῶν πατρικίων

COURT OF JUSTINIAN

of Governor of Pentapolis, to that
country, to serve his basest passions,
but quarrelled with him, and was
straightway sent out of the country. In
consequence of this she fell into want
of common necessaries, with which she
hereafter provided herself by prostitution,
as she had been accustomed to do. She
first went to Alexandria, and afterwards
wandered all through the East, until she
reached Byzantium, plying her trade in
every city on her way—a trade which, I
imagine, Heaven will not pardon a man
for calling by its right name — as if
the powers of evil would not allow any
place on earth to be free from the debaucheries of Theodora. Such was the
birth, and such the training of this
woman, and her name became better
known than that of any other prostitute
of her time.

On her return to Byzantium, Justinian
became excessively enamoured of her.
At first he had intercourse with her
merely as her lover, although he raised
her to the position of a patrician. By

ἀξίωμα. Δύναμιν τοίνυν ἐξαισίαν τινὰ, καὶ χρήματα ἐπιεικῶς μεγάλα περιβαλέσθαι ἡ Θεοδώρα εὐθὺς ἴσχυσε. Πάντων γὰρ ἥδιστον τῷ ἀνθρώπῳ ἐφαίνετο· ὃ δὴ ξυμβαίνειν τοῖς ἐκτόπως ἐρῶσι φιλεῖ, χάριτάς τε πάσας καὶ χρήματα πάντα τῇ ἐρωμένῃ χαρίζεσθαι. Ἐγίνετό τε ἡ πολυτέλεια τοῦ ἔρωτος τοῦδε ὑπέκκαυμα. Ξὺν αὐτῇ τοίνυν πολλῷ ἔτι μᾶλλον τὸν δῆμον διέφθειρεν, οὐκ ἐνταῦθα μόνον, ἀλλ' ἀνὰ πᾶσαν τὴν Ῥωμαίων ἀρχήν. Ἄμφω γὰρ μοίρας τῆς Βενέτων ἐκ παλαιοῦ ὄντες, ἐν πολλῇ ἐξουσίᾳ τούτοις δὴ τοῖς στασιώταις τὰ ἐς τὴν πολιτείαν ἔθεντο πράγματα. Χρόνῳ δὲ πολλῷ ὕστερον τὸ πλεῖστον τοῦ κακοῦ ἐλελωφήκει τρόπῳ τοιῷδε.

ια'. Ἰουστινιανῷ ἐν ἡμέραις πολλαῖς νοσῆσαι ξυνέβη· ἐν δὲ τῇ νόσῳ ταύτῃ ἐς τόσον κινδύνου ἀφίκετο, ὥστε καὶ ἐλέχθη ὅτι δὴ ἀποθάνοι· οἱ μέντοι στασιῶται ταῦτα, ἅπερ ἐρρήθη, ἡμάρτανον, καί τινα Ὑπάτιον, οὐκ ἀφανῆ ἄνδρα, δι' ἡμέρας ἐν τῷ τῆς Σοφίας ἱερῷ διεχρήσαντο. Ἐξειργασμένου δὲ τοῦ

COURT OF JUSTINIAN

this means Theodora was straightway
enabled to gain very great influence and
to amass considerable sums of money.
She charmed Justinian beyond all the
world, and, like most infatuated lovers,
he delighted to show her all the favour
and give her all the money that he
could. This lavishness added fuel to
the flame of passion. In concert with
her he plundered the people more than
ever, not only in the capital, but throughout the Roman Empire; for, as both of
them had for a long time been members
of the Blue faction, they had placed
unlimited power in its hands, although
the evil was subsequently somewhat
checked, in the manner which I will
now relate.

Justinian had for some time suffered
from a dangerous illness; in fact, it was
even reported that he was dead. The
Blue faction were committing the crimes
of which I have spoken, and slew Hypatius,
a person of consequence, in the Church
of St. Sophia, in broad daylight. When
the murderer had accomplished his work,

ΠΡΟΚΟΠΙΟΥ ΑΝΕΚΔΟΤΑ

κακουργοῦντος ἔργον, ταραχὴ ἐς βασιλέα ἦλθε· τῶν τε ἀμφ' αὐτὸν ἕκαστος, ἐπεὶ τῆς 'Ιουστινιανοῦ ἀπουσίας ἐλάβετο, τὴν τῶν πεπραγμένων ἀτοπίαν ἐπὶ μέγα αἴρειν ἐν σπουδῇ ἐποιεῖτο, καταλέγων ἐξ ἀρχῆς ἅπαντα, ὅσα δὴ γενέσθαι τετύχηκε. Τότε δὴ ὁ βασιλεὺς τῷ τῆς πόλεως ἐπάρχῳ ἐπέστελλε τῶν πεπραγμένων ἁπάντων ποιεῖσθαι τὰς τίσεις. Ἦν δὲ οὗτος ὁ ἀνὴρ Θεόδοτος ὄνομα, ὅνπερ Κολοκύνθιον ἐπίκλησιν ἐκάλουν. Καὶ ὃς διερευνώμενος ἅπαντα, πολλοὺς μὲν τῶν κακούργων ἑλεῖν τε καὶ διαχρήσασθαι νόμῳ ἴσχυσε· πολλοὶ δὲ καὶ διαλαθόντες ἐσώθησαν. Μεταξὺ γὰρ ἐπιαπολέσθαι αὐτοὺς πράγμασι 'Ρωμαίων ἔδει.

ιβ'. Ὁ δὲ παράδοξον διασωθεὶς σωτηρίαν, καὶ τὸν Θεόδοτον κτεῖναι, ἅτε φαρμακέα καὶ μάγον, εὐθὺς ἐνεχείρει. Ἐπεὶ δὲ οὐκ εἶχεν ὅτῳ ποτὲ χρώμενος τὸν ἄνθρωπον διαφθείρειε,

COURT OF JUSTINIAN

a clamour was raised which reached the Emperor's ears, and all his courtiers seized upon the opportunity of pointing out the outrageous character of the offence which, owing to Justinian's absence from public affairs, the murderer had been enabled to perpetrate, and enumerated all the crimes that had been committed from the outset. Hereupon the Emperor gave orders to the prefect of the city to punish these crimes. This man was named Theodotus, nicknamed Colocynthius.[1] He instituted an inquiry into the whole matter, and had the courage to seize and put to death, according to the law, many of the malefactors, several of whom, however, hid themselves and so escaped, being destined to perish afterwards together with the Roman Empire. Justinian, who miraculously recovered, straightway began to plan the destruction of Theodotus, on the pretext that he was a magician and used philtres. However, as he found no proofs on which the man

[1] Pumpkin.

τῶν οἱ ἐπιτηδείων τινὰς πικρότατα αἰκισά-
μενος, ἠνάγκαζε λόγους, ὡς ἥκιστα ὑγιεῖς, ἐπ᾽
αὐτῷ φθέγγεσθαι. Πάντων δὲ οἱ ἐκποδὼν
ἱσταμένων, καὶ σιωπῇ τὴν ἐς τὸν Θεόδοτον
ὀδυρομένων ἐπιβουλὴν, μόνος ὁ Πρόκλος, τὴν
τοῦ καλουμένου Κοιαίστορος ἔχων ἀρχὴν,
καθαρὸν ἀπέφαινε τοῦ ἐγκλήματος εἶναι τὸν
ἄνθρωπον, καὶ θανάτου οὐδαμῇ ἄξιον. Διὸ
δὴ Θεόδοτος ἐς τὰ Ἱεροσόλυμα βασιλέως κομίζεται γνώμῃ. Γνοὺς δὲ ἥκειν τινὰς ἐνταῦθα,
οἵπερ αὐτὸν διαφθείρουσιν, ἐν τῷ ἱερῷ ἦν
κρυπτόμενος τὸν ἅπαντα χρόνον, οὕτω τε
διαβιοὺς ἐτελεύτησε. Τὰ μὲν οὖν ἀμφὶ Θεόδοτον ταύτῃ πῃ ἔσχεν.

ιγ΄. Οἱ δὲ στασιῶται σωφρονέστατοι τὸ
ἐντεῦθεν ἐγένοντο ἀνθρώπων ἁπάντων. Οὐ
γὰρ ἔτι τὰ τοιαῦτα ἐξαμαρτάνειν ἠνείχοντο,
καίπερ σφίσι παρὸν ἀδεέστερον τῇ ἐς τὴν
δίαιταν παρανομίᾳ χρῆσθαι. Τεκμήριον δὲ·
ὀλίγων γάρ τινων ὕστερον τόλμαν τὴν ὁμοίαν
ἐνδειξαμένων, τίσις οὐδεμία ἐς αὐτοὺς γέγονεν.
Οἱ γὰρ τοῦ κολάζειν τὴν ἐξουσίαν ἀεὶ ἔχοντες,

COURT OF JUSTINIAN 82

could be condemned, he flogged and
tortured some of his intimates until he
forced them to make most unfounded
accusations against him. When no one
dared to oppose Justinian, but silently
bewailed the plot against Theodotus, Proclus, the Quaestor, alone declared that the
man was innocent and did not deserve
to die. Theodotus was therefore sen-
tenced by the Emperor to banishment
to Jerusalem. But, learning that certain
men had been sent thither to assassinate
him, he took sanctuary in the temple,
where he spent the rest of his life in
concealment until he died. Such was
the end of Theodotus.

From this time forth, however, the
Blue party behaved with the greatest
moderation ; they did not venture to
perpetrate such crimes, although they
had it in their power to abuse their
authority more outrageously and with
greater impunity than before. Here is
a proof of this ; when a few of them
afterwards showed the same audacity in
evil-doing, they were not punished in

ΠΡΟΚΟΠΟΥ ΑΝΕΚΔΟΤΑ

παρρησίαν τοῦ διαλανθάνειν τοῖς τὰ δεινὰ εἰργασμένοις παρείχοντο, ταύτῃ αὐτοὺς τῇ ξυγχωρήσει ἐς τὸ τοῖς νόμοις ἐπεμβαίνειν ἐνάγοντες.

COURT OF JUSTINIAN 83

any way; for those who had the power to punish always gave malefactors an opportunity to escape, and by this indulgence encouraged them to trample upon the laws.

ΚΕΦΑΛΑΙΟΝ Ι´.

α´. Ἕως μὲν οὖν ἡ βασιλὶς περιῆν ἔτι, γυναῖκα ἐγγυητὴν Ἰουστινιανὸς τὴν Θεοδώραν ποιήσασθαι οὐδεμιᾷ μηχανῇ εἶχεν. Ἐν τούτῳ γὰρ μόνον ἀπ᾽ ἐναντίας αὐτῷ ἐχώρει, καίπερ ἀντιστατοῦσα τῶν ἄλλων οὐδέν. Πονηρίας μὲν γὰρ ἡ γυνὴ ἀπωτάτω οὖσα ἐτύγχανεν· ἄγροικος δὲ ἦν κομιδῇ καὶ βάρβαρος γένος, ὥσπερ μοι εἴρηται. Ἀντιλαβέσθαι δὲ ἀρετῆς οὐδαμῇ ἴσχυσεν, ἀλλ᾽ ἀπειροτάτη οὖσα διατετέλεκε τῶν κατὰ τὴν πολιτείαν πραγμάτων· ἥ γε οὐδὲ ξὺν τῷ ὀνόματι τῷ αὑτῆς ἰδίῳ, ἅτε καταγελάστῳ ὄντι, ἐς παλάτιον ἦλθεν, ἀλλ᾽ Εὐφημία ἐπικληθεῖσα. Χρόνῳ δὲ ὕστερον τῇ βασιλίδι μὲν ἀπογενέσθαι ξυνέπεσεν.

β´. Ὁ δὲ [Ἰουστῖνος], ἠλιθιάζων τε καὶ κομιδῇ ἐσχατογέρων γενόμενος, πρὸς τῶν ἀρχομένων γέλωτα ὦφλεν· ὀλιγωρίᾳ τε πολλῇ ἐς αὐτὸν ἐχόμενοι ἅπαντες, ἅτε τῶν πρασσομένων οὐ ξυνιέντος ὑπερεώρων· Ἰουστινιανὸν δέ ξὺν δέει πολλῷ ἐθεράπευον. Κυκῶν γὰρ

COURT OF JUSTINIAN   84

CHAPTER X

As long as the Empress Euphemia was
alive, Justinian could not contrive to marry
Theodora. Though she did not oppose
him on any other point, she obstinately
refused her consent to this one thing.
She was altogether free from vice, although
she was a homely person and of barbarian
descent, as I have already said. She never
cultivated any active virtues, but remained
utterly ignorant of State affairs. She did
not bear her own name, which was a
ridiculous one, when she came to the
palace, but was re-named Euphemia.
Soon afterwards, however, she died.

Justin was in his second childhood and
so sunk in senility that he was the laugh-
ing-stock of his subjects. All despised
him utterly, and disregarded him because
he was incompetent to control State affairs,
but they paid their court to Justinian with

ΠΡΟΚΟΠΙΟΥ ΑΝΕΚΔΟΤΑ

ἀεὶ καὶ ξυνταράσσων ἀνεσόβει ἐφεξῆς ἅπαντας.

γ΄. Τότε δὴ τὴν ἐγγύην πρὸς τὴν Θεοδώραν ἐνεχείρει ποιεῖν. Ἀδύνατον δὲ ὂν ἄνδρα, ἐς ἀξίωμα βουλῆς ἥκοντα, ἑταίρᾳ γυναικὶ ξυνοικίζεσθαι, νόμοις ἄνωθεν τοῖς παλαιοτάτοις ἀπορρηθὲν, λῦσαί τε τοὺς νόμους τὸν βασιλέα νόμῳ ἑτέρῳ ἠνάγκασε, καὶ τοὐνθένδε ἅτε γαμετῇ τῇ Θεοδώρᾳ ξυνῴκησε, καὶ τοῖς ἄλλοις ἅπασι βάσιμον κατεστήσατο τὴν πρὸς ἑταίρας ἐγγύην· τυραννῶν τε αὐτίκα ἐπεβάτευε τῆς τοῦ αὐτοκράτορος τιμῆς, προσχήματι συμπεπλασμένῳ τῆς πράξεως ἐπικαλύπτων τὸ βίαιον. Ἀνεῖπον γὰρ αὐτὸν Βασιλέα ξὺν τῷ θείῳ τῶν Ρωμαίων, εἴ τι δόκιμον ἦν, δειμάτων περιουσίᾳ ἐπὶ ταύτην ἠγμένοι τὴν ψῆφον.

δ΄. Παρέλαβον τοίνυν τὴν βασιλείαν Ἰουστινιανός τε καὶ Θεοδώρα, πρότερον τῆς ἑορτῆς ἡμέραις τρισὶν, ὅτε δὴ οὔτε ἀσπάσασθαι τινα....., οὔτε εἰρηναῖα προσειπεῖν ἔξεστιν. Ἡμέραις δὲ οὐ πολλαῖς ὕστερον, Ἰουστῖνος

COURT OF JUSTINIAN

awe, for he terrified them all by his love of disturbance and reckless innovations.

He then resolved to bring about his marriage with Theodora. It was forbidden by the most ancient laws of the State that anyone of the senatorial order should marry a courtesan; so he prevailed upon the Emperor to repeal the existing law and introduce a new one, whereby he was allowed to live with Theodora as his legitimate wife, and it became possible for anyone else to marry a courtesan. He also straightway assumed the demeanour of absolute despot, veiling his forcible seizure of power under the pretext of reasons of State. He was proclaimed Emperor of the Romans, as his uncle's colleague. Whether this was legal or not may be doubted, since he owed his election to the terror with which he inspired those who gave him their votes.

So Justinian and Theodora ascended the Imperial throne three days before Easter, at a time when it is forbidden to make visits or even to greet one's friends. A few days later Justin was carried off

μὲν ἐτελεύτησε νόσῳ, τῇ ἀρχῇ ἐπιβιοὺς ἔτη ἐννέα· μόνος δὲ Ἰουστινιανὸς ξὺν τῇ Θεοδώρᾳ τὴν βασιλείαν ἔσχεν.

ε΄. (Κεφ. Ι΄ ancien.) Οὕτω γοῦν ἡ Θεοδώρα, ὥσπερ ἐρρήθη, τεχθεῖσά τε καὶ τεθραμμένη καὶ παιδευθεῖσα, ἐς βασιλείας ἀξίωμα, τρόπῳ οὐδενὶ ἐμποδισθεῖσα, ἦλθεν. Οὐδὲ γὰρ τῷ γήμαντι ὕβρεώς τις οἴησις γέγονεν, εἴ οἱ παρὸν ἐκ πάσης ἀπολεξαμένῳ τῆς Ῥωμαίων ἀρχῆς γαμετὴν γυναῖκα ποιήσασθαι, τὴν πασῶν γυναικῶν μάλιστα εὖ τε γεγονυῖαν, καὶ τροφῆς κορυφαίου μεταλαχοῦσαν, τοῦ τε αἰδεῖσθαι οὐκ ἀμελέτητον γεγενημένην, καὶ σωφροσύνῃ ξυνῳκισμένην, πρὸς δὲ τῷ κάλλει ὑπερφυᾶ, καὶ παρθένον τινὰ, καὶ τὸ δὴ λεγόμενον ὀρθοτίτθιον οὖσαν. Ὁ δὲ τὸ κοινὸν ἄγος ἁπάντων ἀνθρώπων αὑτοῦ ἴδιον πεποιῆσθαι οὐκ ἀπηξίου, ἐπ᾽ οὐδενὶ τῶν προδεδηλωμένων καταδυόμενος, καὶ γυναικὶ πλησιάζειν ἄλλα τε πολλὰ περιβεβλημένῃ μεγάλα μιάσματα, καὶ παιδοκτονίας πολλὰς ἐθελουσίων ἀμβλώσεων. Ἄλλο τέ μοι ἐνδεῖν ἤθους πέρι μνημονεῦσαι τοῦδε τοῦ ἀνθρώπου οὐδ᾽ ὁτιοῦν οἶμαι. Ἅπαντα γὰρ αὐτοῦ τὰ τῆς ψυχῆς πάθη οὗτος ἀναξιόχρεως ὁ γάμος σημῆναι διαρκῶς εἴη, ἑρμηνεύς τε καὶ μάρτυς τοῦ τρόπου καὶ λογογράφος γινόμενος. Ἐπεὶ ὅστις ἀλογήσας τὴν ὑπὲρ τῶν πεπραγμένων αἰσχύνην, οὐκ ἀπαξιοῖ τοῖς ἐντυγχάνουσι βδελυρὸς φαίνεσθαι· τούτῳ δὴ οὐδεμία παρανομίας ἀταρπὸς ἄβατος· ἀλλὰ τὴν ἀναίδειαν ἀεὶ τοῦ

COURT OF JUSTINIAN   86

by disease, after a reign of nine years, and Justinian and Theodora reigned alone.

Thus did Theodora, as I have told you, in spite of her birth and bringing-up, reach the throne without finding any obstacle in her way. Justinian felt no shame at having wedded her, although he might have chosen the best born, the best educated, the most modest and virtuously nurtured virgin in all the Roman Empire, with outstanding breasts, as the saying is; whereas he preferred to take to himself the common refuse of all mankind, and without a thought of all that has been told, married a woman stained with the shame of many abortions and many other crimes. Nothing more, I conceive, need be said about this creature's character, for all the vices of his heart are thoroughly displayed in the fact of so unworthy a marriage. When a man feels no shame at an act of this kind, and braves the loathing of the world, there is thereafter no path of wickedness which may not be trodden by him, but, with a face incapable

μετώπου προβεβλημένος, ῥᾳστά τε καὶ οὐδενὶ πόνῳ, ἐς τῶν πράξεων τὰς μιαρωτάτας χωρεῖ.

ϛ΄. Οὐ μὴν οὐδέ τις ἐκ τῆς συγκλήτου βουλῆς, τὸ αἶσχος τοῦτο ἀναδουμένην τὴν πολιτείαν ὁρῶν, δυσφορεῖσθαί τε καὶ τὴν πρᾶξιν ἀπειπεῖν ἔγνω, καίπερ αὐτὴν ἅπαντες ἴσα θεῷ προσκυνήσοντες· Ἀλλ' οὐδέ τις ἱερεύς, δεινοπαθῶν ἔνδηλος γέγονε καὶ ταῦτα Δέσποιναν αὐτὴν προσερεῖν μέλλοντες. Καὶ ὁ πρότερον αὐτῆς θεατὴς δῆμος δοῦλος εὐθὺς οὐδενὶ κόσμῳ αὐτῆς εἶναί τε καὶ ὀνομάζεσθαι ὑπτίαις ἐδικαίου χερσίν. Οὐδέ τις στρατιώτης ἠγρίωτο, εἰ τοὺς ἐν τοῖς στρατοπέδοις κινδύνους ὑπὲρ τῶν τῆς Θεοδώρας πραγμάτων ὑφίστασθαι μέλλοι, οὐδέ τις αὐτῇ ἄλλος ἀπήντησε τῶν ἁπάντων ἀνθρώπων.

ζ΄. Ἀλλὰ πάντες, οἶμαι, τῷ ταῦτα οὕτως δεδόσθαι κεκλημένοι, ἀνεχώρησαν συμπεραίνεσθαι τὸ μίασμα τοῦτο· ὥσπερ τῆς τύχης ἐπίδειξιν τῆς δυνάμεως πεποιημένης ἤδη ἅπαντα πρυτανευούσης τὰ ἀνθρώπεια, ὡς ἥκιστα μέλλει· οὔτε ὅπως ἂν τὰ πραττόμενα εἰκότα εἴη, οὐδὲ ὅπως ταῦτα κατὰ λόγον τοῖς ἀνθρώποις γεγενῆσθαι δοκῇ. Ἐπαίρει γοῦν τινα ἐξαπιναίως ἀλογίστῳ τινὶ ἐξουσίᾳ ἐς ὕψος μέγα,

COURT OF JUSTINIAN   87

of blushing, he plunges, utterly devoid of
scruple, into the deepest baseness.

However, no one in the Senate had
the courage to show dissatisfaction at
seeing the State fasten this disgrace upon
itself, but all were ready to worship
Theodora as if she had been a goddess.
Neither did any of the clergy show any
indignation, but bestowed upon her the
title of "Lady." The people who had
formerly seen her upon the stage now
declared themselves, with uplifted hands,
to be her slaves, and made no secret of
the name. None of the army showed
irritation at having to face the dangers
of war in the service of Theodora, nor
did anyone of all mankind offer her the
least opposition. All, I suppose, yielded
to circumstances, and suffered this disgraceful act to take place, as though
Fortune had wished to display her power
by disposing human affairs so that events
came about in utter defiance of reason,
and human counsel seemed to have no
share in directing them. Fortune does
thus raise men suddenly to great heights

88 ΠΡΟΚΟΠΙΟΥ ΑΝΕΚΔΟΤΑ

ᾧπερ ἐναντιώματα μὲν πολλὰ ξυμπεπλέχθαι δοκεῖ, ἀντιστατεῖ δὲ παρά τι ἔργον τῶν πάντων οὐδὲν, ἀλλ' ἄγεται μηχανῇ πάσῃ ὅπη ποτὲ αὐτῇ διατέτακται, ἁπάντων ἑτοίμως ἐξισταμένων τε καὶ ὑποχωρούντων προϊούσῃ τῇ τύχῃ. Ἀλλὰ ταῦτα μὲν ὅπῃ τῷ θεῷ φίλον, ταύτῃ ἐχέτω τε καὶ λεγέσθω.

η'.· Ἡ δὲ Θεοδώρα εὐπρόσωπος μὲν ἦν, καὶ εὔχαρις ἄλλως· κολοβὸς δὲ, καὶ ὠρακιῶσα οὐ πανταπασι μὲν, ἀλλ' ὅσον ὑπόχλωρος εἶναι, γοργόν τε καὶ συνεστραμμένον ἀεὶ βλέπουσα. Τῶν δὲ δὴ αὐτῇ βεβιωμένων ἐν τῇ θυμέλῃ τὰ μὲν πλεῖστα λέγοντι οὐκ ἂν ὁ πᾶς αἰὼν ἐπαρκέσῃ, ὀλίγα δὲ ἄττα ἐν τοῖς ἔμπροσθεν λόγοις ἀπολεξάμενος, τοῦ τῆς γυναικὸς τρόπου τοῖς ἐπιγενησομένοις ὅλην ἂν πεποιῆσθαι τὴν δήλωσιν ἱκανὸς εἴην.

θ'. Νῦν δὲ αὐτῆς καὶ τἀνδρὸς τὰ πεπραγμένα ἐν ὀλίγῳ δηλωτέον ἡμῖν, ἐπεὶ οὐδέ τι ἀλλήλοιν χωρὶς ἐς τὴν δίαιταν ἐπραξάτην. Χρόνον μὲν γὰρ πολὺν ἔδοξαν ἅπασι ταῖς γνώμαις ἀεὶ καὶ τοῖς ἐπιτηδεύμασι καταντικρὺ ἀλλήλοιν ἰέναι· ὕστερον μέντοι ἐξεπίτηδες αὐτοῖν ξυμπεπλάσθαι ἡ δόκησις αὕτη ἐγνώσθη, τοῦ μὴ ξυμφρονήσαντας τοὺς κατηκόους σφίσιν

COURT OF JUSTINIAN   88

of power, by means in which reason has
no share, in spite of all obstacles that
may bar the way, for nothing can check
her course, but she proceeds straight on
towards her goal, and everything makes
way for her. But let all this be, and be
represented as it pleases God.

Theodora was at this time handsome
and of a graceful figure, but she was
short, without much colour, but rather
of a pale complexion, and with brilliant
and piercing eyes. It would take a lifetime to tell of all her adventures during
her theatrical life, but I think what little
I have selected above will be sufficient
to give an indication of her character.
We must now briefly set forth what she
and her husband did, for during their
married life neither ever did anything
without the other. For a long time they
appeared to all to be at variance both
in their characters and in their actions;
but afterwards this disagreement was
seen to have been purposely arranged
between them, in order that their subjects
might not come to an agreement and rise

ΠΡΟΚΟΠΟΥ ΑΝΕΚΔΟΤΑ

ἐπαναστῆναι, ἀλλὰ διεστάναι τὰς γνώμας ἐπ᾽ αὐτοὺς ἅπασι.

ι΄. Πρῶτα μὲν οὖν τοὺς Χριστιανοὺς διαναστήσαντες, καὶ τὴν ἐναντίαν ἔν γε τοῖς ἀντιλεγομένοις σκηπτομένω ἀλλήλοιν ἰέναι, διεσπάσαντο οὕτως ἅπαντας, ὥσπερ μοι λελέξεται οὐ πολλῷ ὕστερον, ἔπειτα δὲ τοὺς στασιώτας διείλοντο. Καὶ ἡ μὲν δυνάμει τῇ πάσῃ μεταποιεῖσθαι τῶν Βενέτων ἐπλάσσετο, καὶ τὴν ἐξουσίαν αὐτοῖς ἐπὶ τοὺς ἀντιστασιώτας ἀναπετάσασα ἐνεδίδου κόσμῳ ἐν οὐδενὶ ἁμαρτάνειν τε καὶ βιάζεσθαι τὰ ἀνήκεστα. Ὁ δὲ, ὥσπερ ἀγανακτοῦντι μὲν καὶ ἀποσκύζοντι λάθρα ἐῴκει, κελεύσεως δὲ τῇ γυναικὶ ἀντιστατεῖν οὐχ οἷῳ τε ὄντι· πολλάκις δὲ καὶ μεταμπισχόμενοι τὴν τοῦ δύνασθαι δόξαν σφίσιν αὐτοῖς τὴν ἐναντίαν. Ὁ μὲν γὰρ τοὺς Βενέτους οἷα ἐξαμαρτάνοντας κολάζειν ἠξίου, ἡ δὲ, τῷ λόγῳ χαλεπαίνουσα, ἐδυσφορεῖτο ὅτι δὴ οὐχ ἑκοῦσα τἀνδρὸς ἡσσηθείη. Τῶν μέντοι Βενέτων οἱ στασιῶται, ὥσπερ μοι εἴρηται, σωφρονέστατοι ἔδοξαν εἶναι. Τοὺς γὰρ πέλας βιάζεσθαι ὅσα ἐξῆν οὐδαμῆ ἐδικαίουν.

ια΄. Ἔν τε ταῖς περὶ τὰς δίκας φιλονεικίαις ἐδόκει μὲν ἑκάτερος ἑνὶ τῶν διαφόρων

COURT OF JUSTINIAN 89

against them, but might all be divided
in their opinion. First, they split up the
Christians into two parties and brought
them to ruin, as I shall tell you hereafter, by this plan of pretending to take
different sides. Next they created divi-
sions amongst the State factions. Theodora feigned to be an eager partisan of
the Blues, and gave them permission to
commit the greatest atrocities and deeds
of violence against the opposite faction,
while Justinian pretended to be grieved
and annoyed in his secret soul, as though
he could not oppose his wife's orders;
and often they would pretend to act in
opposition. The one would declare that
the Blues must be punished because they
were evil-doers, while the other pretended
to be enraged, and angrily declared that
she was overruled by her husband against
her will. Yet, as I have said, the Blue
faction seemed wondrously quiet, for they
did not outrage their neighbours as much
as they might have done.

In legal disputes, each of them would
pretend to favour one of the litigants,

ἀμύνειν, νικᾶν δὲ αὐτοῖν τὸν λόγῳ τῷ ἀδίκῳ
ξυνιστάμενον ἐπάναγκες ἦν· οὕτω δὲ τὰ
πλεῖστα χρημάτων αὐτοὺς τῶν ἀντιλεγομένων
ληίζεσθαι.

ιβ'. Πολλοὺς μὲν οὖν ὅδε ὁ αὐτοκράτωρ,
ἐν τοῖς αὑτῷ καταλέγων ἐπιτηδείοις, ἐς τὴν
ἐξουσίαν ἀνεβίβαζε, τοῦ βιάζεσθαί τε, καὶ εἰς
τὴν πολιτείαν ἐξαμαρτάνειν ἃ βούλοιντο·
ἐπειδὰν δὲ πλούτου τι χρῆμα περιβεβλημένοι
φανεῖεν, εὐθύς τι προσκεκρουκότες τῇ γυναικὶ,
διάφοροι ἦσαν. Ὧν δὴ κατ᾽ ἀρχὰς μεταποιεῖσθαι πάσῃ προθυμίᾳ οὐδαμῆ ὑπηξίου, ὕστερον
δὲ τὴν ἐς τοὺς ἀνθρώπους μεθεὶς εὔνοιαν, τὰ ἐς
τὴν σπουδὴν τάραχος ἐκ τοῦ αἰφνιδίου ἐγίνετο.
Καὶ ἡ μὲν αὐτίκα εἰργάζετο αὐτοὺς ἀνήκεστα
ἔργα· ὁ δὲ, δῆθεν οὐκ ἐπαισθανόμενος τῶν
πραττομένων, σύμπασαν αὐτῶν τὴν οὐσίαν
κτήσει ἀναισχύντῳ ἠσπάζετο. Τούτοις τε ἀεὶ
τοῖς μηχανήμασιν ἐν σφίσι μὲν αὐτοῖς ξυμ-
φρονοῦντες, ἐς δὲ τὸ ἐμφανὲς στασιάζειν ποιούμενοι, διαστήσασθαί τε τοὺς ὑπηκόους καὶ
τὴν τυραννίδα βεβαιότατα κρατύνεσθαι ἔσχον.

COURT OF JUSTINIAN 90

and of necessity made the man with the worse case win ; by this means they plundered both the parties of most of the disputed property. The Emperor received many persons into his intimacy, and gave them appointments with liberty to do what they pleased in the way of violent injustice and fraud against the State ; but when they were seen to have amassed a considerable amount of wealth, they straightway fell into disgrace for having offended the Empress. At first Justinian would take upon himself to inquire kindly into their case, but soon he would drop the pretence of good-will, and his zeal on their behalf would throw the whole matter into confusion. Upon this, Theodora would treat them in the most shameful way, while he, pretending not to understand what was going on, would shamelessly confiscate their entire property. They used to carry on these machinations by appearing to be at variance, while really playing into each other's hands, and were thus able to set their subjects by their ears and firmly establish their own power.

ΚΕΦΑΛΑΙΟΝ ΙΑ΄.

α΄. Ἐπειδὴ οὖν Ἰουστινιανὸς τὴν βασιλείαν παρέλαβε, συγχεῖν ἅπαντα εὐθὺς ἴσχυσεν. Ἃ γὰρ ἔμπροσθεν νόμῳ ἀπορρηθέντα ἐτύγχανεν, ἐς τὴν πολιτείαν εἰσῆγε, τά τε ὄντα καὶ ξυνειθισμένα καθελὼν σύμπαντα· ὥσπερ ἐπὶ τούτῳ κεκοσμημένος τὸ τῆς βασιλείας σχῆμα, ἐφ' ᾧ ἅπαντα μεταλλάσσοι ἐφ' ἕτερον σχῆμα. Ἀρχάς τε γὰρ τὰς μὲν οὔσας ἀνῄρει· τὰς δὲ οὐκ οὔσας ἐφίστη τοῖς πράγμασι· τούς τε νόμους καὶ τῶν στρατιωτῶν τοὺς καταλόγους, ταυτὸ τοῦτο ἐποίει· οὐ τῷ δικαίῳ εἴκων, οὐδὲ τῷ ξυμφόρῳ ἐς τοῦτο ἠγμένος, ἀλλ' ὅπως δὴ ἅπαντα νεώτερά τε καὶ αὐτοῦ ἐπώνυμα εἴη. Ἦν δέ τι καὶ μεταβαλεῖν ἐν τῷ παραυτίκα ἥκιστα ἴσχυσεν, ἀλλὰ τούτῳ γε τὴν ἐπωνυμίαν τὴν αὑτοῦ ἔθετο.

CHAPTER XI

WHEN Justinian came to the throne, he straightway succeeded in upsetting everything. What had previously been forbidden by the laws he introduced, while he abolished all existing institutions, as though he had assumed the imperial robe for no other purpose than to alter completely the form of government. He did away with existing offices, and established other new ones for the management of affairs. He acted in the same manner in regard to the laws and the army; not that he was led to do so by any love of justice or the public advantage, but merely in order that all institutions might be new and might bear his name; if there was any institution that he was unable to abolish at once, he gave it his name, that at least it might appear new. He could never

β'. Χρημάτων δὲ ἁρπαγῆς, ἢ φόνου ἀνθρώπων, κόρος αὐτὸν οὐδεὶς ἔλαβε πώποτε· ἀλλ' οἰκίας μὲν παμπληθεῖς λησάμενος εὐδαιμόνων ἀνδρῶν ἑτέρας ἐξήτει· προέμενος εὐθὺς τῶν βαρβάρων τισὶν ἢ ἀνοήτοις οἰκοδομίαις λείας τῆς προτέρας τὰ χρήματα. Κατὰ μυρίους δὲ ἴσως λόγῳ οὐδενὶ ἀνελὼν, ἐς πλειόνων ἄλλων ἐπιβουλὴν αὐτίκα μάλα καθίστατο.

γ'. Εἰρήνης τοίνυν 'Ρωμαίοις οὔσης ἐς πάντας ἀνθρώπους, οὐκ ἔχων ὅστις γένηται, τῶν φόνων ἐπιθυμίᾳ πάντας βαρβάρους πρός τε ἀλλήλους ξυνέκρουε· τῶν δὲ Οὔννων τοὺς ἡγουμένους ἐξ αἰτίας οὐδεμιᾶς μετακαλῶν, χρήματα μεγάλα σφίσιν ἀτόπῳ φιλοτιμίᾳ προίετο, φιλίας ἐνέχυρα δῆθεν τῷ λόγῳ ταῦτα ποιούμενος· ὅπερ αὐτὸν ἐρρήθη καὶ ὑπὸ τὸν χρόνον τῆς 'Ιουστίνου βασιλείας πεποιηκέναι. Οἱ δὲ τὰ χρήματα κεκομισμένοι, τῶν ξυναρχόντων τινὰς ξὺν τοῖς ἑπομένοις τοῖς αὐτῶν ἔπεμπον, καταθέειν ἐξ ἐπιδρομῆς γῆν τὴν βασιλέως κελεύοντες, ὅπως καὶ αὐτοὶ τὴν εἰρήνην ἀπεμπολεῖν τῷ ταύτην ὠνεῖσθαι λόγῳ οὐδενὶ βουλομένῳ δυνατοὶ

COURT OF JUSTINIAN

satisfy his insatiable desire, either of
money or blood ; but after he had
plundered one wealthy house, he would
seek for another to rob, and straightway
squander the plunder upon subsidies to
barbarians, or senseless extravagance in
building. After he had destroyed his
victims by tens of thousands, he immediately began to lay plots against even
greater numbers. As the Roman Empire
was at peace with foreign nations, his
impatience of quiet led him, out of un-
controllable love of bloodshed, to set the
barbarians fighting with one another.
Sending for the chieftains of the Huns
for no reason whatever, he took a pride
in lavishing great sums of money upon
them, under the pretext of securing their
friendship, just as he did in the time of
the Emperor Justin, as I have already
told you. These Huns, when they had
got the money, sent to some of their
fellow-chieftains with their retainers, and
bade them make inroads into the Emperor's territory, that they also might
make a bargain with him for the peace

ΠΡΟΚΟΠΙΟΥ ΑΝΕΚΔΟΤΑ

εἶεν. Καὶ οἱ μὲν αὐτίκα ἠνδραπόδιζόν τε τὴν Ῥωμαίων ἀρχὴν, καὶ οὐδέν τι ἧσσον ἔμμισθοι πρὸς τοῦ βασιλέως ἐγίνοντο· ἕτεροι δὲ μετ' ἐκείνους εὐθὺς ἐς τὸ ληΐζεσθαι τοὺς ταλαιπώρους Ῥωμαίους καθίσταντο, καὶ μετὰ τὴν λείαν ἆθλα τῆς ἐφόδου τὴν βασιλέως φιλοτιμίαν ἐδέχοντο. Οὕτω τε ἅπαντες, ξυλλήβδην εἰπεῖν, οὐδένα ἀνιέντες καιρὸν, ἐκ περιτροπῆς ἦγόν τε καὶ ἔφερον ἀπαξάπαντα. Ἀρχόντων γάρ εἰσι τοῖς βαρβάροις τούτοις ξυμμορίαι πολλαὶ, καὶ περιήρχετο πόλεμος τὴν μὲν αἰτίαν ἐκ φιλοτιμίας ἀλογίστου λαβὼν, τὸ δὲ πέρας εὑρέσθαι οὐδαμῇ ἔχων ἀλλ' ἐφ' ἑαυτὸν ἀνακυκλούμενος τὸν πάντα αἰῶνα. Διὸ δὴ χῶρος μέν τις, ἢ ὄρος, ἢ σπήλαιον, ἢ ἄλλο τι τῆς Ῥωμαίων γῆς, ὑπὸ τὸν χρόνον τοῦτον, ἀδῄωτον οὐδαμῇ ἔμεινε, χώραις δὲ πολλαῖς πλέον ἢ πεντάκις ἁλῶναι συνέβη.

δ. Καὶ ταῦτα μέντοι, καὶ ὅσα πρὸς Μήδων τε καὶ Σαρακηνῶν, καὶ Σκλαβηνῶν, καὶ

COURT OF JUSTINIAN

93

which he was so ready to purchase.
These men straightway subjugated the
Empire, and nevertheless remained in
the Emperor's pay; and, following their
examples, others straightway began to
harass the wretched Romans, and, after
they had secured their booty, were
graciously rewarded by the Emperor for
their invasion. Thus the whole Hunnish
nation, one tribe after another, never
ceased at any time to lay waste and
plunder the Empire; for these barbarians
are under several independent chieftains,
and the war, having once begun through
his foolish generosity, never came to an
end, but always kept beginning anew; so
so that, during this time, there was no
mountain, no cave, no spot whatever in
the Roman Empire that remained un-
ravaged, and many countries were harried
and plundered by the enemy more than
five several times.

These calamities, and those which
were brought upon the Empire by the
Medes, the Saracens, the Sclavonians,

Ἀντῶν, καὶ τῶν ἄλλων βαρβάρων, ξυνηνέχθη γενέσθαι, ἐν τοῖς ἔμπροσθέν μοι δεδιήγηται λόγοις· ἀλλ' ὅπερ τοῦδε ἀρχόμενος τοῦ λόγου ὑπεῖπον, τὴν αἰτίαν τῶν ξυμπεπτωκότων ἐνταῦθά μοι ἦν ἀναγκαῖον εἰπεῖν. Καὶ Χοσρόῃ μὲν κεντηναρίων πλῆθος ὑπὲρ τῆς εἰρήνης προέμενος, αὐτογνωμονήσας δὲ οὐδενὶ λόγῳ, αἰτιώτατος τοῦ λελύσθαι τὰς σπονδὰς γέγονεν, Ἀλαμούνδαρόν τε καὶ Οὔννους τοὺς Πέρσαις ἐνσπόνδους σπουδάζων τε καὶ διατεινόμενος ἑταιρίζεσθαι, ὅπερ μοι ἐν λόγοις τοῖς ὑπὲρ αὐτῶν οὐκ ἀπαρακαλύπτως εἰρῆσθαι δοκεῖ.

ε'. Ἐν ᾧ δὲ τὰ ἐκ τῶν στάσεών τε καὶ πολέμων κακὰ Ῥωμαίοις ἀνήγειρε καὶ ἐρρίπιζεν, ἐν τοῦτο βουλευσάμενος, αἵματος ἀνθρωπείου τὴν γῆν πολλαῖς μηχαναῖς ἔμπλεων γίνεσθαι, καὶ χρήματα· ληΐζεσθαι πλείω, φόνον καὶ ἄλλον τῶν ὑπηκόων ἐπενόει πολὺν τρόπῳ τοιῷδε. Χριστιανῶν δόξαι ἀπόβλητοι πολλαί εἰσιν ἐν πάσῃ τῇ Ῥωμαίων ἀρχῇ, ἅσπερ αἱρέσεις καλεῖν νενομίκασι, Μοντανῶν τε καὶ Σαββατιανῶν, καὶ ὅσαις ἄλλαις πλανᾶσθαι αἱ τῶν ἀνθρώπων εἰώθασι γνῶμαι. Τούτους ἅπαντας δόξαν τὴν παλαιὰν ἐκέ-

COURT OF JUSTINIAN 94

the Antes, and other barbarians, I have
described in the previous books of my
history; but, as I have said at the beginning of this story, I was here obliged
to explain the causes which led thereto.

Justinian paid Chosroes many centenars in order to secure peace, and
then, with unreasonable arbitrariness, did
more than anyone to break the truce,
by employing every effort to bring Ala-
mundur and his Huns over to his own
side, as I have already set forth in plain
terms in my history.

While he was stirring up all this
strife and war to plague the Romans,
he also endeavoured, by various devices,
to drench the earth in human blood, to
carry off more riches for himself, and to
murder many of his subjects. He proceeded as follows. There prevail in the
Roman Empire many Christian doctrines
which are known as heresies, such as
those of the Montanists and Sabbatians
and all the others by which men's minds
are led astray. Justinian ordered all these
beliefs to be abandoned in favour of the

ΠΡΟΚΟΠΙΟΥ ΑΝΕΚΔΟΤΑ

λευε μετατίθεσθαι, ἄλλα τε ἀπειλήσας ἀπει-
θοῦσι πολλά, καὶ τὰς οὐσίας ἐς τοὺς παῖδας
ἢ ξυγγενεῖς μηκέτι παραπέμπειν οἷόν τε εἶναι.
Τούτων δὲ τὰ ἱερὰ τῶν αἱρετικῶν καλουμένων, καὶ διαφερόντως οἷσπερ ἡ τοῦ Ἀρείου
ἤσκητο δόξα, πλοῦτόν τινα εἶχεν ἀκοῆς
κρείττω. Οὔτε γὰρ ἡ σύγκλητος βουλὴ ξύμπασα, οὔτε τις ἄλλη μεγίστη μοῖρα τῆς
Ῥωμαίων ἀρχῆς, τά γε εἰς τὴν οὐσίαν εἰκα-
ζεσθαι τούτοις δὴ τοῖς ἱεροῖς ἔσχε. Κειμήλιά
τε γὰρ αὐτοῖς χρυσᾶ τε καὶ ἀργυρᾶ, καὶ
ξυγκείμενα ἐκ λίθων ἐντίμων, ἀμύθητά τε
καὶ ἀναρίθμητα ἦν· οἰκίαι τε καὶ κῶμαι
παμπληθεῖς, καὶ χώρα πολλὴ πανταχόθι τῆς
γῆς, καὶ ὅση ἄλλη πλούτου ἰδέα ἐστί τε καὶ
ὀνομάζεται ἐν πᾶσιν ἀνθρώποις.

ϛ´. Ἅτε οὐδενὸς αὐτὰ τῶν πώποτε
βεβασιλευκότων ὀχλήσαντος, πολλοί τε ἄνθρωποι, καὶ ταῦτα δόξης ὄντες ὀρθῆς, τῇ
τῶν σφετέρων ἐπιτηδευμάτων προφάσει ἐνθένδε ἀεὶ τοῦ βίου τὰς ἀφορμὰς εἶχον. Τούτων μὲν οὖν τῶν ἱερῶν πρῶτον τὰς οὐσίας
δημοσιώσας Ἰουστινιανὸς βασιλεύς, ἀφείλετο
ἐξαπιναίως τὰ χρήματα πάντα, ἐξ οὗ τοῖς
πολλοῖς ἀποκεκλεῖσθαι τὸ λοιπὸν τοῦ βίου
συνέβη. Πολλοὶ δὲ εὐθὺς πανταχόσε πε-
ριιόντες, δόξης τῆς πατρίου τοὺς παραπίπ-

COURT OF JUSTINIAN 95

old religion, and threatened the recusants
with legal disability to transmit their property to their wives and children by will.
The churches of these so-called heretics
—especially those belonging to the Arian
heresy—were rich beyond belief. Neither
the whole of the Senate, or any other of
the greatest corporations in the Roman
Empire, could be compared with these
churches in wealth. They had gold and
silver plate and jewels more than any man
could count or describe ; they owned many
mansions and villages, and large estates
everywhere, and everything else which is
reckoned and called wealth among men.

As none of the previous Emperors had
interfered with them, many people, even
of the orthodox faith, procured, through
this wealth, work and the means of livelihood. But the Emperor Justinian first
of all sequestrated all the property of
these churches, and suddenly took away
all that they possessed, by which many
people lost the means of subsistence.
Many agents were straightway sent out
to all parts of the Empire to force whom-

τοντας ἠνάγκαζον μεταβάλλεσθαι. "Απερ ἐπεὶ ἀνθρώποις ἀγροίκοις οὐχ ὅσια ἔδοξεν εἶναι, τοῖς ταῦτα ἐπαγγέλλουσιν ἀντιστατεῖν ἅπαντες ἔγνωσαν. Πολλοὶ μὲν οὖν πρὸς τῶν στασιωτῶν διεφθείροντο· πολλοὶ δὲ καὶ σφᾶς αὑτοὺς διεχρήσαντο, εὐσεβεῖν μάλιστα ὑπὸ ἀβελτερίας οἰόμενοι· καὶ αὐτῶν ὁ μὲν πλεῖστος ὅμιλος, γῆς τῆς πατρῴας ἐξιστάμενοι, ἔφευγον· Μοντανοὶ δὲ, οἳ ἐν Φρυγίᾳ κατῴκηντο, σφᾶς αὐτοὺς ἐν ἱεροῖς τοῖς σφετέροις καθείρξαντες, τούτους τε τοὺς νεὼς αὐτίκα ἐμπρήσαντες, ξυνδιεφθάρησαν οὐδενὶ λόγῳ· πᾶσά τε ἀπ' αὐτοῦ ἡ Ῥωμαίων ἀρχὴ φόνου τε ἦν καὶ φυγῆς ἔμπλεως.

ζ. Νόμου δὲ τοῦ τοιούτου καὶ ἀμφὶ τοὺς Σαμαρείτας αὐτίκα τεθέντος, ταραχὴ ἄκριτος τὴν Παλαιστίνην κατέλαβεν. Ὅσοι μὲν οὖν ἔν τε Καισαρείᾳ τῇ ἐμῇ κἀν ταῖς ἄλλαις πόλεσιν ᾤκουν, παρὰ φαῦλον ἡγησάμενοι κακοπάθειάν τινα ὑπὲρ ἀνοήτου φέρεσθαι δόγματος, ὄνομα Χριστιανῶν τοῦ σφίσι παρόντος, ἀνταλλαξάμενοι τῷ προ-

COURT OF JUSTINIAN 96

soever they met to change the faith of
his forefathers. These homely people, considering this an act of impiety, decided to
oppose the Emperor's agents. Hereupon
many were put to death by the persecuting
faction, and many made an end of themselves, thinking, in their superstitious
folly, that this course best satisfied the
claims of religion; but the greater part
of them voluntarily quitted the land of
their forefathers, and went into exile.
The Montanists, who were settled in
Phrygia, shut themselves up in their
churches, set them on fire, and perished in
the flames; and, from this time forth,
nothing was to be seen in the Roman
Empire except massacres and flight.

Justinian straightway passed a similar law with regard to the Samaritans,
which produced a riot in Palestine. In
my own city of Caesarea and other cities,
the people, thinking that it was a foolish thing to suffer for a mere senseless dogma, adopted, in place of the
name which they had hitherto borne,
the appellation of " Christians," and so

ΠΡΟΚΟΠΙΟΥ ΑΝΕΚΔΟΤΑ

σχήματι τούτῳ, τὸν ἐκ τοῦ νόμου ἀποσεί-
σασθαι κίνδυνον ἴσχυσαν. Καὶ αὐτῶν ὅσοις
μέν τι λογισμοῦ καὶ ἐπιεικείας μετῆν, πιστοὶ
εἶναι τὰ ἐς δόξαν τήνδε οὐδαμῆ ἀπηξίουν· οἱ
μέντοι πλεῖστοι ὥσπερ ἀγανακτοῦντες, ὅτι δὴ
οὐχ ἑκούσιοι, ἀλλὰ τῷ νόμῳ ἠναγκασμένοι,
δόγμα τὸ πάτριον μετεβάλλοντο, αὐτίκα δὴ
μάλα ἐπί τε Μανιχαίους καὶ τοὺς καλουμένους Πολυθέους ἀπέκλιναν.

η΄. Οἱ δὲ γεωργοὶ ξύμπαντες ἀθρόοι
γεγενημένοι, ὅπλα ἀνταίρειν βασιλεῖ ἔγνωσαν,
βασιλέα σφίσι τῶν τινα λῃστῶν προβεβλη-
μένοι, Ἰουλιανὸν ὄνομα, Σαβάρου υἱόν. Καὶ
χρόνον μέν τινα τοῖς στρατιώταις ἐς χεῖρας
ἐλθόντες, ἀντεῖχον· ἔπειτα δὲ ἡττηθέντες τῇ
μάχῃ, διεφθάρησαν ξὺν τῷ ἡγεμόνι. Καὶ
λέγονται μυριάδες ἀνθρώπων δέκα ἐν τῷ
πόνῳ τούτῳ ἀπολωλέναι· καὶ χώρα ἡ πάσης
γῆς ἀγαθὴ μάλιστα, ἔρημος γεωργῶν ἀπ'
αὐτοῦ γέγονε. Τοῖς τε τῶν χωρίων κυρίοις
Χριστιανοῖς οὖσι τὸ πρᾶγμα τοῦτο ἐς μέγα
κακὸν ἐτελεύτησεν. Ἀναγκαῖον γὰρ γέγονε
σφίσιν οὐδὲν ἐνθένδε μετακομιζομένοις, φόρον

COURT OF JUSTINIAN 97

avoided the danger with which they were threatened by this law. Such of them as had any claims to reason and who belonged to the better class, thought it their duty to remain stedfast to their new faith; but the greater part, as though out of pique at having been forced against their will by the law to abandon the faith of their fathers, adopted the belief of the Manicheans, or what is known as Polytheism.

But all the country people met together in a body and determined to take up arms against the Emperor. They chose a leader of their own, named Julian, the son of Sabarus, and for some time held their own in the struggle with the Imperial troops, but were at last defeated and cut to pieces, together with their leader. It is said that one hundred thousand men fell in this engagement, and the most fertile country on the earth has ever since been without cultivators. This did great harm to the Christian landowners in that country, for, although they received nothing from

13—2

98 ΠΡΟΚΟΠΙΟΥ ΑΝΕΚΔΟΤΑ

τὸν ἐπέτειον, ἀδρόν τινα ὄντα, ἐς τὸν ἅπαντα αἰῶνα βασιλεῖ φέρειν, ἐπεὶ οὐδεμιᾷ φειδοῖ ἡ τοῦ ἔργου τούτου ἐπιτροπὴ γέγονεν.

θ'. Ἐντεῦθεν ἐπὶ τοὺς Ἕλληνας καλουμένους τὴν δίωξιν ἦγεν, αἰκιζόμενός τε τὰ σώματα καὶ τὰ χρήματα ληιζόμενος. Ἀλλὰ καὶ αὐτῶν ὅσοι τοῦ Χριστιανῶν ὀνόματος δῆθεν τῷ λόγῳ μεταλαχεῖν ἔγνωσαν, καιρὸν τὸν παρόντα σφίσιν ἐκκρούοντες, οὗτοι δὴ οὐ πολλῷ ὕστερον ἐπὶ ταῖς σπονδαῖς καὶ θυσίαις καὶ ἄλλοις οὐχ ὁσίοις ἔργοις ἐκ τοῦ ἐπιπλεῖστον ἡλίσκοντο. Τὰ γὰρ ἀμφὶ τοῖς Χριστιανοῖς εἰργασμένα ἐν τοῖς ὄπισθέν μοι λόγοις λελέξεται.

ι'. Μετὰ δὲ καὶ τὸ παιδεραστεῖν νόμῳ ἀπεῖργεν, οὐ τὰ μετὰ τὸν νόμον διερευνώμενος, ἀλλὰ τοὺς πάλαι ποτὲ ταυτῃ δὴ τῇ νόσῳ ἁλόντας. Ἐγίνετό τε ἡ ἐς αὐτοὺς ἀποστροφὴ οὐδενὶ κόσμῳ· ἐπεὶ καὶ κατηγόρου χωρὶς ἐπράσσετο ἡ ἐς αὐτοὺς τίσις· ἑνός τε ἀνδρὸς ἢ παιδὸς λόγος, καὶ τούτου δούλου, ἂν οὕτω τύχοι, καὶ ἀκουσίου μαρτυρεῖν ἐπὶ τὸν κεκτημένον ἀναγκασθέντος, ἔδοξεν εἶναι ἀκριβὴς ἔλεγχος. Τούς τε οὕτως ἁλισκομέ-

COURT OF JUSTINIAN 98

their property, yet they were forced to pay heavy taxes yearly to the Emperor for the rest of their lives, and no abatement or relief from this burden was granted to them.

After this he began to persecute those who were called Gentiles, torturing their persons and plundering their property. All of these people, who decided to adopt the Christian faith nominally, saved themselves for the time, but not long afterwards most of them were caught offering libations and sacrifices and performing other unholy rites. How he treated the Christians I will subsequently relate.

Next he forbade paederasty by law, and he made this law apply not only to those who transgressed it after it had been passed, but even to those who had practised this wickedness long before. The law was applied to these persons in the loosest fashion, the testimony of one man or boy, who possibly might be a slave unwilling to bear witness against his master, was held to be sound evidence. Those who were convicted were

ΠΡΟΚΟΠΙΟΥ ΑΝΕΚΔΟΤΑ

νους τὰ αἰδοῖα περιῃρημένους ἐπόμπευεν. Οὐκ ἐς πάντας μέντοι τὸ κακὸν κατ' ἀρχὰς ἤγετο, ἀλλ' ὅσοι ἢ Πράσινοι εἶναι, ἢ μεγάλα περιβεβλῆσθαι χρήματα ἔδοξαν, ἢ ἄλλο τι προσκεκρουκότες ἐτύγχανον.

ια'. Καὶ μὴν καὶ τοῖς μετεωρολόγοις χαλεπῶς εἶχεν. Διὸ δὴ αὐτοὺς καὶ ἡ ἐπὶ τοῖς κλέπταις τεταγμένη ἀρχὴ ᾐκίζετό τε ἀπ' οὐδεμιᾶς ἄλλης αἰτίας, καὶ ξαίνουσα κατὰ νώτου πολλὰς, ἐπὶ καμήλων φερομένους ἐπόμπευεν ἀνὰ πᾶσαν τὴν πόλιν, γέροντάς τε καὶ ἄλλως ἐπιεικεῖς ὄντας, ἄλλο αὐτοῖς ἐπικαλεῖν οὐδὲν ἔχουσα, πλήν γε δὴ ὅτι σοφοὶ τὰ περὶ τοὺς ἀστέρας ἐν τοιούτῳ χώρῳ ἐβούλοντο εἶναι.

ιβ'. Ἔφευγον τοίνυν ἀνθρώπων διηνεκὴς ὅμιλος πολὺς οὐκ ἐς βαρβάρους μόνον, ἀλλὰ καὶ ἐς τοὺς μακρὰν ᾠκισμένους Ῥωμαίων· ἦν. τε ἰδεῖν ἐν χώρᾳ τε ἀεὶ καὶ πόλει ἑκάστῃ τοὺς πλείστους ξένους. Τοῦ γὰρ διαλαθεῖν ἕνεκα, γῆς τῆς πατρῴας τὴν ἀλλοτρίαν ἠλλάξαντο εὐπετῶς ἕκαστοι, ὥσπερ τῆς πατρίδος αὐτοῖς ὑπὸ πολεμίων ἁλούσης.

COURT OF JUSTINIAN 99

carried through the city, after having had their genitals cut off. This cruelty was not at first practised against any except those who belonged to the Green faction or were thought to be very rich, or had otherwise offended.

Justinian and Theodora also dealt very harshly with the astrologers, so that the officers appointed to punish thieves proceeded against these men for no other cause than that they were astrologers, dealt many stripes on their backs, and paraded them on camels through the city; yet they were old and respectable men, against whom no reproach could be brought except that they dwelt in Byzantium and were learned about the stars.

There was a continual stream of emigration, not only to the lands of the barbarians, but also to the nations most remote from Rome; and one saw a very great number of foreigners both in the country and in each city of the Empire, for men lightly exchanged their native land for another, as though their own country had been captured by an enemy.

ΠΡΟΚΟΠΙΟΥ ΑΝΕΚΔΟΤΑ

ΚΕΦΑΛΑΙΟΝ ΙΒ΄.

α΄. Τὸν μὲν οὖν πλοῦτον τῶν εὐδαιμόνων εἶναι δοκούντων ἐν Βυζαντίῳ καὶ πόλει ἑκάστῃ, μετά γε τοὺς ἐκ τῆς συγκλήτου βουλῆς, τρόποις οἷσπερ εἴρηται Ἰουστινιανός τε καὶ Θεοδώρα λησάμενοι ἔσχον. Ὅπως δὲ καὶ τοὺς ἐκ βουλῆς ἀφαιρεῖσθαι τὰ χρήματα πάντα ἴσχυσαν, αὐτίκα δηλώσω.

(Κεφ. ιβ΄ ancien.) Ἦν τις ἐν Βυζαντίῳ Ζήνων ὄνομα, ἐκείνου Ἀνθεμίου υἱωνὸς, ὅσπερ ἐν τῇ ἑσπερίᾳ τὴν βασιλείαν τὰ πρότερα ἔσχεν. Τοῦτον δὴ ἐξεπίτηδες ἄρχοντα ἐπ᾽ Αἰγύπτου καταστησάμενοι ἔστελλον. Ἀλλ᾽ ὁ μὲν, χρημάτων τὸ πλοῖον τῶν τιμιωτάτων ἐμπλησάμενος, τὰ ἐς τὴν ἀναγωγὴν διετείνετο· ἦσαν γὰρ αὐτῷ σταθμός τε ἀργύρου ἀναρίθμητος, καὶ χρυσώματα μαργάροις τε καὶ σμαράγδοις καλλωπισθέντα, καὶ λίθοις ἄλλοις τοιούτοις ἐντίμοις· οἱ δὲ, τινὰς ἀναπείσαντες τῶν οἱ πιστοτάτων εἶναι δοκούντων, τὰ μὲν

CHAPTER XII

THOSE who were considered the wealthiest persons in Byzantium and the other cities of the Empire, next after members of the Senate, were robbed of their wealth by Justinian and Theodora in the manner which I have described above. I shall now describe how they managed to take away all the property of members of the Senate.

There was at Constantinople one *Zeno*, the grandson of that Anthemius who formerly had been Emperor of the West. They sent this man to Egypt as governor. He delayed his departure, while he loaded his ship with precious valuables; for he had silver beyond any man's counting, and gold plate set with pearls and emeralds, and with other like precious stones. But Justinian and Theodora bribed some of those who passed for his

χρήματα ἐνθένδε ὅτι τάχιστα ἐκφορήσαντες, πῦρ δὲ ἐν κοίλῃ νηὶ ἐμβεβλημένοι, τῷ Ζήνωνι ἀπαγγέλλειν ἐκέλευον ἀπὸ ταὐτομάτου τήν τε φλόγα ἐν τῷ πλοίῳ ξυνηνέχθαι καὶ διολωλέναι τὰ χρήματα. Χρόνῳ δὲ ὕστερον, Ζήνωνι μὲν ἐξαπιναίως ἀπογενέσθαι ξυνέπεσεν, αὐτοὶ δὲ κύριοι. τῆς οὐσίας εὐθὺς, ἅτε κληρονόμοι, γεγόνασι. Διαθήκην γάρ τινες προὔφερον, ἥπερ οὐ παρ᾽ ἐκείνου ξυγκεῖσθαι διατεθρύλληται.

β΄. Καὶ Τατιανοῦ τε καὶ Δημοσθένους καὶ τῆς Ἱλαρᾶς τρόπῳ τῷ ὁμοίῳ σφᾶς αὐτοὺς κληρονόμους πεποίηνται, οἵπερ τά τε ἄλλα καὶ τὸ ἀξίωμα πρῶτοι ἔν γε Ῥωμαίων τῇ βουλῇ ἦσαν. Τινῶν δὲ οὐ διαθήκας, ἀλλ᾽ ἐπιστολὰς διεσκευασμένοι τὴν οὐσίαν ἔσχον. Οὕτω γὰρ Διονυσίου τε κληρονόμοι γεγόνασιν, ὃς ἐν Λιβάνῳ ᾤκει, καὶ Ἰωάννου τοῦ Βασιλείου παιδός, ὃς ἐπιφανέστατος μὲν Ἐδεσσηνῶν ἐγεγόνει πάντων, βίᾳ δὲ πρὸς Βελισαρίου ἐν ὁμήρων λόγῳ ἐκδέδοται τοῖς Πέρσαις, ὥσπερ μοι ἐν τοῖς ἔμπροσθεν λόγοις ἐρρήθη. Τοῦτον γὰρ τὸν Ἰωάννην ὁ μὲν Χοσρόης οὐκέτι ἠφίει, ἐπικαλῶν Ῥωμαίοις ἠλογηκέναι τὰ ξυγκείμενα πάντα, ἐφ᾽ οἷς

COURT OF JUSTINIAN 101

most faithful servants, to take everything out of the ship as fast as they could, set it on fire in the hold, and then go and tell Zeno that his ship had taken fire of its own accord, and that all his property was lost. Some time after this Zeno died suddenly, and they took possession of his property as his heirs, producing a will which, it is currently reported, was never made by him.

In like manner they made themselves the heirs of Tatian, of Demosthenes, and of Hilara, persons who at that time held the first rank in the Roman Senate. They obtained other persons' fortunes by the production, not of formal wills, but of counterfeit conveyances. This was how they became the heirs of Dionysius, who dwelt in Libanus, and of John the son of Basil, who was the leading man in Edessa, and had been delivered up to the Persians as a hostage against his will by Belisarius, as I have told already. Chosroes kept this John a prisoner, and refused to let him go, declaring that the Romans had not performed all the terms

αὐτῷ πρὸς Βελισαρίου δοθεὶς ἐτύγχανεν· ἀποδίδοσθαι μέντοι ἅτε δορυάλωτον γεγονότα ἠξίου. Ἡ δὲ τοῦ ἀνδρὸς μάμμη (περιοῦσα γὰρ ἐτύγχανεν ἔτι), τὰ λύτρα παρεχομένη, οὐχ ἧσσον ἢ δισχιλίας λίτρας ἀργύρου, τὸν υἱωνὸν ὠνήσεσθαι ἐπίδοξος ἦν. Ἀλλ' ἐπεὶ τὰ λύτρα ταῦτα ἐς Δάρας ἦλθε, μαθὼν ὁ βασιλεὺς τὸ συμβόλαιον γενέσθαι οὐκ εἴα· ὡς μὴ ἐς τοὺς βαρβάρους, εἰπὼν, ὁ Ῥωμαίων κομίζηται πλοῦτος. Οὐ πολλῷ δὲ ὕστερον, τῷ μὲν Ἰωάννῃ νοσήσαντι ξυνέβη ἐξ ἀνθρώπων ἀφανισθῆναι· ὁ δὲ τὴν πόλιν ἐπιτροπεύων ἐπιστολὴν ἀναπλάσας τινὰ, ἔφη πρὸς αὐτὸν ἅτε φίλον οὐ πολλῷ ἔμπροσθεν τὸν Ἰωάννην γράψαι, ὥς οἱ αὐτῷ βουλομένῳ εἴη, εἰς τὸν βασιλέα τὴν αὐτοῦ οὐσίαν ἐλθεῖν.

γ'. Πάντων δὲ τῶν ἄλλων τὰ ὀνόματα καταλέγειν οὐκ ἂν δυναίμην ὧνπερ αὐτόματοι κληρονόμοι γεγένηνται. Ἀλλὰ μέχρι μὲν οὖν ἡ τοῦ Νίκα καλουμένη στάσις ἐγένετο, κατὰ μίαν διαλέγεσθαι τὰς τῶν εὐδαιμόνων οὐσίας ἠξίουν· ἐπεὶ δὲ ταύτην, ὥσπερ μοι ἐν τοῖς ἔμπροσθεν λόγοις ἐρρήθη,

COURT OF JUSTINIAN

of the treaty for which John had been given in pledge by Belisarius, but he was prepared to let him be ransomed as a prisoner of war. His grandmother, who was still alive, got together the money for his ransom, not less than two thousand pounds of silver, and would have ransomed her grandson; but when this money arrived at Dara, the Emperor heard of the transaction and forbade it, that the wealth of Romans might not be conveyed to barbarians. Not long after this John fell ill and died; whereupon the governor of the city forged a letter which he said John had written to him as a friend not long before, to the effect that he desired the Emperor to succeed to his property.

I could not give the list of all the other people whose heirs Justinian and Theodora became by the free will of the testators. However, up to the time of the insurrection called Nike, they only plundered rich men of their property one by one; but when this broke out, as I have described in my former works, they

ΠΡΟΚΟΠΙΟΥ ΑΝΕΚΔΟΤΑ

γενέσθαι ξυνέβη, τότε δὴ ἀθρόας εἰπεῖν
σχεδόν τι ἁπάντων τῶν ἀπὸ τῆς συγκλήτου
βουλῆς τὰς οὐσίας δημοσιώσαντες, τὰ μὲν
ἔπιπλα πάντα, καὶ τῶν χωρίων ὅσα κάλ-
λιστα ἦν, ᾗπερ ἐβούλοντο διεχείρησαν· ἀπολέξαντες δὲ τὰ φόρου πικροῦ τε καὶ βαρυ-
τάτου ὑποτελῆ ὄντα, φιλανθρωπίας προσχήματι
τοῖς πάλαι κεκτημένοις ἀπέδοντο. Διὸ δὴ
πρός τε τῶν φορολόγων ἀγχόμενοι καὶ ἀπο-
κναιόμενοι τόκοις ὀφλημάτων ἀειρρύτοις τισὶ
δυσθανατοῦντες ἀκούσιοι διεβίωσαν.

δ΄. Διὸ δὴ ἐμοί τε καὶ τοῖς πολλοῖς
ἡμῶν οὐδεπώποτε ἔδοξαν οὗτοι ἄνθρωποι
εἶναι, ἀλλὰ δαίμονες παλαμναῖοί τινες, καὶ
ὥσπερ οἱ ποιηταὶ λέγουσι βροτολοιγὼ ἤστην,
οἳ δὴ ἐπὶ κοινῆς βουλευσάμενοι, ὅπως ἅπαντα
ἀνθρώπεια γένη τε καὶ ἔργα ὡς ῥᾷστα καὶ
τάχιστα διαφθείρειν ἱκανοὶ εἶεν, ἀνθρώπειόν
τε ἠμπέσχοντο σῶμα καὶ ἀνθρωποδαίμονες
γεγενημένοι, τῷ τρόπῳ τούτῳ ξύμπασαν τὴν
οἰκουμένην κατέσεισαν. Τεκμηριῶσαι δ᾽ ἄν
τις τὸ τοιοῦτο πολλοῖς τε καὶ ἄλλοις καὶ
τῇ τῶν πεπραγμένων δυνάμει.

ε΄. Τὰ γὰρ δαιμόνια τῶν ἀνθρωπείων

COURT OF JUSTINIAN   103

then sequestrated nearly all the property
of the Senate. They laid their hands
upon all movables and the finest parts
of the estates, but set apart such lands
as were burdened with grievous imposts,
and, under pretence of kindness, restored
them to their former possessors. So these
people, oppressed by the tax-gatherers, and
tormented by the never-ceasing interest to
be paid upon their debts, became weary
of their lives.

For the reasons which I have stated,
I, and many of my position, never believed that they were really two human
beings, but evil demons, and what the
poets call scourges of mankind, who
laid their heads together to see how they
could fastest and most easily destroy the
race and the works of man, but who had
assumed human forms, and become something between men and demons, and
thus convulsed the whole world. One
can find proofs of this theory more
particularly in the superhuman power
with which they acted.

There is a wide distinction between

ΠΡΟΚΟΠΙΟΥ ΑΝΕΚΔΟΤΑ

ξυμβαίνει πολλῷ τῷ διαλλάσσοντι διακεκρίσθαι. Πολλῶν ἀμέλει γεγονότων ἐκ τοῦ παντὸς αἰῶνος ἀνθρώπων, τύχῃ ἢ φύσει φοβερῶν ἐς τὰ μάλιστα, οἱ μὲν πόλεις, οἱ δὲ χώρας, ἢ ἄλλο τι τοιοῦτο καθ᾽ αὑτοὺς ἔσφηλαν, ὄλεθρον δὲ ξυμπάντων ἀνθρώπων ξυμφοράς τε γῆς τῆς οἰκουμένης ἀπάσης οὐδείς, ὅτι μὴ οὗτοι ἄνθρωποι, ἐργάζεσθαι ἱκανῶς ἔσχον· ὧν δὴ καὶ ἡ τύχη ὑπούργει τῇ γνώμῃ συγκατεργαζομένη τῶν ἀνθρώπων διαφθοράν. Σεισμοῖς τε γὰρ καὶ λοιμοῖς, καὶ ὑδάτων ποταμίων ἐπιρροαῖς, ὑπὸ τὸν χρόνον τοῦτον, πλεῖστα διολωλέναι τετύχηκεν, ὥς μοι αὐτίκα λελέξεται. Οὕτως οὐκ ἀνθρωπείῳ, ἀλλ᾽ ἑτέρῳ σθένει τὰ δεινὰ ἔπρασσον.

ϛ΄. Λέγουσι δὲ αὐτοῦ καὶ τὴν μητέρα φάναι τῶν ἐπιτηδείων τισίν, ὡς οὐ Σαββατίου, τοῦ αὐτῆς ἀνδρός, οὐδὲ ἀνθρώπων τινὸς υἱὸς εἴη. Ἡνίκα γὰρ αὐτὸν κύειν ἔμελλεν, ἐπιφοιτᾶν αὐτῇ δαιμόνιον οὐχ ὁρώμενον, ἀλλ᾽ αἴσθησίν τινα, ὅτι δὴ πάρεστιν, αὐτῇ παρασχόν, ἅτε ἄνδρα γυναικὶ πλησιάσαντα, καθάπερ ἐν ὀνείρῳ ἀφανισθῆναι.

COURT OF JUSTINIAN 104

the human and the supernatural. Many men have been born in every age who, either by circumstances or their own character, have shown themselves terrible beings, who became the ruin of cities, countries, and whatever else fell into their hands; but to destroy all men and to ruin the whole earth has been granted to none save these two, who have been helped by Fortune in their schemes to destroy the whole human race. For, about this time, much ruin was caused by earthquakes, pestilences and inundations of rivers, as I shall immediately tell you. Thus it was not by mere human power, but by something greater, that they were enabled to work their evil will.

It is said that Justinian's mother told some of her intimates that Justinian was not the son of Sabbatius, her husband, or of any human being; but that, at the time when she became pregnant, an unseen demon companied with her, whom she only felt as when a man has connection with a woman, and who then vanished away as in a dream.

ΠΡΟΚΟΠΙΟΥ ΑΝΕΚΔΟΤΑ

ζ. Τινὲς δὲ τῶν αὐτῷ παρόντων τε πόρρω που τῶν νυκτῶν, καὶ ξυγγινομένων ἐν παλατίῳ δηλονότι, οἷσπερ ἐν καθαρῷ ἡ ψυχὴ ἦν, φάντασμά τι θεάσασθαι δαιμόνιον ἄηθες σφίσιν ἀντ' αὐτοῦ ἔδοξαν. Ὁ μὲν γὰρ ἔφασκεν, ἄφνω μὲν αὐτὸν θρόνου τοῦ βασιλείου ἐξαναστάντα περιπάτους ἐνταῦθα ποιεῖν· συχνὸν γὰρ καθῆσθαι οὐδαμῆ εἴθιστο· τῆς· δὲ κεφαλῆς ἐν τῷ παραυτίκα τῷ Ἰουστινιανῷ ἀφανισθείσης, τὸ ἄλλο οἱ σῶμα τούτους δὴ τοὺς διαύλους ποιεῖν δοκεῖν, αὐτόν τε, ἅτε οἱ τῶν ὀμμάτων περὶ τὴν θέαν ὡς ἥκιστα ὑγιαινόντων, ἀσχάλλοντα καὶ διαπορούμενον ἐπὶ πλεῖστον ἑστάναι. Ὕστερον μέντοι, τῆς κεφαλῆς τῷ σώματι ἐπανηκούσης, τὰ τέως λειπόμενα οἴεσθαι παρὰ δόξαν ἀναπιμπλάναι. Ἄλλος δὲ παρεστάναι οἱ καθημένῳ ἔφη· ἐκ δὲ τοῦ αἰφνιδίου τὸ πρόσωπόν οἱ κρέατι ἀσήμῳ ἰδεῖν ἐμφερὲς γεγονός· οὔτε γὰρ ὀφρῦς, οὔτε ὀφθαλμοὺς ἐπὶ χώρας τῆς αὐτῶν ὄντας, οὔτε ἄλλο τι τὸ παράπαν ἔφερε γνώρισμα· χρόνου μέντοι αὐτῷ τὸ σχῆμα τῆς ὄψεως ἐπανῆκον ἰδεῖν. Ταῦτα οὐκ αὐτὸς

COURT OF JUSTINIAN 105

Some who have been in Justinian's company in the palace very late at night, men with a clear conscience, have thought that in his place they have beheld a strange and devilish form. One of them said that Justinian suddenly arose from his royal throne and walked about (although, indeed, he never could sit still for long), and that at that moment his head disappeared, while the rest of his body still seemed to move to and fro. The man who beheld this stood trembling and troubled in mind, not knowing how to believe his eyes. Afterwards the head joined the body again, and united itself to the parts from which it had so strangely been severed.

Another declared that he stood beside Justinian as he sat, and of a sudden his face turned into a shapeless mass of flesh, without either eyebrows or eyes in their proper places, or anything else which makes a man recognisable ; but after a while he saw the form of his face come back again. What I write here I did not see myself, but I heard it told

θεασάμενος γράφω, ἀλλὰ τῶν τότε θεάσασθαι ἰσχυριζομένων ἀκούσας.

η'. Λέγουσι δὲ καὶ μοναχόν τινα τῷ Θεῷ ἐς τὰ μάλιστα φίλον, πρὸς τῶν αὐτῷ γῆν τὴν ἔρημον ξυνοικούντων ἀναπεισθέντα, σταλῆναι μὲν ἐς Βυζάντιον, τοῖς ἄγχιστα σφίσιν ἐνῳκημένοις ἐπαμυνοῦντα, βιαζομένοις τε καὶ ἀδικουμένοις ἀνύποιστα· ἐνταῦθα δὲ ἀφικόμενον αὐτίκα εἰσόδου τῆς παρὰ τὸν βασιλέα τυχεῖν· μέλλοντα δὲ εἴσω παρ' αὐτὸν γενέσθαι, ἀμεῖψαι μὲν τὸν. ἐκεῖσε οὐδὸν θατέρῳ τὼ πόδε, ἐξαπιναίως δὲ ἀναποδίζοντα ὀπίσω ἰέναι. Εὐνοῦχον μὲν οὖν τὸν εἰσαγωγέα, καὶ τοὺς τῇδε παρόντας, πολλὰ τὸν ἄνθρωπον λιπαρεῖν ἐπίπροσθεν βαίνειν. Τὸν δὲ οὐδέν τι ἀποκρινάμενον, ἀλλὰ καὶ παραπλῆγι ἐοικότα ἐς τὸ δωμάτιον, οὗ δὴ κατέλυε, γεγονότα· τῶν τέ οἱ ἑπομένων ἀναπυνθανομένων, ὅτου ἕνεκα ταῦτα ποιοίη· φάναι λέγουσιν αὐτὸν ἄντικρυς, ὡς τῶν δαιμόνων τὸν ἄρχοντα ἐν τῷ παλατίῳ. ἐπὶ τοῦ θρόνου καθήμενον ἴδοι, ᾧ δὴ ξυγγενέσθαι ἤ τι παρ' αὐτοῦ αἰτεῖσθαι οὐκ ἂν ἀξιοίη. Πῶς δὲ οὐκ ἔμελλεν ὅδε ὁ ἀνὴρ δαίμων τις ἀλιτήριος εἶναι, ὅς γε ποτοῦ,

COURT OF JUSTINIAN 106

by men who were positive that they had
seen it.

They say, too, that a certain monk,
highly in favour with God, was sent
to Byzantium by those who dwelt with
him in the desert, to beg that favour
might be shown to their neighbours, who
had been wronged and outraged beyond
endurance. When he arrived at Byzantium, he straightway obtained an audience
of the Emperor ; but just as he was
about to enter his apartment, he started
back, and, turning round, suddenly withdrew. The eunuch, who was escorting
him, and also the bystanders, besought
him earnestly to go forward, but he made
no answer, but like one who has had a
stroke of the palsy, made his way back
to his lodging. When those who had
come with him asked why he acted thus,
they say that he distinctly stated that
he saw the chief of the devils sitting on
his throne in the midst of the palace,
and he would not meet him or ask
anything of him. How can one believe
this man to have been anything but an

ἢ σιτίων, ἢ ὕπνου εἰς κόρον οὐδέποτε ἦλθεν
ἀλλ' ἀμωσγέπως τῶν παρατεθέντων ἀπογευσάμενος, ἀωρὶ νύκτωρ περιήρχετο τὰ βασίλεια,
καίπερ ἐς τὰ ἀφροδίσια δαιμονίως ἐσπουδακώς.

θ'. Λέγουσι δὲ καὶ τῶν Θεοδώρας ἐραστῶν τινες, ἡνίκα ἐπὶ τῆς σκηνῆς ἦν, νύκτωρ
τι αὐτοῖς ἐπισκῆψαν δαιμόνιον ἐξελάσαι τοῦ
δωματίου, ἵνα δὴ σὺν αὐτῇ ἐνυκτέρευεν· ὀρχηστρὶς δέ τις, Μακεδονία ὄνομα, ἐγεγόνει
τοῖς ἐν 'Αντιοχεῦσι Βενέτοις, δύναμιν περι-
βεβλημένη πολλήν. Γράμματα γὰρ 'Ιου-
στινιανῷ γράφουσα ἔτι 'Ιουστίνου διοικουμένου τὴν βασιλείαν, οὓς ἂν βούλοιτο τῶν
ἐν τοῖς ἑῴοις λογίμων ἀνῄρει οὐδενὶ πόνῳ,
καὶ αὐτῶν τὰ χρήματα ἐποίει ἀνάγραπτα ἐς
τὸ δημόσιον γίνεσθαι.

ι'. Ταύτην τὴν Μακεδονίαν φασὶν ἐξ
Αἰγύπτου καὶ Λιβύης ποτὲ ἥκουσαν τὴν
Θεοδώραν ἀσπασομένην, ἐπειδὴ λίαν δυσφο-
ρουμένην τε αὐτὴν καὶ ἀσχάλλουσαν εἶδεν
οἷς δὴ περιύβριστό τε πρὸς τοῦ 'Εκηβολίου
καὶ τῷ χρήματά οἱ ἐν τῇ ὁδῷ ταύτῃ ἀπολωλέναι, πολλὰ παρηγορεῖν τε καὶ παραθρα-

COURT OF JUSTINIAN 107

evil demon, who never took his fill of
drink, food, or sleep, but snatched at
the meals which were set before him
anyhow, and roamed about the palace at
untimely hours of the night, and yet was
so passionately addicted to venery.

Some of Theodora's lovers, when she
was still on the stage, declare that a demon
had fallen upon them and driven them
out of her bedchamber that it might
pass the night with her. There was a
dancer named Macedonia, who belonged
to the Blue faction at Antioch, and had
very great influence with Justinian. This
woman used to write letters to him while
Justin was still on the throne, and thus
easily made away with any great man
in the East whom she chose, and caused
their property to be confiscated for the
public use. They say that this Macedonia
once greeted Theodora, when she saw her
very much troubled and cast down at
the ill-treatment which she had received
at the hands of Hecebolius, and at the
loss of her money on her journey, and
encouraged and cheered her, bidding her

σύνειν τὴν ἄνθρωπον, ἅτε τῆς τύχης οἵας τε οὔσης καὶ αὖθις αὐτῇ χορηγοῦ γενέσθαι χρημάτων μεγάλων. Τότε λέγουσι τὴν Θεοδώραν εἰπεῖν, ὡς καὶ ὄναρ αὐτῇ ἐπισκῆψαν τὴν νύκτα ἐκείνην, πλούτου ἕνεκα, μηδεμίαν κελεύσαι ποιεῖσθαι φροντίδα. Ἐπειδὰν γὰρ ἐς Βυζάντιον ἵκοιτο, τῷ τῶν δαιμόνων ἄρχοντι ἐς εὐνὴν ἥξειν· τούτῳ τε ἅτε γαμετὴν γυναῖκα ξυνοικήσεσθαι μηχανῇ πασῇ· καὶ ἀπ' αὐτοῦ κυρίαν αὐτὴν πάντων χρημάτων γενήσεσθαι. Ἀλλὰ ταῦτα μὲν οὕτω δὴ δόξης τοῖς πλείστοις εἶχεν.

COURT OF JUSTINIAN 108

remember the fickleness of fortune, which might again grant her great possessions. They say that Theodora used to tell how, that night, she had a dream which bade her take no thought about money, for that, when she came to Byzantium, she would share the bed of the chief of the demons; that she must manage by all means to become his wedded wife, and that afterwards she would have all the wealth of the world at her disposal.

This was the common report in regard to these matters.

ΚΕΦΑΛΑΙΟΝ ΙΓ'.

α'. Ἰουστινιανὸς δὲ τοιοῦτος μὲν τὸ ἄλλο ἦθος, οἷος δεδήλωται· εὐπρόσιτον δὲ παρεῖχεν αὐτὸν, καὶ πρᾷον τοῖς ἐντυγχάνουσιν οὐδενί τε τῶν πάντων ἀποκεκλεῖσθαι τῆς εἰς αὐτὸν εἰσόδου συνέβαινεν· ἀλλὰ καὶ τοῖς οὐκ ἐν κόσμῳ παρ' αὐτὸν ἑστῶσιν, ἢ φθεγγομένοις, οὐδέποτε χαλεπῶς ἔσχεν. Οὐ μέντοι ἠρυθρία τινὰ τῶν πρὸς αὐτοῦ ἀπολουμένων. Οὐ μὴν οὐδὲ ὀργῆς πώποτέ τι ἢ ἀκροχολίας ὑποφαίνων ἐς τοὺς προσκεκρουκότας ἔνδηλος γέγονεν, ἀλλὰ πρᾷος μὲν τῷ προσώπῳ, καθειμέναις δὲ ταῖς ὀφρύσιν, ὑφειμένῃ δὲ τῇ φωνῇ, ἐκέλευε μυριάδας μὲν διαφθαρῆναι μηδὲν ἠδικηκότων ἀνθρώπων, πόλεις δὲ καθελεῖν, χρήματά τε ἀνάγραπτα ἐς τὸ δημόσιον πάντα ποιεῖσθαι. Εἴκασεν ἄν τις, ἐκ τοῦδε τοῦ ἤθους, προβατίου γνώμην τὸν ἄνθρωπον ἔχειν. Ἦν μέντοι τις αὐτὸν ἱλεούμενος, τοὺς παραπεπτωκότας ἱκεσίοις λιταῖς παραιτεῖσθαι

CHAPTER XIII

ALTHOUGH Justinian's character was such as I have already explained, he was easy of access, and affable to those whom he met. No one was ever denied an audience, and he never was angry even with those who did not behave or speak properly in his presence. But, on the other hand, he never felt ashamed of any of the murders which he committed. However, he never displayed any anger or pettishness against those who offended him, but preserved a mild countenance and an unruffled brow, and with a gentle voice would order tens of thousands of innocent men to be put to death, cities to be taken by storm, and property to be confiscated. One would think, from his manner, that he had the character of a sheep; but if anyone, pitying his victims, were to endeavour, by prayers

πειρῷτο, ἐνταῦθα ἠγριωμένος τε καὶ σεσηρὼς μεστοῦσθαι ἐδόκει, ἀλλὰ καὶ τοῦτο ἐπὶ φθόρῳ τῶν κατηκόων.

β΄. Τοῖς τε γὰρ ἱερεῦσιν ἀδεέστερον τοὺς πέλας συνεχώρει βιάζεσθαι, καὶ ληιζομένοις τὰ τῶν ὁμόρων συνέχαιρεν, εὐσεβεῖν ταύτῃ ἀμφὶ τὸ θεῖον οἰόμενος. Δίκας τε τοιαύτας δικάζων, τὰ ὅσια ποιεῖν ᾤετο, ἤν τις ἱερῶν λόγῳ τῶν τι οὐ προσηκόντων ἁρπάσας νενικηκώς τε ἀπιὼν ᾤχετο. Τὸ γὰρ δίκαιον ἐν τῷ περιεῖναι τοὺς ἱερέας τῶν ἐναντίων ᾤετο εἶναι. Καὶ αὐτὸς δὲ κτώμενος ἐξ οὐ προσηκόντων τὰς τῶν περιόντων ἢ τετελευτηκότων οὐσίας, καὶ ταύτας τῶν τινι νεῶν εὐθὺς ἀνατιθεὶς, τῷ τῆς εὐσεβείας ἐφιλοτιμεῖτο παραπετάσματι· ὡς μὴ ἐς τοὺς βιασθέντας ἢ τούτων αὖθις ἐπανίοι κτῆσις. Ἀλλὰ καὶ φόνων ἀριθμὸν ἄκριτον διὰ ταῦτα εἰργάζετο. Εἰς μίαν γὰρ ἀμφὶ τῷ Χριστῷ δόξαν συναγαγεῖν ἅπαντας ἐν σπουδῇ ἔχων,

COURT OF JUSTINIAN 110

and supplications, to make him relent, he
would straightway become savage, show
his teeth, and vent his rage upon his
subjects. As for the priests, he let them
override their neighbours with impunity,
and delighted to see them plunder those
round about them, thinking that in this
manner he was showing piety. Whenever
he had to decide any lawsuit of this sort,
he thought that righteous judgment con-
sisted in letting the priest win his cause
and leave the court in triumph with some
plunder to which he had no right whatever; for, to him, justice meant the
success of the priest's cause. He himself, when by malpractices he had obtained
possession of the property of people, alive
or dead, would straightway present his
plunder to one of the churches, by which
means he would hide his rapacity under
the cloak of piety, and render it impossible for his victims ever to recover their
possessions. Indeed, he committed num-
berless murders through his notion of
piety; for, in his zeal to bring all men
to agree in one form of Christian doctrine,

ΠΡΟΚΟΠΙΟΥ ΑΝΕΚΔΟΤΑ

λόγῳ οὐδενὶ τοὺς ἄλλους ἀνθρώπους διέφθειρε, καὶ ταῦτα ἐν τῷ τῆς εὐσεβείας προσχήματι πράσσων· οὐ γάρ οἱ ἐδόκει φόνος ἀνθρώπων εἶναι, ἤν γε μὴ τῆς αὐτοῦ δόξης οἱ τελευτῶντες τύχοιεν ὄντες.

γ΄. Οὕτως ἦν κατεσπουδασμένος οἱ τῶν ἀνθρώπων ἐσαεὶ φθόρος· ἐπινοῶν τε ξὺν τῇ γαμετῇ, οὔποτε ἀνίει τὰς εἰς τοῦτον φερούσας αἰτίας. Ἄμφω γὰρ τώδε τὼ ἀνθρώπω τὰς ἐπιθυμίας ἐκ τοῦ ἐπιπλεῖστον ἀδελφὰς εἶχον· οὗ δὲ αὐτοῖς καὶ διαλλάσσειν τὸν τρόπον ξυνέβη· πονηρὸς μὲν ἑκάτερος ἦν, τὰ μέντοι ἐναντιώτατα ἐνδεικνύμενοι, τοὺς ὑπηκόους διέφθειρον. Ὁ μὲν γὰρ κονιορτοῦ τὰ ἐς τὴν γνώμην κουφότερος ἦν, ὑποκείμενος τοῖς ἀεὶ παράγειν, ὅποι ποτ᾿ ἐδόκει, βουλομένοις αὐτόν, ἢν μὴ τὸ πρᾶγμα ἐς φιλανθρωπίαν ἢ ἀκερδίαν ἄγοι· θῶπάς τε λόγους ἐνδελεχέστατα προσιέμενος. Ἔπειθον γὰρ αὐτὸν οἱ κολακεύοντες οὐδενὶ πόνῳ, ὅτι μετέωρος ἀρθείη καὶ ἀεροβατοίη. Καί ποτε αὐτῷ παρεδρεύων Τριβωνιανὸς ἔφη περιδεὴς ἀτεχνῶς εἶναι, μή ποτε αὐτὸς ὑπὸ εὐσεβείας ἐς τὸν οὐρανὸν ἀναληφθεὶς λάθοι. Τοιούτους δὲ τοὺς

COURT OF JUSTINIAN 111

he recklessly murdered all who dissented therefrom, under the pretext of piety, for he did not think that it was murder, if those whom he slew were not of the same belief as himself. Thus, his thoughts were always fixed upon slaughter, and, together with his wife, he neglected no excuse which could bring it about; for both of these beings had for the most part the same passions, but sometimes they played a part which was not natural to them; for each of them was thoroughly wicked, and by their pretended differences of opinion, brought their subjects to ruin. Justinian's character was weaker than water, and anyone could lead him whither he would, provided it was not to commit any act of kindness or incur the loss of money. He especially delighted in flattery, so that his flatterers could easily make him believe that he should soar aloft and tread upon the clouds. Once indeed, Tribonianus, when sitting by him, declared that he was afraid that some day Justinian would be caught up into heaven because of his righteousness, and would be lost to men.

ἐπαίνους ἤτοι σκώμματα ἐν τῷ τῆς διανοίας ἐποιεῖτο βεβαίῳ.

δ΄. Ἀλλὰ καὶ του θαυμάσας, ἂν οὕτω τύχοι, τὴν ἀρετήν, ὀλίγῳ ὕστερον ἅτε πονηρῷ ἐλοιδορεῖτο· καὶ κακίσας τῶν τινα ὑπηκόων, αὖθις αὐτοῦ ἐπαινέτης ἐγίνετο οὐδενὶ λόγῳ, ἐξ οὐδεμιᾶς μεταβεβλημένος αἰτίας. Τὰ γὰρ τῆς γνώμης αὐτῷ ἐξ ἐναντίας ᾔει, ὧν τε αὐτὸς ἔλεγε καὶ ἐβούλετο ἔνδηλος εἶναι. Ὅπως μέντοι ὁ τρόπος αὐτῷ τὰ ἐς φιλίαν τε καὶ ἔχθος εἶχεν, ὑπεῖπον ἤδη, τοῖς τῷ ἀνθρώπῳ ἐκ τοῦ ἐπιπλεῖστον εἰργασμένοις τεκμηριώσας. Ἐχθρὸς μὲν γὰρ ἀσφαλής τε καὶ ἄτρεπτος ἦν, ἐς δὲ τοὺς φίλους ἄγαν ἀβέβαιος. Ὥστε ἀμέλει τῶν μέν οἱ ἐσπουδασμένων κατειργάσατο πλείστους, φίλος δὲ τῶν πώποτε μισουμένων οὐδενὶ γέγονεν. Οὓς δὲ μάλιστα γνωρίμους καὶ ἐπιτηδείους ἔδοξεν ἔχειν, τούτους τῇ ὁμοζύγι ἢ ἄλλῳ ὁτῳοῦν χαριζόμενος, ἀπολουμένους οὐκ ἐς μακρὰν προύδωκε, καίπερ εὖ εἰδώς, ὅτι δὴ ἐς αὐτὸν εὐνοίας ἕνεκα τεθνήξονται μόνης. Ἄπιστος γὰρ ἐν πᾶσι πλήν γε δὴ τῆς τε ἀπανθρω-

COURT OF JUSTINIAN   112

Such praises, or rather sneers, as these
he constantly bore in mind; yet, if he
admired any man for his goodness, he
would shortly afterwards upbraid him for
a villain, and after having railed at one
of his subjects without any cause, he
would suddenly take to praising him,
having changed his mind on no grounds
whatever; for what he really thought was
always the opposite of what he said, and
wished to appear to think. How he was
affected by emotions of love or hate I
think I have sufficiently indicated by what
I have said concerning his actions. As
an enemy, he was obstinate and relentless;
as a friend, inconstant; for he made
away with many of his strongest par-
tisans, but never became the friend of
anyone whom he had once disliked.
Those whom he appeared to consider his
nearest and dearest friends he would in
a short time deliver up to ruin to please
his wife or anyone else, although he
knew well that they died only because
of devotion for him; for he was untrust-
worthy in all things save cruelty and

πίας καὶ φιλοχρηματίας διαφανὴς ἦν. Ταύτης γὰρ αὐτὸν ἀποστῆσαι δυνατὸν οὐδενὶ γέγονεν.

ε΄. Ἀλλὰ καὶ ἐς ἃ πείθειν αὐτὸν ἡ γαμετὴ οὐκ εἶχε, χρημάτων αὐτῷ μεγάλων ἐλπίδας ἐκ τοῦ ἔργου ἐσομένων ἐμβαλομένη, εἰς τὴν πρᾶξιν ἥνπερ ἐβούλετο, οὔτι ἐθελούσιον τὸν ἄνδρα ἐφεῖλκε. Κέρδους γὰρ οὐκ εὐπρεποῦς ἔνεκα, καὶ νόμους τιθέναι, καὶ αὖ πάλιν αὐτοὺς καθελεῖν, οὐδαμῆ ἀπηξίου. Ἐδίκαζέ τε οὐ κατὰ τοὺς νόμους, οὓς αὐτὸς ἔγραψεν· ἀλλ᾽ ἔνθα ἂν αὐτὸν μείζων τε ὀφθεῖσα, καὶ μεγαλοπρεπεστέρα ἡ τῶν χρημάτων ὑπόσχεσις ἄγοι. Καὶ κατὰ μικρὸν γὰρ κλέπτοντι ἀφαιρεῖσθαι τὰς τῶν ὑπηκόων οὐσίας, αἰσχύνην αὐτῷ φέρειν τινὰ οὐδαμῆ ᾤετο· ἡνίκα δὴ οὐχ ἀπαξάπαντα ἀφελέσθαι λόγῳ τινὶ εἶχεν ἢ ἔγκλημα ἐπενεγκὼν ἀπροσδόκητον, ἢ διαθήκης οὐ γεγενημένης προσχήματι.

ϛ΄. Ἔμεινέ τε, αὐτοῦ Ῥωμαίων ἄρχοντος, οὐ πίστις πρὸς θεὸν ἀσφαλής, ἡ δόξα, οὐ νόμος ὀχυρός, οὐ πρᾶξις βεβαία, οὐ συμβόλαιον οὐδέν. Στελλομένων δὲ πρὸς αὐτοῦ τῶν οἱ ἐπιτηδείων τινὲς ἐπί τινα πρᾶξιν, εἰ μὲν δὴ αὐτοῖς ἀπολωλεκέναι ξυνέβη, τῶν σφίσι παραπεπτωκότων πολλοὺς καὶ χρημάτων τι λήίσασθαι πλῆθος, οὗτοι δὴ εὐδόκιμοι τῷ αὐτοκράτορι ἐδόκουν τε εἶναι καὶ ὀνομά-

COURT OF JUSTINIAN 113

avarice, from which nothing could restrain him. Whenever his wife could not persuade him to do a thing, she used to suggest that great gain was likely to result from it, and this enabled her to lead him into any course of action against his will. He did not blush to make laws and afterwards repeal them, that he might make some infamous profit thereby. Nor did he give judgment according to the laws which he himself had made, but in favour of the side which promised him the biggest and most splendid bribe. He thought it no disgrace to steal away the property of his subjects, little by little, in cases where he had no grounds for taking it away all at one swoop, either by some unexpected charge or a forged will. While he was Emperor of the Romans neither faith in God nor religion was secure, no law continued in force, no action, no contract was binding. When he intrusted any business to his officials, if they put to death numbers of those who fell into their hands and carried off great wealth as plunder, they were looked upon

ζεσθαι, ἅτε δὴ ἅπαντα ἐς τὸ ἀκριβὲς τὰ
ἐπηγγελμένα ἐπιτελέσαντες· εἰ δὲ φειδοῖ τινι
ἐς ἀνθρώπους χρησάμενοι, παρ' αὐτὸν ἴκοιντο,
δύσνους τε αὐτοῖς τὸ λοιπὸν καὶ πολέμιος
ἦν. Ἀπογνούς τε ὥσπερ ἀρχαιότροπόν τινα
τὴν τῶν ἀνδρῶν φύσιν, ἐς τὴν ὑπουργίαν
οὐκέτι ἐκάλει. Ὥστε καὶ πολλοὶ ἐν σπουδῇ
ἐποιοῦντο ἐνδείκνυσθαι αὐτῷ, ὡς πονηροὶ
εἶεν, καίπερ σφίσι τῶν ἐπιτηδευμάτων οὐ
ταύτῃ ἐχόντων. Ὑποσχόμενος δέ τισι πολλάκις, καὶ ὅρκῳ ἢ γράμμασι τὴν ὑπόσχεσιν
ὀχυρωτέραν πεποιημένος, εὐθὺς ἐθελούσιος ἐς
λήθην ἀφῖκτο, δόξης τι φέρειν αὐτῷ τὸ
ἔργον τοῦτο οἰόμενος. Καὶ ταῦτα Ἰουστινιανὸς οὐ μόνον ἐς τοὺς ὑπηκόους ἐπράσσετο,
ἀλλὰ καὶ ἐς τῶν πολεμίων πολλούς, ὥσπερ
μοι εἴρηται ἔμπροσθεν.

ζ'. Ἦν τε ἄοκνος τε καὶ ἄϋπνος, ἐπιπλεῖστον εἰπεῖν, καὶ σιτίοις μὲν ἢ ποτῷ
κατακορὴς οὐδαμῇ γέγονεν, ἀλλὰ σχεδόν τι
ἄκρῳ δακτύλῳ ἀπογευσάμενος ἀπηλλάσσετο·
ὥσπερ γάρ τι αὐτῷ πάρεργον τῆς φύσεως
ἀγγαρευούσης τὰ τοιαῦτα ἐφαίνετο εἶναι·
ἐπεὶ καὶ ἀπόσιτος ἡμέρας τε καὶ νύκτας δύο

COURT OF JUSTINIAN 114

as faithful servants of the Emperor, and
were spoken of as men who had accurately
carried out his instructions; but, if they
came back after having shown any mercy,
he took a dislike to them and was their
enemy for life, and never again would
employ them, being disgusted with their
old-fashioned ways. For this reason many
men were anxious to prove to him that
they were villains, although they really
were not such. He would often make
men repeated promises, and confirm his
promise by an oath or by writing, and
then purposely forget all about it, and
think that such an action did him credit.
Justinian behaved in this manner not
only towards his own subjects, but also
towards many of his enemies, as I have
already told. As a rule he dispensed
with both rest and sleep, and never took
his fill of either food or drink, but merely
picked up a morsel to taste with the tips
of his fingers, and then left his dinner,
as if eating had been a bye-work imposed
upon him by nature. He would often go
without food for two days and nights,

τὰ πολλὰ ἔμενεν, ἄλλως τε ἡνίκα ὁ πρὸ τῆς πασχαλίας καλουμένης ἑορτῆς χρόνος ἐνταῦθα ἄγοι. Τότε γὰρ πολλάκις ἡμέραιν δυοῖν, ὥσπερ εἴρηται, γεγονὼς ἄσιτος ὕδατί τε βραχεῖ ἀποζῆν ἐπηξίου, καὶ βοτάναις ἀγρίαις τισὶν, ὥραν τε, ἂν οὕτω τύχοι, καταδραθὼν μίαν, εἶτα περιπάτους ἀεὶ ποιούμενος τὸν ἄλλον κατέτριβε χρόνον.

η΄. Καίτοι εἰ τοῦτον αὐτὸν καιρὸν ἐς πράξεις δαπανᾶν ἀγαθὰς ἤθελεν, ἐπὶ μέγα ἄν τι εὐδαιμονίας ἐκεχωρήκει τὰ πράγματα. Νῦν δὲ τῇ φύσεως ἰσχύϊ ἐπὶ τῷ Ῥωμαίων πονηρῷ χρώμενος, ξύμπασαν αὐτῶν τὴν πολιτείαν ἐς τὸ ἔδαφος καθελεῖν ἴσχυσεν. Ἐγρηγορέναι τε γὰρ διηνεκὲς καὶ ταλαιπωρεῖν καὶ πονεῖσθαι οὐκ ἄλλου του ἕνεκα ἔργου πεποίηται ἢ ὥστε κομπωδεστέρας ἀεὶ καθ' ἑκάστην τοῖς ὑπηκόοις ἐπιτεχνᾶσθαι τὰς συμφοράς. Ἦν γὰρ, ὅπερ εἴρηται, διαφερόντως ὀξὺς ἐπινοῆσαί τε καὶ ταχὺς ἀποτελέσαι ἀνόσια ἔργα, ὥστε αὐτῷ καὶ τὰ τῆς φύσεως ἀγαθὰ ἐπὶ λύμῃ τῶν ὑπηκόων ἀποκεκρίσθαι ξυνέβαινε.

COURT OF JUSTINIAN 115

especially when fasting was enjoined on the eve of the feast of Easter, when he would often fast for two days, taking no sustenance beyond a little water and a few wild herbs, and sleeping, as it might be, for one hour only, passing the rest of the time in walking to and fro. Had he spent all this time in useful works, the State would have flourished exceedingly; but, as it was, he used his natural powers to work the ruin of the Romans, and succeeded in thoroughly disorganizing the constitution. His constant wakefulness, his privations, and his labour were undergone for no other purpose than to make the sufferings of his subjects every day more grievous; for, as I have said before, he was especially quick in devising crimes, and swift to carry them out, so that even his good qualities seemed to have been so largely bestowed upon him merely for the affliction of his people.

ΚΕΦΑΛΑΙΟΝ ΙΔ'.

α'. Πραγμάτων γὰρ ἦν ἀωρία πολλὴ, καὶ τῶν εἰωθότων οὐδὲν ἔμεινεν, ὧνπέρ μοι ὀλίγων ὑπομνησθέντι, σιωπῇ δοτέον τὰ λοιπὰ, ὡς μή μοι ὁ λόγος ἀπέραντος εἴη. Πρῶτα μὲν γὰρ οὐδὲν ἐς βασιλικὸν ἀξίωμα ἐπιτηδείως ἔχον, οὔτε αὐτὸς εἶχεν, οὔτε ξυμφυλάσσειν ἠξίου· ἀλλὰ τήν τε γλῶτταν καὶ τὸ σχῆμα καὶ τὴν διάνοιαν ἐβαρβάριζεν. Ὅσα τε γράφεσθαι πρὸς αὐτοῦ βούλοιτο, οὐ τῷ τὴν Κοιαίστωρος ἔχοντι τιμὴν, ἧπερ εἰώθει, ἐπέστελλεν προέσθαι· ἀλλ' αὐτός τε τὰ πλεῖστα, καίπερ οὕτω τῆς γλώττης ἔχων, ἐκφέρειν ἠξίου καὶ τῶν παρατυχόντων πολὺς ὅμιλος, ὥστε τοὺς ἐνθένδε ἠδικημένους οὐκ ἔχειν ὅτῳ ἐπικαλοῖεν.

CHAPTER XIV

EVERYTHING was done at the wrong time, and nothing that was established was allowed to continue. To prevent my narrative being interminable, I will merely mention a few instances, and pass over the remainder in silence. In the first place, Justinian neither possessed in himself the appearance of Imperial dignity, nor demanded that it should be respected by others, but imitated the barbarians in language, appearance, and ideas. When he had to issue an Imperial decree, he did not intrust it to the Quaestor in the usual way, but for the most part delivered it himself by word of mouth, although he spoke his own language like a foreigner; or else he left it in the hands of one of those by whom he was surrounded, so that those who had been injured by such resolutions

ΠΡΟΚΟΠΙΟΥ ΑΝΕΚΔΟΤΑ

β'. Τοῖς δὲ Ἀσηκρῆτις καλουμένοις οὐκ ἀπεκέκριτο τὸ ἀξίωμα ἐς τὸ τὰ βασιλέως ἀπόρρητα γράφειν, ἐφ' ὧνπερ τὸ ἀνέκαθεν ἐτετάχατο ἀλλὰ τά τε ἄλλα ἔγραφεν αὐτὸς ὡς εἰπεῖν ἅπαντα· καὶ εἴ που διατάσσειν τοὺς διαιτῶντας ἐν πόλει δεήσειεν, ἠγνόουν ὅποι ποτὲ αὐτοῖς τὰ ἐς τὴν γνῶσιν ἰτέον εἴη. Οὐ γὰρ εἴα τινὰ ἔν γε τῇ Ῥωμαίων ἀρχῇ γνώμῃ αὐτονόμῳ τὰς ψήφους διδόναι· ἀλλὰ αὐθαδιαζόμενος ἀλογίστῳ τινὶ παρρησίᾳ, κρίσεις τε αὐτὸς τὰς ἐσομένας ἐρρύθμιζεν, ἀκοῆς λόγον πρός του τῶν διαφερομένων λαβὼν, καὶ ἀνύδικα εὐθὺς τὰ δεδικασμένα ἐποίει, οὐ νόμῳ τινὶ ἢ δικαίῳ ἠγμένος, ἀλλ' ἀπαρακαλύπτως αἰσχροκερδείᾳ· ἡσσώμενος. Δωροδοκῶν γὰρ ὁ βασιλεὺς οὐκ ᾐσχύνετο, πᾶσαν αὐτοῦ τὴν αἰδῶ τῆς ἀπληστίας ἀφελομένης.

γ'. Πολλάκις δὲ τὰ συγκλήτῳ βουλῇ καὶ τῷ αὐτοκράτορι δεδοκιμασμένα εἰς ἑτέραν τινὰ ἐτελεύτησε κρίσιν. Ἡ μὲν γὰρ βουλὴ ὥσπερ ἐν εἰκόνι ἐκάθητο, οὐδὲ τῆς

COURT OF JUSTINIAN   117

did not know to whom to apply. Those who were called A Secretis,[1] and had from very ancient times fulfilled the duty of writing the secret dispatches of the Emperor, were no longer allowed to retain their privileges ; for he himself wrote them nearly all, even the sentences of the municipal magistrates, no one throughout the Roman world being permitted to administer justice with a free hand. He took everything upon himself with un-reasoning arrogance, and so managed cases that were to be decided, that, after he had heard one of the litigants, he immediately pronounced his verdict and obliged them to submit to it, acting in accordance with no law or principle of justice, but being evidently overpowered by shameful greed. For the Emperor was not ashamed to take bribes, since his avarice had deprived him of all feel-ings of shame. It frequently happened that the decrees of the Senate and the edicts of the Emperor were opposed to each other ; for the Senate was as it were but an empty shadow, without the

[1] Private secretaries.

ψήφου οὐδὲ τοῦ καλοῦ κυρία οὖσα· σχήματος δὲ μόνου καὶ νόμου ξυνειλεγμένη παλαιοῦ ἕνεκα· ἐπεὶ οὐδὲ φωνὴν ἀφεῖναί τινα ὁτῳοῦν τῶν ἐνταῦθα ξυνειλεγμένων τὸ παράπαν ἐξῆν, ἀλλ' ὅ τε βασιλεὺς καὶ ἡ σύνοικος ἐκ τῶν ἐπιπλεῖστον διαλαγχάνειν μὲν ἀλλήλοιν τῶν διαφερομένων ἔσκηπτον· ἐνίκα δὲ τὰ ἐν σφίσιν αὐτοῖς ὑπὲρ τούτων ξυγκείμενα. Ἦν δέ τῳ δόξειεν οὐκ ἀσφαλὲς εἶναι παρανενο-μηκότι νενικηκέναι, ὅδε καὶ ἄλλο τι χρυσίον τῷ βασιλεῖ τούτῳ προέμενος, νόμον εὐθὺς διεπράττετο ἀπ' ἐναντίας ἁπάντων ἐλθόντα τῶν πρόσθε κειμένων. Ἦν δὲ καί τις ἕτερος τοῦτον δὴ τὸν νόμον τὸν ἀπολωλότα ἐπιζη-τοίη, αὖθις αὐτὸν μετακαλεῖν τε καὶ ἀντικα-θιστάναι αὐτοκράτωρ οὐδαμῆ ἀπηξίου.

δ'. Οὐδέν τε ἐν τῷ τῆς δυνάμεως βεβαίῳ ἑστήκει, ἀλλ' ἐπλανᾶτο πανταχόσε περι-φερομένη ἡ τῆς δίκης ῥοπή, ὅπη ἂν αὐτὴν βαρήσας ὁ πλείων χρυσὸς ἀνθέλκειν ἰσχύοι. Ἔκειτό τε ἐν τῷ δημοσίῳ τῆς ἀγορᾶς, καὶ ταῦτα ἐκ παλατίου, καὶ προὐτίθετο οὐ δικα-

COURT OF JUSTINIAN 118

power of giving its vote or of keeping up
its dignity; it was assembled merely for
form's sake and in order to keep up an
ancient custom, for none of its members
were allowed to utter a single word. But
the Emperor and his consort took upon
themselves the consideration of questions
that were to be discussed, and whatever
resolutions they came to between themselves prevailed. If he whose cause had
·been victorious had any doubt as to the
legality of his success, all he had to do
was to make a present of gold to the
Emperor, who immediately promulgated
a law contrary to all those formerly in
force. If, again, anyone else desired the
revival of the law that had been repealed,
the autocrat did not disdain to revoke
the existing order of things and to re-
establish it. There was nothing stable in
his authority, but the balance of justice
inclined to one side or the other, according to the weight of gold in either scale.
In the market-place there were buildings
under the management of palace officials,
where traffic was carried on, not only in

στικῆς μόνον, ἀλλὰ καὶ νομοθετικῆς πωλητήρια.

ε΄. Τοὺς δὲ Ῥαιφερενδαρίους καλουμένους οὐκέτι ἀπέχρη ἀνενεγκεῖν ἐς τὸν
βασιλέα τὰς τῶν ἱκετευόντων δεήσεις, ἐς δὲ
τὰς ἀρχὰς ἀναγγεῖλαι μόνον, ᾗπερ εἰώθει, ὅ
τι ἂν αὐτῷ ἀμφὶ τῷ ἱκέτῃ δοκῇ, ἀλλὰ
ξυμφορήσαντες ἐκ πάντων ἀνθρώπων τὸν
ἄδικον λόγον, φενακισμοῖς μὲν τὸν Ἰουστινιανὸν καὶ παραγωγαῖς τισιν ἐξηπάτων,
τοῖς ταῦτα ἐπιτηδεύουσιν ὑποκείμενον φύσει.
Ἔξω δὲ αὐτίκα γενόμενοι, καὶ τῶν σφίσιν
ὡμιληκότων τοὺς ἀντιδίκους καθείρξαντες,
χρήματα οὐδενὸς ἀμυνομένου (ἀνεξελέγκτως)
ἐπράσσοντο ὅσα ἂν αὐτοῖς διαρκῆ εἴη.

ϛ΄. Καὶ στρατιῶται οἱ τὴν ἐν παλατίῳ
φρουρὰν ἔχοντες, ἐν τῇ βασιλείῳ στοᾷ παρὰ
τοὺς διαιτῶντας γενόμενοι, βιαίᾳ χειρὶ τὰς
δίκας ἐσῆγον. Πάντες τε ὡς εἰπεῖν τὴν
αὐτῶν ἐκλιπόντες τάξιν, ὁδοὺς τότε κατ'
ἐξουσίαν ἐβάδιζον ἀπόρους τε καὶ ἀστιβή-
τους σφίσι τὰ πρότερα οὔσας· καὶ τὰ πράγ-

COURT OF JUSTINIAN 119

judicial, but also in legislative decisions. The officers called " Referendars " (or mediators) found it difficult to present the requests of petitioners to the Emperor, and still more difficult to bring before the council in the usual manner the answer proper to be made to each of them; but, gathering together from all quarters worthless and false testimony, they deceived Justinian, who was naturally a fit subject for deception, by fallacious reports and misleading statements. Then, immediately going out to the contending parties, without acquainting them with the conversation that had taken place, they extorted from them as much money as they required, without anyone venturing to oppose them.

Even the soldiers of the Praetorian guard, whose duty it was to attend the judges in the court of the palace, forced from them whatsoever judgments they pleased. All, so to speak, abandoned their own sphere of duty, and followed the paths that pleased them, however difficult or untrodden they had previously

ματα πλημμελῶς πάντα ἐφέρετο, οὐδὲ ὀνό-
ματός τινος ἰδίου μεταλαχόντα· ἐῴκει τε ἡ
πολιτεία βασιλίδι παιζόντων παιδίων. Ἀλλὰ
τἄλλα μοι παριτέον, ὥσπερ τοῦδε ἀρχόμενος
τοῦ λόγου ὑπεῖπον.

ζ. Δελέξεται δὲ ὅστις ἀνὴρ πρῶτος
δικάζοντα δωροδοκεῖν τὸν βασιλέα τοῦτον
ἀνέπεισε. Δέων ἦν τις, Κίλιξ μὲν γένος, ἐς
δὲ φιλοχρηματίαν δαιμονίως ἐσπουδακώς.
Οὗτος ὁ Δέων κράτιστος ἐγένετο κολάκων
ἁπάντων, καὶ οἷος ταῖς τῶν ἀμαθῶν διανοίαις
(τὸ) δόξαν ὑποβαλέσθαι. Πειθὼ γάρ οἵ τινα
ξυναιρομένην ἐς τοῦ τυράννου τὴν ἀβελτηρίαν
ἐπὶ φθόρῳ τῶν ἀνθρώπων εἶχεν. Οὗτος (ὁ)
ἀνὴρ πρῶτος Ἰουστινιανὸν ἀναπείθει ἀπεμ-
πολᾶν χρημάτων τὰς δίκας.

η΄. Ἐπειδή τε κλέπτειν ὅδε ὁ ἀνὴρ
τρόπῳ τῷ εἰρημένῳ ἔγνω, οὐκέτι ἀνίει, ἀλλ'
ὁδῷ προϊὸν τὸ κακὸν τοῦτο ἐπὶ μέγα ἐχώρει,
ὅστις τε δίκην λαχεῖν ἄδικον τῶν τινι
ἐπιεικῶν ἐν σπουδῇ εἶχεν, εὐθὺς παρὰ τὸν
Δέοντα ᾔει, καὶ μοῖραν τῶν ἀντιλεγομένων
τινὰ ὁμολογήσας τῷ τε τυράννῳ καὶ αὐτῷ

COURT OF JUSTINIAN 120

been. Everything was out of gear; offices were degraded, not even their names being preserved. In a word, the Empire resembled a queen over boys at play. But I must pass over the rest, as I hinted at the commencement of this work.

I will now say something about the man who first taught the Emperor to traffic in the administration of justice. His name was Leo; he was a native of Cilicia, and passionately eager to enrich himself. He was the most utterly shameless of flatterers, and most apt in ingratiating himself with the ignorant, and with the Emperor, whose folly he made use of in order to ruin his subjects. It was this Leo who first persuaded Justinian to barter justice for money. When this man had once discovered these means of plunder, he never stopped. The evil spread and reached such a height that, if anyone desired to come off victorious in an unjust cause against an honest man, he immediately repaired to Leo, and, promising to give half of his claim to be divided between the latter and the Em-

κείσεσθαι, αὐτίκα νενικηκὼς, οὐ δέον, ἀπηλλάσσετο ἐκ τοῦ παλατίου. Καὶ Λέων μὲν χρήματα ἐνθένδε περιβαλέσθαι μεγάλα κομιδῇ ἴσχυσε, χώρας τε πολλῆς κύριος γέγονε, Ῥωμαίοις δὲ τὴν πολιτείαν αἰτιώτατος γέγονεν ἐς γόνυ ἐλθεῖν.

θ. Ἦν τε οὐδὲν τοῖς ξυμβεβηκόσιν ὀχύρωμα, οὐ νόμος, οὐχ ὅρκος, οὐ γράμματα, οὐ ποινὴ ξυγκειμένη, οὐκ ἄλλο τῶν ἁπάντων οὐδὲν, ὅτι μὴ Λέοντι καὶ βασιλεῖ χρήματα προέσθαι. Οὐ μὴν οὐδὲ τοῦτο ἐν τῷ βεβαίῳ τῆς γνώμης τῆς τοῦ Λέοντος ἔμενεν, ἀλλὰ μισθαρνεῖν καὶ πρὸς τῶν ἐναντίων ἠξίου. Κλέπτων γὰρ ἀεὶ καὶ ἐφ' ἑκάτερα τῶν ἐπ' αὐτῷ προστεθαρρηκότων ὀλιγωρεῖν τε καὶ ἀπ' ἐναντίας ἰέναι οὐδαμῇ αἰσχύνην ὑπώπτευεν εἶναι. Οὐδὲν γὰρ αἰσχρὸν, εἰ μόνον τὸ κερδαίνειν προσῇ, ἐδόξαζέν οἱ αὐτῷ ἐπαμφοτερίζοντι ἔσεσθαι. Ὁ μὲν οὖν Ἰουστινιανὸς τοιοῦτός τις ἦν.

COURT OF JUSTINIAN   121

peror, left the palace, having already gained his cause, contrary to all principles of right and justice. In this manner Leo acquired a vast fortune, and a great quantity of land, and became the chief cause of the ruin of the State. There was no longer any security in contracts, in law, in oaths, in written documents, in any penalty agreed upon, or in any other security, unless money had been previously given to Leo and the Emperor. Nor was even this method certain, for Justinian would accept bribes from both parties; and, after having drained the pockets of both of those who had put confidence in him, he was not ashamed to cheat one or other of them (no matter which), for, in his eyes, there was nothing disgraceful in playing a double part, provided only that it turned out profitable for him.

Such a man was Justinian.

ΚΕΦΑΛΑΙΟΝ ΙΕʹ.

αʹ. Θεοδώρα δὲ ἐν τῷ βεβαίῳ τῆς ἀπανθρωπίας ἐνδελεχέστατα ἐπεπήγει τὴν γνώμην. Ἄλλῳ μὲν γὰρ ἀναπεισθεῖσα ἢ ἀναγκασθεῖσα εἰργάζετο οὐδὲν πώποτε· αὐτὴ δὲ τὰ δόξαντα ἐπετέλει αὐθαδιαζομένη δυνάμει τῇ πάσῃ, οὐδενὸς ἐξαιτεῖσθαι τὸν παραπεπτωκότα τολμῶντος. Οὐδὲ γὰρ χρόνου μῆκος, οὐ κολάσεως πλησμονὴ, οὐχ ἱκετείας μηχανὴ, οὐ θανάτου ἀπειλή, ὅτι δὴ ἐξ οὐρανοῦ πεσεῖται τῷ παντὶ γένει ἐπίδοξος οὖσα, καταθέσθαι αὐτήν τι τῆς ὀργῆς ἔπειθε. Καὶ συλλήβδην Θεοδώραν τῷ προσκεκρουκότι καταλλαγεῖσαν οὐδείς ποτε εἶδεν, ἢ ζῶντι, ἢ ἐξ ἀνθρώπων ἀφανισθέντι· ἀλλὰ τοῦ τετελευτηκότος ὁ παῖς διαδεξάμενος τὸ τῆς βασιλίδος ἔχθος, ὥσπερ ἄλλο τι τοῦ πατέρος, ἐς τριγονίαν παρέπεμπεν.

CHAPTER XV

As for Theodora, her disposition was governed by the most hardened and inveterate cruelty. She never did anything either under persuasion or compulsion, but employed all her self-willed efforts to carry out her resolutions, and no one ventured to intercede in favour of those who fell in her way. Neither length of time, nor fulness of punishment, nor carefully drawn-up prayers, nor the fear of death, nor the vengeance of Heaven, by awe of which the whole human race is impressed, could persuade her to abate her wrath. In a word, no one ever saw Theodora reconciled to one who had offended her, either during his lifetime or after his death; for the children of the deceased father inherited the hatred of the Empress, as if it were part of his patrimony; and, when he died, left it in turn

ΠΡΟΚΟΠΙΟΥ ΑΝΕΚΔΟΤΑ

Ὁ γὰρ θυμὸς αὐτῇ κινεῖσθαι μὲν εἰς ἀνθρώπων φθορὰν ἑτοιμότατος ἦν, ἐς δὲ τὸ λωφῆσαι ἀμήχανος.

β'. Τὸ μέντοι σῶμα ἐθεράπευε μειζόνως μὲν ἢ κατὰ τὴν χρείαν, ἐλασσόνως δὲ ἢ κατὰ τὴν αὐτῆς ἐπιθυμίαν. Ταχύτατα μὲν γὰρ ἐς τὸ βαλανεῖον εἰσῄει, ὀψιαίτατα δὲ ἀπαλλαγεῖσα καὶ καταλουσαμένη ἐς τὸ ἀκρατίζεσθαι ἐνθένδε ἐχώρει. Ἀκρατισαμένη δὲ ἡσυχίαν ἦγεν. Ἀριστῶσα μέντοι καὶ δεῖπνον αἱρουμένη ἐς πᾶσαν ἰδέαν ἐδωδίμων τε καὶ ποτῶν ἤρχετο· ὕπνοι τε αὐτῆς ἀεὶ μακρότατοι ἀντελαμβάνοντο, ἡμερινοὶ μὲν ἄχρι πρώτων νυκτῶν, νυκτερινοὶ δὲ ἄχρις ἡλίου ἀνίσχοντος. Εἰς πᾶσάν τε οὕτως ἀκρασίας ἐκπεπτωκυῖα τρίβον ἐς τόσον ἡμέρας καιρὸν ἅπασαν διοικεῖσθαι ἠξίου τὴν Ῥωμαίων ἀρχήν.

γ'. Καὶ ἢν τῳ ἐπιστείλειε πρᾶξίν τινα ὁ βασιλεὺς οὐκ αὐτῆς γνώμῃ, ἐς τοῦτο τύχης περιειστήκει τούτῳ δὴ τῷ ἀνθρώπῳ τὰ πράγματα, ὥστε οὐ πολλῷ ὕστερον τῆς τε τιμῆς παραλυθῆναι σὺν ὕβρει μεγάλῃ, καὶ ἀπολωλέναι θανάτῳ αἰσχίστῳ.

δ'. Τῷ μὲν Ἰουστινιανῷ ἅπαντα πράσσειν ῥάδιον ἦν· οὐχ ὅσον τῷ τῆς διανοίας

COURT OF JUSTINIAN   123

to his sons. Her mind was ever most readily stirred to the destruction of men, and was incapable of being checked. She bestowed upon her person greater care than necessity demanded, but less than her desire prompted her to. She entered the bath very early in the morning; and, having spent a long time over her ablutions, went to breakfast, and afterwards again retired to rest. At dinner and supper she partook of every kind of food and drink. She slept a great deal : during the day, till nightfall, and, during the night, till sunrise. And, although she thus abandoned herself to every intemperance, she considered that the little time she had left was sufficient for the conduct of 'the affairs of the Roman Empire. If the Emperor intrusted anyone with a commission without having previously consulted Theodora, the unfortunate man soon found himself deprived of his office, in the deepest disgrace, and perished by a most dishonourable death.

Justinian was speedy in the conduct of business of all kinds, not only owing

εὐκόλῳ, ἀλλ' ὅτι καὶ ἄϋπνος ἐπιπλεῖστον, ὥσπερ εἴρηται, καὶ εὐπρόσοδος πάντων μάλιστα. Πολλὴ γὰρ ἀνθρώποις ἐξουσία ἐγίνετο, καίτοι ἀδόξοις τε καὶ ἀφανέσι παντάπασιν οὖσιν· οὐχ ὅτι ἐντυχεῖν τῷ τυράννῳ τούτῳ, ἀλλὰ καὶ κοινολογεῖσθαι καὶ ἐξ ἀπορρήτων συγγίνεσθαι.

ε΄. Παρὰ δὲ τὴν βασιλίδα οὐδὲ τῶν ἀρχόντων τινὶ ὅτι μὴ χρόνῳ τε πολλῷ καὶ πόνῳ εἰσιτητὰ ἦν, ἀλλὰ προσήδρευον μὲν ἀεὶ ἅπαντες, ἀνδραποδώδη τινὰ προσεδρίαν ἐν δωματίῳ στενῷ τε καὶ πνιγηρῷ τὸν ἅπαντα χρόνον. Κίνδυνος γὰρ ἀπολελεῖφθαι τῶν ἀρχόντων τινὶ ἀνύποιστος ἦν. Ἵσταντο δὲ διηνεκὲς ἐπ' ἄκρων δακτύλων, καθυπέρτερον ἕκαστος τῶν πέλας διατεινόμενος τὸ πρόσωπον ἔχειν, ὅπως αὐτὸν ἔνδοθεν ἐξιόντες εὐνοῦχοι ὁρῷεν. Ἐκαλοῦντο δὲ αὐτῶν τινες μόλις τε καὶ ἡμέραις πολλαῖς ὕστερον· ἐσιόντες δὲ παρ' αὐτὴν ξὺν δέει πολλῷ, ὅτι τάχιστα ἀπηλλάσσοντς, προσκυνήσαντες μόνον, καὶ ταρσοῦ ἑκατέρου ποδὸς ἄκρῳ χείλει ἀψάμενοι. Φθέγ-

COURT OF JUSTINIAN   124

to his continual sleeplessness (as has been
mentioned before), but also by reason of
his easiness of temper, and, above all,
his affability. For he allowed people to
approach him, although they were altogether obscure and unknown; and the
interview was not limited to mere admission to the presence of the Emperor,
but he permitted them to converse and
associate with him on confidential terms.
With the Empress the case was different;
even the highest officials were not admitted until they had waited a long time,
and after a great deal of trouble. They
all waited patiently every day, like so
many slaves, in a body, in a narrow and
stifling room; for the risk they ran if
they absented themselves was most serious.
There they remained standing all the time
on tip-toe, each trying to keep his face
above his fellow's, that the eunuchs, as
they came out, might see them. Some
were invited to her presence, but rarely,
and after several days of attendance; when
at last they were admitted, they merely
did obeisance to her, kissed both her

γεσθαι γὰρ ἢ αἰτεῖσθαί τι, μὴ ἐκείνης ἐγκελευομένης, οὐδεμία παρρησία ἐγίνετο.

ϛ'. Ἐς δουλοπρέπειαν γὰρ ἡ πολιτεία ἦλθε, δουλοδιδάσκαλον αὐτὴν ἔχουσα. Οὕτω τε Ῥωμαίοις τὰ πράγματα διεφθείρετο, τοῦ μὲν τυράννου τῷ ἄγαν εὐήθει δοκοῦντι εἶναι, Θεοδώρας δὲ τῷ χαλεπῷ καὶ λίαν δυσκόλῳ. Ἐν μὲν γὰρ τῷ εὐήθει τὸ ἀβέβαιον ἦν· ἐν δὲ τῷ δυσκόλῳ τὸ ἄπρακτον. Ἐν τοῖς μὲν οὖν τῆς τε γνώμης αὐτοῖς καὶ τῆς διαίτης τὸ διαλλάσσον ἐφαίνετο· κοινὰ δὲ ἦν αὐτοῖς ἥ τε φιλοχρηματία, καὶ ἡ τῶν φόνων ἐπιθυμία, καὶ τὸ μηδενὶ ἀληθίζεσθαι. Ἄμφω γὰρ ἐπιτηδείως ἐς τὰ μάλιστα ψεύδεσθαι εἶχον.

ζ'. Καὶ ἦν μέν τις τῶν Θεοδώρᾳ προσκεκρουκότων ἁμαρτάνειν λέγοιτό τι βραχύ τε καὶ λόγου οὐδαμῇ ἄξιον, αἰτίας εὐθὺς ἀναπλάσσουσα τῷ ἀνθρώπῳ οὐδὲν προσηκούσας, ἐς μέγα τι κακοῦ τὸ πρᾶγμα ἦρεν.

COURT OF JUSTINIAN 125

feet, and then hastily retired in great awe; for they were not allowed to address her or to prefer any request except at her bidding; so slavishly had the spirit of Roman society degenerated under the instruction of Theodora, and to such a state of decay had the affairs of the Empire sunk, partly in consequence of the too great apparent easiness of the Emperor, partly owing to the harsh and peevish nature of Theodora; for the easiness of the one was uncertain, while the peevishness of the other hindered the transaction of public business.

There was this difference in their disposition and manner of life; but, in their love of money, thirst of blood, and aversion to truth, they were in perfect accord. They were, both of them, exceedingly clever inventors of falsehoods; if any one of those who had incurred the displeasure of Theodora was accused of any offence, however trivial and unimportant, she immediately trumped up against him charges with which he was in no way concerned, and greatly

Ἐγκλημάτων τε ἠκούετο πλῆθος, καὶ καταλύσεως πέρι τῶν κατηκόων ληΐζεσθαι δικαστήριον ἦν· καὶ δικασταὶ ξυνελέγοντο πρὸς αὐτῆς ἀγειρόμενοι, οἳ δὴ ἔμελλον διαμαχέσασθαι πρὸς ἀλλήλους, ὅστις ἂν αὐτῶν μᾶλλον τῶν ἄλλων ἀρέσκειν τῇ ἐς τὴν γνῶσιν ἀπανθρωπίᾳ τῇ βασιλίδι τὸ βούλημα ἱκανὸς γένοιτο. Οὕτω τε τοῦ παραπεπτωκότος τὴν μὲν οὐσίαν αὐτίκα ἐς τὸ δημόσιον ἀνάγραπτον ἐποίει· πικρότατα δὲ αὐτὸν αἰκισαμένη, καίπερ ἴσως εὐπατρίδην τὸ ἀνέκαθεν ὄντα, ἢ φυγῇ ζημιοῦν ἢ θανάτῳ οὐδαμῆ ἀπηξίου.

η'. Ἦν δέ γε τῶν αὐτῇ ἐσπουδασμένων τινὶ ἐπὶ φόνοις ἀδίκοις, ἢ ἑτέρῳ τῳ τῶν μεγίστων ἀδικημάτων ἁλῶναι ξυμβαίνῃ, διασύρουσα καὶ χλενάζουσα τὴν τῶν κατηγόρων ὁρμήν σιωπᾶν τὰ προσπεσόντα οὔτι ἐθελουσίους ἠνάγκαζεν. Ἀλλὰ καὶ τῶν πραγμάτων τὰ σπουδαιότατα εἰς γελωτοποιίαν μεταβάλλειν, ὅταν αὐτῇ δοκῇ, ὥσπερ ἐν σκηνῇ καὶ θεάτρῳ ἔργον πεποίηται.

θ'. Καὶ ποτέ τις τῶν πατρικίων γέρων τε καὶ χρόνον πολὺν ἐν ἀρχῇ γεγονὼς (οὗπερ

COURT OF JUSTINIAN 126

aggravated the matter. A number of accusations were heard, and a court was immediately appointed to put down and plunder the subjects; judges were called together by her, who would compete amongst themselves to see which of them might best be able to accommodate his decision to the cruelty of Theodora. The property of the accused was immediately confiscated, after he had first been cruelly flogged by her orders (although he might be descended from an illustrious family), nor had she any scruples about banishing, or even putting him to death. On the other hand, if any of her favourites were found guilty of murder or any other great crime, she pulled to pieces and scoffed at the efforts of the accusers, and forced them, against their will, to abandon proceedings. Whenever it pleased her, she turned affairs of the greatest importance into ridicule, as if they were taking place upon the stage of the theatre. A certain patrician, of advanced age, and who had for a long time held office (whose name is known to me,

ΠΡΟΚΟΠΙΟΥ ΑΝΕΚΔΟΤΑ

ἐγὼ τὸ ὄνομα ἐξεπιστάμενος ὡς ἥκιστα ἐπι-
μνήσομαι, ὡς μὴ ἀπέραντον τὴν ἐς αὐτὸν
ὕβριν ποιήσωμαι), τῶν αὐτῇ ὑπηρετούντων
τινὰ, ὀφείλοντά οἱ χρήματα μεγάλα εἰσπρά-
ξασθαι οὐχ οἷός τε ὢν, ἐσῆλθε παρ᾽ αὐτὴν,
τόν τε συμβαλόντα αἰτιασόμενος καὶ δεηθησό-
μενος αὐτῷ βοηθῆσαι τὰ δίκαια. Ὅπερ ἡ
Θεοδώρα προμαθοῦσα, τοῖς εὐνούχοις ἐπέστελλεν, ἐπειδὰν ὁ πατρίκιος πρὸς αὐτὴν
ἵκοιτο, κυκλώσασθαι μὲν αὐτὸν ἅπαντας,
ἐπακούειν δὲ αὐτῇ φθεγγομένῃ, ὑπειποῦσα ὅ
τι αὐτοὺς ἀντιφθέγγεσθαι δεῖ. Ἐπεὶ δὲ ὁ
πατρίκιος ἐς τὴν γυναικωνῖτιν εἰσῆλθε, προσ-
εκύνησε μὲν ὥσπερ αὐτὴν προσκυνεῖν εἴθιστο,
δεδακρυμένῳ δὲ εοικώς·

ι'. "Ὦ δέσποινα," ἔφη, "χαλεπὸν πα-
"τρικίῳ ἀνδρὶ χρημάτων δεῖσθαι. Ἃ γὰρ τοῖς
"ἄλλοις συγγνώμην τε καὶ ἔλεον φέρει, ταῦτα
"ἐς ὕβριν τῷδε ξυμβαίνει τῷ ἀξιώματι ἀπο-
"κεκρίσθαι. Ἄλλῳ μὲν γὰρ ὁτῳοῦν ἀπο-
"ρουμένῳ τὰ ἔσχατα πάρεστιν αὐτὸ τοῦτο
"εἰπόντι τοῖς χρήσταις ὄχλου τοῦ ἐνθένδε
"εὐθὺς ἀπηλλάχθαι· πατρίκιος δὲ ἀνὴρ, οὐκ

COURT OF JUSTINIAN 127

although I will not disclose it, in order to avoid bringing infinite disgrace upon him), being unable to recover a large sum of money which was owing to him from one of Theodora's attendants, applied to her, intending to press his claim against the debtor, and to beg her to assist him in obtaining his rights. Having heard of this beforehand, Theodora ordered her eunuchs to surround the patrician in a body on his arrival, and to listen to what was said by her, so that they might reply in a set form of words previously suggested by her. When the patrician entered her chamber, he prostrated himself at her feet in the usual manner, and, with tears in his eyes, thus addressed her:

"O sovereign lady! it is hard for a patrician to be in want of money; for that which in the case of others excites pity and compassion, becomes, in the case of a person of rank, a calamity and a disgrace. When any ordinary individual is in great straits, and informs his creditors, this immediately affords him relief from his trouble; but a patrician, when

ΠΡΟΚΟΠΙΟΥ ΑΝΕΚΔΟΤΑ

"ἔχων ὅθεν ἂν ἐκτῖσαι τοῖς χρήσταις τὰ
"ὀφλήματα ἱκανὸς εἴη, μάλιστα μὲν τοῦτο
"ἂν εἰπεῖν αἰσχυνθείη· εἰπὼν δὲ οὐκ ἂν
"ποτε πείσῃ, ὡς οὐχ οἷόν τε ὂν τῷδε πενίαν
"τῷ τάγματι ξυνοικίζεσθαι. Ἢν δέ γε καὶ
"πείσῃ, τὰ πάντων αὐτῷ αἴσχιστά τε καὶ
"ἀνιαρότατα πεπονθέναι ξυμβήσεται. Οὐ-
"κοῦν, ὦ δέσποινα, εἰσί μοι χρῆσται, οἱ μὲν
"δανείσαντες τὰ σφέτερα αὐτῶν, οἱ δὲ παρ'
"ἐμοῦ δεδανεισμένοι. Καὶ τοὺς μὲν δανεί-
"σαντας ἐνδελεχέστατα ἐγκειμένους οὐχ οἷός
"τέ εἰμι αἰδοῖ τοῦ ἀξιώματος ἀποκρούσασθαι·
"οἱ δέ γε ὀφείλοντες, οὐ γὰρ πατρίκιοι
"τυγχάνουσιν ὄντες, εἰς σκήψεις τινὰς ἀπαν-
"θρώπους χωροῦσιν. Ἀντιβολῶ τοίνυν καὶ
"ἱκετεύω καὶ δέομαι βοηθῆσαί τέ μοι τὰ
"δίκαια, καὶ τῶν παρόντων ἀπαλλάξαι
"κακῶν." Ὁ μὲν ταῦτα εἶπεν. Ἡ δὲ γυνὴ
ἀπεκρίνατο ἐμμελῶς· "Πατρίκιε, ὁ δεῖνα·"
καὶ ὁ τῶν εὐνούχων χορὸς ὑπολαβὼν ἀντεφθέγξατο, "μεγάλην κήλην ἔχεις." Αὖθις
δὲ τοῦ ἀνθρώπου ἱκετεύσαντός τε καὶ ῥῆσίν
τινα ἐμφερῆ τοῖς ἔμπροσθεν εἰρημένοις
εἰπόντος, κατὰ ταὐτὰ πάλιν ἥ τε γυνὴ
ἀπεκρίνατο, καὶ ὁ χορὸς ἀντεφθέγξατο, ἕως

COURT OF JUSTINIAN 128

unable to pay his creditors, would, in the first place, be ashamed to own it; and, if he did so, he would never make them believe it, since the world is firmly convinced that poverty can never be associated with our class; even if he *should* persuade them to believe it, it would be the greatest blow to his dignity and reputation that could happen. Well, my lady, I owe money to some, while others owe money to me. Out of respect for my rank, I cannot cheat my creditors, who are pressing me sorely, whereas my debtors, not being patricians, have recourse to cruel subterfuges. Wherefore, I beg and entreat and implore your majesty to assist me to gain my rights, and to deliver me from my present misfortunes!"

Such were his words. Theodora then commenced to sing, " O patrician," and the eunuchs took up her words and joined in chorus, "you have a large tumour." When he again entreated her, and added a few words to the same effect as before, her only answer was the same refrain, which was taken up by the chorus of

ΠΡΟΚΟΠΙΟΥ ΑΝΕΚΔΟΤΑ

ὢν ἀπειπὼν ὁ ταλαίπωρος προσεκύνησέ τε
ᾗπερ εἰώθει, καὶ ἀπιὼν ᾤχετο οἴκαδε.

ια΄. Ἐν προαστείοις δὲ τοῖς ἐπιθαλατ-
τίοις τὸ πλεῖστον τοῦ ἔτους καὶ οὐχ ἥκιστα
ἐν τῷ καλουμένῳ Ἡραίῳ διατριβὴν εἶχε, καὶ
αὐτοῦ τῶν ἑπομένων ὁ πολὺς ὅμιλος κακοπαθείᾳ πολλῇ εἴχετο. Τῶν τε γὰρ ἀναγκαίων
ἐσπάνιζον, καὶ θαλαττίοις ὡμίλουν κινδύνοις,
ἄλλως τε καὶ χειμῶνος, ἂν οὕτω τύχοι,
ἐπιπεσόντος, ἢ τοῦ κήτους ἐνταῦθά ποι
ἐπισκήψαντος. Ἀλλ᾽ αὐτοὶ τὰ πάντων
ἀνθρώπων κακὰ οὐδὲν πρᾶγμα ᾤοντο εἶναι,
ὅσον ἦν γε μόνον αὐτοῖς τρυφᾶν ἐξείη.

COURT OF JUSTINIAN 129

eunuchs. At length the unhappy man, tired of the whole affair, did reverence to the Empress in the usual manner, and returned home.

During the greater part of the year, Theodora resided in the suburbs on the coast, chiefly in the Heraeum, where her numerous retinue and attendants suffered great inconvenience, for they were short of the necessaries of life, and were exposed to the perils of the sea, of sudden storms, or the attacks of sea-monsters. However, they regarded the greatest misfortunes as of no importance, if only they had the means of enjoying the pleasures of the court.

ΚΕΦΑΛΑΙΟΝ ΙϚ'.

α'. Ὁποῖος δὲ ὁ Θεοδώρας τρόπος πρὸς τοὺς προσκεκρουκότας ἐφαίνετο, αὐτίκα δηλώσω, ὀλίγων δηλονότι ἐπιμνησθεὶς, ὡς μὴ ἀτελεύτητα πονεῖν δόξαιμι. Ἡνίκα Ἀμαλασοῦνθα τῆς ἐν Γότθοις ἀπαλλαξείουσα διατριβῆς μεταμπίσχεσθαι τὸν βίον ἔγνω, καὶ τὴν ἐπὶ τὸ Βυζάντιον διενοεῖτο πορεύεσθαι, ὥσπερ μοι ἐν τοῖς ἔμπροσθεν λόγοις ἐρρήθη, λογισαμένη ἡ Θεοδώρα, ὡς εὐπατρίδης τε ἡ γυνὴ καὶ βασιλὶς εἴη, καὶ ἰδεῖν μὲν εὐπρεπὴς ἄγαν, ἐπινοεῖν δὲ ὅ τι ἂν βούλοιτο γοργὸς μάλιστα, ὕποπτον δὲ αὐτῆς ποιησαμένη τό τε μεγαλοπρεπὲς καὶ διαφερόντως ἀρρενωπόν, ἅμα δὲ καὶ τὸ τοῦ ἀνδρὸς ἐλαφρὸν δείσασα, οὐκ ἐπὶ μικροῖς τὴν ζηλοτυπίαν ἐξήνεγκεν, ἀλλ' ἐνεδρεύειν τὴν γυναῖκα, μέχρις ἐς θάνατον, ἐν βουλῇ ἔσχεν.

CHAPTER XVI

I WILL now relate how Theodora treated those who had offended her, merely giving a few details, that I may not seem to have undertaken a task without end.

When Amalasunta, as I have narrated in the earlier books, desiring to abandon her connection with the affairs of the Goths, resolved to change her manner of life, and to retire to Byzantium, Theodora, considering that she was of illustrious descent and a princess, that she was of singular beauty, and exceedingly active in forming plans to carry out her wishes, was seized with suspicion of her distinguished qualities and eminent courage, and at the same time with apprehensions on account of her husband's fickleness. This made her exceedingly jealous; and she determined to compass the death of her rival by intrigue.

ΠΡΟΚΟΠΙΟΥ ΑΝΕΚΔΟΤΑ

β΄. Αὐτίκα τοίνυν ἀναπείθει τὸν ἄνδρα, Πέτρον μόνον αὐτὸν ἅτε πρεσβεύσοντα, ἐς Ἰταλίαν πέμψαι. Ὧι δὴ στελλομένῳ βασιλεὺς μὲν ἐπέστελλεν, ἅπερ μοι ἐν τοῖς ἐγκαίροις δεδιήγηται λόγοις, ἵνα δή μοι τῶν πεπραγμένων ἐκπύστους ποιεῖσθαι τὰς ἀληθείας δέει τῆς βασιλίδος ἀδύνατα ἦν. Αὐτὴ δὲ τοῦτο ἐπήγγελλε μόνον, ὅτι τάχιστα τὴν γυναῖκα ἐξ ἀνθρώπων ἀφανιεῖν, ἐπ᾽ ἐλπίδος ὀχεῖσθαι μεγάλων ἀγαθῶν, ἢν τὰ ἐπηγγελμένα ποιοίη, καταστησαμένη τὸν ἄνθρωπον. Καὶ ὃς ἐν Ἰταλίᾳ γενόμενος (οὐ γὰρ εἶδεν ἀνθρώπου φύσις ὀκνηρῶς ἐς ἄδικον φόνον ἰέναι, ἀρχῆς τινος ἴσως ἢ χρημάτων ἐν ἐλπίσι κειμένων μεγάλων), οὐκ οἶδα ἥντινα Θευδάτῳ παραίνεσιν ποιησάμενος, διαχρήσασθαι τὴν Ἀμαλασοῦνθαν ἀνέπεισε. Καὶ ἀπ᾽ αὐτοῦ ἔς τε τὸ τοῦ μαγίστρου ἀξίωμα ἦλθε, καὶ ἐπὶ πλεῖστον δυνάμεως, καὶ μάλιστα πάντων ἐχθρῶν. Τὰ μὲν οὖν κατὰ τὴν Ἀμαλασοῦνθαν ἐς τοῦτο ἐτελεύτα.

COURT OF JUSTINIAN   131

She immediately persuaded the Emperor to send a man named Peter, by himself, to Italy, as ambassador to her. On his setting out, the Emperor gave him the instructions which I have mentioned in the proper place, where it was impossible for me to inform my readers of the truth, for fear of the Empress. The only order she gave the ambassador was to compass the death of Amalasunta with all possible despatch, having bribed him with the promise of great rewards if he successfully carried out his instructions. This man, expecting either preferment or large sums of money (for under such circumstances men are not slow to commit an unjust murder), when he reached Italy, by some arguments or other persuaded Theodatus to make away with Amalasunta. After this, Peter was advanced to the dignity of " Master of Offices," and attained to the highest influence, in spite of the detestation with which he was universally regarded. Such was the end of the unhappy Amalasunta.

γ΄. Ἦν δέ τις Ἰουστινιανῷ ἐπιστολογράφος, Πρίσκος ὀνόματι, ἄγαν πονηρὸς μὲν καὶ Παφλαγών, καὶ πρέπων τοῦ προστάτου τὸν τρόπον ἀρέσκειν· λίαν δὲ πρὸς αὐτὸν εὐνοϊκῶς ἔχων, καὶ πρὸς αὐτοῦ τυγχάνειν τῶν ὁμοίων οἰόμενος· διὸ δὴ καὶ χρημάτων μεγάλων ὧν κύριος ὑπῆρχε οὐκ ἐν δίκῃ τάχιστα γέγονε. Τοῦτον δὴ ἅτε ὀφρυάζοντά τε καὶ οἱ ἀντιτείνειν πειρώμενον ἡ Θεοδώρα ἐς τὸν ἄνδρα διέβαλε. Καὶ τὰ μὲν πρῶτα οὐδὲν ἤνυσεν· οὐ πολλῷ δὲ ὕστερον αὐτὴ μὲν τὸν ἄνθρωπον εἰς ναῦν ἐμβιβάσασα, ὅπῃ ἐβούλετο ἔπεμψε, καὶ ἀποθρίξασα ἱερέα οὔτι ἑκούσιον ἠνάγκασεν εἶναι. Αὐτὸς δὲ δόκησιν παρεχόμενος, ὅτι δὴ τῶν ποιουμένων οὐδὲν εἰδείη, Πρίσκον μὲν οὐ διηρευνᾶτο ὅπῃ γῆς εἴη, οὐδὲ ἐν μνήμῃ τὸ λοιπὸν εἶχεν, ἀλλὰ σιωπῇ ὥσπερ ληθάργῳ ἁλοὺς καθῆστο, τὰ μέντοι χρήματα ὀλίγων οἱ ἀπολελειμμένων ἐληίσατο πάντα.

δ΄. Ὑποψίας δὲ ἐμπεσούσης αὐτῇ εἰς

COURT OF JUSTINIAN   132

Justinian had a secretary named Priscus, a Paphlagonian by birth, a man distinguished in every kind of villainy, a likely person to please the humour of his master, to whom he was exceedingly devoted, and from whom he expected to receive similar consideration; and by these means, in a short time, he unjustly amassed great wealth. Theodora, unable to endure his insolence and opposition, accused him to the Emperor. At first she was unsuccessful, but, shortly afterwards, she put him on board a ship, sent him away to a place she had previously determined upon, and having ordered him to be shaved, forced him to become a priest. In the meantime, Justinian, pretending that he knew nothing of what was going on, neither inquired to what part of the world Priscus had been banished, nor ever thought of him again afterwards, but remained silent, as if he had fallen into a state of lethargy. However, he seized the small fortune that he had left behind him.

Theodora had become suspicious of

τῶν οἰκετῶν ἕνα, Ἀρεοβίνδον ὄνομα, βάρβα-
ρον μὲν γένος, εὐπρεπῆ δὲ καὶ νεανίαν, ὅνπερ
ταμίαν αὐτὴ καταστησαμένη ἐτύγχανεν, ἀπο-
λύσασθαι βουλομένη τὸ ἔγκλημα, καίπερ, ὥς
φασι, τοῦ ἀνθρώπου δαιμονίως ἐρῶσα, ἐν μὲν
τῷ παρόντι πικρότατα αὐτὸν ἀπ᾽ οὐδεμιᾶς
αἰτίας αἰκίζεσθαι ἔγνω· τὸ δὲ λοιπὸν οὐδέν
τι ἀμφ᾽ αὐτῷ ἔγνωμεν· οὐδέ τις αὐτὸν ἄχρι
νῦν εἶδεν. Ἦν γάρ τι τῶν πρασσομένων
ἀποκρύπτεσθαι αὐτῇ βουλομένη εἴη, τοῦτο δὴ
ἄρρητόν τε καὶ ἀμνημόνευτον ἅπασιν ἔμεινε,
καὶ οὔτε τῷ ἐπισταμένῳ ἀγγεῖλαι τῶν τινι
ἀναγκαίων ἐξῆν, οὔτε τῷ μανθάνειν βουλομένῳ
πυνθάνεσθαι, κἂν πάνυ τις περίεργος ἦν.

ε΄. Τοιοῦτο γὰρ δέος, ἐξ οὗ γεγόνασιν
ἄνθρωποι, ἐκ τυράννων οὐδενὸς γέγονεν· ἐπεὶ
οὐδὲ λαθεῖν τι τὸν προσκεκρουκότα οἷόν τε
ἦν. Πλῆθος γὰρ κατασκόπων αὐτῇ τὰ λεγόμενα καὶ πρασσόμενα ἔν τε τῇ ἀγορᾷ καὶ
ταῖς οἰκίαις ἐσήγγελλον. Ἡνίκα τοίνυν τοῦ
παραπεπτωκότος τὴν κόλασιν ἐκφέρεσθαι οὐ-

COURT OF JUSTINIAN 133

one of her servants named Areobindus, a barbarian by birth, but a youth of great comeliness, whom she had appointed her steward. Wishing to purge the imagined offence, (although, as was said) she was violently enamoured of him, she caused him to be cruelly beaten with rods, for no apparent reason. What became of him afterwards we do not know; nor has anyone seen him up to the present day. For when Theodora desired to keep any of her actions secret, she took care to prevent their being talked about or remembered. None of those who were privy to them were permitted to disclose them even to their nearest relations, or to any who desired to obtain information on the subject, however curious they might be. No tyrant had ever yet inspired such fear, since it was impossible for any word or deed of her opponents to pass unnoticed. For she had a number of spies in her employ who informed her of everything that was said and done in public places and private houses. When she desired to punish anyone who had

ΠΡΟΚΟΠΙΟΥ ΑΝΕΚΔΟΤΑ

δαμῆ ἤθελεν, ἐποίει τάδε. Τὸν ἄνθρωπον μετακαλεσαμένη, ἥν τις τῶν λογίμων ἐτύγχανεν ὤν, μόνη τε αὐτὴ τῶν ὑπουργούντων τινὶ παραδοῦσα μόνῳ, ἐπήγγελλεν εἰς τὰς ἐσχατιὰς αὐτὸν μετακομίσαι τῆς Ῥωμαίων ἀρχῆς. Καὶ ὃς ἀωρὶ τῶν νυκτῶν κατακεκαλυμμένον αὐτὸν καὶ δεθέντα εἰς ναῦν ἐμβιβάσας, καὶ σὺν αὐτῷ γεγονὼς, οὗ οἱ πρὸς τῆς γυναικὸς ἐπετέτακτο, ἐνταῦθα παρεδίδου λαθραιότερον τῷ ἐς ταύτην τὴν ὑπουργίαν ἱκανῶς ἔχοντι, φυλάσσειν τε ὡς ἀσφαλέστατα ἐπιστείλας τὸν ἄνθρωπον, καὶ ἐπειπὼν μηδενὶ φράζειν, ἕως ἂν ἢ τὸν ταλαίπωρον ἡ βασιλὶς οἰκτίζηται, ἢ χρόνον πολὺν τῇ ἐνταῦθα κακοπαθείᾳ δυσθανατήσας τε καὶ καταμαρανθεὶς τελευτήσειεν, ἀπηλλάσσετο.

ϛʹ. Καὶ Βασιανὸν δέ τινα Πράσινον, οὐκ ἀφανῆ νέον ὄντα, αὐτῇ διαλοιδορησάμενον δι᾿ ὀργῆς ἔσχε. Διὸ δὴ ὁ Βασιανὸς (οὐ γὰρ ἀνήκοος ταύτης δὴ τῆς ὀργῆς ἐγεγόνει), ἐς

offended her, she adopted the following plan. If he were a patrician, she sent for him privately, and handed him over to one of her confidential attendants, with instructions to carry him to the furthest boundaries of the empire. In the dead of night, her agent, having bound the unfortunate man and muffled his face, put him on board a ship, and, having accompanied him to the place whither he had been instructed to convey him, departed, having first delivered him secretly to another who was experienced in this kind of service, with orders that he was to be kept under the strictest watch, and that no one should be informed of it, until either the Empress took pity upon the unfortunate man, or, worn out by his sufferings, he at length succumbed and died a miserable death.

A youth of distinguished family, belonging to the Green faction, named Basianus, had incurred the Empress's displeasure by speaking of her in sarcastic terms. Hearing that she was incensed against him, he fled for refuge

ΠΡΟΚΟΠΙΟΥ ΑΝΕΚΔΟΤΑ

τοῦ Ἀρχαγγέλου τὸν νεὼν φεύγει. Ἡ δέ οἱ ἐπέστησεν αὐτίκα τὴν τῷ δήμῳ ἐφεστῶσαν ἀρχήν, οὐδὲν μέντοι λοιδορίας ἐπικαλεῖν ἐπαγγείλασα, ὅτι δὲ παιδεραστοίη ἐπενεγκοῦσα. Καὶ ἡ μὲν ἀρχὴ ἐκ τοῦ ἱεροῦ τὸν ἄνθρωπον ἀναστήσασα, ᾐκίζετο ἀνυποίστῳ τῇ κολάσει· ὁ δὲ δῆμος ἅπας, ἐπεὶ ἐν τοιαύταις ξυμφοραῖς εἶδε σῶμα ἐλευθέριόν τε καὶ ἀνειμένῃ ἄνωθεν διαίτῃ ἐντραφέν, ἀπήλγησέ τε τὸ πάθος εὐθὺς, καὶ σὺν οἰμωγῇ ἀνέκραγον οὐράνιον ὅσον ἐξαιτούμενοι τὸν νεανίαν. Ἡ δὲ αὐτὸν ἔτι μᾶλλον κολάσασα, καὶ τὸ αἰδοῖον ἀποτεμομένη διέφθειρεν ἀνεξελέγκτως, καὶ τὴν οὐσίαν ἐς τὸ δημόσιον ἀνεγράψατο. Οὕτως, ἡνίκα ὀργῴη τὸ γύναιον τοῦτο, οὔτε ἱερὸν ὀχυρὸν ἐγεγόνει, οὔτε νόμου του ἀπαγόρευσις, οὔτε πόλεως ἀντιβόλησις ἐξελέσθαι τὸν παραπεπτωκότα ἱκανὴ ἐφαίνετο οὖσα, οὔτε ἄλλο αὐτῇ ἀπήντα τῶν ἁπάντων οὐδέν.

COURT OF JUSTINIAN 135

to the church of St. Michael the Arch-
angel. Theodora immediately sent the
Praetor of the people to seize him, bidding him charge him, however, not with
insolence towards herself, but with the
crime of sodomy. The magistrate, having
dragged him from the church, subjected
him to such intolerable torments, that
the whole assembled people, deeply
moved at seeing a person of such noble
mien, and one who had been so deli-
cately brought up, exposed to such
shameful treatment, immediately com-
miserated his sufferings, and cried out
with loud lamentations that reached the
heavens, imploring pardon for the young
man. But Theodora persisted in her
work of punishment, and caused his
death by ordering him to be castrated,
although he had been neither tried nor
condemned. His property was confiscated
by the Emperor. Thus this woman, when
infuriated, respected neither the sanctuary
of the church, nor the prohibitive authority of the laws, nor the intercession of
the people, nor any other obstacle what-

136 ΠΡΟΚΟΠΟΥ ΑΝΕΚΔΟΤΑ

ζ. Καὶ Διογένην δέ τινα οἷα Πράσινον ὄντα δι' ὀργῆς ἔχουσα, ἄνδρα ἀστεῖον καὶ ποθεινὸν ἅπασί τε καὶ αὐτῷ τῷ βασιλεῖ, οὐδέν τι ἧσσον γάμων ἀνδρείων ἐν σπουδῇ συκοφαντεῖν εἶχε. Δύο γοῦν ἀναπείσασα τῶν αὑτοῦ οἰκετῶν κατηγόρους τε καὶ μάρτυρας τῷ κεκτημένῳ ἐπέστησε. Τοῦ δὲ οὐ κρύβδην ἐξεταζομένου καὶ λαθραίως, ᾗπερ εἰώθει, ἀλλ' ἐν δημοσίῳ, δικαστῶν ᾐρημένων πολλῶν τε καὶ οὐκ ἀδόξων, διὰ τὴν Διογένους δόξαν, ἐπεὶ οὐκ ἐδόκουν ἀκριβολογουμένοις τοῖς δικασταῖς οἱ τῶν οἰκετῶν λόγοι ἀξιόχρεοι ἐς τὴν κρίσιν εἶναι, ἄλλως τε καὶ παιδαρίων ὄντων,

η'. Θεόδωρον τῶν Διογένει ἀναγκαίων τινὰ ἐν τοῖς εἰωθόσιν οἰκιδίοις καθεῖρξεν. Ἐνταῦθα πολλαῖς μὲν θωπείαις, πολλοῖς δὲ

COURT OF JUSTINIAN 136

soever. Nothing was able to save from her vengeance anyone who had given her offence. She conceived a hatred, on the ground of his belonging to the Green faction, for a certain Diogenes, a native of Constantinople, an agreeable person, who was liked by the Emperor and everyone else. In her wrath, she accused him, in like manner, of sodomy, and, having suborned two of his servants, put them up to give evidence against and to accuse their master. But, as he was not tried secretly and in private, as was the usual custom, but in public, owing to the reputation he enjoyed, a number of distinguished persons were selected as judges, and they, scrupulous in the discharge of their duties, rejected the testimony of his servants as insufficient, especially on the ground of their not being of legal age. The Empress thereupon caused one of the intimate friends of Diogenes, named Theodorus, to be shut up in one of her ordinary prisons, and endeavoured to win him over, at one time by flattery,

18

ΠΡΟΚΟΠΙΟΥ ΑΝΕΚΔΟΤΑ

τὸν ἄνθρωπον αἰκισμοῖς περιῆλθεν. Ἐπεί τέ οἱ οὐδὲν προὐχώρει, νευρὰν βοείαν ἐς τοῦ ἀνθρώπου τὴν κεφαλὴν ἀμφὶ τὰ νῶτα περιελίξαντες, τὴν νευρὰν στρέφειν τε καὶ σφίγγειν ἐκέλευε. Καὶ τοὺς μὲν οἱ ὀφθαλμοὺς Θεοδώρα ἐκπεπηδηκέναι τὴν οἰκείαν λιπόντας χώραν ὑπώπτευεν, οὐδὲν μέντοι τῶν οὐ γεγονότων ἀπαγγέλλειν ἔγνω. Διὸ δὴ οἱ μὲν δικασταὶ ἅτε ἀμαρτυρήτου δίκης ἀπέγνωσαν· ἡ δὲ πόλις ἑορτὴν ἀπ᾽ αὐτοῦ πανδημεὶ ἦγεν. Ἀλλὰ τοῦτο μὲν τῇδε ἐχώρησεν.

COURT OF JUSTINIAN   137

at another by ill-treatment. When none
of these measures proved successful, she
ordered a cord of ox-hide to be bound
round his head, over his forehead and
ears, and then to be twisted and tightened.
She expected that, under this treatment,
his eyes would have started from their
sockets, and that he would have lost his
sight. But Theodorus refused to tell a
lie. The judges, for want of proof, acquitted him; and his acquittal was made
the occasion of public rejoicing.

Such was the manner in which Theodorus was treated.

ΠΡΟΚΟΠΙΟΥ ΑΝΕΚΔΟΤΑ

ΚΕΦΑΛΑΙΟΝ ΙΖ΄.

α΄. Ἐρρήθη δὲ ἀρχομένῳ μοι τοῦδε τοῦ λόγου, καὶ ὅσα Βελισάριόν τε, καὶ Φώτιον, καὶ Βούζην, αὐτὴ ἐργασθείη. Στασιῶται δὲ Βένετοι δύο, Κίλικες γένος, Καλλινίκῳ τῷ Κιλικίας δευτέρας ἄρχοντι, σὺν θορύβῳ πολλῷ ἐπιστάντες, χειρῶν ἀδίκων ἐπ᾽ αὐτὸν ἦρξαν· τόν τε αὐτοῦ ἱπποκόμον ἄγχιστά που ἑστῶτα, καὶ ἀμύνειν τῷ κεκτημένῳ πειρώμενον, ἔκτειναν, τοῦ τε ἄρχοντος καὶ τοῦ δήμου θεωμένου παντός. Καὶ ὁ μὲν τοὺς στασιώτας ἄλλων τε πολλῶν καὶ τοῦδε ἁλόντας τοῦ φόνου, ἐν δίκῃ ἀνεῖλεν· ἡ δὲ μαθοῦσα, ὅτι καὶ τοὺς Βενέτους προσποιεῖται, ἐνδεικνυμένη, ἔτι αὐτὸν τὴν ἀρχὴν ἔχοντα ἐν τῷ τῶν φονέων

CHAPTER XVII

As for the manner in which she treated Belisarius, Photius, and Buzes, I have already spoken of it at the commencement of this work.

Two Cilicians, belonging to the Blue faction, during a mutiny, laid violent hands upon Callinicus, governor of the second Cilicia, and slew his groom, who was standing near him, and endeavoured to defend his master, in the presence of the governor and all the people. Callinicus condemned them to death, since they had been convicted of several other murders besides this. When Theodora heard of this, in order to show her devotion to the party of the Blues, she ordered that the governor, while he still held office, should be crucified in the place where the two offenders had been

ΠΡΟΚΟΠΙΟΥ ΑΝΕΚΔΟΤΑ

τάφῳ ἐνεσκολόπισεν οὐδενὶ λόγῳ. Βασιλεὺς δὲ κλάειν τε καὶ ὀδύρεσθαι τὸν ἀπολωλότα σκηπτόμενος, καθῆστο γρυλλίζων· πολλά τε τοῖς ἐς τὴν πρᾶξιν ὑπουργηκόσιν ἀνατεινάμενος, οὐδὲν ἔδρασε· τὰ μέντοι χρήματα τοῦ τετελευτηκότος ληΐζεσθαι ὡς ἥκιστα ἀπηξίωσεν· ἀλλὰ καὶ ὑπὲρ ἁμαρτάδων τῶν ἐς τὸ σῶμα κολάσεις τῇ Θεοδώρᾳ ἐπινοεῖν ἐπιμελὲς ἦν.

β΄. Πόρνας ἀμέλει, πλέον ἢ πεντακοσίας ἀγείρασα ἐν ἀγορᾷ μέσῃ ἐς τριώβολον, ὅσον ἀποζῆν μισθαρνούσας ἔς τε τὴν ἀντιπέρας ἤπειρον στείλασα, ἐν τῳ καλουμένῳ (Μετανοίας) μοναστηρίῳ καθεῖρξε τὸν βίον μεταμφιέσασθαι ἀναγκάζουσα.. Ὧν δή τινες ἐρρίπτουν αὑτὰς ἀφ᾽ ὑψηλοῦ νύκτωρ, ταύτῃ τε τῆς ἀκουσίου μεταβολῆς ἀπηλλάσσοντο.

γ΄. Δύο δὲ κόραι ἐν Βυζαντίῳ ἀδελφαὶ ἤτην, οὐκ ἐκ πατρός τε καὶ τριγονίας ὑπάτων

COURT OF JUSTINIAN 139

executed, although he had committed no crime. The Emperor, pretending that he bitterly lamented his loss, remained at home, grumbling and threatening all kinds of vengeance upon the perpetrators of the deed. He did nothing, however; but, without scruple, appropriated the property of the dead man to his own use. Theodora likewise devoted her attention to punishing those women who prostituted their persons. She collected more than five hundred harlots, who sold themselves for three obols in the market-place, thereby securing a bare subsistence, and transported them to the other side of the Bosphorus, where she shut them up in the Monastery of Repentance, with the object of forcing them to change their manner of life. Some of them, however, threw themselves from the walls during the night, and in this manner escaped a change of life so contrary to their inclinations.

There were at Byzantium two young sisters, illustrious not only by the consulships of their father and grandfather,

140   ΠΡΟΚΟΠΙΟΥ ΑΝΕΚΔΟΤΑ

μονον, ἀλλ' ἀνέκαθεν αἵματος τοῦ πρώτου ἔν γε τῇ συγκλήτῳ βουλῇ γεγοννυῖαι. Ταύταις ἤδη ἐς γάμον ἐλθούσαις ἀπολωλότων τῶν ἀνδρῶν ˙χήραις γεγονέναι ξυνέπεσεν. Αὐτίκα δὲ ἄνδρας ἡ Θεοδώρα δύο ἀγελαίους τε καὶ βδελυροὺς ἀπολέξασα, ξυνοικεῖν αὐταῖς ἐν σπουδῇ εἶχεν, ἐπικαλοῦσα μὴ σωφρόνως βιοῦν. Ὅπερ ἵνα μὴ γένηται, δείσασαι ἐς τὸ τῆς Σοφίας ἱερὸν φεύγουσιν· ἔς τε τὸν θεῖον λουτρῶνα ἐλθοῦσαι, τῆς ἐνταῦθα. κολυμβήθρας ἀπρὶξ εἴχοντο. Ἀλλὰ τοσαύτην αὐταῖς ἀνάγκην τε καὶ κακοπάθειαν προσετρίψατο ἡ βασίλισσα, ὥστε αὐταῖς ἀπαλλαξειούσαις τῶν ἐνθένδε κακῶν τὸν γάμον αὐτῶν ἀνταλ- λάξασθαι ἐν σπουδῇ γέγονεν. Οὕτως αὐτῇ ἄχραντος οὐδεὶς ἢ ἄσυλος μεμένηκε χῶρος. Αὗται μὲν οὖν ἀνδράσι πτωχοῖς τε καὶ ἀπερριμμένοις πολλῷ ἀπὸ τῆς σφετέρας ἀξίας ἀκούσιαι ξυνῳκίσθησαν καίπερ εὐπα- τριδῶν σφίσι παρόντων μνηστήρων. Ἡ δὲ μήτηρ αὐταῖς, χήρα καὶ αὐτὴ γεγοννυῖα, οὔτε ἀνοιμῶξαι, οὔτε ἀποκλαῦσαι τολμῶσα τὸ πάθος, παρῆν τῇ ἐγγύῃ. Ὕστερον . δὲ ἀπο-

COURT OF JUSTINIAN   140

but by a long descent of nobility, and
belonging to one of the chief families of
the Senate. They had married early and
lost their husbands. Theodora, charging
them with living an immoral life, selected
two debauchees from the common people
and designed to make them their husbands. The young widows, fearing that
they might be forced to obey, took refuge
in the church of St. Sophia, and, approaching the sacred bath, clung closely to
the font. But the Empress inflicted such
privations and cruel treatment upon them,
that they preferred marriage in order to
escape from their immediate distress. In
this manner Theodora showed that she
regarded no sanctuary as inviolable, no
spot as sacred. Although suitors of noble
birth were ready to espouse these ladies,
they were married against their will to
two men, poor and outcast, and far
below them in rank. Their mother, who
was a widow like themselves, was present
at the marriage, but did not venture to
cry out or express her sorrow at this
atrocious act. Afterwards, Theodora, re-

ΠΡΟΚΟΠΙΟΥ ΑΝΕΚΔΟΤΑ

σειομένη ἡ Θεοδώρα τὸ μίασμα, δημοσίαις αὐτὰς παρηγορῆσαι ξυμφοραῖς ἔγνω. Ἄρχοντα γὰρ ἑκάτερον κατεστήσατο. Καὶ ταῖς μὲν κόραις παραψυχὴ οὐδ᾽ ὡς γέγονε· πάθη δὲ ἀνήκεστα καὶ ἀνύποιστα τοῖς ὑπηκόοις σχεδὸν ἅπασι πρὸς τῶν ἀνδρῶν τούτων ξυνηνέχθη παθεῖν· ἅπερ μοι ἐν τοῖς ἔμπροσθεν λόγοις λελέξεται. Θεοδώρᾳ γὰρ οὔτε ἀρχῆς οὔτε πολιτείας ἀξίωσις, οὔτε τι ἄλλο ἐπιμελὲς ἦν, εἰ τὸ βούλημα περανεῖται μόνον.

δ'. Ἐτύγχανε δὲ ὑπό του κυήσασα τῶν ἐραστῶν, ἡνίκα ἔτι ἐπὶ σκηνῆς ἦν· τοῦ δὲ κακοῦ ὀψὲ τοῦ καιροῦ αἰσθομένη, πάντα μὲν ἐς τὸ ἀμβλύσκειν, ὥσπερ εἰώθει, ἐποίει· ἄωρον δὲ ἀποκτιννύναι τὸ βρέφος οὐδεμιᾷ μηχανῇ εἶχεν, ἐπεὶ οὐ πολλῷ ἀπελέλειπτο τὸ ἀνθρωποειδὲς γένος γεγονέναι. Διὸ δὴ ἐπεὶ οὐδὲν προὐχώρει, τῆς πείρας ἀφεμένη, τίκτειν ἠνάγκαστο. Ὁρῶν δὲ αὐτὴν ὁ τοῦ τεχθέντος πατὴρ

COURT OF JUSTINIAN 141

penting of what she had done, endeavoured
to console them by promoting their husbands to high offices to the public detri-
ment. But even this was no consolation
to these young women, for their husbands
inflicted incurable and insupportable woes
upon almost all their subjects, as I will
describe later; for Theodora paid no heed
to the dignity of the office, the interests
of the State, or any other consideration,
provided only she could accomplish her
wishes.

While still on the stage, she became
with child by one of her friends, but did
not perceive her misfortune until it was
too late. She tried all the means she
had formerly employed to procure abortion, but she was unable prematurely to
destroy the living creature by any means
whatsoever, since it had nearly assumed
the form of a human being. Therefore,
finding her remedies unsuccessful, she
abandoned the attempt, and was obliged
to bring forth the child. Its father,
seeing that Theodora was at a loss what
to do, and was indignant because, now

ΠΡΟΚΟΠΙΟΥ ΑΝΕΚΔΟΤΑ

ἀπορουμένην τε καὶ ἀσχάλλουσαν, ὅτι μήτηρ γενομένη τῷ σώματι ὁμοίως ἐργάζεσθαι οὐκέτι δυνατὴ εἴη, ἐπεὶ καὶ ἀληθῶς δὴ ὑπήσθετο, ὡς διαχρήσεται τὸ παιδίον, ἀνείλετό τε καὶ Ἰωάννην ἐπονομάσας, ἐπεὶ ἄρσεν ἦν, ἐς τὴν Ἀραβίαν, ἐς ἥνπερ ὥρμητο, ἀπιὼν ᾤχετο. Ἐπεὶ δὲ αὐτὸς μὲν τελευτᾶν ἔμελλεν, Ἰωάννης τε ἤδη μειράκιον ἦν, τὸν πάντα λόγον αὐτῷ ἀμφὶ τῇ μητρὶ ὁ πατὴρ ἔφρασε. Καὶ ὅς πάντα ἐπὶ τῷ πατέρι τὰ νόμιμα ποιήσας ἐξ ἀνθρώπων ἀφανισθέντι, χρόνῳ τινὶ ὕστερον ἐς Βυζάντιον ἦλθε, καὶ τοῖς περὶ τὴν μητέρα τὰς εἰσόδους ἀεὶ ποιουμένοις τὸ πρᾶγμα ἀγγέλλει. Οἱ δὲ οὐδὲν ἀπὸ τοῦ ἀνθρωπείου τρόπου αὐτὴν λογιεῖσθαι ὑποτοπήσαντες, ἐπαγγέλλουσι τῇ μητρί, ὅτι δὴ αὐτῆς Ἰωάννης ὁ υἱὸς ἥκοι. Δείσασα δὲ γυνὴ, μὴ ἐς τὸν ἄνδρα ἔκπυστος ὁ λόγος γένηται, τὸν παῖδά οἱ ἐς ὄψιν ἐκέλευεν ἥκειν. Ἐπεί τε εἶδε παραγενόμενον, τῶν οἰκείων τινὶ ἐνεχείρισεν, ᾧπερ ἀεὶ τὰ τοιαῦτα ἐπιστέλλειν εἰώθει. Καὶ τρόπῳ μὲν ὅτῳ ὁ

COURT OF JUSTINIAN   142

that she had become a mother, she was
no longer able to traffic with her person
as before, and being with good reason in
fear for the child's life, took it up, named
it John, and carried it away with him to
Arabia, whither he had resolved to retire.
The father, just before his death, gave
John, who was now grown up, full information concerning his mother.

John, having performed the last offices
for his dead father, some time afterwards
repaired to Byzantium, and explained the
state of affairs to those who were charged
with the duty of arranging admission to
an audience with the Empress. They,
not suspecting that she would conceive
any inhuman designs against him, an-
nounced to the mother the arrival of
her son. She, fearing that the report
might reach the ears of the Emperor,
ordered her son to be brought to her.
When she saw him approaching, she
went to meet him and handed him over
to one of her confidants, whom she
always intrusted with commissions of
this kind. In what manner the unfor-

ταλαίπωρος ἐξ ἀνθρώπων ἠφάνισται, οὐκ ἔχω εἰπεῖν, οὐδεὶς δὲ αὐτὸν ἄχρι δεῦρο ἰδεῖν οὐδὲ ἀπογενομένης τῆς βασιλίδος ἔσχεν.

ε΄. Τότε καὶ ταῖς γυναιξὶ σχεδόν τι ἁπάσαις τὸν τρόπον διεφθάρθαι ξυνέβη. Ἐξήμαρτον γὰρ ἐς τοὺς ἄνδρας ἐξουσίᾳ τῇ πάσῃ, οὐ φέροντος αὐταῖς κίνδυνόν τινα ἢ βλάβην τοῦ ἔργου· ἐπεὶ καὶ ὅσαι μοιχείας ἁλοῖεν, αὐταὶ μὲν κακῶν ἀπαθεῖς ἔμενον, παρὰ δὲ τὴν βασιλίδα αὐτίκα ἰοῦσαι, ἀντίστροφοί τε γενόμεναι, καὶ δίκην οὐ γεγονότων ἐγκλημάτων ἀντιλαχοῦσαι, τοὺς ἄνδρας ὑπῆγον. Περιῆν τε αὐτοῖς ἀνεξελέγκτοις οὖσι, τὴν μὲν προῖκα ἐν διπλασίῳ ἀποτιννύναι· μεμαστιγωμένοις δὲ ἐκ τοῦ ἐπιπλεῖστον ἐς τὸ δεσμωτήριον ἀπαχθῆναι· καὶ αὖ πάλιν τὰς μοιχευτρίας ἐπιδεῖν, κεκομψευμένας τε καὶ πρὸς τῶν μοιχῶν ἀδεέστερον λαγνευομένας. Τῶν δὲ μοιχῶν πολλοὶ ἀπ᾽ αὐτοῦ τοῦ ἔργου καὶ τιμῆς ἔτυχον. Διόπερ οἱ πλεῖστοι τὸ λοιπὸν πάσχοντες

COURT OF JUSTINIAN   143

tunate youth disappeared I cannot say.
He has never been seen to this day—
not even after his mother's death.

At that time the morals of women
were almost without exception corrupt.
They were faithless to their husbands
with absolute licence, since the crime of
adultery brought neither danger nor harm
upon them.   When convicted of the
offence, they escaped punishment, thanks
to the Empress, to whom they immediately applied.   Then, getting the
verdict quashed on the ground that the
charges were not proved, they in turn
accused their husbands, who, although
not convicted, were condemned to refund
twice the amount of the dower, and,
for the most part, were flogged and led
away to prison, where they were permitted to look upon their adulterous
wives again, decked out in fine garments
and in the act of committing adultery
without the slightest shame with their
lovers, many of whom, by way of recompense, received offices and rewards.   This
was the reason why most husbands after-

πρὸς τῶν γυναικῶν ἀνόσια ἔργα, ἀσμενέστατα
ἀμαστίγωτοι σιωπῇ ἔμενον, τὴν παρρησίαν
αὐταῖς, τῷ μὴ πεφωρᾶσθαι δοκεῖν, ἐνδιδόντες.

ς'. Αὕτη ἅπαντα πρυτανεύειν αὐτογνω-
μονοῦσα τὰ ἐν τῇ πολιτείᾳ ἠξίου. Τάς τε γὰρ
ἀρχὰς καὶ ἱερωσύνας ἐχειροτόνει, ἐκεῖνο μόνον
διερευνωμένη καὶ φυλασσομένη ἐνδελεχέστατα,
μὴ καλὸς κἀγαθός τις ὁ τὸ ἀξίωμα μετιὼν
εἴη, καὶ οὐχ οἷός τέ οἱ ἐσόμενος ἐς τὰ ἐπαγ-
γελλόμενα ὑπουργήσειν.

ζ'. Καὶ τοὺς γάμους ἅπαντας τῇ θείᾳ
ἐξουσίᾳ τινὶ διῳκεῖτο, τό τε γαμεῖν πρῶτον
οὐδεμίαν ἄνθρωποι ἐγγύην ἑκουσίαν πεποίηνται.
Γυνὴ ἑκάστῳ ἐξαπιναίως ἐγίνετο, οὐχ ὅτι δὴ
αὐτὸν ἤρεσκεν, ὅπερ κἂν τοῖς βαρβάροις εἰώθει,
ἀλλ' ὅτι βουλομένῃ τῇ Θεοδώρᾳ εἴη. Ὅπερ
αὖ καὶ ταῖς γαμουμέναις ἀνάπαλιν ξυνέβαινε
πάσχειν, ἀνδράσι ξυνιέναι οὐδαμῇ ἐθελούσιαι
ἠναγκάζοντο. Πολλάκις δὲ καὶ τὴν νύμφην

COURT OF JUSTINIAN 144

wards put up with unholy outrages on the part of their wives, and gladly endured them in silence in order to escape the lash. They even afforded them every opportunity to avoid being surprised.

Theodora claimed complete control of the State at her sole discretion. She appointed magistrates and ecclesiastical dignitaries. Her only care and anxiety was—and as to this she made the most careful investigation—to prevent any office being given to a good and honourable man, who might be prevented by his conscience from assisting her in her nefarious designs.

She ordered all marriages as it were by a kind of divine authority; men never made a voluntary agreement before marriage. A wife was found for each without any previous notice, not because she pleased him (as is generally the case even amongst the barbarians) but because Theodora so desired it. Brides also had to put up with the same treatment, and were obliged to marry husbands whom they did not desire. She often turned the

ἐκ τῆς παστάδος ἀποβιβάσασα, λόγῳ οὐδενὶ ἀνυμέναιον τὸν νύμφιον ἀφῆκε, τοῦτο μόνον ξὺν ἀκροχολίᾳ εἰποῦσα, ὅτι δὴ αὐτὴν ἀπαρέσκει. Ὅπερ ἄλλους τε πολλοὺς ἔδρασε καὶ Λεόντιον, ὅσπερ ῥαιφερενδάριος ἦν τὴν τιμὴν, καὶ Σατορνῖνον, τὸν Ἑρμογένους τοῦ μαγίστρου γεγονότος ἐπὶ μνηστῇ.

η′. Τούτῳ γὰρ τῷ Σατορνίνῳ ἦν τις ἀνεψιαδῆ παρθένος μνηστὴ, ἐλευθέριος καὶ κοσμία, ἥνπερ οἱ Κύριλλος ὁ πατὴρ κατηγγύησεν, Ἑρμογένους τοῦ βίου ἤδη ἀπολυθέντος. πεπηγυίας τε αὐτοῖς τῆς παστάδος, τὸν νυμφίον καθεῖρξεν, ὃς ἐς τὴν ἑτέραν παστάδα ἤχθη· ἔγημέ τε κωκύων καὶ οἰμώζων ὅσον τὴν Χρυσομαλλοῦς παῖδα. Χρυσομαλλὼ δὲ αὕτη πάλαι μὲν ὀρχηστρὶς ἐγεγόνει, καὶ αὖθις ἑταίρα· τότε δὲ ξὺν ἑτέρᾳ Χρυσομαλλοῖ καὶ Ἰνδαροῖ ἐν παλατίῳ δίαιταν εἶχεν. Ἀντὶ γὰρ τοῦ φαλλοῦ καὶ τῆς ἐν θεάτρῳ δια-

COURT OF JUSTINIAN 145

bride out of bed herself, and, without any
reason, dismissed the bridegroom before
the marriage had been consummated,
merely saying, in great anger, that she
disapproved of her. Amongst others
whom she treated in this manner was
Leontius the "referendary," and Saturninus, the son of Hermogenes the late
Master of Offices, whom she deprived
of their wives. This Saturninus had a
young maiden cousin of an age to marry,
free-born and modest, whom Cyrillus, her
father, had betrothed to him after the
death of Hermogenes. After the bridal
chamber had been made ready and everything prepared, Theodora imprisoned the
youthful bridegroom, who was afterwards
conducted to another chamber, and forced,
in spite of his violent lamentations and
tears, to wed the daughter of Chrysomallo.
This Chrysomallo had formerly been a
dancer and a common prostitute, and at
that time lived with another woman like
her, and with Indaro, in the palace, where,
instead of devoting themselves to phallic
worship and theatrical amusements, they

19—2

146 ΠΡΟΚΟΠΙΟΥ ΑΝΕΚΔΟΤΑ

τριβῆς τῇδε διῳκοῦντο τὰ πράγματα. Ξυγ-
καταδαρθὼν δὲ ὁ Σατορνῖνος τῇ νύμφῃ, καὶ
διαπεπαρθενευμένην εὑρὼν, ἔς τινα τῶν ἐπιτηδείων ἐξήνεγκεν, ὅτι δὴ οὐκ ἄτρητον γήμοι.
Ὅπερ ἐπεὶ ἐς Θεοδώραν ἦλθε, τοὺς ὑπηρέτας
ἐκέλευεν, ἄτε ἀποσεμνυνόμενον καὶ ὁρκωθέντα
οὐδὲν αὐτῷ προσῆκον, μετέωρον αἴρειν, οἷα
τὰ ἐς γραμματιστοῦ φοιτῶντα παιδία, ξαί-
νουσά τε κατὰ τῶν νώτων πολλὰς, ἀπεῖπεν
αὐτῷ μὴ φλυάρῳ εἶναι.

θ'. Οἷα μέντοι καὶ Ἰωάννην τὸν Καππαδόκην εἰργάσατο, ἐν τοῖς ἔμπροσθεν λόγοις
ἐρρήθη, ἅπερ αὐτῇ διαπέπρακται τῷ ἀνθρώπῳ
χαλεπαινούσῃ, οὐχ ὑπὲρ ὧν ἐς τὴν πολιτείαν
ἡμάρτανε (τεκμήριον δὲ· τῶν γὰρ ὕστερον
δεινότερα ἐς τοὺς ὑπηκόους ἐργασαμένων οὐδένα τοῦτο πεποίηται·) ἀλλ' ὅτι τά τε ἄλλα
τῇ γυναικὶ καταντικρὺ ἐτόλμα ἰέναι, καὶ αὐτὴν
ἐς τὸν βασιλέα διέβαλλεν, ὥστε αὐτῇ καὶ τὸν
ἄνδρα ἐκπεπολεμῶσθαι παρ' ὀλίγον ἐλθεῖν.

COURT OF JUSTINIAN 146

occupied themselves with affairs of State together with Theodora.

Saturninus, having lain with his new wife and discovered that she had already lost her maidenhead, informed one of his friends that his wife was no virgin. When this reached the ears of Theodora, she ordered the servants to hoist him up, like a boy at school, upbraiding him with having behaved too saucily and having taken an unbecoming oath. She then had him severely flogged on the bare back, and advised him to restrain his talkative tongue for the future.

In my former writings I have already related her treatment of John of Cappadocia, which was due to a desire to avenge personal injuries, not to punish him for offences against the State, as is proved by the fact that she did nothing of the kind in the case of those who committed far greater cruelties against their subjects. The real cause of her hatred was, that he ventured to oppose her designs and accused her to the Emperor, so that they nearly came to open

ΠΡΟΚΟΠΙΟΥ ΑΝΕΚΔΟΤΑ

Τῶν γὰρ αἰτιῶν, ὅπερ ὑπεῖπον, ἐνταῦθά μοι μάλιστα τὰς ἀληθεστάτας ἀναγκαῖον εἰπεῖν. Ἡνίκα τε αὐτὸν ἐπ' Αἰγύπτου καθεῖρξε, πεπονθότα ὅσα μοι ἀμφ' αὐτῷ προδεδήλωται, οὐδ' ὥς τινα ἔλαβε τῆς τοῦ ἀνθρώπου κολάσεως κόρον, ἀλλὰ ψευδομάρτυρας ἐπ' ἐκείνῳ διερευνωμένη, οὐδέποτε ἀνίει. Τέτρασι δὲ ἐνιαυτοῖς ὕστερον Πρασίνους εὑρέσθαι δύο, τῶν ἐν Κυζίκῳ στασιωτῶν, ἴσχυσεν, οἵπερ τῶν τῷ ἐπισκόπῳ ἐπαναστάντων ἐλέγοντο εἶναι. Καὶ αὐτοὺς θωπείαις τε καὶ λόγοις καὶ ἀπειλαῖς κατορρωδήσας, καὶ ταῖς ἐλπίσιν ἐπαρθεὶς, τὸ μίασμα τοῦ φόνου ἐς Ἰωάννην ἀνήνεγκεν. Ὁ δὲ δὴ ἕτερος τῆς ἀληθείας ἀπεναντίας ἐλθεῖν οὐδαμῆ ἔγνω, καίπερ οὕτως ἐκ τῆς βασάνου καταταθεὶς, ὥστε ὅτι δὴ καὶ τεθνήξεται αὐτίκα μάλα ἐπίδοξος ἦν. Διὸ δὴ τὸν μὲν Ἰωάννην τούτῳ δὴ τῷ παραπετάσματι διαχρήσασθαι οὐδεμιᾷ μηχανῇ ἔσχε, τοῖν δὲ νεανίαιν τούτοιν χεῖρας τὰς δεξιὰς ἔτεμε· τοῦ μὲν, ὅτι ψευδομαρτυρεῖν οὐδαμῆ ἤθελε· τοῦ

COURT OF JUSTINIAN 147

hostilities. I mention this here because, as I have already stated, in this work I am bound to state the real causes of events. When, after having inflicted upon him the sufferings I have related, she had confined him in Egypt, she was not even then satisfied with his punishment, but was incessantly on the look out to find false witnesses against him. Four years afterwards, she succeeded in finding two of the Green faction who had taken part in the sedition at Cyzicus, and were accused of having been accessory to the assault upon the Bishop. These she attacked with flattery, promises, and threats. One of them, alarmed and inveigled by her promises, accused John of the foul crime of murder, but the other refused to utter falsehoods, although he was so cruelly tortured that he seemed likely to die on the spot. She was, therefore, unable to compass the death of John on this pretext, but she caused the young men's right hands to be chopped off—that of the one because he refused to bear false witness; that of the

148 ΠΡΟΚΟΠΙΟΥ ΑΝΕΚΔΟΤΑ

δὲ, ὅπως μὴ ἐπιφανὴς ἡ ἐπιβουλὴ ἐς τὸ πᾶν γένηται. Τούτων δὲ οὕτως ἐν τῷ δημοσίῳ πρασσομένων τῆς ἀγορᾶς, ἐποιεῖτο τῶν πρασσομένων μηδένα τὸ παράπαν ξυνεῖναι.

COURT OF JUSTINIAN 148

other, to prevent her intrigue becoming universally known, for she endeavoured to keep secret from others those things which were done in the open market-place.

ΚΕΦΑΛΑΙΟΝ ΙΗ΄.

α΄. Ὅτι δὲ οὐκ ἄνθρωπος, ἀλλα δαίμων τις, ὥσπερ εἴρηται, ἀνθρωπόμορφος ἦν, τεκμηριώσαιτο ἄν τις τῷ μεγέθει σταθμώμενος ὧν εἰς τοὺς ἀνθρώπους κακῶν ἔδρασεν. Ἐν γὰρ τῷ ὑπερβάλλοντι τῶν πεπραγμένων καὶ ἡ τοῦ δεδρακότος δύναμις ἔνδηλος γίνεται. Τὸ μὲν οὖν μέτρον ἐς τὸ ἀκριβὲς τῶν ὑπ' αὐτοῦ ἀνῃρημένων εἰπεῖν οὐκ ἄν ποτέ μοι δοκεῖ τῶν πάντων τινὶ ἢ τῷ θεῷ δυνατὰ εἶναι. Θᾶσσον γάρ τις, οἶμαι, τὴν πᾶσαν ψάμμον ἐξαριθμήσειεν, ἢ ὅσους βασιλεὺς οὗτος ἀνῄρηκε. Τὴν δὲ χώραν ἐπιπλεῖστον διαριθμούμενος, ἥνπερ ἔρημον τῶν ἐνοικούντων ξυμπέπτωκεν εἶναι, μυριάδας μυριάδων μυρίας φημὶ ἀπολωλεκέναι. Λιβύην μὲν γὰρ, ἐς τοσοῦτον διήκουσαν μέτρον, οὕτω ἀπολώλεκεν, ὥστε ὁδὸν ἰόντι πολλὴν, ἀνδρὶ ἐντυχεῖν χαλεπόν τε καὶ λόγου ἄξιον εἶναι. Καίτοι Βανδίλων μὲν τῶν ὅπλα ἀργυριουμένων ἐνταῦθα μυριάδες ὀκτὼ

CHAPTER XVIII

THAT Justinian was not a man, but a demon in human shape, as I have already said, may be abundantly proved by considering the enormity of the evils which he inflicted upon mankind, for the power of the acting cause is manifested in the excessive atrocity of his actions. I think that God alone could accurately reckon the number of those who were destroyed by him, and it would be easier for a man to count the grains of sand on the sea-shore than the number of his victims. Considering generally the extent of country which was depopulated by him, I assert that more than two millions of people perished. He so devastated the vast tract of Libya that a traveller, during a long journey, considered it a remarkable thing to meet a single man; and yet there were eighty thousand Vandals who bore

ΠΡΟΚΟΠΙΟΥ ΑΝΕΚΔΟΤΑ

ἐτύγχανον οὖσαι· γυναίων δὲ καὶ παιδαρίων καὶ θεραπόντων αὐτῶν, τίς ἂν εἰκάσειε μέτρον; Λιβύων δὲ τῶν ἐν ταῖς πόλεσιν ᾠκημένων τὰ πρότερα, καὶ γῆν γεωργούντων, ἐργασίαν τε τὴν κατὰ θάλασσαν ἐργαζομένων, ὅπερ μοι αὐτόπτῃ ἐπιπλεῖστον γεγονέναι τετύχηκε, πῶς ἄν τις τὸ πλῆθος διαριθμεῖσθαι τῶν πάντων ἀνθρώπων ἱκανὸς εἴη; τούτων δὲ πολλῷ ἔτι πλείους Μαυρούσιοι ἦσαν ἐνταῦθα, οἷς δὴ ἅπασι ξύν τε γυναιξὶ καὶ γόνῳ διεφθάρθαι ξυνέβη. Πολλοὺς δὲ αὖ καὶ Ῥωμαίων στρατιωτῶν, καὶ τῶν αὐτοῖς ἐκ Βυζαντίου ἐπισπομένων, ἡ γῆ ἔκρυψεν· ὥστε εἴ τις μυριάδας ἀνθρώπων ἔν τε Λιβύῃ πεντακοσίας ἰσχυρίζεται ἀπολωλέναι, οὐκ ἂν ποτε τῷ πράγματι, οἶμαι, διαρκῶς εἴποι.

β΄. Αἴτιον δὲ ὅτι Βανδίλων εὐθὺς ἡσσημένων, οὐχ ὅπως κρατύνοιτο τὴν τῆς χώρας ἐπικράτησιν ἐπιμελές οἱ ἐγίνετο, οὐδ᾽ ὅπως οἱ ἡ τῶν ἀγαθῶν φυλακὴ ἐν τῷ ἀσφαλεῖ, εὐνοίᾳ τῶν κατηκόων, εἴη, προὐνόησεν, ἀλλὰ Βελισάριον αὐτίκα μελλήσει οὐδεμιᾷ μετεπέμπετο, τυραννίδα οἱ οὐδαμόθεν προσήκουσαν

COURT OF JUSTINIAN 150

arms, besides women, children and servants without number. In addition to these, who amongst men could enumerate the ancient inhabitants who dwelt in the cities, tilled the land, and traded on the coast, of whom I myself have seen vast numbers with my own eyes? The natives of Mauretania were even still more numerous, and they were all exterminated, together with their wives and children. This country also proved the tomb of numbers of Roman soldiers and of their auxiliaries from Byzantium. Therefore, if one were to assert that five millions perished in that country, I do not feel sure that he would not under-estimate the number. The reason of this was that Justinian, immediately after the defeat of the Vandals, did not take measures to strengthen his hold upon the country, and showed no anxiety to protect his interests by securing the goodwill of his subjects, but immediately recalled Belisarius on a charge of aspiring to royal power (which would by no means have suited him) in order that he might

ἐπεγκαλέσας, ὅπως τὸ ἐνθένδε διοικούμενος κατ᾽ ἐξουσίαν Λιβύην καταπιὼν ὅλην ληίζηται. Τιμητὰς ἀμέλει τῆς γῆς ἔπεμπε καὶ φόρους ἐπετίθει πικροτάτους τινὰς, οὐ πρότερον ὄντας. Καὶ τῶν χωρίων προσεποιεῖτο, εἴ τι ἄριστον ἦν, καὶ Ἀρειανοὺς τῶν ἐν σφίσιν αὐτοῖς μυστηρίων εἶργε. Κἂν ταῖς στρατιωτικαῖς δυνάμεσιν ὑπερήμερος ἦν, καὶ ἄλλως τοῖς στρατιώταις ἐγεγόνει βαρὺς, ἐξ ὧν αἱ στάσεις φυόμεναι τετελευτήκασιν εἰς ὄλεθρον μέγαν. Οὐ γὰρ μένειν ἐν τοῖς καθεστῶσί ποτε ἴσχυεν, ἀλλὰ ξυγχεῖν τε καὶ ἀναθολοῦν ἐπεφύκει πάντα.

γ΄. Ἰταλία δὲ οὐχ ἧσσον ἢ τριπλασία Λιβύης οὖσα, ἔρημος ἀνθρώπων πολλῷ μᾶλλον ἢ ἔτι ἐκείνη πανταχόθι γεγένηται· ὥστε δὴ μέτρου τῶν κἀνταῦθα ἀνῃρημένων ἡ δήλωσις ἔσται· (ἥ τε) γὰρ αἰτία τῶν ἐν Ἰταλίᾳ ξυμπεπτωκότων ἤδη μοι ἔμπροσθεν δεδιήγηται. Ἅπαντα γὰρ ὅσα ἐν Λιβύῃ, κἀνταῦθα αὐτῷ ἡμαρτήθη τε, καὶ τοὺς καλουμένους

COURT OF JUSTINIAN 151

manage the affairs of the country at his own discretion, and ravage and plunder the whole of Libya. He sent commissioners to value the province, and imposed new and most harsh taxes upon the inhabitants. He seized the best and most fertile estates, and prohibited the Arians from exercising the rites of their religion. He was dilatory in keeping his army well supplied and in an effective condition, while in other respects he was a severe martinet, so that disturbances arose which ended in great loss. He was unable to abide by what was established, but was by nature prone to throw everything into a state of confusion and disturbance.

Italy, which was three times larger than Libya, was depopulated far more than the latter throughout its whole extent, whence a computation may be made of 'the number of those who perished there, for I have already spoken of the origin of the events that took place in Italy. All his crimes in Africa were repeated in Italy; having despatched

Λογοθέτας προσεπιπέμψας, ἀνεχαίτισέ τε καὶ διέφθειρεν εὐθὺς ἅπαντα.

δ'. Κατέτεινε δὲ ἡ Γότθων ἀρχὴ πρὸ τοῦδε τοῦ πολέμου ἐκ Γάλλων τῆς γῆς ἄχρι τῶν Δακίας ὁρίων· οὗ δὴ πόλις τὸ Σίρμιόν ἐστι. Γαλλίας μὲν οὖν καὶ Βενετίων γῆν τὴν πολλὴν Γερμανοὶ ἔσχον, ἐπειδὴ ἀφίκετο ἐς Ἰταλίαν ὁ Ῥωμαίων στρατός. Σίρμιον δὲ καὶ τὰ ἐκείνῃ πεδία Γήπαιδες κατέχουσιν· ἅπαντα μέντοι, συλλήβδην εἰπεῖν, ἀνθρώπων παντελῶς ἔρημα. Τοὺς μὲν γὰρ ὁ πόλεμος, τοὺς δὲ νόσος τε καὶ λιμὸς διεχρήσαντο, ἃ δὴ τῷ πολέμῳ ἕπεσθαι πέφυκεν. Ἰλλυρίους δὲ καὶ Θρᾴκην ὅλην, εἴη δ' ἂν ἐκ κόλπου τοῦ Ἰονίου μέχρι ἐς τὰ Βυζαντίων προάστεια, ἐν τοῖς Ἑλλάς τε καὶ Χερρονησιτῶν ἡ χώρα ἐστὶν, Οὖννοί τε καὶ Σκλαβηνοὶ καὶ Ἄνται σχεδόν τι ἀνὰ πᾶν καταθέοντες ἔτος, ἐξ οὗ Ἰουστινιανὸς παρέλαβε τὴν Ῥωμαίων ἀρχὴν, ἀνήκεστα ἔργα εἰργάσαντο τοὺς ταύτῃ ἀνθρώπους. Πλέον γὰρ ἐν ἑκάστῃ ἐμβολῇ οἶμαι ἢ κατὰ μυριάδας εἴκοσιν εἶναι τῶν τε ἀνῃρημένων καὶ ἠνδραποδισμένων ἐνταῦθα Ῥω-

COURT OF JUSTINIAN   152

Logothetae to this country also, he immediately overthrew and ruined everything.

Before the Italian war, the Empire of the Goths extended from the territory of the Gauls to the boundaries of Dacia, and the city of Sirmium ; but, when the Roman army arrived in Italy, the greater part of Cisalpine Gaul and of the territory of the Venetians was in the occupation of the Germans. Sirmium and the adjacent country was in the hands of the Gepidae. The entire tract of country, however, was utterly depopulated ; war and its attendant evils, disease and famine, had exterminated the inhabitants. Illyria and the whole of Thrace, that is to say, the countries between the Ionian Gulf and the suburbs of Byzantium, including Hellas and the Chersonese, were overrun nearly every year after the accession of Justinian by the Huns, Slavs and Antes, who inflicted intolerable sufferings upon the inhabitants. I believe that, on the occasion of each of these inroads, more than two hundred thousand Romans were either slain or carried away into slavery, so that the

153 ΠΡΟΚΟΠΙΟΥ ΑΝΕΚΔΟΤΑ

μαίων, ὥστε τὴν Σκυθῶν ἐρημίαν ἀμέλει ταύτης πανταχόσε τῆς γῆς ξυμβαίνειν.

ε΄. Τὰ μὲν οὖν ἐν Διβύῃ τε καὶ Εὐρώπῃ κατὰ τὸν πόλεμον ξυνενεχθέντα τοιαῦτα ἐστι. Σαρακηνοὶ δὲ τοὺς ἑφους Ῥωμαίους, ἐκ γῆς Αἰγύπτου μέχρι τῶν Περσίδος ὁρίων, πάντας τοῦτον τὸν χρόνον διηνεκῶς καταθέοντες, οὕτω δὴ ἐνδελεχέστατα κατειργάσαντο, ὥστε ὀλιγανθρωπότατα ξύμπαντα ἐγεγόνει τὰ ἐκείνῃ χωρία, καὶ οὐ μήποτε ἀνθρώπῳ, οἶμαι, δυνατὰ ἔσται τὸ μέτρον τῶν οὕτως ἀπολωλότων διερευνωμένῳ εὑρέσθαι. Πέρσαι τε καὶ Χοσρόης τρὶς μὲν ἐμβάλλοντες ἐς τὴν ἄλλην Ῥωμαίων ἀρχὴν, τάς τε πόλεις καθεῖλον, καὶ τοὺς ἀνθρώπους οὓς ἂν λάβοιεν ἔν τε πόλεσι ταῖς ἁλισκομέναις καὶ χώρᾳ ἑκάστῃ, τοὺς μὲν κτείνοντες, τοὺς δὲ ξὺν αὑτοῖς ἐπαγόμενοι, ἔρημον τὴν γῆν κατεστήσαντο τῶν ἐνοικούντων, ἧπερ αὐτοὺς ἐπισκῆψαι ξυνέπεσεν. Ἐξ οὗ δὲ καὶ εἰς γῆν τὴν Κολχίδα εἰσήλασαν, αὐτοῖς τε καὶ Λαζοῖς καὶ Ῥωμαίοις διαφθείρεσθαι μέχρι δεῦρο ξυμβαίνει.

ϛ΄. Οὐ μέντοι οὐδὲ Πέρσαις, ἢ Σαρακηνοῖς, ἢ Οὔννοις, ἢ τῷ Σκλαβηνῶν γένει, ἢ τῶν ἄλλων βαρβάρων τισὶν, ἀκραιφνέσιν ἐκ Ῥωμαίων τῆς γῆς ξυνηνέχθη ἀπαλλαγῆναι.

COURT OF JUSTINIAN 153

solitude of Scythia overspread these
provinces.

Such were the results of the wars in
Libya and Europe. During all this time,
the Saracens also made perpetual inroads
upon the Eastern Romans, from Egypt
to the Persian frontiers, and harassed
them so persistently, that those districts
gradually became depopulated. I believe
it would be impossible for anyone to
estimate correctly the number of men
who perished there.

The Persians under Chosroes thrice
invaded the rest of the Roman territory,
destroyed the cities, slew or carried off
those whom they found in the captured
towns in each district, and depopulated
the country wherever they attacked it.
From the time they entered Colchis, the
losses were divided between themselves,
the Lazes, and the Romans, as up to the
present day.

However, neither Persians, Saracens,
Huns, Slavs, nor any other barbarians
were themselves able to evacuate Roman
territory without considerable loss, for,

"Εν τε γὰρ ταῖς ἐφόδοις, καὶ πολλῷ ἔτι μᾶλλον ἔν τε πολιορκίαις καὶ ξυμβολαῖς, ἐναντιώμασι πολλοῖς προσεπταικότες, οὐδέν τι ἧσσον ξυνδιεφθάρησαν. Οὐ γὰρ Ῥωμαῖοι μόνον, ἀλλὰ καὶ βάρβαροι σχεδόν τι πάντες, τῇ Ἰουστινιανοῦ μιαιφονίᾳ ἀπώναντο. Ἦν μὲν γάρ τοι καὶ Χοσρόης αὐτός τε πονηρὸς τὸ ἦθος καὶ, ὥς μοι ἐν λόγοις εἴρηται τοῖς καθήκουσι, τὰς μὲν αἰτίας αὐτῷ τοῦ πολέμου ὅδε παρείχετο πάσας. Οὐ γὰρ ἠξίου τοῖς καιροῖς ἐναρμόζειν τὰς πράξεις, ἀλλ' ἀπὸ καιροῦ πάντα εἰργάζετο, ἐν μὲν εἰρήνῃ καὶ σπονδαῖς ἐξαρτώμενος ἀεί, νῷ δολερῷ, ἐπὶ τοὺς πέλας πολέμου αἰτίας, ἐν δὲ τῷ πολέμῳ ἀναπεπτωκώς τε οὐδενὶ λόγῳ καὶ τὴν τῶν ἔργων παρασκευὴν ὀκνηρῶς ἄγαν, διὰ φιλο- χρηματίαν, ποιούμενος, ἀντί τε σπουδῆς τῆς περὶ ταῦτα περισκοπῶν μὲν τὰ μετέωρα, περίεργος δὲ ἀμφὶ τῇ τοῦ θεοῦ φύσει γινό- μενος, καὶ οὔτε τὸν πόλεμον μεθιεὶς, τῷ

COURT OF JUSTINIAN 154

in their inroads, and still more in their
sieges and engagements, they often met
with numerous reverses which inflicted
equal disasters upon them. Thus not
only the Romans, but almost all the
barbarians, felt the bloodthirstiness of
Justinian. Chosroes (as I have stated
in the proper place) was certainly a
man of depraved character, but it was
Justinian who always took the initiative
in bringing about war with this prince,
for he took no care to adapt his policy
to circumstances, but did everything at
the wrong moment. In time of peace
or truce, his thoughts were ever craftily
engaged in endeavouring to find pretexts
for war against his neighbours. In war,
he lost heart without reason, and, owing
to his meanness, he never made his preparations in good time ; and, instead of
devoting his earnest attention to such
matters, he busied himself with the investigation of heavenly phenomena and
with curious researches into the nature
of God. Nevertheless, he would not
abandon war, being by nature tyrannical

μιαιφόνος τις καὶ τυραννικὸς εἶναι, οὔτε περιεῖναι τῶν πολεμίων οἷός τε ὤν, τῷ μὴ τὰ
δέοντα ὑπὸ σμικρολογίας περιεργάζεσθαι.

ζ΄.   Ταύτῃ τε αὐτοῦ βασιλεύοντος ἡ γῆ
ξύμπασα ἔμπλεως αἵματος ἀνθρωπείου ἔκ
τε Ῥωμαίων καὶ βαρβάρων σχεδόν τι πάντων διαρκῶς γέγονε. Ταῦτα μέντοι κατὰ τὸν
πόλεμον πανταχόθι τῆς Ῥωμαίων, ξυλλήβδην
εἰπεῖν, ὑπὸ τοῦτον τὸν χρόνον ξυνηνέχθη
γενέσθαι. Τὰ δὲ κατὰ στάσιν ἔν τε Βυζαντίῳ καὶ πόλει ἑκάστῃ ξυνενεχθέντα διαριθμούμενος, οὐκ ἐλάσσω ἀνθρώπων φόνον
ταύτῃ ξυμβῆναι ἢ κατὰ τὸν πόλεμον οἴομαι.
Τοῦ γὰρ δικαίου καὶ τῆς ὁμοίας ἐπιστροφῆς
ἐπὶ τοῖς ἁμαρτανομένοις ὡς ἥκιστα ὄντων,
ἀλλὰ κατεσπουδασμένου τῷ βασιλεῖ θατέρου
τοῖν μεροῖν μάλιστα, ἡσυχίαν οὐδὲ θάτεροι
ἦγον· ἀλλ᾽ οἱ μὲν τῷ ἐλασσοῦσθαι, οἱ δὲ τῷ
θαρσεῖν, εἰς ἀπόγνωσίν τε καὶ ἀπόνοιαν ἀεὶ
ἔβλεπον· καὶ πὴ μὲν ἀθρόοι ἐπ᾽ ἀλλήλους
ἰόντες, πὴ δὲ κατ᾽ ὀλίγους μαχόμενοι, ἢ καὶ
κατ᾽ ἄνδρα ἕνα τὰς ἐνέδρας, ἂν οὕτω τύχοι,
ποιούμενοι, ἐς δύο καὶ τριάκοντα ἐνιαυτοὺς

COURT OF JUSTINIAN   155

and bloodthirsty, although he was unable to overcome his enemies, since his meanness prevented him from making the necessary preparations. Thus, during the reign of this prince, the whole world was deluged with the blood of nearly all the Romans and barbarians.

Such were the events that took place, during the wars abroad, throughout the whole of the Roman Empire; but the disturbances in Byzantium and every other city caused equal bloodshed; for, since no regard was had to justice or impartiality in meting out punishment for offences, each faction being eager to gain the favour of the Emperor, neither party was able to keep quiet. They alternately abandoned themselves to the madness of despair or presumptuous vanity, according as they failed or succeeded in ingratiating themselves with him. Sometimes they attacked one another *en masse*, sometimes in small bands, sometimes in single combat, or set ambuscades for each other at every opportunity. For thirty-two years without in-

οὐδένα ἀνιέντες καιρὸν, αὐτοὶ τε εἰργάζοντο ἀλλήλους ἀνήκεστα ἔργα, καὶ πρὸς τῆς τῷ δήμῳ ἐφεστώσης ἀρχῆς ὡς τὰ πολλὰ διεφθείροντο. Ἡ μέντοι τίσις τῶν ἁμαρτανομένων ἐκ τοῦ ἐπιπλεῖστον εἰς τοὺς Πρασίνους ἐγίνετο.

η΄. Ἔτι μὴν καὶ ἡ ἐς τοὺς Σαμαρείτας καὶ τοὺς καλουμένους Αἱρετικοὺς κόλασις φόνου ἐνέπλησε τὴν Ῥωμαίων ἀρχήν. Ταῦτα δέ μοι ὅσον ἐν κεφαλαίῳ εἰρῆσθαι ἀπομνημονευέσθω τανῦν, ἐπεί μοι ἱκανῶς ὀλίγῳ ἔμπροσθεν δεδιήγηται. Ταῦτα μὲν κατὰ τὸν ἐν σώματι γενόμενον δαίμονα τετύχηκε γενέσθαι ἐς πάντας ἀνθρώπους, ὧνπερ τὰς αἰτίας αὐτὸς, ἅτε βασιλεὺς καταστὰς, ἔδωκεν· ὅσα μέντοι κατακεκρυμμένῃ δυνάμει καὶ φύσει δαιμονίᾳ διειργάσατο ἀνθρώπους κακά, ἐγὼ δηλώσω·

θ΄. Τούτῳ γὰρ Ῥωμαίων διοικουμένῳ, τὰ πράγματα πολλὰ καὶ ἄλλα πάθη ξυνηνέχθη γενέσθαι, ἅπερ οἱ μὲν τῇ τοῦ πονηροῦ δαίμονος τῇδε παρουσίᾳ ἰσχυρίζοντο καὶ μηχανῇ ξυμβῆναι, οἱ δὲ αὐτοῦ τὸ θεῖον τὰ ἔργα μισῆσαν ἀποστραφέν τε ἀπὸ τῆς Ῥωμαίων ἀρχῆς, χώραν δαίμοσι τοῖς παλαμναίοις ἐν-

COURT OF JUSTINIAN 156

termission they inflicted horrible cruelties
upon one another. They were frequently
put to death by the Praefect of the city,
although punishment for offences fell most
heavily upon the Green faction. The
punishment of the Samaritans also, and
other so-called heretics, deluged the
Roman Empire with blood. Let it
suffice, on the present occasion, to recall
briefly what I have already narrated in
greater detail. These calamities, which
afflicted the whole world, took place
during the reign of this demon in the
form of a man, for which he himself,
when Emperor, was responsible. I will
now proceed to relate the evils he
wrought by some hidden force and de-
moniacal power.

During his control of the Empire,
numerous disasters of various kinds occurred, which some attributed to the
presence and artifices of his evil genius,
while others declared that the Divinity,
in detestation of his works, having turned
away in disgust from the Roman Empire,
had given permission to the avenging

δεδωκέναι, ταῦτα διαπράξασθαι τῇδε. Ἔδεσσαν μὲν γὰρ Σκιρτὸς ἐπικλύσας ὁ ποταμὸς, μυρίων δημιουργὸς τοῖς ἐκείνῃ ἀνθρώποις συμφορῶν γέγονεν, ὥς μοι ἐν τοῖς ἔμπροσθεν λόγοις γέγραπται. Νεῖλος δὲ ἀναβὰς μὲν ᾗπερ εἰώθει, χρόνοις δὲ οὐκ ἀποβὰς τοῖς καθήκουσι, δεινὰ τοὺς ᾠκημένους εἰργάσατο ἔργα, ἅπερ μοι καὶ πρότερον δεδιήγηται. Κύδνος δὲ Ταρσὸν περιβαλλόμενος, σχεδόν τι πᾶσαν ἡμέρας τε αὐτὴν ἐπικλύσας πολλὰς, οὐ πρότερον ἀπέστη ἢ ὡς αὐτὴν ἀνήκεστα κακὰ ἔδρασε.

ι΄. Σεισμοὶ δὲ Ἀντιόχειάν τε καθεῖλον τὴν τῆς ἑῴας πρώτην, καὶ Σελεύκειαν, ᾗπερ αὐτῆς ἐκ γειτόνων οἰκεῖται, καὶ τὴν ἐν Κιλικίᾳ ἐπιφανεστάτην Ἀνάζαρβον. Ἐν αἷς τῶν ἀπολωλότων τὸ μέτρον τίς ἂν διαριθμεῖσθαι δυνατὸς εἴη; προσθείη δὲ ἄν τις τά τε Ἴβωρα, καὶ Ἀμάσειαν, ἢ πρώτη ἐν Πόντῳ ἐτύγχανεν οὖσα, Πολύβοτόν τε τὴν ἐν Φρυγίᾳ, καὶ ἢν Πισίδαι Φιλομήδην καλοῦσι, Λύχνιδόν τε τὴν ἐν Ἠπειρώταις, καὶ Κόρινθον, αἳ δὴ πολυανθρωπόταται ἐκ παλαιοῦ ἦσαν. Ταύταις γὰρ ἁπαξαπάσαις ὑπὸ τοῦτον τὸν χρόνον

COURT OF JUSTINIAN 157

deities to inflict these misfortunes. The river Scirtus overflowed Edessa, and brought the most grievous calamities upon the inhabitants of the district, as I have already related. The Nile, having overflown its banks as usual, did not subside at the ordinary time, and caused great suffering among the people. The Cydnus was swollen, and nearly the whole of Tarsus lay for several days under water; and it did not subside until it had wrought irreparable damage to the city.

Several cities were destroyed by earthquake—Antioch, the chief city of the East, Seleucia, and Anazarbus, the most famous town in Cilicia. Who could calculate the numbers of those who were thereby destroyed? To these cities we may add Ibora, Amasea (the chief city of Pontus), Polybotus in Phrygia (called Polymede by the Pisidians), Lychnidus in Epirus, and Corinth, cities which from ancient times had been thickly populated. All these cities were overthrown at that time by an earthquake, during which nearly

ΠΡΟΚΟΠΙΟΥ ΑΝΕΚΔΟΤΑ

σεισμῷ τε καταπεσεῖν, καὶ τοῖς ᾠκημένοις σχεδόν τι πᾶσι ξυνδιολωλέναι τετύχηκεν. Ἐπιγενόμενος δὲ καὶ ὁ λοιμός, οὗ πρόσθεν ἐμνήσθην, τὴν ἡμίσειαν μάλιστα τῶν περιγινομένων ἀνθρώπων ἀπήνεγκε μοῖραν. Τοσούτων μὲν ἀνθρώπων ἐγίνετο φθόρος, Ἰουστινιανοῦ πρότερον Ῥωμαίοις διοικουμένου τὴν πολιτείαν, καὶ ὕστερον τὴν αὐτοκράτορα ἀρχὴν ἔχοντος.

COURT OF JUSTINIAN 158

all their inhabitants perished. Afterwards the plague (which I have spoken of before) began to rage, and swept away nearly half the survivors. Such were the disasters that afflicted mankind, from the day when Justinian first commenced to manage the affairs of the kingdom to the time, and after he had ascended the Imperial throne.

ΠΡΟΚΟΠΙΟΥ ΑΝΕΚΔΟΤΑ

ΚΕΦΑΛΑΙΟΝ ΙΘ'.

α'. "Οπως δὲ καὶ τὰ χρήματα ἀφείλετο ἀπαξάπαντα, ἐρῶν ἔρχομαι, ὄψιν ὀνείρου ὑπειπὼν πρότερον, ἥνπερ κατ᾽ ἀρχὰς τῆς Ἰουστινιανοῦ βασιλείας τῶν τινι ἐπιφανῶν ἰδεῖν ξυνηνέχθη. Ἔφη γάρ οἱ δοκεῖν ἐν τῷ ὀνείρῳ ἑστάναι μέν που ἐν Βυζαντίῳ παρὰ τὴν τῆς θαλάσσης ἠϊόνα, ἣ δὴ Χαλκηδόνος καταντικρύ ἐστιν, ὁρᾶν δὲ τοῦτον κατὰ τὸν ἐκείνῃ πορθμὸν ἑστῶτα μέσον. Καὶ πρῶτον μέντοι τὸ ὕδωρ τῆς θαλάσσης αὐτὸν ἐκπιεῖν ὅλον, ὥστε οἴεσθαι τὸ λοιπὸν αὐτὸν ἐπὶ τῆς ἠπείρου ἑστάναι, οὐκέτι τοῦ πορθμοῦ ταύτῃ ἐπιόντος· ἔπειτα ὕδωρ ἄλλο ῥύπου τε πολλοῦ καὶ φωρυτοῦ γέμον βρύσαν ἐξ ὑπονόμων ἑκατέρωθεν ὄντων ἐνταῦθα γενέσθαι· καὶ αὐτὸ μὲν τοῦτον ἐκπιεῖν ἅμα, γυμνόν τε αὖθις ἐξεργάσασθαι τοῦ πορθμοῦ χῶρον. Ἡ μὲν τοῦ ὀνείρου ὄψις ἐδήλου τοιαῦτα.

CHAPTER XIX

I WILL now relate the manner in which he got possession of the wealth of the world, after I have first mentioned a vision which was seen in a dream by a person of distinction at the commencement of his reign. He thought he was standing on the coast at Byzantium, opposite Chalcedon, and saw Justinian standing in the midst of the channel. The latter drank up all the water of the sea, so that it seemed as if he were standing on dry land, since the water no longer filled the strait. After this, other streams of water, full of filth and rubbish, flowing in from the underground sewers on either side, covered the dry land. Justinian again swallowed these, and the bed of the channel again became dry. Such was the vision this person beheld in his dream.

β'. Ἰουστινιανὸς δὲ οὗτος, ἡνίκα οἱ ὁ θεῖος Ἰουστῖνος τὴν βασιλείαν παρέλαβε, χρημάτων δημοσίων ἔμπλεων τὴν πολιτείαν εὗρεν. Ἀναστάσιος γὰρ, προνοητικώτατός τε ἅμα καὶ οἰκονομητικώτατος πάντων αὐτοκρα· τόρων γενόμενος, δείσας, ὅπερ ἐγένετο, μή οἱ ὁ τὴν βασιλείαν ἐκδεξόμενος, χρημάτων ὑπο· σπανίζων, ἴσως τοὺς κατηκόους ληΐζηται, χρυσοῦ τοὺς θησαυροὺς ἅπαντας κατακόρως ἐμπλη· σάμενος, τὸν βίον ξυνεμετρήσατο. Οὔσπερ ἅπαντας Ἰουστινιανὸς ὡς τάχιστα διεσπάσατο, ποῖ μὲν θαλασσίοις οἰκοδομίαις λόγον οὐκ ἐχούσαις, ποῖ δὲ τῇ ἐς τοὺς βαρβάρους φιλό· τητι· καίτοι ᾠήθη [. . . . .] ἄν τις αὐτὸ βασιλεῖ ἐς ἄγαν ἀσώτῳ ἐσομένῳ ἐτῶν ἑκατὸν ἐπαρκέσειν. Ἰσχυρίζοντο γὰρ οἱ τοῖς θησαυροῖς τε καὶ ἄλλοις ἅπασι τοῖς βασιλι· κοῖς χρήμασιν ἐφεστῶτες, Ἀναστασίου μὲν Ῥωμαίων ἔτη πλέον ἢ ἑπτὰ καὶ εἴκοσιν ἄρξαν· τος, διακόσια καὶ τρισχίλια χρυσοῦ κεντηνάρια ἐς τὴν βασιλείαν εἰσκομισθῆναι οὐδενὶ πόνῳ, καὶ τούτων ἁπάντων οὐδ' ὁτιοῦν ἀπολελεῖφθαι, ἀλλ', ἔτι περιόντος Ἰουστίνου, πρὸς τοῦδε τοῦ ἀνθρώπου δεδαπανῆσθαι, ᾗπέρ μοι ἐν τοῖς ἔμπροσθεν λόγοις εἴρηται.

γ'. Ἅπερ γὰρ αὐτὸς ἐν τῷ παντὶ χρόνῳ σφετερίζεσθαί τε οὐ δέον καὶ ἀναλοῦν ἴσχυσεν,

COURT OF JUSTINIAN 160

This Justinian, when his uncle Justin succeeded to the throne, found the treasury well filled, for Anastasius, the most provident and economical of all the Emperors, fearing (what actually happened) that his successor, if he found himself in want of money, would probably plunder his subjects, filled the treasure-houses with vast stores of gold before his death. Justinian exhausted all this wealth in a very short time, partly by senseless buildings on the coast, partly by presents to the barbarians, although one would have imagined that a successor, however profligate and extravagant, would have been unable to have spent it in a hundred years; for the superintendents of the treasures and other royal possessions asserted that Anastasius, during his reign of more than twenty-seven years, had without any difficulty accumulated 320,000 centenars, of which absolutely nothing remained, it having all been spent by this man during the lifetime of his uncle, as I have related above. It is impossible to describe or estimate the vast sums

οὐδ' ἄν τινα λόγον ἢ λογισμὸν ἢ μέτρον φανῆναι μηχανή τις οὐδεμία ἐστίν. Ὥσπερ γάρ τις ποταμὸς ἀέννaos, ἐς ἡμέραν ἑκάστην ἐκδηιούμενος κατελήιζετο τοὺς ὑπηκόους· ἐπέρρει δὲ ἅπαντα τοῖς βαρβάροις εὐθύς.

δ'. Πλοῦτον οὕτω τὸν δημόσιον εὐθὺς ἐκφορήσας, ἐπὶ τοὺς κατηκόους τὸ βλέμμα ἦγε· πλείστους τε αὐτίκα τὰς οὐσίας ἀφείλετο, ἁρπάζων τε καὶ βιαζόμενος οὐδενὶ λόγῳ, τῶν ἐγκλημάτων τε οὐδαμῆ γεγονότων, ὑπάγων τοὺς εὐδαίμονας ἔν τε Βυζαντίῳ καὶ πόλει ἑκάστῃ δοκοῦντας εἶναι.

ε'. Καὶ τοῖς μὲν πολυθείαν, τοῖς δὲ δόξης ἐν Χριστιανοῖς οὐκ ὀρθῆς αἵρεσιν, τοῖς δὲ παιδεραστίας, ἑτέροις ἱερῶν γυναικῶν ἔρωτας, ἢ ἄλλας τινὸς οὐ θεμιτὰς μίξεις, ἄλλοις στάσεως ἀφορμὴν, ἢ μέρους Πρασίνου στοργὴν, ἢ ἐς αὐτὸν ὑβρίζειν, ἢ ὄνομα ὁτιοῦν ἄλλο ἐπενεγκὼν, ἢ κληρονόμος αὐτόματος τοῖς τετελευτηκόσιν, ἢ καὶ περιοῦσιν, ἂν οὕτω τύχοι, γενόμενος. Αἱ γὰρ δὴ σεμνόταται τῶν πράξεων αὐτῷ τοιαῦται

COURT OF JUSTINIAN 161

which he appropriated to himself during his lifetime by illegal means and wasted in extravagance; for he swallowed up the fortunes of his subjects like an ever-flowing river, daily absorbing them in order to disgorge them amongst the barbarians. Having thus squandered the wealth of the State, he cast his eyes upon his private subjects. Most of them he immediately deprived of their possessions with unbounded rapacity and violence, at the same time bringing against the wealthy inhabitants of Byzantium, and those of other cities who were reputed to be so, charges utterly without foundation. Some were accused of polytheism, others of heresy; some of sodomy, others of amours with holy women; some of unlawful intercourse, others of attempts at sedition; some of favouring the Green faction, others of high treason, or any other charge that could be brought against them. On his own responsibility he made himself heir not only of the dead, but also of the living, as opportunity offered. In such matters he showed

21—2

162 ΠΡΟΚΟΠΙΟΥ ΑΝΕΚΔΟΤΑ

ἦσαν. Ὅπως δὲ καὶ τὴν γενομένην ἐπ' αὐτὸν στάσιν, ἣν Νίκα ἐκάλουν, διοικησάμενος, πᾶσι κληρονόμος τοῖς ἐκ βουλῆς εὐθὺς γέγονεν, ἤδη μοι ἔναγχος δεδιήγηται· καὶ ὅπως, τῆς στάσεως οὐκ ὀλίγῳ πρότερον, αὐτὸς ἰδίᾳ ἑκάστου τὴν οὐσίαν ἀφείλετο.

ς΄. Τοὺς δὲ βαρβάρους ἅπαντας, οὐδένα ἀνιεὶς καιρὸν, χρήμασιν ἐδωρεῖτο μεγάλοις, ἑῴους τε καὶ ἑσπερίνους, πρός τε ἄρκτον καὶ μεσημβρίαν, ἄχρι ἐς τοὺς ἐν Βρεττανίαις ᾠκημένους, καὶ γῆς πανταχόθι τῆς οἰκουμένης, ὧνπερ τὰ ἔθνη οὐδὲ ὅσον ἀκοῇ πρότερον εἴχομεν, ἀλλὰ πρῶτον ἰδόντες εἶτα τοῦ γένους ὄνομα ἔγνωμεν. Αὐτοί τε γὰρ πυνθανόμενοι τὸ τοῦ ἀνδρὸς ἦθος, ἐπ' αὐτὸν δὴ ἐκ πάσης γῆς ξυνέρρεον ἐς Βυζάντιον. Καὶ ὃς οὐδεμιᾷ ὀκνήσει, ἀλλ' ὑπερηδόμενος τῷ ἔργῳ τούτῳ, καί τι καὶ ἕρμαιον εἶναι οἰόμενος τὸν μὲν Ῥωμαίων ἐξαντλεῖν πλοῦτον, βαρβάροις δὲ ἀνθρώποις, ἢ ῥοθίοις τισὶ θαλαττίοις προτέσθαι, ἀεὶ καθ'

COURT OF JUSTINIAN 162

himself an accomplished diplomatist. I have
already mentioned above how he profited
by the sedition named Nika which was
directed against him, and immediately
made himself heir of all the members of
the Senate, and how, shortly before the
sedition broke out, he obtained possession
of the fortunes of private individuals. On
every occasion he bestowed handsome
presents upon all the barbarians alike,
those of East and West, and North and
South, as far as the inhabitants of the
British Islands and of the whole world,
nations of whom we had not even heard
before, and whose names we did not
know, until we became acquainted with
them through their ambassadors. When
these nations found out Justinian's disposition, they flocked to Byzantium from
all parts of the world to present themselves to him. He, without any hesitation, overjoyed at the occurrence, and
regarding it as a great piece of good luck
to be able to drain the Roman treasury
and fling its wealth to barbarians or the
waves of the sea, dismissed them every

ΠΡΟΚΟΠΙΟΥ ΑΝΕΚΔΟΤΑ

ἑκάστην αὐτῶν ἕκαστον ξὺν ἁδροῖς χρήμασιν ἀπεπέμπετο.

ζ. Ταύτῃ τε οἱ βάρβαροι ἅπαντες κύριοι τοῦ Ῥωμαίων παντάπασι γεγένηνται πλούτου, ἢ τὰ χρήματα πρὸς τοῦ βασιλέως κεκομισμένοι, ἢ ληιζόμενοι τὴν τῶν Ῥωμαίων ἀρχὴν, ἢ τοὺς αἰχμαλώτους ἀποδιδόμενοι, ἢ τὴν ἐκεχειρίαν ἀπεμπολοῦντες· τήν τε τοῦ ὀνείρου ὄψιν, ἧς ἄρτι ἐμνήσθην, ἐς τοῦτο τῷ ἰδόντι ἀποκεκρίσθαι τετύχηκε.

COURT OF JUSTINIAN 163

day loaded with handsome presents. In this manner the barbarians became absolute masters of the wealth of the Romans, either by the donations which they received from the Emperor, their pillaging of the Empire, the ransom of their prisoners, or their trafficking in truces. This was the signification of the dream which I have mentioned above.

ΠΡΟΚΟΠΙΟΥ ΑΝΕΚΔΟΤΑ

ΚΕΦΑΛΑΙΟΝ Κ΄.

α΄. Καὶ ἄλλους μέντοι ἐπιτεχνήσασθαι τῆς τῶν κατηκόων ληλασίας τρόπους ἴσχυσεν, οἵπερ, ἐς ὅσον δυνατὸς ἂν εἴην, αὐτίκα μάλα λελέξονται, δι' ὧν οὐκ ἀθρόως, ἀλλὰ κατὰ βραχὺ τὰς πάντων οὐσίας ληΐζεσθαι διαρκῶς ἔσχε. Πρῶτα τῷ δήμῳ (οἱ) ἔπαρχον ἐκ τοῦ ἐπὶ πλεῖστον ἐφίστη· ὃς δὴ ἔμελλε τοῖς τὰ πωλητήρια ἔχουσι πόρου ἔνου ἐνθένδε διαλαγχάνων ἐς τὴν ἐξουσίαν αὐτοὺς ἐμβιβάζειν τοῦ τὰ ὤνια, ὅπῃ βούλοιντο, ἀποδίδοσθαι. Καὶ περιειστήκει τοῖς τῇδε ἀνθρώποις ὠνεῖσθαι τὰ ἐπιτήδεια τριπλασίονα μὲν καταβαλλομένοις τιμήματα· ὅτῳ δὲ ἂν διὰ ταῦτα ἐπικαλοῖεν, οὐδαμῆ ἔχουσι. Μέγα τε τὸ ἀπὸ τοῦ ἔργου βλάβος ἠγείρετο. Μέρος γὰρ τῆς βασιλείας τοῦδε φερομένης τοῦ πόρου πλουτεῖν ἀπ' αὐτοῦ ἡ τῷ πράγματι ἐφεστῶσα ἀρχὴ ἤθελε. Τὸ δὲ ἐνθένδε, οἵ τε τῆς ἀρχῆς ὑπηρέται, τῆς αἰσχρᾶς

CHAPTER XX

BESIDES this, Justinian found other
means of contriving to plunder his subjects, not *en masse* and at once, but by
degrees and individually. These methods
I will now proceed to describe as well
as I am able. First of all he appointed
a new magistrate, who had the right of
conferring upon all those who kept shops
the privilege of selling their wares at
whatever price they pleased, on payment
of a yearly rent to the Emperor. The
citizens were compelled to make their
purchases in the market, where they paid
three times as much as elsewhere; nor,
although he suffered severe loss, was the
purchaser allowed to claim damages from
anyone, for part of the profit went to the
Emperor, and part to increase the salary
of these officials. Purchasers were equally

ΠΡΟΚΟΠΙΟΥ ΑΝΕΚΔΟΤΑ

ταύτης ὑπουργίας ἐπειλημμένοι, καὶ οἱ τὰ πωλητήρια ἔχοντες τῆς τοῦ παρανομεῖν ἐξουσίας δραξάμενοι, ἀνήκεστα ἔργα τοὺς τότε ὠνεῖσθαι δεομένους εἰργάζοντο, οὐχ ὅσον, ὡς εἴρηται, πολλαπλάσια τὰ τιμήματα κομιζόμενοι, ἀλλὰ καὶ δολώσεις ἐν τοῖς ὠνίοις μηχανώμενοι ἀμυθήτους τινάς.

β'. Ἔπειτα δὲ πολλὰ καταστησάμενος τὰ καλούμενα μονοπώλια, τήν τε κατηκόων ἐλευθερίαν ἀπεμπολήσας τοῖς τὸ ἄγος τοῦτο ἐνεργολαβεῖν ἀξιοῦσιν, αὐτὸς μὲν τίμημα τοῦ ἔργου τούτου ἀντιφορτισάμενος, ἀπηλλάσσετο· τοῖς δὲ αὐτῷ ξυμβεβληκόσι παρείχετο τὴν ἐργασίαν ᾗ βούλοιντο διοικήσασθαι· ὅπερ ἀπαρακαλύπτως ἡμαρτάνετο κἀν ταῖς ἄλλαις ἀπάσαις ἀρχαῖς. Βασιλέως γὰρ ἀεὶ μοῖράν τινα οὐ πολλὴν τῶν φωρίων κομιζομένου, αἵ τε ἀρχαὶ ἀπ' αὐτοῦ καὶ οἱ πράγματι ἐφεστῶτες ἑκάστῳ ἀδεέστερον τοὺς σφίσι παραπίπτοντας ἐληΐζοντο.

γ'. Ὥσπερ δὲ οἱ οὐχ ἱκανῶν ἐς τοῦτο

COURT OF JUSTINIAN 165

cheated by the magistrates' servants, who took part in these disgraceful transactions, while the shopkeepers, who were allowed to put themselves beyond reach of the law, inflicted great hardships upon their customers—not merely by raising their prices many times over, but by being guilty of unheard-of frauds in regard to their wares. Afterwards, Justinian instituted several "monopolies," as they were called, and sold the liberty of the subject to any who were willing to undertake this disgraceful traffic, after having settled with them the price that was to be paid. This done, he allowed those with whom he had made the bargain to carry out the management of the affair in whatever way they thought fit. He made these disgraceful arrangements, without any attempt at concealment, with all the other magistrates, who plundered their subjects with less apprehension, either themselves or through their agents, since some part of the profits of the plunder always fell to the share of the Emperor. Under the pretence that the former

166 ΠΡΟΚΟΠΙΟΥ ΑΝΕΚΔΟΤΑ

οὐσῶν τῶν πάλαι διατεταγμένων ἀρχῶν, ἑτέρας δύο ἐπὶ τῇ πολιτείᾳ ἐπετεχνήσατο· καίτοι
ἅπαντα μετῄει πρότερον τὰ ἐγκλήματα ἡ τῷ
δήμῳ ἐφεστῶσα Ἀρχή. Ἀλλ' ὅπως ἀεὶ πλείους τέ οἱ συκοφάνται εἶεν, καὶ πολλῷ ἔτι θᾶσσον τῶν οὐδὲν ἐπταικότων τὰ σώματα αἰκί-
ζοιτο, ταύτας δὴ τὰς ἀρχὰς ἐπινοεῖν ἔγνω.
Καὶ αὐταῖν τὴν ἑτέραν μὲν τοῖς κλέπταις δῆθεν τῷ λόγῳ ἐπέστησεν, ὄνομα ταύτῃ ἐπιθεὶς
Πραίτωρα δήμου· τῇ δὲ δὴ ἑτέρᾳ τούς τε
παιδεραστοῦντας ἐς ἀεὶ τίννυσθαι καὶ γυναιξὶν
οὐ νόμιμα μιγνυμένους ἐπήγγελλε, καὶ εἴ τῳ
τὰ ἐς τὸ θεῖον οὐκ ὀρθῶς ἤσκηται, ὄνομα ταύτῃ
ἐπιθεὶς Κοιαίστωρα.

δ'. Ὁ μὲν οὖν Πραίτωρ, εἴ τινα ἐν τοῖς
φωρίοις λόγου πολλοῦ ἄξια εὗρε, ταῦτα δὴ τῷ
αὐτοκράτορι ἀποφέρειν ἠξίου, φάσκων οὐδαμῆ
φαίνεσθαι τοὺς τούτων κυρίους. Ταύτῃ τε
χρημάτων ἀεὶ τῶν τιμιωτάτων διαλαγχάνειν ὁ
βασιλεὺς εἶχεν. Ὁ δὲ δὴ Κοιαίστωρ καλούμενος, τοὺς παραπεπτωκότας κατεργαζόμενος,
ἃ μὲν βούλοιτο ἔφερεν· αὐτὸς δὲ οὐδὲν ἧσσον
ἐπλούτει τοῖς ἀλλοτρίοις οὐδενὶ νόμῳ. Οἱ γὰρ

COURT OF JUSTINIAN 166

magistrates were insufficient to carry
out these arrangements (although the
city prefect had previously been able to
deal with all criminal charges) he created
two new ones. His object in this was,
that he might have at his disposal a
larger number of informers, and that he
might the more easily inflict punishment
and torture upon the innocent. One of
these was called Praetor of the People,
whose nominal duty it was to deal with
thieves; the second was called the Commissioner, whose function it was to punish
all cases of paederasty, buggery, superstition and heresy. If the Praetor found
any articles of value amongst stolen
goods, he handed them over to the Emperor, declaring that no owner could be
found for them, and in this manner
Justinian every day got possession of something of very great value. The Commissioner, after he had condemned offenders,
confiscated what he pleased out of their
estates and bestowed it upon the Emperor,
who thus, in defiance of the law, enriched
himself out of the fortunes of others; for

ΠΡΟΚΟΠΙΟΥ ΑΝΕΚΔΟΤΑ

δὴ τούτων τῶν ἀρχῶν ὑπηρέται οὔτε κατ᾽
ἀρχὰς κατηγόρους ἐπήγοντο, οὔτε μάρτυρας
τῶν πεπραγμένων παρείχοντο· ἀλλὰ διηνεκὲς
πάντα τοῦτον τὸν χρόνου ἀκατηγόρητοί τε καὶ
ἀνεξέλεγκτοι, ὡς λαθραιότατα, ἐντυχόντες, ἐκ-
τείνοντό τε καὶ ἀφῃροῦντο τὰ χρήματα.

ε΄. Ὕστερον δὲ ὁ παλαμναῖος οὗτος ταύταις τε καὶ τῇ τῷ δήμῳ ἐφεστώσῃ ἀρχῇ πάντων ὁμοίως ἐπιμελεῖσθαι τῶν ἐγκλημάτων ἐπέστελλεν, ἐρίζειν σφίσιν πρὸς ἀλλήλους εἰπὼν,
ὅστις αὐτῶν πλείους τε καὶ θᾶσσον διαφθείρειν
ἱκανὸς εἴη. Καὶ αὐτῶν ἕνα μὲν αὐτὸν εὐθὺς
ἐρέσθαι φασίν· ἢν ἐς τοὺς τρεῖς τίς ποτε δια-
βάλλοιτο, τίνος ἂν αὐτῶν ἡ τοῦ πράγματος
διάγνωσις εἴη· τὸν δὲ ὑπολαβόντα φάναι, ὅστις
ἂν αὐτῶν προτερήσας τοὺς ἄλλους φθάνοι.

ς΄. Ἀλλὰ καὶ τὴν τοῦ Κοιαίστωρος
καλουμένην ἀρχὴν διέθετο οὐδενὶ κόσμῳ, ᾗσπερ
διαφερόντως ἐπεμελῶντο οἱ πρότερον βεβασιλευκότες, ὡς εἰπεῖν, ἅπαντες, ὅπως τά τε
ἄλλα ἔμπειροι καὶ σοφοὶ, καὶ τὰ ἐς τοὺς

COURT OF JUSTINIAN 167

the servants of these magistrates did not even take the trouble at the commencement of the trial to bring forward accusers or to produce any witnesses to the offences, but, during the whole of this period, without intermission, unexamined and unconvicted, the accused were secretly punished by death and the confiscation of their property by the Emperor.

Afterwards, this accursed wretch ordered both these magistrates and the city prefect to deal with all criminal affairs indifferently, bidding them enter into rivalry to see which of them could destroy the greatest number of citizens in the shortest time. It is said that, when one of them asked him which of them should have the decision if anyone was accused before all three, he replied, " Whichever of you has anticipated the others."

He debased the office of Quaestor, which almost all the preceding Emperors had held in especial regard, so that it was only filled by men of wisdom and experience, who above all were learned

168 ΠΡΟΚΟΠΙΟΥ ΑΝΕΚΔΟΤΑ

νόμους μάλιστα εἶεν οἱ ταύτην διαχειρίσαντες, καὶ χρημάτων διαφανῶς ἀδωρότατοι, ὡς οὐκ ἄνευ μεγάλου ὀλέθρου τούτου γε τῇ πολιτείᾳ γενησομένου, εἴπερ οἱ ταύτην τὴν ἀρχὴν ἔχοντες ἢ ἀπειρίᾳ τινὶ ἔχοιντο ἢ φιλοχρηματίᾳ ἐφεῖντο.

ζ. Ὁ δὲ βασιλεὺς οὗτος πρῶτον μὲν ἐπὶ ταύτης Τριβωνιανὸν κατεστήσατο, οὗπερ τὰ ἐπιτηδεύματα ἐν τοῖς ἔμπροσθεν λόγοις διαρκῶς εἴρηται. Ἐπεὶ δὲ ὁ Τριβωνιανὸς ἐξ ἀνθρώπων ἠφάνιστο, μοῖραν μὲν αὐτοῦ τῆς οὐσίας ἀφείλετο, καίτοι παιδός τέ οἱ ἀπολελειμμένου καὶ πλήθους ἐκγόνων· ἐπεγένετο τῷ ἀνθρώπῳ ἡ τέλειος ἡμέρα τοῦ βίου. Ἰούνιλον δὲ, Λίβυν γένος, ἐπὶ τῆς τιμῆς κατεστήσατο ταύτης, νόμου δὲ οὐδὲ ὡς ἀκοὴν ἔχοντα, ἐπεὶ οὐδὲ τῶν ῥητόρων τις ἦν, γράμματα δὲ Λατῖνα μὲν ἐξεπιστάμενον, Ἑλληνικῶν μέντοι ἔνεκα οὐδὲ πεφοιτηκότα πρὸς γραμματιστοῦ πώποτε, οὐδὲ τὴν γλῶτταν αὐτὴν ἑλληνίζειν δυνάμενον. Πολλάκις ἀμέλει φωνὴν Ἑλληνίδα προθυμηθεὶς ἀφεῖναι, πρὸς τῶν ὑπηρετούντων γέλωτα ὦφλε· ἐς δὲ τὴν αἰσχροκέρδειαν δαιμονίως ἐσπουδακότα, ὅς γε γράμματα μὲν τὰ βασιλέως ἐν δημοσίῳ ἀπεμπολῶν ὡς ἥκιστα κατεδέετο. Ἑνὸς δὲ στατῆρος χρυσοῦ

COURT OF JUSTINIAN   168

in the law and free from all suspicion of corruptibility, for it was felt that it would unavoidably be disastrous to the State if it were to be filled by men without experience or who were the slaves of avarice. This Emperor first bestowed it upon Tribonianus, whose character and misdeeds I have sufficiently described elsewhere. After his death, Justinian seized part of his estate, although he had left a son and several relatives who survived him. He then appointed Junilus (a Libyan by birth), a man who had not so much as a hearsay knowledge of law, for he had not even studied it in the public schools. Although he had a knowledge of Latin, he had never had any tuition in Greek, and was unable to speak the language. Frequently, when he attempted to say a few words in Greek, he was laughed at by his own servants. He was so mad after filthy lucre, that he had not the least scruple in publicly selling letters of office signed by the Emperor, and was never ashamed to stretch out his hand to those who

22

ΠΡΟΚΟΠΙΟΥ ΑΝΕΚΔΟΤΑ

ἔνεκα τὴν χεῖρα ὀρέγειν τοῖς ἐντυγχάνουσιν οὐδαμῆ ὤκνει. Οὐχ ἦσσόν τε ἢ ἑπτὰ ἐνιαυτῶν χρόνον τούτου ἡ πολιτεία τὸν γέλωτα ὦφλεν.

θ'. Ἐπεὶ δὲ καὶ Ἰούνιλος ἐς τὸ μέτρον τοῦ βίου ἀφίκετο, Κωνσταντῖνον ἐπὶ τοῦδε τοῦ ἀξιώματος κατεστήσατο, νόμων μὲν ὄντα οὐκ ἀμελέτητον, νέον δὲ κομιδῆ, καὶ οὔπω ἀγωνίας δικανικῆς εἰς πεῖραν ἐλθόντα, κλεπτίστατον δὲ καὶ ἀλαζονικώτατον ἀνθρώπων ἀπάντων. Οὗτος Ἰουστινιανῷ ποθεινότατός τε ἄγαν καὶ φίλτατος ἐν τοῖς μάλιστα ἐγεγόνει, ἐπεὶ καὶ δι' αὐτοῦ κλέπτειν τε καὶ δικάζειν ὁ βασιλεὺς οὗτος ἀεὶ οὐδαμῆ ἀπηξίου. Διὸ δὴ χρήματα μεγάλα, χρόνου ὀλίγου, Κωνσταντῖνος ἔσχε, καὶ ὑπερφυεῖ τινι κόμπῳ ἐχρῆτο, ἀεροβατῶν τε καὶ πάντας ἀνθρώπους περιφρονῶν· κἂν μέν τινες αὐτῷ πολλὰ βούλοιντο χρήματα προέσθαι, ταῦτα δὴ κατατιθέντες τῶν οἱ πιστοτάτων τισί, τὰ σφίσιν ἐσπουδασμένα κατορθοῦν ἴσχυον. Αὐτῷ μέντοι ἐντυχεῖν ἢ ξυγγενέσθαι τῶν πάντων οὐδενὶ γέγονε δυνατόν, ὅτι μὴ ἐς βασιλέα δρόμῳ ἰόντι, ἢ ἀπαλλασσομένῳ ἐνθένδε, οὐ

COURT OF JUSTINIAN 169

had to do with him for a stater of gold. For no less than seven years the State endured the shame and ridicule brought upon it by this officer.

On the death of Junilus, Justinian elevated to this office Constantine, who was not unacquainted with law, but was very young and had never yet taken part in a trial; besides which, he was the most abandoned thief and braggart in the world. Justinian entertained the highest regard for him and showed him very great favour, condescending to make him the chief instrument of his extortion and sole arbiter in legal decisions. By this means Constantine in a short time amassed great wealth, but his insolence was outrageous, and his pride led him to treat everyone with contempt. Even those who were desirous of making him considerable presents were obliged to intrust them to those who seemed to be most in his confidence, for no one was permitted to approach or converse with him, except when he was hurrying to or returning from the Emperor. Even then

ΠΡΟΚΟΠΙΟΥ ΑΝΕΚΔΟΤΑ

βάδην, ἀλλὰ σπουδῇ τε καὶ τάχει πολλῷ, τοῦ μή τινά οἱ ἀκερδῆ ἀσχολίαν τοὺς προσιόντας προστρίβεσθαι. Ταῦτα μὲν οὖν τῇδε βασιλεῖ τῷδε εἶχεν.

COURT OF JUSTINIAN 170

he did not slacken his pace, but walked on hastily, for fear that those who approached him might waste his time without paying for it. Such was the manner in which Justinian dealt with the Quaestorship.

ΚΕΦΑΛΑΙΟΝ ΚΑ'.

α'. Πρὸς δὲ τοῦ τῶν Πραιτωρίων ἐπάρχου ἀνὰ πᾶν ἔτος πλέον ἢ τριάκοντα κεντηνάρια πρὸς τοῖς δημοσίοις ἐπράσσετο φόροις, οἷς δὴ ὄνομα τὸ ἀερικὸν ἐπιτέθεικεν, ἐκεῖνο, οἶμαι, παραδηλῶν, ὅτι δὴ οὐ τεταγμένη τις, οὐδὲ ξυνειθισμένη οὖσα ἡ φορὰ ἐτύγχανεν αὕτη, ἀλλὰ τύχῃ τινὶ ὥσπερ ἐξ ἀέρος ἀεὶ αὐτὴν φερομένην ἐλάμβανε, δέον τῆς πονηρίας τῆς αὐτοῦ ταῦτα ἐπικαλεῖν ἔργα. Ὧν δὴ τῷ ὀνόματι οἱ ἐπὶ τῆς ἀρχῆς τεταγμένοι ἀδεέστερον ἀεὶ ταῖς ἐς τοὺς κατηκόους λῃστείαις ἐχρῶντο. Καὶ ταῦτα μὲν τῷ αὐτοκράτορι ἀποφέρειν ἠξίουν· αὐτοὶ δὲ πλοῦτον βασιλικὸν περιεβάλλοντο οὐδενὶ πόνῳ. Ὧνπερ Ἰουστινιανὸς ἐπιστροφὴν οὐδεμίαν ἐδικαίου ποιεῖσθαι, καιροφυλακῶν ὅπως, ἐπειδὰν τάχιστα πλούτου τι μέγα περιβάλλονται χρῆμα, ὅ τι

CHAPTER XXI

THE Praefect of the supreme tribunals, besides the public tax, annually paid to the Emperor more than thirty centenars of gold. This sum was called the "aerial tribute," doubtless because it was no regular or usual one, but seemed to have fallen as it were by chance from Heaven, whereas it ought rather to have been called "the impost of his wickedness," for it served as a pretext to those functionaries, who were invested with high power, to plunder their subjects incessantly without fear of punishment. They pretended that they had to hand over the tribute to the Emperor, and they themselves, without any difficulty, acquired sufficient sums to secure regal affluence for themselves. Justinian allowed them to go on unchecked and unheeded, waiting until they had amassed great wealth,

δὴ αὐτοῖς ἐπενεγκὼν ἀπροφάσιστον, ἀθρόον αὐτοῖς ἀφαιρεῖσθαι τὴν οὐσίαν ἱκανὸς εἴη, ὅπερ Ἰωάννην τὸν Καππαδόκην εἰργάσατο.

β'. Ἅπαντες οὖν ἀμέλει, ὅσοι τῆς τιμῆς ὑπὸ τὸν χρόνον τοῦτον ἐλάμβανον, πλούσιοι ἐξαπιναίως οὐδενὶ γεγένηνται μέτρῳ· δυοῖν μέντοι χωρὶς, Φωκᾶ τε, οὗπερ ἐν τοῖς ἔμπροσθεν λόγοις ἐμνήσθην, (ἅτε τοῦ δικαίου ἐς τὸ ἀκρότατον ἐπιμελητοῦ γεγονότος· κέρδους γὰρ ὁτουοῦν οὗτος ὁ ἀνὴρ ἐν τῷ ἀξιώματι καθαρὸς ἔμεινε)· καὶ Βάσσου, ὃς δὴ ἐν χρόνῳ τῷ ὑστέρῳ τὴν ἀρχὴν ἔλαβεν. Ὧνπερ οὐδέτερος ἐνιαυτὸν διασώσασθαι τὴν τιμὴν ἔσχεν, ἀλλ' ἀχρεῖοί τε καὶ τοῦ καιροῦ τὸ παράπαν ἀλλόκοτοι μηνῶν που ὀλίγων τοῦ ἀξιώματος ἔξω γεγένηνται. Ἵνα δὲ μὴ, τὸ καθ' ἕκαστόν μοι διηγουμένῳ, ἀτελεύτητος ὁ λόγος εἴη, ταὐτὰ κἂν ταῖς ἄλλαις ἐπράσσετο ταῖς ἐν Βυζαντίῳ ἀρχαῖς.

γ'. Πανταχόθι μέντοι τῆς Ῥωμαίων γῆς ὁ Ἰουστινιανὸς ἐποίει τάδε. Τοὺς πονηροτάτους τῶν ἀνθρώπων ἀπολεξάμενος, διεφ-

COURT OF JUSTINIAN 172

when it was his practice to bring against them some charge from which they could not readily clear themselves, and to confiscate the whole of their property, as he had treated John of Cappadocia. All those who held this office during his reign became wealthy to an extraordinary degree, and suddenly, with two exceptions. One of these was Phocas, of whom I have spoken in my previous writings—a man in the highest degree observant of integrity and honesty; who, during his tenure of office, was free from all suspicion of illegal gain. The other was Bassus, who was appointed later. Neither of them enjoyed their dignity for a year. At the end of a few months they were deprived of it as being incapable and unsuited to the times. But, not to go into details in every case, which would be endless, I will merely say that it was the same with all the other magistrates of Byzantium.

In all the cities throughout the Empire, Justinian selected for the highest offices the most abandoned persons he

ΠΡΟΚΟΠΙΟΥ ΑΝΕΚΔΟΤΑ

θάρθαι ἀπεδίδοτο τὰς ἀρχὰς σφίσι χρημάτων μεγάλων. Σώφρονι γὰρ ἀνδρὶ, ἢ ξυνέσεως ὁπωστιοῦν μεταλαχόντι, ἔννοια οὐδεμία ἐγένετο χρήματα οἰκεῖα προΐεσθαι, ἐφ' ᾧ δὴ τοὺς οὐδὲν ἠδικηκότας ληΐζηται. Τοῦτό τε τὸ χρυσίον πρὸς τῶν ξυμβαλλόντων κεκομισμένος, ἐς τὴν ἐξουσίαν αὐτοὺς ἐνεβίβαζε τοῦ τοὺς κατηκόους πάντα ἐργάζεσθαι. Ἀφ' ὧν ἔμελλον τὰς χώρας αὐτοῖς ἀνθρώποις ἀπολοῦντες ἀπάσας πλούσιοι τὸ λοιπὸν ἔσεσθαι αὐτοί. Οἱ δὲ τὰς τῶν πόλεων τιμὰς ἐπὶ τόκοις ἀδροῖς τισιν ἀπὸ τῆς τραπέζης δεδανεισμένοι, καὶ τῷ ἀποδεδομένῳ ἀπαριθμήσαντες, ἐπειδὴ ἐγένοντο ἐν ταῖς πόλεσι, πᾶσαν κακοῦ ἰδέαν ἐς τοὺς ἀρχομένους ἀεὶ ἐνδεικνύμενοι, οὐκ ἄλλου του ἐν ἐπιμελείᾳ καθίσταντο, ἢ ὅπως τοῖς χρήσταις τὰ ὡμολογημένα τελέσειαν, καὶ αὐτοὶ τὸ λοιπὸν ἐν τοῖς πλουσιωτάτοις τετάξονται, οὐκ ἔχοντος αὐτοῖς κίνδυνόν τινα ἢ ὕβριν τοῦ ἔργου· φέροντος δέ τι καὶ δόξης μᾶλλον, ὅσῳ καὶ

COURT OF JUSTINIAN 173

could find, and sold to them for vast sums the positions which they degraded. In fact, no honest man, possessed of the least common sense, would ever have thought of risking his own fortune in order to plunder those who had committed no offence. When Justinian had received the money from those with whom he made the bargain, he gave them full authority to deal with their subjects as they pleased, so that, by the destruction of provinces and populations, they might enrich themselves in the future; for, since they had borrowed large sums from the bankers at heavy rates of interest to purchase their magistracies, and had paid the sum due to him who sold them, when they arrived in the cities, they treated their subjects with every kind of tyranny, paying heed to nothing save how they might fulfil their engagements with their creditors and lay up great wealth for themselves. They had no apprehension that their conduct would bring upon them the risk of punishment; on the contrary, they expected that the greater

πλείους τῶν σφίσι παραπεπτωκότων οὐδενὶ
λόγῳ ἀποκτείναντες ληΐζεσθαι ἴσχυον. Τὸ
γὰρ τοῦ φονέως τε καὶ λῃστοῦ ὄνομα ἐς τὸ
τοῦ δραστηρίου αὐτοῖς ἀποκεκρίσθαι ξυνέβαινεν. Ὅσους μέντοι τῶν ἐχόντων ἀρχὰς
ᾔσθετο πλούτῳ ἀκμάζοντας, τούτους δὲ σκή-
ψεσι σαγηνεύσας, εὐθὺς ἅπαντα συλλήβδην
ἀφῃρεῖτο τὰ χρήματα.

δ΄. Μετὰ δὲ νόμον τοὺς τὰς ἀρχὰς
ἔγραψε μετιόντας ὀμνύναι, ἦ μὴν καθαροὺς
ἀπὸ πάσης κλοπῆς σφᾶς αὐτοὺς ἔσεσθαι,
καὶ μήτε τι δώσειν τῆς ἀρχῆς ἕνεκα, μήτε
λήψεσθαι· ἀράς τε πάσας ἐπέβαλεν, ὅσαι
πρὸς τῶν παλαιοτάτων ὠνομασμέναι εἰσίν,
ἤν τις τῶν γεγραμμένων ἐκβαίη. Ἀλλὰ
τοῦ νόμου τεθέντος οὔπω ἐνιαυτὸν, αὐτὸς
μὲν τῶν γεγραμμένων καὶ κατηραμένων ὀλιγω-
ρήσας καὶ τῆς ὑπὲρ τούτων αἰσχύνης ἀδεέστερον τὰ τιμήματα τῶν ἀρχῶν, οὐκ ἐν
παραβύστῳ, ἀλλ᾽ ἐς τὸ δημόσιον τῆς ἀγορᾶς,
ἔπραττεν. Οἱ δὲ τὰς ἀρχὰς ὠνημένοι, διώ-
μοτοι μᾶλλον ἢ πρότερον, πάντα ἐσύλων.

COURT OF JUSTINIAN   174

the number of those whom they plundered or put to death without cause, the greater the reputation they would attain, for the name of murderer and robber was regarded as a proof of activity. But when Justinian learned that they had amassed considerable wealth during office, he entangled them in his net, and on some pretence or other deprived them of all their riches in a moment.

He had published an edict that candidates for offices should swear that they would keep themselves free from extortion, that they would neither give nor receive anything for their offices, and uttered against those who transgressed the law the most violent curses of ancient times. The law had not been in force a year when, forgetting its terms and the malediction which had been pronounced, he shamelessly put up these offices for sale, not secretly, but publicly in the market-place, and those who purchased them, in spite of their oaths to the contrary, plundered and ravaged with greater audacity than before.

ε΄. Ύστερον δὲ καὶ ἄλλο τι ἐπετεχνήσατο, ἀκοῆς κρεῖσσον. Τῶν ἀρχῶν, ἅσπερ ἀξιωτάτας ἔν τε Βυζαντίῳ καὶ πόλεσι ταῖς ἄλλαις ᾤετο εἶναι, οὐκέτι ἀπεμπολεῖν ἔγνω ᾗπερ τὰ πρότερα, μισθωτοὺς δὲ διερευνώμενος, ἐχειροτόνει· τάξας αὐτοῖς ὅ τι δὴ μισθαρνοῦντας ἀποφέρειν αὑτῷ τὰ χωρία πάντα. Οἱ δὲ τὴν μίσθωσιν κεκομισμένοι, ἀδεέστερον ξυμφορήσαντες ἐκ πάσης γῆς ἅπαντα ἔφερον, καὶ περιήρχετο μισθοφόρος ἐξουσία, τῷ τῆς ἀρχῆς ὀνόματι, καταληϊζομένη τοὺς ὑπηκόους.

ς΄. Οὕτως ὁ βασιλεὺς ἀκριβολογούμενος τὸν ἅπαντα χρόνον, ἐκείνους ἐφίστη τοῖς πράγμασιν, οἳ δὴ πάντων κατὰ τὸν ἀληθῆ λόγον μιαρώτατοι ἦσαν, ἀεί τε τὸ κακὸν τοῦτο ἰχνηλατῶν κατετύγχανεν. Ἡνίκα οὖν ἀμέλει τοὺς πρώτους πονηροὺς ἐπὶ τῆς ἀρχῆς κατεστήσατο, ἐς φῶς τε αὐτῶν ἡ τῆς δυνάμεως ἐξουσία τὴν κακοτροπίαν ἐξήνεγκεν, ἐθαυμάζομέν γε ὅπως δὴ κακότητα τοσαύτην ἀνθρώπου φύσις ἐχώρησεν. Ἐπεὶ δὲ αὐτοὺς οἱ χρόνῳ τῳ

COURT OF JUSTINIAN 175

He afterwards thought of another contrivance, which may seem incredible. He resolved no longer to put up for sale, as before, the offices which he believed to be of greatest repute in Byzantium and other cities, but sought out a number of hired persons, whom he appointed at a fixed salary, and ordered to bring all the revenues to himself. These men, having received their salary, shamelessly got together from every country and carried off everything that they could. The stipendiary commission went from one place to another, plundering the subjects of the Empire in the name of their office.

Thus the Emperor exercised in every case the greatest care in the selection of these agents of his, who were truly the greatest scoundrels in the world; nor were his efforts and industry in this detestable business unsuccessful. When he advanced the first of his wicked agents to high offices, and the licence of authority revealed their corruption, we were astounded to think how the nature of man could be capable of such enormity. But

176 ΠΡΟΚΟΠΙΟΥ ΑΝΕΚΔΟΤΑ

ἀρχὰς ἐκδεξάμενοι πολλῷ τῷ περιόντι παρελᾶν ἴσχυσαν, διηποροῦντο πρὸς ἀλλήλους οἱ ἄνθρωποι, ὅντινα τρόπον οἱ πρόσθεν πονηρότατοι δόξαντες τοσούτῳ παραλόγῳ, ἅτε αὐτοὶ καλοὶ καὶ ἀγαθοὶ γεγονότες ἐν τοῖς σφετέροις ἐπιτηδεύμασι πρὸς τῶν ἐπιγεγενημένων ἡσσήθησαν, αὖθίς τε οἱ τρίτοι τοὺς δευτέρους ὑπερηκόντισαν πονηρίᾳ τῇ πάσῃ, καὶ μετ' ἐκείνους ἕτεροι, τοῖς τῶν ἐγκλημάτων καινοτομήμασιν, ὄνομα χρηστὸν τοῖς φθάσασι προσετρίψαντο. Μηκυνομένου δὲ τοῦ κακοῦ, πᾶσιν ἐκμεμαθηκέναι τῷ ἔργῳ ξυνέβη, ὅτι δὴ τοῖς ἀνθρώποις ἐπ' ἄπειρον μὲν ἡ πονηρία φύεσθαι εἴωθε, μαθήσει δὲ τῶν προγεγενημένων ἐκτρεφομένη, καὶ τῇ τῆς παρουσίας ἐξουσίᾳ ἐς τὸ λυμαίνεσθαι τοῖς παραπίπτουσιν ἐξαγομένη, ἐς τοσόνδε ἀεὶ ἐξικνεῖσθαι δοκεῖ, ἐς ὅσον δύναται ἡ τῶν βλαπτομένων σταθμᾶσθαι δόξα. Ῥωμαίοις μὲν οὖν τά γε ἀμφὶ τοῖς ἄρχουσι ταύτῃ πῃ εἶχε.

ζ'. Πολλάκις δὲ καὶ Οὔννων πολεμίων στρατῷ ἀνδραποδίσασί τε καὶ ληισαμένοις

COURT OF JUSTINIAN 176

when those who succeeded them far outdid them, men were at a loss to understand how their predecessors could have appeared the most wicked of mankind, since, in comparison with their successors, who had surpassed them in evil-doing, they might be considered good and honest men. But the third set and their successors so far outstripped the second in every kind of villainy, and in their cleverness in inventing new accusations, that they secured for their predecessors a certain reputation and a good name. As the misfortunes of the State increased, all learned by experience that there is no limit to the innate wickedness of man, and that, when it is supported by the knowledge of precedents, and encouraged by the power in its hands to torment its victims, no man can tell how far it will extend, but only the thoughts of the oppressed are capable of estimating it. Such was the state of affairs in regard to the magistrates.

The hostile armies of the Huns had often reduced to slavery and plundered

ΠΡΟΚΟΠΙΟΥ ΑΝΕΚΔΟΤΑ

τὴν Ῥωμαίων ἀρχὴν οἱ Θρᾳκῶν τε καὶ Ἰλλυριῶν στρατηγοί, βεβουλευμένοι ἀναχωροῦσιν ἐπιθήσεσθαι, ἀνεπήδησαν, ἐπεὶ βασιλέως Ἰουστινιανοῦ γράμματα εἶδον, ἀπεροῦντα σφίσι τὴν ἐς τοὺς βαρβάρους ἐπίθεσιν, ἀναγκαίων αὐτῶν ἐς ξυμμαχίαν Ῥωμαίοις ὄντων ἐπὶ Γότθους ἴσως ἢ ἐπὶ ἄλλους πολεμίων τινάς.

η΄. Καὶ ἀπ᾽ αὐτοῦ οἱ βάρβαροι οὗτοι ἐληΐζοντο μὲν ὡς πολέμιοι, καὶ ἠνδραποδίζοντο τοὺς τῇδε Ῥωμαίους· ξὺν δὲ τῇ ἄλλῃ λείᾳ καὶ τοῖς αἰχμαλώτοις, ἅτε φίλοι καὶ ξύμμαχοι Ῥωμαίοις ὄντες, ἐπ᾽ οἴκου ἀπεκομίζοντο. Πολλάκις δὲ καὶ γεωργῶν τῶν ἐνταῦθά τινες, παίδων τε σφετέρων καὶ γυναικῶν πόθῳ ἐξηνδραποδισμένων ἠγμένοι, ἀθρόοι τε γεγενημένοι, ἀναχωροῦσι πολλοὺς κτείναντες, καὶ αὐτῶν τοὺς ἵππους ἴσχυσαν ξὺν πάσῃ ἀφελέσθαι τῇ λείᾳ· πραγμάτων μέντοι ἐς πεῖραν ἦλθον ἐνθένδε δυσκόλων. Ἐκ Βυζαντίου γάρ τινες ἐσταλμένοι, αἰκίζεσθαί τε

COURT OF JUSTINIAN   177

the inhabitants of the Empire. The
Thracian and Illyrian generals resolved to
attack them on their retreat, but turned
back, when they were shown letters
from the Emperor forbidding them to
attack the barbarians, on pretence that
their help was necessary to the Romans
against the Goths and other enemies of
the Empire.

Making use of this opportunity, these
barbarians plundered the country like
enemies, and carried away the inhabitants
into slavery; and in this manner these
pretended friends and allies of the Romans
returned home with their plunder and a
number of prisoners. Frequently, some
of the peasants in those parts, urged on
by a longing for their wives and children
who had been carried away into slavery,
formed themselves into bands, marched
against the barbarians, slew a number of
them, and succeeded in capturing their
horses together with their plunder. This
success, however, proved very unfortunate
for them ; for agents were sent from Byzantium, who had no hesitation in beating

23—2

ΠΡΟΚΟΠΙΟΥ ΑΝΕΚΔΟΤΑ

αὐτῶν καὶ λωβᾶσθαι τὰ σώματα, καὶ χρήμασι ζημιοῦν οὐδεμιᾷ ὀκνήσει ἠξίουν, ἕως τοὺς ἵππους ἅπαντας δοῖεν, οὕσπερ τοὺς βαρβάρους ἀφείλοντο.

and wounding them and seizing their property, until they had restored all the horses that they had taken from the barbarians.

ΚΕΦΑΛΑΙΟΝ ΚΒ'.

α'. Ἡνίκα δὲ βασιλεύς τε καὶ Θεοδώρα τὸν Καππαδόκην Ἰωάννην ἀνεῖλον, ἀντικαθιστάναι μὲν ἐς τιμὴν τὴν αὐτοῦ ἤθελον, ἄνδρα δέ τινα πονηρότερον εὑρεῖν ἐπὶ κοινῆς ἐποιοῦντο· περισκοπούμενοί τε τὸ τοιοῦτο τῆς τυραννίδος ὄργανον καὶ ἁπάσας διερευνῶντες τὰς τῶν ἀνθρώπων γνώμας, ὅπως ἔτι θᾶσσον τοὺς ὑπηκόους ἀπολεῖν δύνωνται. Ἐν μὲν οὖν τῷ παραυτίκα Θεόδοτον ἀντ' αὐτοῦ ἐπὶ τῆς ἀρχῆς κατέστησαν, ἄνδρα οὐ κακοήθη μὲν, οὐ σφόδρα δὲ ἀρέσκειν αὐτοῖς ἱκανὸν γεγονότα. Ὕστερον δὲ ἅπαν διερευνώμενοι περιήρχοντο. Εὗρον δὲ παρὰ δόξαν ἀργυράμοιβόν τινα Πέτρον ὀνόματι, Σύρον γένος, ὅνπερ ἐπίκλησιν Βαρσύμην ἐκάλουν, ὃς πάλαι μὲν ἐπὶ τῆς τοῦ χαλκοῦ τραπέζης καθήμενος, κέρδη αἰσχρότατα ἐκ ταύτης δὴ ἐπορίζετο τῆς ἐργασίας, τὴν περὶ τοὺς ὀβολοὺς

CHAPTER XXII

AFTER the Emperor and Empress had destroyed John of Cappadocia, they were desirous of appointing someone else to his office, and agreed to search for a man even more vicious than he. They looked around to find this instrument of tyranny, and examined the dispositions of all, in order that they might the more speedily be able to ruin their subjects. They temporarily conferred the office upon Theodotus, who, though certainly not an honourable man, was not sufficiently wicked to satisfy them. They continued their search in all directions, and at last by accident found a banker named Peter, a Syrian by birth, surnamed Barsyames. He had long sat at the copper money-changer's counter, and had amassed large sums by his disgraceful malpractices. He

κλοπὴν εὖ μάλα τεχνάζων καὶ τοὺς αὐτῷ ξυμβάλλοντας ἀεὶ τῷ τῶν δακτύλων τάχει ἐκκρούων. Δεξιὸς γὰρ ἦν κλέψαι μὲν τὰ τῶν αὐτῷ περιπεπτωκότων ἀναίδην, ἁλοὺς δὲ ὀμόσαι, καὶ τῶν χειρῶν τὸ ἁμάρτημα τῷ τῆς γλώττης περικαλύψαι θράσει.

β. Ἐν δὲ τοῖς τῶν ὑπάρχων στρατιώταις καταλεχθεὶς, ἐς τοσοῦτον ἀτοπίας ἐλήλακεν, ὥστε Θεοδώρᾳ ἀρέσκειν τε ἐν τοῖς μάλιστα, καὶ ἐκ τῶν ἀδίκων αὐτῇ βουλημάτων ῥᾷστα ὑπουργεῖν τὰ ἀμήχανα. Διὸ δὴ Θεόδοτον μὲν, ὅνπερ μετὰ τὸν Καππαδόκην καταστησάμενοι ἔτυχον, τῆς τιμῆς αὐτίκα παρέλυσαν, Πέτρον δὲ ταύτῃ ἐπέστησαν, ὅσπερ αὐτοῖν διεπράξατο κατὰ νοῦν ἅπαντα. Τούς τε γὰρ στρατευομένους ἀποστερῶν τὰς ξυντάξεις ἁπάσας, οὔτε αἰσχυνθεὶς οὔτε δείσας πώποτε ὤφθη, ἀλλὰ καὶ ὠνίους τὰς ἀρχὰς ἔτι μᾶλλον ἢ πρότερον προὔθηκεν, ἀτιμοτέρας τε αὐτὰς καταστησάμενος ἀπε-

COURT OF JUSTINIAN 180

was exceedingly cunning at thieving obols, ever deceiving his customers by the quickness of his fingers. He was very clever at filching without ado what fell into his hands, and, when detected, he swore that it was the fault of his hands, and made use of most impudent language in order to conceal his guilt.

This Barsyames, having been enrolled in the praetorian guard, behaved so outrageously that he approved himself beyond all others to Theodora, and was selected by her to assist in carrying out those of her nefarious schemes which required the most inventive genius. For this reason Justinian and Theodora immediately deprived Theodotus of the dignity bestowed upon him as the successor of the Cappadocian, and appointed Peter in his stead, who in every respect acted in accordance with their wishes.

He not only, without the least fear or shame, cheated the soldiers of their pay, but offered commands and offices for sale to a greater extent than before. Having thus degraded them, he sold them to

δίδοτο τοῖς ταύτην δὴ οὐκ ἀποκνοῦσι τὴν ἀνοσίαν ἐμπορίζεσθαι πρᾶξιν, ἐφιεὶς διαρρήδην τοῖς τὰς ἀρχὰς ὠνησαμένοις ταῖς τῶν ἀρχομένων ψυχαῖς τε καὶ οὐσίαις ᾗ βούλοιντο χρήσασθαι. Αὐτῷ τε γὰρ εὐθὺς καὶ τῷ τῆς χώρας καταβεβληκότι τὸ τίμημα ἡ. τοῦ συλᾶν τε καὶ ἄλλως ἁρπάζειν ἐξουσία ξυνέκειτο.

γʹ. Καὶ προῄει μὲν ἐκ τοῦ κεφαλαίου τῆς πολιτείας ἡ τῶν βίων ὠνή· ἐπράττετό τε τὸ συμβόλαιον τῆς τῶν πόλεων διαφθορᾶς, ἔν τε τῶν δικαστηρίων τοῖς προὔχουσι καὶ τῷ δημοσίῳ τῆς ἀγορᾶς περιήρχετο λῃστὴς ἔννομος, ὄνομα τῇ πράξει τιθεὶς τὴν συλλογὴν τῶν ἐπὶ τοῖς τιμήμασι τῆς ἀρχῆς καταβεβλημένων χρημάτων οὐκ ἐχούσης τινὰ ἐλπίδα τῆς τῶν ἁμαρτανομένων ἐπιστροφῆς. Ἐκ πάντων δὲ τῶν τῇ ἀρχῇ ὑπηρετούντων, πολλῶν τε καὶ δοκίμων ὄντων, τοὺς πονηροὺς ἀεὶ ἐς αὐτὸν εἷλκε.

δʹ. Τοῦτο δὲ οὐκ αὐτὸς ἐξήμαρτε μόνος, ἀλλὰ καὶ ὅσοι ταύτην πρότερόν τε καὶ ὕστερον τὴν τιμὴν ἔσχον. Ἡμαρτάνετο δὲ τοιοῦτο

COURT OF JUSTINIAN   181

persons who were not ashamed to engage
in this unholy traffic, giving express permission to the purchasers to deal as they
pleased with the lives and properties of
those who were subject to their authority;
for Barsyames claimed for himself and
granted to anyone who had paid down
the price of a province the right of
plundering and ravaging it at pleasure.
It was from the chief of the State that
this traffic in lives proceeded, and agree-
ments were entered into for the ruin of
the cities. In the chief courts and in
the public market - place the legalised
brigand went round about, who was
called "collector" from his duty of col-
lecting the money paid for the purchase
of dignities, which they exacted from the
oppressed, who had no hope of redress.
Of all those who were promoted to his
service, although several were men of repute, Barsyames always preferred such
as were of depraved character.

He was not the only offender in this
respect; all his predecessors and successors were equally guilty. The " Master

κἂν τῇ τοῦ Μαγίστρου καλουμένῃ ἀρχῇ, κἂν τοῖς Παλατίνοις, οἳ δὴ ἀμφί τε τοὺς θησαυροὺς καὶ τὰ πριβάτα καλούμενα, τό τε πατριμόνιον ἐπιτελεῖν ἀεὶ τὴν ὑπουργίαν εἰώθασιν, ἐν πάσαις τε, συλλήβδην εἰπεῖν, ταῖς ἐν Βυζαντίῳ καὶ πόλεσι ταῖς ἄλλαις τεταγμέναις ἀρχαῖς. Ἐξ οὗ γὰρ ὅδε ὁ τύραννος τὰ πράγματα διῳκήσατο, ἐν ἀρχῇ ἑκάστῃ τοὺς τοῖς ὑπηρετοῦσι προσήκοντας πόρους, πῇ μὲν αὐτός, πῇ δὲ ὁ τὴν τιμὴν ἔχων, προσεποιοῦντο οὐδενὶ λόγῳ· οἵ τε αὐτοῖς ἐπιτάττουσιν ὑπουργοῦντες, πενόμενοι τὰ ἔσχατα πάντα τοῦτον τὸν χρόνον, δουλο-πρεπέστατα ὑπουργεῖν ἠναγκάζοντο.

ε΄. Σίτου δὲ πολλοῦ κομιδῇ ἐς Βυζάν-τιον κεκομισμένου, ἐσεσήπει μὲν ὁ πλεῖστος ἤδη· αὐτὸς δὲ τοῦτον πόλεσι ταῖς ἑῴαις ἐπέβαλλε κατὰ λόγον ἑκάστῃ, καίπερ οὐκ ἔχοντα ἐπιτηδείως εἰς βρῶσιν ἀνθρώπων· ἐπέβαλλέ τε οὐχ ᾗπερ ἀποδίδοσθαι τὸν κάλλιστον σῖτον εἰώθει, ἀλλὰ καὶ πολλῷ ἀξιώτερον· ἦν τε τοῖς ὠνουμένοις ἐπάναγκες χρήματα μεγάλα προεμένοις ἐπὶ τιμήμασι φορτικωτάτοις, εἶτα τὸν σῖτον ἐς τὴν θάλασ-σαν, ἢ ἔς τινα ὑδροχόαν ἀπορριπτεῖν. Ἐπεὶ

COURT OF JUSTINIAN 182

of Offices " did the same, likewise the
officials of the imperial treasury, and those
who had the duty of superintending the
Emperor's private and personal estate—
in a word, all who held public appointments in Byzantium and other cities.
In fact, from the time that this tyrant
had the management of affairs, either he
or his minister claimed the subsidies
suitable to each office, and those who
served their superiors, suffering extreme
poverty, were compelled to submit to be
treated as if they were the most worthless slaves.

The greater part of the corn that had
been imported to Byzantium was kept
until it rotted ; but, although it was not
fit for human consumption, he forced the
cities of the East to purchase it in proportion to their importance, and he demanded payment, not at the price paid
even for the best corn, but at a far
higher rate ; and the poor people, who
had been forced to purchase it at an
outrageously heavy price, were compelled
to throw it into the sea or the drains.

δὲ καὶ σίτου ἀκραιφνοῦς τε καὶ οὔπω σεσηπότος μέγα τι πλῆθος ἐνταῦθα ἀπέκειτο, καὶ τοῦτο πλείσταις τῶν πόλεων ταῖς σίτου ὑποσπανιζούσαις ἀπεμπολεῖν ἔγνω. Ταύτῃ γὰρ διπλάσια τὰ χρήματα ἐποίει ἤπερ τοῖς ὑποτελέσι τὸ δημόσιον ὑπὲρ τουτουὶ τοῦ σίτου τὰ πρότερα ἐλελόγιστο.

ϛʹ. Ἀλλ' ἐπεὶ ἐς νέωτα οὐκέτι ὁμοία ἡ τῶν καρπῶν φορὰ ἤκμαζεν, ἐνδεεστέρως δὲ ἢ κατὰ τὴν χρείαν ἐς Βυζάντιον ὁ σιταγωγὸς στόλος ἀφίκετο, Πέτρος τοῖς παροῦσι διαπορούμενος, ἐκ τῶν ἔν τε Βιθυνίᾳ καὶ Φρυγίᾳ καὶ Θρᾴκῃ χωρίων πρίασθαι μέγα τι χρῆμα σίτου ἠξίου. Ἦν τε ἀναγκαῖον τοῖς ταύτῃ οἰκοῦσι μέχρι μὲν ἐς τὴν θάλασσαν πόνῳ πολλῷ τὰ φορτία φέρειν, ἐς Βυζάντιον δὲ ξὺν κινδύνῳ αὐτὰ ἐσκομίζεσθαι, καὶ βραχέα μὲν τιμήματα δῆθεν τῷ λόγῳ πρὸς αὐτοῦ φέρεσθαι, τὴν ζημίαν δὲ αὐτοῖς ἐς τοσόνδε μεγέθους καθίστασθαι, ὥστε ἀγαπᾶν, ἤν τις αὐτοὺς ἐφῄη τόν τε σῖτον τῷ δημοσίῳ χαρίζεσθαι καὶ τίμημα ἕτερον ὑπὲρ αὐτοῦ κατατιθέναι. Τοῦτ' ἔστι τὸ ἄχθος, ὅπερ καλεῖν συνωνὴν νενο-

COURT OF JUSTINIAN 183

That which was sound and not yet spoilt, of which there was great abundance in the capital, the Emperor determined to sell to those cities which were scantily supplied. In this manner he realised twice the amount that had formerly been obtained by the receivers of the public tribute in the provinces. The next year the supply of corn was not so abundant, and the transports did not bring a sufficient quantity to supply the needs of the capital. Peter, disconcerted at the state of affairs, conceived the idea of buying up a great quantity of corn from Bithynia, Phrygia and Thrace. The inhabitants of those provinces were forced to bring it down to the coasts themselves (a work of great labour), and to convey it at considerable risk to Byzantium, where they had to be satisfied with an absurdly low price. Their losses were so considerable, that they would have preferred to have given the corn gratuitously to the public granaries, and even to have paid twice as much. This burdensome duty was

μίκασιν. Ἐπεὶ δὲ οὐδ' ὡς σῖτος ἐν Βυζαντίῳ κατὰ τὴν χρείαν ἱκανὸς ἐγεγόνει, πολλοὶ τὸ πρᾶγμα ἐς βασιλέα διέβαλλον. Ἅμα δὲ καὶ οἱ στρατευόμενοι σχεδόν τι ἅπαντες, ἅτε τὰς εἰωθυίας οὐ κεκομισμένοι ξυντάξεις, θορύβῳ τε ἀνὰ τὴν πόλιν καὶ ταραχῇ πολλῇ εἴχοντο. Βασιλεὺς μὲν οὖν ἤδη τε αὐτῷ χαλεπῶς ἔχειν ἔδοξε καὶ παραλύειν αὐτὸν τῆς ἀρχῆς ἤθελε, διά τε ταῦτα, ἅπερ ἐρρήθη, καὶ ὅτι χρήματα δαιμονίως μεγάλα ἠκηκόει αὐτῷ ἀποκεκρύφθαι, ἅπερ ἐκ τοῦ δημοσίου σεσυληκὼς ἔτυχε. Καὶ ἦν δὲ οὕτως.

ζ'. Θεοδώρα δὲ τὸν ἄνδρα οὐκ εἴα· ἐκτόπως γὰρ τὸν Βαρσυάμην ἠγάπα. Ἐμοὶ δὲ δοκεῖ τῆς τε πονηρίας ἕνεκα καὶ τοῦ τοῖς κατηκόοις διαφερόντως λυμαίνεσθαι. Αὐτή τε γὰρ ὠμοτάτη ἦν, καὶ ἀπανθρωπίας ἀτεχνῶς ἔμπλεως, καὶ τοὺς ὑπουργοῦντας ἠξίου τὰ ἐς τὸν τρόπον αὐτῇ ὡς μάλιστα ἐπιτηδείως ἔχειν. Φασὶ δὲ αὐτὴν καὶ κατα-

COURT OF JUSTINIAN 184

called Synōnē, or provisioning the capital
with corn from the provinces. But, as
even then the supply of corn was not
sufficient for the needs of the city, many
complaints were made to the Emperor.
At the same time the soldiers, hardly any
of whom had as yet received their pay,
assembled and created a great disturbance in the city. The Emperor appeared
greatly irritated against Peter, and resolved to deprive him of his office, both
for the reasons stated and also because
it was reported to him that he had
amassed extraordinary wealth, which he
kept hidden away, by robbing the public
treasury; and this in fact was the case.
But Theodora opposed her husband's
intention, being exceedingly enamoured
of Barsyames, apparently on account of
his evil character and the remarkable
cruelty with which he treated his subjects; for, being herself exceedingly cruel
and utterly inhuman, she was anxious
that the character of her agents should
be in conformity with her own. It is
also said that Theodora, against her will,

μαγευθεῖσαν πρὸς τοῦ Πέτρου ἀκούσιον αὐτῷ εὐνοϊκῶς ἔχειν. Περί τε γὰρ τοὺς φαρμακέας καὶ τὰ δαιμόνια περιέργως ἐσπουδάκει ὁ Βαρσνάμης οὗτος, καὶ τοὺς καλουμένους Μανιχαίους ἐτεθήπει τε καὶ αὐτῶν προστατεῖν ἐκ τοῦ ἐμφανοῦς οὐδαμῇ ἀπηξίου. Καίτοι καὶ ταῦτα ἡ βασιλὶς ἀκούσασα, οὐ μεθῆκε τὴν ἐς τὸν ἄνθρωπον εὔνοιαν, ἀλλὰ μᾶλλον ἔτι διὰ ταῦτα περιστέλλειν τε καὶ ἀγαπᾶν ἔγνω. Μάγοις τε γὰρ καὶ φαρμακεῦσι καὶ αὐτὴ ὁμιλήσασα ἐκ παιδὸς, ἅτε τῶν ἐπιτηδευμάτων αὐτὴν ἐς τοῦτο ἀγόντων, διεβίω πιστεύουσά τε τῷ πράγματι τούτῳ καὶ αὐτῷ τὸ θαρσεῖν ἐς ἀεὶ ἔχουσα.

η'. Λέγουσι δὲ καὶ τὸν Ἰουστινιανὸν οὐ τοσοῦτον θωπεύουσα χειροήθη ποιήσασθαι, ὅσον τῇ ἐκ τῶν δαιμονίων ἀνάγκῃ. Οὐ γάρ τις ἦν εὔφρων ἢ δίκαιος ὅδε ἀνὴρ, ἢ ἐς τὸ ἀγαθὸν βέβαιος· ὥστε κρείσσων ποτὲ τῆς τοιαύτης ἐπιβουλῆς εἶναι, ἀλλὰ φόνων μὲν καὶ χρημάτων ἔρωτος διαφανῶς ἥσσων, τοῖς δὲ αὐτὸν ἐξαπατῶσι καὶ κολακεύουσιν οὐ χαλεπῶς εἴκων, ἔν τε πράξεσι ταῖς

COURT OF JUSTINIAN

had been forced by the enchantments of Barsyames to become his friend; for this man had devoted great attention to sorcerers and supernatural beings, admired the Manichaeans, and was not ashamed openly to profess himself their supporter. Although the Empress was not ignorant of this, she did not withdraw her favour, but resolved on this account to show even greater interest and regard for him than before, for she herself also, from her earliest years, had associated with sorcerers and magicians, since her character and pursuits inclined her towards them. She had great faith in their arts, and placed the greatest confidence in them. It is even said that she did not render Justinian susceptible to her influence so much by her flatteries as by the irresistible power of evil spirits; for Justinian was not sufficiently kindly, or just, or persistent in well-doing to be superior to such secret influence, but was manifestly dominated by a thirst for blood and riches, and fell an easy prey to those who deceived and flattered him. In

μάλιστά οἱ ἐσπουδασμέναις μετεβάλλετό τε οὐδενὶ λόγῳ καὶ κονιορτῷ ἐνδελεχέστατα ἐμφερὴς ἐγεγόνει. Ταῦτά τοι οὐδέ τις τῶν αὐτοῦ ξυγγενῶν ἢ ἄλλως γνωρίμων ἐλπίδα τινά ποτε ἀσφαλῆ ἐπ᾽ αὐτῷ ἔσχεν, ἀλλὰ μεταναστάσεις αὐτῷ ἐς ἀεὶ τῆς ἐς τὰ ἐπιτηδεύματα ἐγίνοντο γνώμης. Οὕτω τε καὶ τοῖς φαρμακεῦσιν, ὅπερ ἐρρήθη, εὐέφοδος ὢν, καὶ τῇ Θεοδώρᾳ πόνῳ οὐδενὶ ὑποχείριος ἐγεγόνει, καὶ ἀπ᾽ αὐτοῦ μάλιστα ἡ βασιλὶς ἅτε σπουδαῖον τὰ τοιαῦτα Πέτρον ὄντα ὑπερηγάπα.

θ΄. Ἀρχῆς μὲν οὖν, ἧς τὰ πρότερα εἶχε, βασιλεὺς αὐτὸν παρέλυσε μόλις, Θεοδώρας τε ἐγκειμένης, οὐ πολλῷ ὕστερον ἄρχοντα τῶν θησαυρῶν αὐτὸν κατεστήσατο, Ἰωάννην παραλύσας ταύτης δὴ τῆς τιμῆς, ὅσπερ αὐτὴν παρειληφὼς μησί που ὀλίγοις πρότερον ἔτυχεν. Ἦν δὲ οὗτος ὁ ἀνὴρ γένος μὲν Παλαιστῖνος, πρᾷος δὲ καὶ ἀγαθὸς ἄγαν, καὶ οὐδὲ πορίζεσθαι χρημάτων ἰδικῶν πόρους εἰδὼς, οὐδέ τῳ λυμηνάμενος πώποτε

COURT OF JUSTINIAN 186

undertakings which needed the greatest attention, he changed his plans without any reason and showed himself as light as the dust swept before the wind. Thus none of his kinsmen or friends had the least confidence in his stability, but, in the execution of his purpose, his opinion perpetually changed with the greatest rapidity. Being, as I have said, an easy object of attack for the sorcerers, he in like manner readily fell a victim to Theodora, who, for this reason, entertained the highest affection for Peter as one devoted to the study of these arts.

The Emperor only succeeded with great difficulty in depriving him of his office, and, at the pressing entreaty of Theodora, soon afterwards appointed him chief of the treasury, and deprived John of these functions, although he had only been invested with them a few months previously. This John was a native of Palestine, a good and gentle man, who did not even know how to find out the means of increasing his private fortune, and had never done injury to a single

τῶν πάντων ἀνθρώπων. Ἀμέλει καὶ διαφερόντως ἠγάπων αὐτὸν ὁ λεὼς ἅπας. Διά τοι τοῦτο Ἰουστινιανόν τε καὶ τὴν ὁμόζυγα οὐδαμῆ ἤρεσκεν· οἵπερ ἐπειδὴ τῶν σφίσιν ὑπουργούντων καλόν τε καὶ ἀγαθὸν παρὰ δόξαν τινὰ ἴδοιεν, ἰλιγγιῶντές καὶ δυσφορούμενοι ἐς τὰ μάλιστα πάσῃ μηχανῇ αὐτὸν ὅτι τάχιστα διωθεῖσθαι ἐν σπουδῇ ἐποιοῦντο.

ι΄. Οὕτω γοῦν καὶ τοῦτον τὸν Ἰωάννην ὁ Πέτρος ἐκδεξάμενος, θησαυρῶν τε τῶν βασιλικῶν προὔστη, καὶ συμφορῶν αὖθις μεγάλων αἰτιώτατος ἅπασι γέγονεν. Ἀποτεμνόμενος γὰρ τῶν χρημάτων τὸ πλεῖστον μέρος, ἅπερ ἐν παραψυχῆς λόγῳ πολλοῖς χορηγεῖσθαι ἀνὰ πᾶν ἔτος πρὸς βασιλέως ἐκ παλαιοῦ διατέτακται, αὐτὸς μὲν τοῖς δημοσίοις οὐ δέον ἐπλούτει, καὶ μοῖραν ἐνθένδε βασιλεῖ ἀνέφερεν. Οἱ δὲ τὰ χρήματα περιῃρημένοι, ἐν πένθει μεγάλῳ περιεκάθηντο, ἐπεὶ καὶ τὸ χρυσοῦν νόμισμα οὐχ ᾗπερ εἰώθει ἐκφέρειν ἠξίου, ἀλλ' ἔλασσον αὐτὸ καταστησάμενος, πρᾶγμα οὐδεπώποτε γεγονὸς πρότερον. Τὰ μὲν ἀμφὶ τοῖς ἄρχουσι βασιλεῖ ταύτῃ πῃ εἶχεν.

COURT OF JUSTINIAN   187

individual. The more decided the affection of the people for him, the less he met with the approval of Justinian and his partner, who, as soon as they found amongst their agents, contrary to expectation, a good and honourable man, were quite dumbfounded, showed their indignation, and endeavoured by every possible means to get rid of him with the least delay. Thus Peter succeeded John as chief of the royal treasury, and was one of the chief causes of great misery to all the inhabitants of the Empire. He embezzled the greater part of the fund, which, in accordance with an ancient custom, was annually distributed by the Emperor to a number of families by way of assisting them. Part of this public money he sent to the Emperor, and kept part for himself, whereby he acquired illgotten wealth. Those who were thus deprived of this money lived in a pitiable state. He did not even coin the same amount of gold as before, but less—a thing which had never been done before. Such was the manner in which Justinian dealt with the magistracies.

ΚΕΦΑΛΑΙΟΝ ΚΓ'.

α'. Ὅπως δὲ τοὺς τὰ χωρία κεκτημέ-νους πανταχοῦ πη διέφθειρεν, ἐρῶν ἔρχομαι. Ἀπέχρη μὲν οὖν ἡμῖν εἰπεῖν τῶν ἐς τὰς πόλεις ἁπάσας στελλομένων ἀρχόντων ἐπιμ-νησθεῖσιν οὐ πολλῷ πρότερον καὶ τούτων δὴ τῶν ἀνθρώπων σημῆναι τὰ πάθη. Πρώ-τους γὰρ οἱ ἄνθρωποι οὗτοι τοὺς τῶν χωρίων κυρίους βιαζόμενοι ἐληΐζοντο καὶ ὡς δὲ τἄλλα ἃ εἴρηται πάντα.

β'. Πρῶτα μὲν εἰθισμένον ὂν ἐκ πα-λαιοῦ, ἕκαστον τὴν Ῥωμαίων ἀρχὴν ἔχοντα, οὐχ ἅπαξ μόνον, ἀλλὰ καὶ πολλάκις τοῖς τῶν δημοσίων ὀφλημάτων λειψάνοις τοὺς κατηκόους δωρεῖσθαι πάντας, τοῦ μήτε τοὺς ἀπορουμένους τε καὶ ὅθεν ἂν ἐκτίνοιεν τὰ λείψανα ταῦτα οὐδαμῆ ἔχοντας διηνεκὲς ἀποπνίγεσθαι, μήτε τοῖς φορολόγοις σκήψεις παρέχεσθαι, συκοφαντεῖν ἐγχειροῦσι τῶν τοῦ φόρου ὑποτελῶν τοὺς οὐδὲν ὀφείλοντας, οὗτος ἐς δύο καὶ τριάκοντα ἐτῶν χρόνον

CHAPTER XXIII

I WILL now relate how he everywhere ruined the possessors of estates, although, to show their misery, it would really be sufficient to refer to what has been said, just before this, concerning the governors dispatched to all the provinces and cities, for it was they who plundered those who possessed landed estates, as before related.

It had long been an established custom that the Roman Emperor should, not only once, but on several occasions, remit to his subjects all the arrears that were owing to the treasury, so that those who were in difficulties and had no means of settling these arrears might not be continually pressed, and that the tax collectors might not have an excuse for vexatiously attempting to exact money from those liable to tribute, where in many cases it was not due. Justinian,

οὐδὲν τοιοῦτο ἐς τοὺς κατηκόους εἰργάσατο·
καὶ ἀπ' αὐτοῦ τοῖς μὲν ἀπορουμένοις ἀναγκαῖον ἦν ἀποδρᾶναί τε γῆν, καὶ μηκέτι
ἐπανιέναι. Καὶ οἱ συκοφάνται τοὺς ἐπιεικεστέρους ἀπέκναιον κατηγορίαν ἐπανασείον-
τες, ἅτε τὸ τέλος ἐνδεεστέρως ἐκ παλαιοῦ
καταβάλλοντας τῆς ἐγκειμένης τῷ χωρίῳ
φορᾶς. Οὐ γὰρ ὅσον οἱ ταλαίπωροι τὴν
καινὴν τοῦ φόρου ἀπαγωγὴν ἐδεδίεσαν, ἀλλὰ
καὶ χρόνων τοσούτων τὸ πλῆθος οὐδὲν
προσῆκον βαρύνεσθαι φόροις. Πολλοὶ γοῦν
ἀμέλει τὰ σφέτερα αὐτῶν τοῖς συκοφάνταις ἢ τῷ δημοσίῳ προέμενοι ἀπηλλάσσοντο.

γ: Ἔπειτα δὲ Μήδων μὲν καὶ Σαρακηνῶν τῆς Ἀσίας γῆν τὴν πολλὴν, τῶν δὲ
δὴ Οὔννων καὶ Σκλαβηνῶν ξύμπασαν Εὐρώ-
πην λῃσαμένων, καὶ τῶν πόλεων τὰς μὲν
καθελόντων εἰς ἔδαφος, τὰς δὲ ἀργυρολο-
γησάντων ἐς τὸ ἀκριβὲς μάλιστα, τοὺς δὲ
ἀνθρώπους ἐξανδραποδισάντων ξὺν χρήμασι
πᾶσιν, ἔρημόν τε τῶν οἰκητόρων κατα-
στησαμένων χώραν ἑκάστην ταῖς καθ'
ἡμέραν ἐπιδρομαῖς, φόρον μὲν οὐδενὶ τῶν

COURT OF JUSTINIAN 189

however, for thirty-two years made no concession of the kind to his subjects, the result of which was that the poor people were forced to quit the country without any hope of return. The more honest were perpetually harassed by these false accusers, who threatened to charge them with having paid less than the amount at which they were rated. These unhappy individuals were less afraid of the imposition of new taxes than of the insupportable weight of the unjust exactions which for many years they had been compelled to pay, whereupon many of them abandoned their property to their accusers or to the fisc.

The Medes and Saracens had ravaged the greater part of Asia, and the Huns and Slavs had plundered the whole of Europe. Cities had been razed to the ground or subjected to severe exactions; the inhabitants had been carried away into slavery with all they possessed, and every district had been deserted by its inhabitants in consequence of the daily inroads. Justinian, however, remitted no

ἁπάντων ἀφῆκε, πλήν γε δὴ ὅσον ἐνιαυτοῦ ταῖς ἁλούσαις τῶν πόλεων μόνον. Καίτοι εἰ καθάπερ Ἀναστάσιος βασιλεὺς ἑπτάετες ταῖς ἁλούσαις τὰ τέλη ἐπιχωρεῖν ἔγνω, οἶμαι δ᾽ ἂν οὐδ᾽ ὣς αὐτὸν πεποιῆσθαι τὰ δέοντα.

δ΄. Ἐπεὶ Καβάδης μὲν ταῖς οἰκοδομίαις ὡς ἥκιστα λυμηνάμενος ἀπιὼν ᾤχετο· Χοσρόης δὲ ἅπαντα πυρπολήσας καθεῖλεν εἰς ἔδαφος, μείζω τε προσετρίψατο τοῖς περιπεπτωκόσι τὰ πάθη. Καὶ τούτοις μὲν τοῖς ἀνθρώποις, οἷσπερ τὸ γελοιῶδες τοῦτο τοῦ φόρου ἀφῆκε, καὶ τοῖς ἄλλοις ἅπασι, πολλάκις μὲν δεξαμένοις τὸν Μήδων στρατόν, διηνεκὲς δὲ Οὔννων τε καὶ βαρβάρων Σαρακηνῶν γῆν τὴν Ἑῴαν λῃσαμένων, οὐδὲν δὲ ἧσσον καὶ ἐπὶ τῆς Εὐρώπης βαρβάρων ταῦτα ἐργαζομένων ἀεὶ καὶ καθ᾽ ἑκάστην τοὺς ἐκείνῃ Ῥωμαίους, βασιλεὺς οὗτος χαλεπώτερος εὐθὺς γέγονε βαρβάρων ἁπάντων. Συνωναῖς τε γὰρ καὶ ταῖς καλου-

COURT OF JUSTINIAN   190

tax or impost to any one of them, except
in the case of cities that had been taken
by the enemy, and then only for a year,
although, had he granted them exemption
for seven years, as the Emperor Anastasius had done, I do not think that even
then he would have done enough: for
Cabades retired after having inflicted
but little damage upon the buildings,
but Chosroes, by ravaging the country
with fire and sword and razing all its
dwellings to the ground, brought greater
calamities upon the inhabitants. Justinian only granted this absurd remission of
tribute to these people and to others who
had several times submitted to an invasion of the Medes and the continuous
depredations of the Huns and Saracen
barbarians in the East, while the Romans,
settled in the different parts of Europe,
who had equally suffered by the attacks
of the barbarians, found Justinian more
cruel than any of their foreign foes; for,
immediately after the enemy withdrew,
the proprietors of estates found themselves overwhelmed with requisitions for

μέναις ἐπιβολαῖς τε καὶ διαγραφαῖς οἱ τῶν χωρίων κύριοι, τῶν πολεμίων ἀνακεχωρηκότων, αὐτίκα μάλα ἡλίσκοντο.

ε΄. Ὅ τι δὲ τὰ ὀνόματά ἐστί τε καὶ βούλεται ταῦτα, ἐγὼ δηλώσω. Τοὺς τὰ χωρία κεκτημένους ἀναγκάζουσι τὸν Ῥωμαίων ἐκτρέφειν στρατὸν, κατὰ τὸ μέτρον τῆς κειμένης ἑκάστῳ φορᾶς τιμημάτων καταβαλλομένων, οὐχ ᾗπερ ἐφίησιν ὁ παρὼν τῇ χρείᾳ καιρὸς, ἀλλ᾽ ᾗπερ ἔξεστι καὶ διώρισται. Οὐ διερευνώμενοι δὲ, εἴπερ αὐτοῖς ἐπιτήδεια ἐν τῇ χώρᾳ ξυμβαίνει, περιέστηκέ τε τοὺς δειλαίους τούτους ἀνάγκη, τὰ μὲν ἐπιτήδεια στρατιώταις τε καὶ ἵπποις ἐσκομίζεσθαι, πάντα ὠνουμένους αὐτὰ τιμημάτων πολλῶν ἐς ἄγαν ἀξιωτέρων, καὶ ταῦτα ἐκ χώρας μακράν που οὔσης, ἂν οὕτω τύχοι, ἐς τὸ χωρίον ἀποκομίζειν, οὗ δὴ τὸ στρατόπεδον ξυμβαίνει εἶναι, μετρεῖν τε τοῖς τῶν στρατιωτῶν χορηγοῖς, οὐ καθάπερ πᾶσιν ἀνθρώποις νόμος, ἀλλ᾽ ᾗπερ ἐκείνοις ἂν βουλομένοις εἴη. Καὶ τοῦτ᾽ ἔστι τὸ πρᾶγμα, ὅπερ Συνωνὴ καλεῖται, ἐξ οὗ δὴ ἅπασιν ἐκνενευρίσθαι τοῖς τῶν χωρίων κυρίοις ξυμβαίνει. Φόρον γὰρ ἀπ᾽ αὐτοῦ τὸν ἐπέτειον οὐχ ἥσσονα ἢ δεκαπλασίονα κατατιθέναι σφίσιν ἐπάναγκες, οἷς γε οὐ μόνον τῷ στρατῷ χορηγεῖν, ἀλλὰ καὶ σῖτον ἐς Βυ-

COURT OF JUSTINIAN 191

provisions,[1] impositions,[2] and edicts[3] of various kinds, the meaning of which I will now explain. Those who possessed landed property were obliged to furnish provisions for the soldiers in proportion to the amount imposed upon each, and these dues were fixed, not in consideration of the necessities of the moment, but according to an authorised imperial assessment; and, if at any time they had not a sufficient supply upon their lands for the needs of the horses and soldiers, these unhappy persons were forced to purchase them even at a price far above their proper value, and to convey them in many cases from a considerable distance to the place where the troops were encamped, and to distribute them to the adjutants in what quantity and at what rate the latter pleased, not at a fair and reasonable price. This import was called "the import of victualling," which, as it were, cut the sinews of all the landed proprietors; for they had to pay an annual tribute ten times greater than before, and were obliged not only to furnish supplies

[1] Synōnē.　　　[2] Epibolē.　　　[3] Diagraphē.

ζάντιον πολλάκις διακομίζειν ταῦτα πεπονθόσι ξυνέπεσεν· ἐπεὶ οὐχ ὁ Βαρσυάμης
καλούμενος μόνος τὸ τοιοῦτο ἄγος ἐξαμαρτάνειν τετόλμηκεν, ἀλλὰ καὶ πρότερον μὲν
ὁ Καππαδόκης, ὕστερον δὲ οἱ μετὰ τὸν
Βαρσυάμην τοῦτο δὴ τὸ τῆς ἀρχῆς παρα-
λαβόντες ἀξίωμα. Τὰ μὲν οὖν τῆς Συνωνῆς
ταύτῃ πῃ ἔχει.

ϛ΄. Τὸ δὲ τῆς Ἐπιβολῆς ὄνομα ὄλε-
θρός τίς ἐστιν ἀπρόοπτος, ἐξαπιναίως τοῖς
τὰ χωρία κεκτημένοις ἐπιγενόμενος, πρόρρι-
ζόν τε αὐτοῖς ἐκτρίβων τὴν τοῦ βίου
ἐλπίδα. Χωρίων γὰρ τὸ τέλος τῶν ἐρήμων
τε καὶ ἀπόρων γεγενημένων, ὧν δὴ τοῖς τε
κυρίοις καὶ τοῖς γεωργοῖς ἤδη τετύχηκεν ἡ
παντάπασιν ἀπολωλέναι, ἢ γῆν πατρῴαν
ἀπολιποῦσι τοῖς ἐγκειμένοις σφίσι διὰ ταῦτα
κακοῖς κρύπτεσθαι, οὐκ ἀπαξιοῦσιν ἐπιφέ-
ρειν τοῖς οὕτω διεφθαρμένοις παντάπασι.
Τοιοῦτο μὲν καὶ τὸ τῆς Ἐπιβολῆς ὄνομά
ἐστιν, ἐπιπολάσαν ὡς τὸ εἰκὸς ἐπὶ τὸν
χρόνον μάλιστα τοῦτον.

ζ΄. Τὰ δὲ τῶν Διαγραφῶν ὡς συντο-
μώτατα φράσαντι ἀπηλλάχθαι τῇδέ πῃ
ἔχει. Ζημίαις πολλαῖς, ἄλλως τε καὶ ὑπὸ
τοὺς χρόνους τούτους, περιβαλέσθαι τὰς
πόλεις ἦν ἀνάγκη, ὧνπερ τάς τε ἀφορμὰς
καὶ τοὺς τρόπους ἀφίημι λέγειν ἐν τῷ
παρόντι, ὡς μή μοι ὁ λόγος ἀπέραντος
εἴη. Ταύτας οἱ τὰ χωρία ἔχοντες κατατι-

COURT OF JUSTINIAN   192

for the soldiers, but on several occasions
to convey corn to Byzantium. Barsyames
was not the only man who had the audacity to introduce this cursed exaction.
John of Cappadocia had set the example,
and the successors of Barsyames in his
office followed it. Such was the nature
of the Synōnē, as it was called.

The "Epibolē" was a kind of unforeseen ruin, which suddenly attacked
the landed proprietors and utterly deprived
them of the hope of subsistence; for, in the
case of estates that were deserted and un-
productive, the owners or tenants of which
had either died or abandoned their country
and hidden themselves after the misfortunes they had undergone, Justinian did
not hesitate to impose a tax. Such were
these "impositions," which were of frequent occurrence during that time.

A few words will suffice for the impost
called "Diagraphē." At this time especially, the cities were afflicted with
heavy losses, the causes and extent of
which I will say nothing about, for it
would be an endless tale. These losses

θέντες, κατὰ λόγον τῆς ἐγκειμένης ἑκάστῳ
φορᾶς, οὐκ ἄχρι δὲ τούτων αὐτοῖς τὸ κακὸν
ἔστη, ἀλλὰ καὶ τοῦ λοιμοῦ ξύμπασαν περι-
λαβόντος τήν τε ἄλλην οἰκουμένην καὶ
οὐχ ἥκιστα τὴν τῶν Ῥωμαίων ἀρχὴν, τῶν
τε γεωργῶν ἀφανίσαντος μέρος τὸ πλεῖστον,
καὶ ἀπ᾿ αὐτοῦ ἐρήμων ὡς τὸ εἰκὸς γεγενημένων τῶν χωρίων, οὐδεμιᾷ φειδοῖ ἐχρήσατο
ἐς τοὺς τούτων κυρίους. Φόρον γὰρ τὸν
ἐπέτειον οὐ τότε ἀνίει πραττόμενος, οὐχ
ἥπερ ἑκάστῳ ἐπέβαλλε μόνον, ἀλλὰ καὶ
γειτόνων τῶν ἀπολωλότων τὴν μοῖραν.
Προσῆν δὲ αὐτοῖς καὶ τἄλλα τάντα ὧνπερ
ἐμνήσθην ἀρτίως, ἅτε τοῖς τῶν χωρίων
δεδυστυχηκόσι τὴν κτῆσιν ἀεὶ ἐγκειμένων·
ἔτι μέντοι καὶ τοῖς μὲν στρατιώταις ἀνὰ
τὰ κάλλιστά τε καὶ τιμιώτατα δωματίων
τῶν σφετέρων ᾠκημένοις ὑπηρετεῖν, αὐτοῖς
δὲ πάντα τοῦτον τὸν χρόνον ἐν τοῖς φαυλο-
τάτοις τε καὶ ἀπημελημένοις τῶν οἰκιδίων
δίαιταν ἔχειν.

η΄. Ἅπερ ἅπαντα ὑπὸ τὴν Ἰουστινιανοῦ τε καὶ Θεοδώρας βασιλείαν τοῖς ἀνθρώποις ἀεὶ γίνεσθαι ξυνέβη, ἐπεὶ οὔτε πόλεμον
οὔτε τι ἄλλο τῶν μεγίστων κακῶν, ἐν
τούτῳ δὴ τῷ χρόνῳ, λελωφηκέναι τετύχηκεν.
Ἐπεὶ δὲ δωματίων ἐμνήσθην, οὐδὲ τοῦτο

COURT OF JUSTINIAN 193

had to be repaired by the landed proprietors in proportion to the rate at which they were assessed. Their misery, however, did not stop there, but, although pestilence had attacked the whole world, and, especially, the Roman Empire; although most of the farmers had fallen victims, and their properties had become deserted, Justinian did not show the least clemency towards the owners. He continued to exact the yearly tribute from them, not only their own proportion, but that of their neighbours who had died of the plague.[1] Further, they were obliged to treat the soldiers with the greatest civility, and to allow them to take up their quarters in their finest and richest apartments, while they themselves all the time had to content themselves with the poorest and meanest rooms. Such were the calamities that without intermission befell mankind during the reign of Justinian and Theodora, for there was no cessation of war or any other most terrible calamities. Since I have mentioned the word "quarters," I must not forget to

[1] Here the text is corrupt.

ΠΡΟΚΟΠΙΟΥ ΑΝΕΚΔΟΤΑ

παριτέον ἡμῖν, ὅτι δὴ οἱ κεκτημένοι τὰς ἐν Βυζαντίῳ οἰκίας, βαρβάροις ἐνταῦθα καταλύειν παρεχόμενοι, ἑπτακισμυρίοις μάλιστα οὖσιν, οὐχ ὅπως τῶν σφετέρων ὀνίνασθαι οὐδαμῆ εἶχον, ἀλλὰ καὶ προσετρίβοντο δυσκόλοις ἑτέροις.

COURT OF JUSTINIAN   194

say that at one time there were 70,000
barbarians at Constantinople, whom house
owners were obliged to quarter, being thus
shut out from all enjoyment of their own,
and in many other ways inconvenienced.

ΚΕΦΑΛΑΙΟΝ ΚΔ'.

α'. Οὐ μὴν οὐδὲ τὰ ἐς τοὺς στρατιώτας αὐτῷ εἰργασμένα σιωπῇ δοτέον· οἷς δὴ τούτους ἐπέστησεν, ἀνθρώπων ἁπάντων χρήματα σφᾶς ὅτι πλεῖστα ξυλλέγειν ἐνθένδε κελεύσας, εὖ εἰδότας ὡς μοῖρα τῶν πορισθησομένων ἡ δωδεκάτη αὐτοῖς κείσεται. Ὄνομα δὲ Λογοθέτας αὐτοῖς ἔθετο. Οἱ δὲ ἀνὰ πᾶν ἔτος ἐπενόουν τάδε. Τὰς στρατιωτικὰς συντάξεις οὐχ ὁμοίως νόμος χορηγεῖσθαι ἐφεξῆς ἅπασιν, ἀλλὰ νέοις μὲν ἔτι αὐτοῖς οὖσι, καὶ στρατευσαμένοις ἀρτίως, ἐλάσσων ὁ πόρος· πεπονηκόσι δὲ καὶ μέσοις που ἤδη καταλόγου γεγενημένοις, ἐπὶ μεῖζον χωρεῖ. Γεγηρακόσι μέντοι καὶ μέλλουσι τῆς στρατείας ἀφίεσθαι, πολλῷ ἔτι κομπωδεστέρα ἡ σύνταξις, ὅπως αὐτοί τε τὸ λοιπὸν ἰδίᾳ βιοῦντες, ἐς τὸ ἀποζῆν διαρκῶς ἔχοιεν, καὶ ἐπειδὰν αὐτοῖς ξυμμετρήσασθαι τὸν βίον ξυμβαίη, παραψυχήν τινα τῶν οἰκείων ἀπολιπεῖν τοῖς κατὰ τὴν

CHAPTER XXIV

I MUST not, however, omit to mention the manner in which Justinian treated the soldiers. He appointed commissioners, called Logothetae,[1] with directions to squeeze as much money as they could out of them, a twelfth part of the sum thus obtained being assured to them. The following was their mode of operation every year. It was an established custom that the soldiers should not all have the same pay. Those who were young, and had just joined, received less than those who had undergone hardships in the field and were already half-way up the list; while the veterans, whose term of service was all but over, received a more considerable sum, that they might have sufficient to live upon as private individuals, and, after their death, might be able to leave a small inheritance by way

[1] Chancellors, or, Commissioners.

196 ΠΡΟΚΟΠΙΟΥ ΑΝΕΚΔΟΤΑ

οἰκίαν δυνατοὶ εἶεν. Ὁ τοίνυν χρόνος τῶν στρατιωτῶν τοὺς καταδεεστέρους ἐς τῶν τετελευτηκότων, ἢ τῆς στρατείας ἀφεμένων τοὺς βαθμοὺς ἀεὶ ἀναβιβάζων, πρυτανεύει κατὰ πρεσβεῖα τὰς ἐκ τοῦ δημοσίου συντάξεις ἑκάστῳ. Ἀλλ᾽ οἱ λογοθέται καλούμενοι οὐκ εἴων ἐκ τῶν καταλόγων ἀφαιρεῖσθαι τὰ τῶν τετελευτηκότων ὀνόματα, καίπερ ὁμοῦ διαφθειρομένων, ἄλλως τε καὶ κατὰ τοὺς πολέμους συχνοὺς γινομένους τῶν πλείστων. Οὐ μὴν οὐδὲ τοὺς καταλόγους ἔτι ἐπλήρουν, καὶ ταῦτα χρόνου συχνοῦ.

β. Καὶ ἀπ᾽ αὐτοῦ περιειστήκει τῇ μὲν πολιτείᾳ τὸν τῶν στρατευομένων ἀριθμὸν ἐνδεέστερον ἀεὶ εἶναι, τῶν στρατιωτῶν τοῖς περιοῦσι πρὸς τῶν πάλαι τετελευτηκότων διωθουμένοις, ἐπὶ μοίρας παρὰ τὴν ἀξίαν τῆς καταδεεστέρας ἀπολελεῖφθαι, τάς τε ξυντάξεις ἐλασσόνως ἢ κατὰ τὴν προσήκουσαν κομίζεσθαι τάξιν, τοῖς δὲ λογοθέταις διαλαγχάνειν Ἰουστινιανῷ τῶν στρατιωτικῶν χρημάτων πάντα τοῦτον τὸν χρόνον. Ἔτι μέντοι καὶ ἄλλαις ζημιῶν ἰδέαις πολλαῖς τοὺς στρατιώτας ἀπέκναιον, ὥσπερ ἀμειβόμενοι τῶν ἐν τοῖς πολέμοις κινδύνων, ἐπικαλοῦντες τοῖς μὲν ὡς Γραῖκοι εἶεν, ὥσπερ οὐκ ἐξὸν τῶν ἀπὸ τῆς τὸ παράπαν τινὶ γενναίῳ γενέσθαι, τοῖς δὲ ὡς οὐκ ἐπιτεταγμένον πρὸς βασιλέως σφίσι στρατεύεσ-

COURT OF JUSTINIAN 196

of consolation to their families. Thus, in course of time, the soldiers gradually rose in rank, according as their comrades died or retired from the service, and their pay from the public funds was regulated in accordance with their seniority. But these commissioners would not allow the names of those who had died or fallen in battle to be struck out, or the vacancies to be filled, until a long interval had elapsed. The result was, that the army was short of men, and the survivors, after the death of the veterans, were kept in a position far inferior to their merits, and received less pay than they ought to have done, while in the meantime the commissioners handed over to Justinian the money they thus purloined from the soldiers. In addition, they harassed the soldiers with several other kinds of injustices, by way of recompense for the dangers they had undergone in the field ; they were taunted with the name of Greeks, as if Greece could never produce a brave soldier ; others were cashiered, as not having been ordered by the

ΠΡΟΚΟΠΙΟΥ ΑΝΕΚΔΟΤΑ

θαι, καίπερ ἀμφὶ τούτῳ γράμματα βασιλέως ἐνδεικνυμένοις, ἅπερ οἱ λογοθέται διαβάλλειν οὐδεμιᾷ ὀκνήσει ἐτόλμων, ἄλλοις δὲ, ὅτι δὴ τῶν ἑταίρων ἡμέρας σφίσιν ἀπολελεῖφθαί τινας ξυμβαίη.

γ΄. Ὕστερον καὶ τῶν ἐν παλατίῳ φυλάκων τινὲς, ἀνὰ πᾶσαν στελλόμενοι τὴν Ῥωμαίων ἀρχὴν, διηρευνῶντο δῆθεν τῷ λόγῳ ἐν τοῖς καταλόγοις τοὺς ἐς τὸ στρατεύεσθαι ἐπιτηδείους ὄντας ὡς ἥκιστα, καὶ αὐτῶν τινὰς μὲν, ἅτε ἀχρείους ὄντας καὶ γεγηρακότας, ἀφαιρεῖσθαι τὰς ζώνας ἐτόλμων, οἵπερ τὸ λοιπὸν ἐκ τῶν εὐσεβούντων ἐν τῷ δημοσίῳ τῆς ἀγορᾶς προσαιτοῦντες τροφήν, δακρύων τε καὶ ὀλοφύρσεως ἀεὶ προφάσεις τοῖς ἐντυγχάνουσιν ἐγίνοντο πᾶσι, τοὺς δὲ λοιποὺς, ὅπως δὴ μὴ ταῦτα καὶ αὐτοὶ πείσωνται, χρήματα μεγάλα ἐπράττετο· ὥστε πάντων τοὺς στρατιώτας, ἅτε τρόποις ἐκνενευρισμένους πολλοῖς, πτωχοτέρους τε γεγονέναι, καὶ οὐδαμῇ ἐς τὸ πολεμεῖν προθυμεῖσθαι ξυνέβη.

δ΄. Ὅθεν Ῥωμαίοις καὶ τὰ ἐν Ἰταλίᾳ πράγματα λελύσθαι ξυνέπεσεν, οὗ δὴ Ἀλέξανδρος ὁ λογοθέτης σταλεὶς, τοῖς μὲν στρατιώταις ταῦτα ἐπικαλεῖν οὐδεμιᾷ ὀκνήσει

COURT OF JUSTINIAN 197

Emperor to serve, although they showed their commissions, the genuineness of which the Logothetae did not hesitate to call in question; others, again, were disbanded for having absented themselves a short time from their quarters. Afterwards, some of the Palace Guards were sent into every part of the Empire to take an exact inventory of the soldiers who were or were not fit for service. Some were deprived of their belts, as being useless and too old, and for the future were obliged to solicit alms from the charitable in the open market-place —a sad and melancholy spectacle to all beholders. The rest were reduced to such a state of terror that, in order to avoid similar treatment, they offered large sums of money to buy themselves out, so that the soldiers, being thus rendered destitute and in many ways enfeebled, conceived an utter aversion to the service.

This endangered the authority of the Romans, especially in Italy. Alexander, who was sent thither as commissioner, unhesitatingly reproached the soldiers for

ΠΡΟΚΟΠΙΟΥ ΑΝΕΚΔΟΤΑ

ἐθάρρει· τοὺς δὲ Ἰταλοὺς χρήματα ἔπραττεν, τῶν ἐς Θευδέριχον καὶ Γότθους πεπολιτευμένων ἀμύνεσθαι φάσκων. Οὐ μόνοι δὲ οἱ στρατιῶται πενίᾳ τε καὶ ἀπορίᾳ πρὸς τῶν λογοθετῶν ἐπιέζοντο, ἀλλὰ καὶ οἱ πᾶσιν ὑπηρετοῦντες τοῖς στρατηγοῖς παμπληθεῖς τε καὶ δόξῃ μεγάλῃ τὰ πρότερα ὄντες, λιμῷ καὶ πενίᾳ δεινῇ ἤχθοντο. Οὐ γὰρ εἶχον ὅθεν τὰ εἰωθότα σφίσι πορίσονται.

έ. Προσθήσω δέ τι τούτοις καὶ ἕτερον, ἐπεί με ὁ τῶν στρατιωτῶν λόγος ἐς τοῦτο ἄγει. Οἱ Ῥωμαίων βεβασιλευκότες ἐν τοῖς ἄνω χρόνοις πανταχόσε τῶν τῆς πολιτείας ἐσχατιῶν πάμπολυ κατεστήσαντο στρατιωτῶν πλῆθος, ἐπὶ φυλακῇ τῶν ὁρίων τῆς Ῥωμαίων ἀρχῆς, καὶ κατὰ τὴν ἑῴαν μάλιστα μοῖραν ταύτῃ τὰς ἐφόδους Περσῶν τε καὶ Σαρακηνῶν ἀναστέλλοντες, οὕσπερ Λιμιταναίους ἐκάλουν. Τούτοις ὁ βασιλεὺς κατ' ἀρχὰς μὲν οὕτω δὴ παρέργως τε καὶ φαύλως ἐχρῆτο, ὥστε τεσσάρων ἢ πέντε αὐτοῖς ἐνιαυτῶν τῶν συντάξεων τοὺς χορηγοὺς ὑπερημέρους εἶναι· καὶ ἐπειδὰν Ῥωμαίοις τε καὶ Πέρσαις εἰρήνη

COURT OF JUSTINIAN 198

this. He also exacted large sums of money from the Italians, under the pretence of punishing them for their negotiations with Theoderic and the Goths. The soldiers were not the only persons who were reduced to poverty and privation by the commissioners; but those who had accompanied the generals in different capacities and had formerly enjoyed a high reputation, found themselves in great distress, as they had no means of procuring the ordinary necessaries. Since I am speaking of the soldiers, I will give a few additional details. Preceding Emperors had, for a very long time past, carefully posted upon all the frontiers of the Empire a large military force to protect its boundaries, and particularly, in the Eastern provinces, in order to repel the inroads of the Persians and Saracens, they had established garrisons called "frontier troops." Justinian at first treated these troops with such shameful neglect that their pay was four, or even five years in arrear; and, when peace was concluded between

γένοιτο, ἠναγκάζοντο οἱ ταλαίπωροι οὗτοι,
ἅτε καὶ αὐτοὶ τῶν ἐκ τῆς εἰρήνης ἀγαθῶν
ἀπολαύσοντες, χρόνου ῥητοῦ τὰς ὀφειλομένας
σφίσι συντάξεις τῷ δημοσίῳ χαρίζεσθαι· ὕστερον δὲ καὶ αὐτὸ τῆς στρατείας ὄνομα αὐτοὺς
ἀφείλετο οὐδενὶ λόγῳ. Τὸ λοιπὸν τὰ μὲν
ὅρια τῆς Ῥωμαίων ἀρχῆς φυλακτηρίων ἐκτὸς
ἔμεινε, οἱ δὲ στρατιῶται ἐξαπιναίως ἔβλεπον
εἰς τῶν εὐσεβεῖν εἰωθότων τὰς χεῖρας.

ς΄. Ἕτεροι στρατιῶται, οὐχ ἥσσους ἢ
πεντακόσιοι καὶ τρισχίλιοι, τὰ ἐξ ἀρχῆς ἐπὶ
φυλακῇ τοῦ παλατίου κατεστήσαντο, οὕσπερ
Σχολαρίους καλοῦσιν. Καὶ αὐτοῖς συντάξεις
ἀνέκαθεν, πλείους ἢ τοῖς ἄλλοις ἅπασι, τὸ
δημόσιον ἀεὶ χορηγεῖν εἴωθε. Τούτους οἱ πρότερον μὲν ἀριστίνδην ἀπολέξαντες ἐξ Ἀρμε-
νίων, ἐς ταύτην δὴ τὴν τιμὴν ἦγον· ἐξ οὗ δὲ
Ζήνων τὴν βασιλείαν παρέλαβε, πᾶσιν ἐξουσία ἐγένετο, καὶ ἀνάνδροις καὶ ἀπολέμοις
οὖσι παντάπασι, τούτου δὴ τοῦ ὀνόματος ἐπι-
βατεύειν. Προϊόντος δὲ τοῦ χρόνου, καὶ ἀνδρά-
ποδα κατατιθέντες τίμημα τὴν στρατείαν
ὠνοῦντο ταύτην. Ἡνίκα τοίνυν Ἰουστῖνος
τὴν βασιλείαν παρέλαβεν, οὗτος Ἰουστινιανὸς πολλοὺς εἰς τὴν τιμὴν κατεστήσατο ταύτην, χρήματα μεγάλα περιβαλλόμενος. Ἐπεὶ
δὲ τούτοις καταλόγοις οὐδένα ἐνδεῖν τὸ λοιπὸν

COURT OF JUSTINIAN 199

Rome and Persia, these unhappy individuals, who expected to enjoy the advantages of peace, were obliged to make a present to the treasury of the money due to them; and the Emperor finally disbanded them most unjustly. Thus the frontiers of the Roman Empire remained ungarrisoned, and the troops had nothing to subsist upon except the benevolence of the charitable.

There was a certain body of soldiers, about 3,500 in number, called "Scholares," who had been originally appointed as an imperial palace-guard, and received a larger pay from the imperial treasury than the rest of the army. They were first chosen according to merit from the Armenians; but, from the reign of Zeno, anyone, however cowardly and unwarlike, was allowed to enter this body. In course of time, even slaves, on payment of a sum of money, were admitted to their ranks. When Justin succeeded to the throne, Justinian enrolled a large number on payment of considerable sums of money. When the list was filled up,

ἤσθετο, ἑτέρους αὐτοῖς ἐς δισχιλίους ἐντέθεικεν, οὕσπερ Ὑπεραρίθμους ἐκάλουν. Ἐπειδὴ δὲ αὐτὸς τὴν βασιλείαν ἔσχεν, τούτους δὴ τοὺς Ὑπεραρίθμους ἀπεσείσατο αὐτίκα μάλα, τῶν χρημάτων οὐδ' ὁτιοῦν ἀποδοὺς σφίσιν.

ζ'. Ἐς μέντοι τοὺς ἐντὸς τοῦ τῶν Σχολαρίων ἀριθμοῦ ὄντας ἐπενόει τάδε. Ἡνίκα στράτευμα ἐπὶ Λιβύην ἢ Ἰταλίαν ἢ ἐπὶ Πέρσας ὡς σταλήσεται ἐπίδοξον ἦν, καὶ αὐτοῖς ὡς ξυστρατεύσουσιν ἐπήγγελλε συσκευάζεσθαι, καίπερ ἐξεπιστάμενος ἐπιτηδείως αὐτοὺς ἐς τὸ στρατεύεσθαι ὡς ἥκιστα ἔχειν· οἱ δὲ, τοῦτο ἵνα μὴ γένηται δείσαντες, χρόνου οἱ ῥητοῦ τὰς συντάξεις ἀφίεσαν. Ταῦτα μὲν τοῖς Σχολαρίοις πολλάκις ξυνηνέχθη παθεῖν.

Καὶ Πέτρος δὲ, τὸν ἅπαντα χρόνον ἡνίκα τὴν τοῦ Μαγίστρου καλουμένου εἶχεν ἀρχὴν, ἀεὶ καθ' ἡμέραν αὐτοὺς κλοπαῖς ἀμυθήτοις ἀπέκναιε. Πρᾶος μὲν γὰρ ἦν, καὶ ὡς ἥκιστα ὑβρίζειν εἰδὼς, κλεπτίστατος δὲ ἀνθρώπων ἁπάντων, καὶ ῥύπου αἰσχροῦ ἀτεχνῶς ἔμπλεως. Τούτου τοῦ Πέτρου κἀν τοῖς ἔμπροσθεν λόγοις ἐμνήσθην, ἅτε τὸν Ἀμαλασούνθης φόνον, τῆς Θευδερίχου παιδὸς, εἰργασμένου.

η'. Εἰσὶ δὲ καὶ ἕτεροι τῶν ἐν παλατίῳ πολὺ ἀξιώτεροι· ἐπεὶ καὶ πλείω τὸ δημόσιον αὐτοῖς χορηγεῖν εἴωθεν, ἅτε καὶ μείζω κατα-

COURT OF JUSTINIAN   200

he added about 2,000 more who were
called "Supernumeraries," but disbanded
them, when he himself came to the
throne, without any reimbursement. In
regard to these "Scholares," he invented
the following plan : Whenever it was
probable that an expedition would be
despatched to Italy, Libya, or Persia, he
ordered them to make ready to take part
in the campaign, although he knew that
they were utterly unfit for war; and they,
being afraid of this, surrendered their
salaries to the Emperor. This was a
frequent occurrence. When Peter was
"Master of Offices," he daily harassed
them with monstrous thefts. This man,
although he was of a mild and by no
means overbearing disposition, was the
greatest thief in the world and an absolute
slave to sordid avarice. He it was who
(as I have related) contrived the murder
of Amalasunta, the daughter of Theodoric.

There are in the imperial household
other officers of much higher rank, who,
having purchased their positions for a
larger sum, receive better pay in pro-

26

ΠΡΟΚΟΠΙΟΥ ΑΝΕΚΔΟΤΑ

τιθεῖσι τοῦ τῆς στρατείας ὀνόματος τὰ τιμήματα, οἱ δὴ Δομέστικοί τε καὶ Προτήκτορες
ἐπικαλοῦνται, καὶ ἀνέκαθεν ἀμελέτητοί εἰσι
πολεμίων ἔργων. Τάξεως γὰρ καὶ προσώπου
ἕνεκα μόνον ἐν παλατίῳ εἰώθασι καταλέγεσ-
θαι. Καὶ αὐτῶν οἱ μὲν ἐν Βυζαντίῳ, οἱ δὲ
ἐπί τε Γαλατίας ἐκ παλαιοῦ καὶ χωρίων
ἑτέρων ἵδρυνται. Ἀλλὰ καὶ τούτους Ἰουστινιανὸς, τρόπῳ ἀεὶ δεδισσόμενος τῷ εἰρημένῳ,
μεθίεσθαι ἠνάγκαζε τῶν προσηκουσῶν σφίσι
συντάξεων.

θ'. Ἐν κεφαλαίῳ δὲ τοῦτο εἰρήσεται.
Νόμος ἦν ἀνὰ πενταετηρίδα ἑκάστην τὸν
βασιλέα τῶν στρατιωτῶν ἕκαστον δωρεῖσθαι
χρυσίῳ τακτῷ. Πέμποντες δὲ ἀνὰ πεντάετες
πανταχόσε τῆς Ῥωμαίων ἀρχῆς, παρείχοντο
στατῆρας χρυσοῦς στρατιώτῃ ἑκάστῳ πέντε.
Καὶ τοῦτο οὐχ οἷόν τε ἦν μὴ πράσσεσθαι ἀεὶ
μηχανῇ πάσῃ. Ἐξ ὅτου δὲ ἀνὴρ ὅδε διῳκήσατο τὴν πολιτείαν, τοιοῦτο οὐδὲν οὔτε
διεπράξατο, οὔτε ἐμέλλησε, καίπερ χρόνου δύο
καὶ τριάκοντα ἐνιαυτῶν τριβέντος ἤδη, ὥστε
καὶ λήθην τοῦ ἔργου τούτου τοῖς ἀνθρώποις
γενέσθαι.

COURT OF JUSTINIAN 201

portion. These are called "Domestics" and "Protectors." They have always been exempt from military service, and are only reckoned members of the palace on account of their dignity and rank. Some of them are constantly in Byzantium, while others have long been established in Galatia or other provinces. Justinian frightened these in the same manner into abandoning their salaries to him. In conclusion, it was the custom that, every five years, the Emperor should present each of the soldiers with a fixed sum in gold. Accordingly, every five years, commissioners were despatched to all parts of the Empire, to bestow five staters of gold upon every soldier as a gift from the Emperor. This had long been an established and inviolable practice. But, from the day that Justinian assumed the management of affairs, he did nothing of the kind, and showed no intention of doing so during the thirty-two years of his reign, so that the custom was almost completely forgotten.

ΠΡΟΚΟΠΙΟΥ ΑΝΕΚΔΟΤΑ

ΚΕΦΑΛΑΙΟΝ ΚΕ'.

α'. Τινὰ τρόπον δὲ καὶ ἄλλον τῆς ἐς τοὺς κατηκόους λεηλασίας ἐρῶν ἔρχομαι. Οἱ βασιλεῖ τε καὶ ταῖς ἀρχαῖς ἐν Βυζαντίῳ, ἢ ὁπλιζόμενοι, ἢ γράμματα διαχειρίζοντες, ἢ ἄλλο ὁτιοῦν ὑπηρετοῦντες, τάσσονται μὲν ἐν τοῖς καταλόγοις ἀρχὴν ἔσχατοι. Προϊόντος δὲ τοῦ χρόνου ἀναβαίνοντες ἀεὶ ἐς τῶν ἀπο-γινομένων ἢ ὑπεξιόντων τὴν χώραν, τάξεως ἕκαστοι τῆς κατ' αὐτοὺς ἐς τόδε χωροῦσιν, ἕως ἄν τις βαθμοῦ ἐπιβεβηκὼς τοῦ πρώτου, ἤδη ἐς τὸ τῆς τιμῆς ἀφίκηται πέρας.

Καὶ τοῖς ἐς τοῦτο ἀξιώματος ἥκουσι χρήματα ἐκ παλαιοῦ διατέτακται τοσαῦτα τὸ πλῆθος, ὥστε πλέον ἀνὰ πᾶν ἔτος ἢ ἐς ἑκατὸν χρυσοῦ ἀγείρεσθαι κεντηνάρια τούτοις, (καὶ) αὐτούς τε γηροκομεῖσθαι καὶ τῶν ἄλλων πολ-λοὺς μετέχειν αὐτοῖς ὠφελείας ἐκ τοῦ ἐπὶ πλεῖστον τοῖς ἔνθεν ξυνέβαινε, τῆς τε πολιτείας τὰ πράγματα ἐπὶ μέγα εὐπορίας ἀεὶ ταύτῃ

COURT OF JUSTINIAN   202

CHAPTER XXV

I WILL now proceed to mention
another mode in which he plundered
his subjects. Those who, at Byzantium,
serve the Emperor or magistrates, either
as secretaries, or in a military or any
other capacity, are placed last upon the
list of officials. As time goes on, they
are gradually promoted to the place of
those who have died or retired, until they
reach the highest rank and supreme
dignity. Those who had attained to this
honour, in accordance with an ancient
institution, had the right to the enjoyment of a fund of not less than 100
centenars of gold yearly, so that they
might have a comfortable means of subsistence for their old age, and might be
able to assist others as much as possible;
and this was of great influence in bringing
about a successful administration of the

ΠΡΟΚΟΠΙΟΥ ΑΝΕΚΔΟΤΑ

ἐχώρει. Ἀλλὰ βασιλεὺς ὅδε, τούτων αὐτοὺς ἀποστερήσας σχεδόν τι ἁπάντων, αὐτοῖς τε καὶ τοῖς ἄλλοις ἀνθρώποις κακὰ ἤνεγκεν. Ἁψαμένη γὰρ αὐτῶν ἡ πενία πρῶτον, εἶτα καὶ διὰ τῶν ἄλλων ἐχώρει, οἷς τι καὶ πρότερον ὠφελείας μετῆν. Καὶ ἤν τις τὴν ξυμπεπτωκυῖαν αὐτοῖς ἐνθένδε ζημίαν ἐς ἔτη δύο καὶ τριάκοντα διαριθμοῖτο, εὑρήσει τὸ μέτρον, ὧνπερ αὐτοὺς ἀποστερεῖσθαι ξυνέπεσε. Τοὺς μὲν στρατευομένους οὕτως ὁ τύραννος διεχρήσατο.

β΄. Ἅπερ δὲ αὐτ ῳ εἰς ἐμπόρους τε καὶ ναύτας καὶ βαναύσους καὶ ἀγοραίους ἀνθρώπους, δι᾽ αὐτῶν τε καὶ ἐς τοὺς ἄλλους ἅπαντας εἴργασται, φράσων ἔρχομαι. Πορθμὼ δύο ἑκατέρωθεν Βυζαντίου ἐστόν, ἕτερος μὲν ἐφ᾽ Ἑλλησπόντου ἀμφὶ Σηστόν τε καὶ Ἄβυδον, ὁ δὲ δὴ ἕτερος ἐπὶ τοῦ στόματος τοῦ Εὐξείνου καλουμένου Πόντου, οὗ τὸ Ἱερὸν ὀνομάζεται. Ἐν μὲν οὖν τῷ Ἑλλησπόντου πορθμῷ τελωνεῖον μὲν ἐν δημοσίῳ ὡς ἥκιστα ἦν. Ἄρχων δέ τις ἐκ βασιλέως στελλόμενος ἐν Ἀβύδῳ καθῆστο, διερευνώμενος μὲν, ἢν ναῦς ὅπλα φέρουσα ἐς Βυζάντιον οὐ βασιλέως ἴοι γνώμῃ,

COURT OF JUSTINIAN 203

affairs of state. But Justinian deprived
them of all their privileges, and did great
harm, not only to them, but to many
others besides, for the poverty which
attacked them extended to all those who
formerly shared their prosperity. If anyone were to calculate the sums of which
they were thus deprived during these
thirty-two years, he would find that the
amount was very considerable. Such was
the shameful manner in which the tyrant
treated his soldiers.

I will now relate how he behaved
towards merchants, mariners, artisans,
shopkeepers and others. There are two
narrow straits on either side of Byzantium, the one in the Hellespont, between
Sestos and Abydos, the other at the
mouth of the Euxine Sea, close to the
chapel of the Holy Mother. In the strait
upon the Hellespont, there was no public
custom-house, but an officer was sent by
the Emperor to Abydos, to see that no
ship loaded with arms should pass on
the way to Byzantium without the Emperor's leave, and also that no person

καὶ ἤν τις ἐκ Βυζαντίου ἀνάγοιτο, οὐ φερόμενος γράμματα τῶν ἀνδρῶν καὶ σημεῖα, οἷς
ἐπίκειται ἡ τιμὴ αὕτη· (οὐ γὰρ θέμις τινὰ
ἐκ Βυζαντίου ἀνάγεσθαι οὐκ ἀφειμένον πρὸς
τῶν ἀνδρῶν, οἳ τῇ τοῦ Μαγίστρου καλουμένου
ἀρχῇ ὑπουργοῦσι·) πραττόμενος δὲ τοὺς τῶν
πλοίων κυρίους, τέλος οὐδενὶ αἴσθησιν παρεχόμενον ἐλάμβανεν· ὁ δὲ ἐπὶ πορθμοῦ τοῦ
ἑτέρου στελλόμενος μισθὸν ἀεὶ πρὸς βασιλέως
κεκομισμένος ἦν, καὶ διερευνώμενος ἐς τὸ ἀκριβὲς ταῦτα, ἅπερ μοι εἴρηται, καὶ ἤν τι ἐς τοὺς
βαρβάρους κομίζοιτο, οἳ παρὰ τὸν Εὔξεινον
ἵδρυνται πόντον, ὧνπερ οὐ θέμις ἐκ ᾽Ρωμαίων
τῆς γῆς ἐς τοὺς πολεμίους κομίζεσθαι· οὐδὲν
μέντοι ἐξῆν τῷ ἀνδρὶ τούτῳ πρὸς τῶν τῇδε
ναυτιλλομένων προσίεσθαι.

γ'. ᾽Εξ οὗ δὲ ᾽Ιουστινιανὸς τὴν βασιλείαν παρέλαβε, τελωνεῖόν τε δημόσιον κατεστήσατο ἐν πορθμῷ ἑκατέρῳ, καὶ μισθοφόρους
ἄρχοντας δύο ἐς ἀεὶ πέμπων, μίσθωσιν μὲν
αὐτοῖς παρείχετο τὴν ξυγκειμένην, ἐπήγγελλε
δὲ χρήματά οἱ ὅτι πλεῖστα ἐνθένδε ἀποφέρειν
δυνάμει τῇ πάσῃ. Οἱ δὲ ἄλλο οὐδὲν ἢ εὔνοιαν
τὴν ἐπ' αὐτὸν ἐνδείκνυσθαι ἐν σπουδῇ ἔχοντες,
ἁπαξάπαντα πρὸς τῶν πλεόντων τὰ τῶν φορτίων τιμήματα ληιζόμενοι, ἀπηλλάσσοντο. ᾽Εν
μὲν οὖν πορθμῷ ἑκατέρῳ ταῦτα ἐποίει.

COURT OF JUSTINIAN   204

should put out to sea from Byzantium
without letters of licence signed by the
proper official, no ship being allowed to
leave the city without the permission of
the secretaries of the Master of Offices.
The amount which the praetor exacted
from the shipmasters under the name of
toll was so insignificant that it was disregarded. A praetor was also sent to
the other strait, who received his salary
regularly from the Emperor, and whose
duties were the same—to take care that
no one transported to the barbarians on
the Euxine any wares, the export of
which to hostile countries was forbidden;
but he was not allowed to exact any
duties from these navigators. But, from
the day that Justinian succeeded to the
government of affairs, he established a
custom-house on both straits, and sent
thither two officials to collect the dues
at a fixed salary, who were ordered to
get in as much money as they could.
These officials, who desired nothing better
than to show their devotion to him, extorted duty upon all kinds of merchandise

δ΄. Ἐν δὲ Βυζαντίῳ ἐπενόει τάδε. Τῶν τινά οἱ ἐπιτηδείων προὐστήσατο, Σύρον μὲν γένος, ὄνομα δὲ Ἀδδεον, ᾧ δὴ ἐπήγγελλεν ἐκ νηῶν τῶν ἐνταῦθα καταιρουσῶν ὄνησίν τινά οἱ πορίζεσθαι. Ὁ δὲ πλοῖα ἅπαντα τὰ καταίροντα ἐς τὸν Βυζάντιον λιμένα οὐκέτι ἠφίει, ἀλλὰ τοὺς ναυκλήρους ἢ τοῖς τιμήμασιν ἐζημίου νηῶν τῶν σφετέρων, ἢ ἀναφορεῖν ἔς τε Λιβύην καὶ Ἰταλίαν ἠνάγκαζε. Καὶ αὐτῶν οἱ μὲν οὔτε ἀντιφορτίζεσθαι οὔτε θαλαττουργεῖν ἔτι ἤθελον, ἀλλὰ καύσαντες τὰ σφέτερα πλοῖα, εὐθὺς ἄσμενοι ἀπηλλάσσοντο. Ὅσοις μέντοι ἐπάναγκες ἦν ἐκ ταύτης δὴ τῆς ἐργασίας τὸν βίον ποιεῖσθαι, οὗτοι τριπλασίαν πρὸς τῶν ἐμπόρων τὴν μίσθωσιν κεκομισμένοι, τὸ λοιπὸν ἐφορτίζοντο, τοῖς τε ἐμπόροις περιειστήκει ταύτην σφίσιν αὐτοῖς τὴν ζημίαν πρὸς τῶν τὰ φορτία ὠνουμένων ἰάσασθαι, οὕτω τε λιμοκτονεῖσθαι πάσῃ μηχανῇ τοὺς Ῥωμαίους ξυνέβαινεν.

ε΄. Ἀλλὰ ταῦτα μὲν τῇδε κατὰ τὴν πολιτείαν ἐφέρετο. Ἃ δὲ καὶ ἐς τὰ κέρματα

COURT OF JUSTINIAN 205

In regard to the port of Byzantium, he made the following arrangement : — He put it in charge of one of his confidants, a Syrian by birth, named Addeus, whom he ordered to exact duty from all vessels which put in there. This Addeus would not allow those ships which had been any length of time in the harbour to leave it, until the masters had paid a sum of money to free them, or else he compelled them to take on board a freight for Libya or Italy. Some, resolved not to take in a return cargo or to remain at sea any longer, burned their ships and thus escaped all anxiety, to their great rejoicing. But all those who were obliged to continue their profession in order to live, for the future demanded three times the usual amount from merchants for the hire of the ships, and thus the merchants had no means of covering their losses except by requiring a higher price from purchasers ; and thus, by every possible contrivance, the Romans were reduced to the danger of starvation. Such was the general state of affairs. I must not, how-

τοῖς βασιλεῦσιν εἴργασται, οὔ μοι παριτέον οἴομαι εἶναι. Τῶν γὰρ ἀργυραμοιβῶν πρότερον δέκα καὶ διακοσίους ὀβολοὺς, οὓς φόλεις καλοῦσιν, ὑπὲρ ἑνὸς στατῆρος χρυσοῦ προίεσθαι τοῖς ξυμβάλλουσιν εἰωθότων, αὐτοὶ ἐπιτεχνώμενοι κέρδη οἰκεῖα, ὀγδοήκοντα ἑκατὸν μόνους ὑπὲρ τοῦ στατῆρος δίδοσθαι τοὺς ὀβολοὺς διετάξαντο. Ταύτην δὲ νομίσματος ἑκάστου χρυσοῦ ἕκτην ἀπέτεμον μοῖραν πάντων ἀνθρώπων.

ζ. Ἐπεὶ δὲ οἱ βασιλεῖς οὗτοι, τῶν ὠνίων τὰ πλεῖστα εἰς τὰ καλούμενα περιστήσαντες μονοπώλια, τούς τι ὠνήσασθαι βουλομένους ἀεὶ καθ' ἑκάστην ἀπέπνιγον· μόνα δὲ αὐτοῖς ἀνέφαπτα τὰ τῆς ἐσθῆτος ἐλέλειπτο πωλητήρια, μηχανῶνται καὶ ἀμφ' αὐτοῖς τάδε. Ἱμάτια τὰ ἐκ μετάξης, ἐν Βηρυτῷ μὲν καὶ Τύρῳ πόλεσι, ταῖς ἐπὶ Φοινίκης, ἐργάζεσθαι ἐκ παλαιοῦ εἰώθει. Οἵ τε τούτων ἔμποροί τε καὶ ἐπιδημιουργοὶ καὶ τεχνῖται ἐνταῦθα τὸ ἀνέκαθεν ᾤκουν, ἐνθένδε τε ἐς γῆν ἅπασαν φέρεσθαι τὸ ἐμπόλημα τοῦτο ξυνέβαινεν. Ἐπὶ δὲ Ἰουστινιανοῦ βασιλεύοντος, οἱ ἐπὶ ταύτῃ τῇ ἐργασίᾳ ἔν τε Βυζαντίῳ καὶ πόλεσι ταῖς ἄλλαις ὄντες, ἀξιωτέραν ἀπεδίδοντο τὴν ἐσθῆτα ταύτην, αἰτιώμενοι μεῖζον μὲν ἢ πρότερον ἐν χρόνῳ τῷ παρόντι ὑπὲρ αὐτῆς καταβάλλεσθαι τὸ τίμημα Πέρσαις, πλείω

COURT OF JUSTINIAN 206

ever, omit to state the manner in which the rulers dealt with the small coinage. The money-changers had formerly been accustomed to give 210 obols (called Pholes) for a single gold stater. Justinian and Theodora, for their own private gain, ordered that only 180 obols should be given for the stater, and by this means deprived the public of a sixth part of each piece of gold. Having established "monopolies" upon most wares, they incessantly harassed would-be purchasers. The only thing left free from duty was clothes, but, in regard to these also, the imperial pair contrived to extort money. Silken garments had for a long time been made in Berytus and Tyre, cities of Phoenicia. The merchants and workmen connected with the trade had been settled there from very early times, and from thence the business had spread throughout the world. During the reign of Justinian, those who lived in Byzantium and other cities raised the price of their silks, on the plea that at the present time they were dearer in Persia, and that the

δὲ νῦν τὰ δεκατευτήρια εἶναι ἐν γῇ τῇ Ῥωμαίων, δόκησιν ἄπασιν ὁ αὐτοκράτωρ παρεχόμενος, ὅτι δὴ ἐπὶ τούτῳ ἀγανακτοίη, νόμῳ
ἄπασιν ἀπεῖπε, μὴ πλέον ἢ ὀκτὼ χρυσῶν
τῆς τοιαύτης ἐσθῆτος τὴν λίτραν εἶναι. Καὶ
προστίμημα ἔκειτο τοῖς παραβησομένοις τὸν
νόμον, τῶν ὑπαρχόντων στερεῖσθαι χρημάτων. Ταῦτα ἀνθρώποις ἀμήχανά τε καὶ ἄπορα
ἐδόκει παντάπασιν εἶναι. Οὐ γὰρ οἷόν τε ἦν
τοὺς ἐμπόρους, μείζονος τιμῆς τὰ φορτία ἐωνη-
μένους, ἐλάσσονος τιμῆς τοῖς ξυμβάλλουσιν
ἀποδίδοσθαι. Διὸ δὴ ταύτην μὲν τὴν ἐμπο-
ρίαν ἐργολαβεῖν οὐκέτι ἠξίουν, ἐπικλοπώτερον
δὲ φορτίων τῶν σφίσιν ἀπολελειμμένων ἐποιοῦντο κατὰ βραχὺ τὰς πράσεις, δηλονότι τῶν
γνωρίμων τισὶν, οἷσπερ τὰ τοιαῦτα καλλωπί-
ζειν τὰ σφέτερ' αὐτῶν προϊεμένοις ἐν ἡδονῇ ἦν,
ἢ τρόπῳ τῳ ἀναγκαῖον ἐγίνετο.

η'. Ὧν δὴ ἡ βασιλὶς ἐπιψιθυριζόντων
τινῶν αἰσθομένη, καίπερ οὐ βασανίσασα τὰ
θρυλούμενα, ξύμπαντα εὐθὺς τὰ φορτία τοὺς
ἀνθρώπους ἀφείλετο, καὶ χρυσίον αὐτοὺς ἐς
κεντηνάριον ἐπιτιμησαμένη. Ἄρχει δὲ ταύ-

COURT OF JUSTINIAN   207

import tithes were higher. The Emperor pretended to be exceedingly indignant at this, and subsequently published an edict forbidding a pound of silk to be sold for more than eight gold pieces; anyone who disobeyed the edict was to be punished by the confiscation of his property. This measure appeared altogether impracticable and absurd. For it was not possible for the merchants, who had bought their wares at a much higher price, to sell it to customers at a lower rate. They accordingly resolved to give up this business, and secretly and without delay disposed of their remaining wares to certain well-known persons, who took delight in wasting their money upon such adornments, and to whom it had become in a manner an absolute necessity. Theodora heard of this from certain persons who whispered it confidentially, and, without taking the trouble to verify the report, she immediately deprived these persons of their wares, and, in addition, inflicted upon them a fine of a centenar of gold. At the present time, the imperial

της ἔν γε Ῥωμαίοις τῆς ἐργασίας ὁ τοῖς βασιλικοῖς ἐφεστὼς θησαυροῖς. Πέτρον οὖν τὸν Βαρσυάμην ἐπίκλησιν ἐπὶ ταύτης καταστησάμενοι τῆς τιμῆς, οὐ πολλῷ ὕστερον ἐπεχώρουν αὐτῷ πράσσειν ἀνόσια ἔργα. Τοὺς μὲν ἄλλους ἅπαντας τὸν νόμον ἐς τὸ ἀκριβὲς ἐδικαίου τηρεῖν, τοὺς δὲ τοῦ ἔργου τούτου τεχνίτας αὐτῷ νόμῳ ἀναγκάζων ἐργάζεσθαι ἐπεδίδοτο, οὐκέτι ἐπικρυπτόμενος, ἀλλ' ἐν τῷ δημοσίῳ τῆς ἀγορᾶς, βαφῆς μὲν τῆς προστυχούσης τὴν οὐγκίαν οὐχ ἧσσον ἢ κατὰ ἓξ χρυσῶν, βάμματος δὲ τοῦ βασιλικοῦ, ὅπερ καλεῖν ὁλόβηρον νενομίκασι, πλέον ἢ τεσσάρων καὶ εἴκοσι χρυσῶν.

θ΄. Καὶ βασιλεῖ μὲν ἐνθένδε μεγάλα χρήματα ἔφερεν· αὐτὸς δὲ περιβαλλόμενος πλείω ἐλάνθανεν, ὅπερ ἀπ' αὐτοῦ ἀρξάμενον ἐς ἀεὶ ἔμεινε. Μόνος γὰρ ἐς τόδε τοῦ χρόνου ἔμπορός τε ἀπαρακαλύπτως καὶ κάπηλος τοῦ ἐμπολήματος τοῦδε καθίσταται. Ἔμποροι μὲν οὖν ὅσοι πρότερον τὴν ἐργασίαν ταύτην μετῄεσαν, ἔν τε Βυζαντίῳ καὶ πόλει ἑκάστῃ, θαλαττουργοί τε καὶ ἔγγειοι, ἐφέροντο, ὡς τὸ εἰκὸς, τὰ ἐκ τῆς ἐργασίας κακά. Ἐν δὲ πόλεσιν ὁ δῆμος σχεδόν τι ὅλος ταῖς εἰρημέναις προσ-

COURT OF JUSTINIAN 208

treasurer is charged with the superintend-
ence of this trade. When Peter Barsyames held the office, they soon allowed
him all manner of licence in carrying out
his nefarious practices. He demanded
that all the rest should carefully observe
the law, and compelled those who were
engaged in the silk factories to work for
himself alone. Without taking any trouble
to conceal it, he sold an ounce of any
ordinary coloured silk in the public
market-place for six pieces of gold, but
if it was of the royal dye, called Holovere,
he asked more than four-and-twenty for
it. In this manner he procured vast
sums of money for the Emperor, and even
larger sums, which he kept privately for
himself; and this practice, begun by him,
continued. The grand treasurer is at this
moment avowedly the only silk merchant
and sole controller of the market. All
those who formerly carried on this business, either in Byzantium or any other
city, workers on sea or land, felt the loss
severely. Nearly the whole population
of the cities which existed by such manu-

ΠΡΟΚΟΠΙΟΥ ΑΝΕΚΔΟΤΑ

αιτητὴς ἐξαπιναίως ἐγένετο. Βάναυσοι γὰρ ἄνθρωποι καὶ χειρωνάκται λιμῷ παλαίειν, ὡς τὸ εἰκὸς, ἠναγκάζοντο· πολλοί τε ἀπ' αὐτοῦ τὴν πολιτείαν μεταβαλλόμενοι, φεύγοντες ᾤχοντο ἐς τὰ Περσῶν ἤθη. Μόνος δὲ ἀεὶ ὁ τῶν θησαυρῶν ἄρχων, ἐνεργολαβὼν τὸ ἐμπόλημα τοῦτο, μοῖραν μὲν βασιλεῖ, ὥσπερ εἴρηται, πόρων τῶν ἐνθένδε ἀποφέρειν ἠξίου· αὐτὸς δὲ τὰ πλείω φερόμενος, δημοσίαις συμφοραῖς ἐπλούτει. Ταῦτα μὲν οὖν τῇδε κεχώρηκεν.

COURT OF JUSTINIAN

factories were reduced to begging. Artisans and mechanics were forced to struggle against hunger, and many of them, quitting their country, fled to Persia. None but the chief treasurer was allowed to have anything to do with that branch of industry, and, while he handed over part of his gains to the Emperor, he kept the greater part for himself, and thus grew wealthy at the expense of the unfortunate public.

ΠΡΟΚΟΠΙΟΥ ΑΝΕΚΔΟΤΑ

ΚΕΦΑΛΑΙΟΝ ΚϚ'.

α'. "Οντινα δὲ τρόπον τῶν πόλεων τοὺς κόσμους καὶ τὰ ἐγκαλλωπίσματα πάντα, ἔν τε Βυζαντίῳ καὶ πόλει ἑκάστῃ, καθελεῖν ἴσχυσεν, αὐτίκα ἐροῦμεν.

Πρῶτα μὲν καταλύειν τὸ τῶν ῥητόρων ἀξίωμα ἔγνω. Τά τε γὰρ ἔπαθλα ἀφείλετο αὐτοὺς ἅπαντα, οἷσπερ τρυφᾶν τε τὰ πρότερα καὶ ἐγκαλλωπίζεσθαι τῆς συνηγορίας ἀφειμένοι εἰώθασι, καὶ διωμότους συνίστασθαι τοὺς διαφερομένους ἐκέλευσε, καὶ ἀπ' αὐτοῦ περιυβρισμένοι ἐν πολλῇ ἀσημίᾳ ἐγένοντο. Ἐπεὶ δὲ τῶν· τε ἀπὸ τῆς συγκλήτου βουλῆς καὶ τῶν ἄλλων εὐδαιμόνων δοκούντων εἶναι ἔν τε Βυζαντίῳ καὶ πάσῃ τῇ Ῥωμαίων ἀρχῇ πάσας, ὥσπερ ἐρρήθη, τὰς οὐσίας ἀφείλετο, ἀργεῖν τὸ λοιπὸν τῷ ἐπιτηδεύματι τούτῳ ἐλέλειπτο. Οὐ γὰρ εἶχον ἄνθρωποι λόγου ὁτουοῦν οὐδὲν ἄξιον, οὗπερ ἂν ἀμφισβητοῖεν ἀλλήλοις. Αὐτίκα τοίνυν ἐκ πολλῶν μὲν ὀλίγοι, ἐξ ἐνδόξων δὲ λίαν κομιδῇ ἄδοξοι πανταχόθι γεγονότες τῆς

CHAPTER XXVI

I MUST now relate how he robbed Byzantium and other cities of their ornaments. In the first place he resolved to humiliate the lawyers. He deprived them of all the fees, which, after they had finished their case, were considerable, and enriched them and increased their distinction. He ordered that litigants should come to an agreement upon oath, which brought the lawyers into contempt and insignificance. After he had seized the estates of the Senators and other families reputed wealthy, in Byzantium and throughout the Empire, the profession had little to do, for the citizens no longer possessed property worth disputing about. Thus, of the numerous and famous orators who once composed this order there remained only a few, who were everywhere despised and lived in the

γῆς, πενίᾳ μὲν, ὡς τὸ εἰκὸς, πολλῇ εἴχοντο, μόνην δὲ ὕβριν τὴν ἀπὸ τοῦ ἔργου φερόμενοι ἀπηλλάσσοντο.

β΄. Ἀλλὰ καὶ τοὺς ἰατρούς τε καὶ διδασκάλους τῶν ἐλευθερίων τῶν ἀναγκαίων στερεῖσθαι πεποίηκε. Τάς τε γὰρ σιτήσεις, ἃς οἱ πρότερον βεβασιλευκότες ἐκ τοῦ δημοσίου χορηγεῖσθαι τούτοις δὴ τοῖς ἐπιτηδεύμασιν ἔταξαν, ταύτας δὴ οὗτος ἀφείλετο πάσας.

γ΄. Καὶ μὴν καὶ ὅσους οἱ τὰς πόλεις οἰκοῦντες ἁπάσας πολιτικῶν σφίσιν ἢ θεωρητικῶν οἴκοθεν πεποίηνται πόρους, καὶ· τούτους μεταγαγὼν φόροις ἀναμίξαι τοῖς δημοσίοις ἐτόλμησε. Καὶ οὔτε ἰατρῶν τις ἢ διδασκάλων τὸ λοιπὸν ἐγίνετο λόγος, οὔτε δημοσίας τις ἔτι οἰκοδομίας προνοεῖν ἴσχυσεν, οὔτε λύχνα ταῖς πόλεσιν ἐν δημοσίῳ ἑκάστῃ, οὔτε τις ἦν ἄλλη παραψυχὴ τοῖς ταύτας οἰκοῦσι. Τά τε γὰρ θέατρα καὶ ἱππόδρομοι καὶ κυνηγέσια ἐκ τοῦ ἐπιπλεῖστον ἅπαντα ἤργει, οὗ δή οἱ τὴν γυναῖκα τετέχθαι τε καὶ τετράφθαι καὶ πεπαιδεῦσθαι ξυνέβαινεν. Ὕστερον δὲ ταῦτα δὴ ἀργεῖν ἐν Βυζαντίῳ ἐκέλευσε τὰ θεάματα, τοῦ μὴ τὰ εἰωθότα χορηγεῖν τὸ δημόσιον, πολλοῖς τε καὶ σχεδόν τι ἀναρίθμοις οὖσιν, οἷς ἐνθένδε ὁ βίος· ἦν τε

COURT OF JUSTINIAN   211

greatest poverty, finding that their profession brought them nothing but insult.
He also caused physicians and professors
of the liberal arts to be deprived of the
necessaries of life. He cut off from them
all the supplies which former emperors
had attached to these professions, and
which were paid out of the State funds.
Further, he had no scruple about trans-
ferring to the public funds all the revenues which the inhabitants of the cities
had devoted either to public purposes or
for providing entertainments. From that
time no attention was paid to physicians
or professors; no one ventured to trouble
himself about the public buildings; there
were no public lights in the cities, or
any enjoyments for the inhabitants; the
performances in the theatres and hippo-
dromes and the combats of wild beasts,
in which Theodora had been bred and
brought up, were entirely discontinued.
He afterwards suppressed public exhibi-
tions in Byzantium, to save the usual
State contribution, to the ruin of an
almost countless multitude who found

ἰδίᾳ τε καὶ κοινῇ λύπη τε καὶ κατήφεια, ὥσπερ ἄλλο τι τῶν ἀπ' οὐρανοῦ ἐπισκήψασθαι πάθος, καὶ βίος πᾶσιν ἀγέλαστος. Ἄλλο τε τὸ παράπαν οὐδὲν ἐφέρετο τοῖς ἀνθρώποις ἐν διηγήμασιν, οἴκοι τε οὖσι καὶ ἀγοράζουσι, κἂν τοῖς ἱεροῖς διατρίβουσιν, ἢ συμφοραί τε καὶ πάθη καὶ καινοτέρων ἀτυχημάτων ὑπερβολή. Ταῦτα μὲν οὕτω ταῖς πόλεσιν εἶχεν.

δ'. Ὁ δὲ τῷ λόγῳ λείπεται, τοῦτο εἰπεῖν ἄξιον. Ὕπατοι Ῥωμαίων ἀνὰ πᾶν ἔτος ἐγινέσθην δύο, ἅτερος μὲν ἐν Ῥώμῃ, ὁ δὲ δὴ ἕτερος ἐν Βυζαντίῳ. Ὅστις δὲ εἰς τὴν τιμὴν ἐκαλεῖτο ταύτην, πλέον ἢ κεντηνάρια χρυσοῦ εἴκοσιν ἐς τὴν πολιτείαν ἀναλοῦν ἔμελλεν, ὀλίγα μὲν οἰκεῖα, τὰ δὲ πλεῖστα πρὸς βασιλέως κεκομισμένος. Ταῦτά τε τὰ χρήματα ἔς τε τοὺς ἄλλους, ὧνπερ ἐμνήσθην, καὶ ἐκ τοῦ ἐπὶ πλεῖστον ἐς τῶν βίων τοὺς ἀπορωτέρους φερόμενα καὶ διαφερόντως ἐς τοὺς ἐπὶ σκηνῆς, ἅπαντα τὰ πράγματα ἐς ἀεὶ τῇ πόλει ἀνίστη. Ἐξ οὗ δὲ Ἰουστινιανὸς τὴν βασιλείαν παρέλαβεν, οὐκέτι καιροῖς τοῖς καθήκουσι ταῦτα

COURT OF JUSTINIAN   212

their means of support in these entertainments. Their life, both in public and private, became sad and dejected and utterly joyless, as if some misfortune had fallen upon them from Heaven. Nothing was spoken of in conversation at home, in the streets, or in the churches, except misfortune and suffering. Such was the state of the cities.

I have still something important to mention. Every year two consuls were appointed—one at Rome, the other at Byzantium. Whoever was advanced to that dignity was expected to expend more than twenty centenars of gold upon the public. This sum was to a small extent furnished by the consuls themselves, while the greater part was due to the liberality of the Emperor. This money was distributed amongst those whom I have mentioned, above all to the most necessitous, and principally to those employed upon the stage, which materially increased the comfort of the citizens. But, since the accession of Justinian, the elections never took place at the proper

ΠΡΟΚΟΠΙΟΥ ΑΝΕΚΔΟΤΑ

ἐπράσσετο, ἄλλοτε μὲν πολλοῦ Ῥωμαίοις ὕπατος καθίστατο χρόνου, τελευτῶντες δὲ οὐδὲ ὄναρ τὸ πρᾶγμα ἑώρων· ἐξ οὗ δὴ πενίᾳ τινὶ ἐνδελεχέστατα ἐσφίγγετο τὰ ἀνθρώπεια, τὰ μὲν εἰωθότα οὐκέτι τοῖς ὑπηκόοις παρεχομένου, τὰ δὲ ὑπάρχοντα τρόποις ἅπασι πανταχόθεν ἀφαιρουμένου.

ε΄. Ὡς μὲν οὖν τὰ δημόσια καταπιὼν ξύμπαντα χρήματα, τοὺς ἐκ τῆς συγκλήτου βουλῆς ὁ λυμεὼν οὗτος ἕκαστόν τε ἰδίᾳ καὶ κοινῇ ξύμπαντας τὰς οὐσίας ἀφῄρηται, διαρκῶς δεδιηγῆσθαι οἶμαι. Ὡς δὲ καὶ τοὺς ἄλλους, εὐδαίμονας δοκοῦντας εἶναι, συκοφαντίᾳ περιιὼν ἀφαιρεῖσθαι τὰ χρήματα ἴσχυσεν, ἱκανώτατά μοι εἰρῆσθαι νομίζω. Ἐν μέντοι στρατιώταις τε καὶ ἄρχουσι πᾶσιν ὑπηρετοῦντας, καὶ τοὺς ἐν παλατίῳ στρατευομένους, γεωργούς τε καὶ χωρίων κτήτορας καὶ κυρίους, καὶ οἷς ἐν λόγοις τὰ ἐπιτηδεύματά ἐστιν, ἀλλὰ μὴν ἐμπόρους τε καὶ ναυκλήρους καὶ ναύτας, βαναύσους τε

COURT OF JUSTINIAN 213

time; sometimes one consul remained in office for several years, and at last people never even dreamed of a fresh appointment. This reduced all to the greatest distress; since the Emperor no longer granted the usual assistance to his subjects, and at the same time deprived them of what they had by every means in his power.

I think I have given a sufficient account of the manner in which this destroyer swallowed up the property of the members of the Senate and deprived them all of their substance, whether publicly or privately. I also think that I have said enough concerning the fraudulent accusations which he made use of, in order to get possession of the property of other families which were reputed to be wealthy. Lastly, I have described the wrongs he inflicted upon the soldiers and servants of those in authority and the militia in the palace; upon countrymen, the possessors and proprietors of estates, and professors of the arts and sciences; upon merchants, ship-

214 ΠΡΟΚΟΠΙΟΥ ΑΝΕΚΔΟΤΑ

καὶ χειρώνακτας, καὶ ἀγοραίους, καὶ οἷς ἀπὸ τῶν ἐπὶ τῆς σκηνῆς ἐπιτηδευμάτων ὁ βίος, καὶ μὴν καὶ τοὺς ἄλλους ὡς εἰπεῖν ἅπαντας, ἐς οὓς διϊκνεῖσθαι βλάβος τὸ ἐς τούσδε συμβαίνει. Οἷα δὲ τούς τε προσαιτητὰς καὶ ἀγελαίους ἀνθρώπους, καὶ πτωχούς τε καὶ λώβῃ πάσῃ ἐχομένους εἰργάσατο, αὐτίκα ἐροῦμεν· τὰ γὰρ ἀμφὶ τοῖς ἱερεῦσιν αὐτῷ πεπραγμένα ἐν τοῖς ὄπισθεν λόγοις λελέξεται. Πρῶτα μὲν, ὅπερ εἴρηται, ἅπαντα περιβεβλημένος τὰ πωλητήρια, καὶ ὠνίων τῶν ἀναγκαιοτάτων τὰ λεγόμενα καταστησάμενος μονοπώλια, πλέον ἢ τριπλάσια τιμήτατα πάντας ἀνθρώπους ἐπράττετο. Καὶ τὰ μὲν ἄλλα, ἐπεὶ ἀνάριθμά μοι ἔδοξεν εἶναι, οὐκ ἂν ἔγωγε λόγῳ ἀτελευτήτῳ καταλέγειν φιλονεικοίην.

ς'. Ἀπὸ δὲ τῶν τοὺς ἄρτους ὠνουμένων πικρότατα ἐς πάντα τὸν αἰῶνα ἐσύλει, οὓς δὴ καὶ χειρώνακτας, καὶ πτωχούς, καὶ πάσῃ λώβῃ ἐχομένους ἀνθρώπους (μὴ) οὐκ ὠνεῖσθαι ἀδύνατον. Αὐτὸς μὲν γὰρ ἐς τρία κεντηνάρια φέρεσθαι ἀνὰ πᾶν ἔτος ἠξίου ἐνθένδε, ὅπως οἱ ἄρτοι ὦσι καὶ σποδοῦ ἔμπλεοι· οὐδὲ γὰρ

COURT OF JUSTINIAN 214

masters and sailors; mechanics, artisans, and retail dealers; those who gained their livelihood by performing upon the stage; in a word, upon all who were affected by the misery of these. I must now speak of his treatment of the poor, the lower classes, the indigent, and the sick and infirm. I will then go on to speak of his treatment of the priests.

At first, as has been said, he got all the shops into his own hands, and having established monopolies of all the most necessary articles of life, exacted from his subjects more than three times their value. But if I were to enter into the details of all these monopolies, I should never finish my narrative, for they are innumerable.

He imposed a perpetual and most severe tax upon bread, which the artisans, the poor, and infirm were compelled to purchase. He demanded from this commodity a revenue of three centenars of gold every year, and those poor wretches were obliged to support themselves upon bread full of dust, for the Emperor did

ΠΡΟΚΟΠΙΟΥ ΑΝΕΚΔΟΤΑ

ἐς τοῦτο δὴ τὸ αἰσχροκερδίας ἀσέβημα ὁ βασιλεὺς οὗτος ὀκνηρὸς ᾔει· ταύτῃ δὲ τῇ σκήψει οἰκεῖα κέρδη ἐπιτεχνώμενοι, οἷς ἐπέκειτο ἡ τιμὴ αὕτη, αὐτοὶ μὲν ῥᾷστα ἐς πλοῦτόν τινα περιΐσταντο μέγαν, λιμὸν δὲ τοῖς πτωχοῖς χειροποίητον, ἐν εὐθηνοῦσι χρόνοις, ἀεὶ παρὰ δόξαν εἰργάζοντο· ἐπεὶ οὐδὲ σῖτον ἑτέρωθέν τινι εἰσκομίζεσθαι τὸ παράπαν ἐξῆν, ἀλλὰ ἀναγκαῖον ἦν ἅπασι τούτους δὴ ὠνουμένους ἄρτους ἐσθίειν.

ζ. Τὸν δὲ τῆς πόλεως ὀχετὸν διερρωγότα τε ὁρῶντες, καὶ μοῖραν ὕδατος οὐκ ὀλίγην τινὰ ἐς τὴν πόλιν εἰσάγοντα, ὑπερεώρων τε καὶ οὐδ᾽ ὁτιοῦν αὐτῷ προέσθαι ἤθελον, καίπερ ὁμίλου ἀεὶ ἀμφὶ τὰς κρήνας ἀποπνιγομένου πολλοῦ, καὶ τῶν βαλανείων ἀποκεκλεισμένων ἁπάντων· καίτοι ἐς οἰκοδομίας θαλασσίους τε καὶ ἀνοήτους ἄλλας μέγεθος χρημάτων οὐδενὶ λόγῳ προΐετο, πανταχόθι τῶν προαστείων ἐπιτεχνώμενος, ὥσπερ τῶν βασιλείων αὐτοὺς οὐ χωρούντων, ἐν οἷς δὴ ἅπαντες οἱ πρότερον βεβασιλευκότες διαβιοῦν ἐς ἀεὶ ἤθελον. Οὕτως οὐ χρημάτων φειδοῖ, ἀλλὰ

COURT OF JUSTINIAN 215

not blush to carry his avarice to this
extent. Seizing upon this as an excuse,
the superintendents of the markets, eager
to fill their own pockets, in a short
time acquired great wealth, and, in spite
of the cheapness of food, reduced the
poor to a state of artificial and unexpected
famine; for they were not allowed to import corn from any other parts, but were
obliged to eat bread purchased in the city.

One of the city aqueducts had broken,
and a considerable portion of the water
destined for the use of the inhabitants
was lost. Justinian, however, took no
notice of it, being unwilling to incur any
expense for repairs, although a great
crowd continually thronged round the
fountains, and all the baths had been
shut. Nevertheless, he expended vast
sums without any reason or sense upon
buildings on the seashore, and also built
everywhere throughout the suburbs, as if
the palaces, in which their predecessors
had always been content to live, were no
longer suitable for himself and Theodora;
so that it was not merely parsimony, but

φθόρου ἀνθρώπων ἔνεκα, τῆς τοῦ ὀχετοῦ οἰκοδομίας ὀλιγωρεῖν ἔγνω· ἐπεὶ οὐδεὶς ἐκ τοῦ παντὸς χρόνου Ἰουστινιανοῦ τοῦδε ἑτοιμότερος γέγονεν ἀνθρώπων ἁπάντων χρήματα προσποιεῖσθαι κακῶς, καὶ ταῦτα χειρόνως αὐτίκα δὴ μάλα προέσθαι. Δυοῖν τοίνυν ἀπολελειμμένοιν ἔν τε ποτῷ καὶ (τοῖς) ἐδωδίμοις, τοῖς (τε) τὰ ἔσχατα πενομένοις καὶ πτωχοῖς οὖσιν, ὕδατος καὶ ἄρτου, δι' ἀμφοῖν αὐτοὺς, ὥσπερ μοι δεδιήγηται, βασιλεὺς ὅδε ἔβλαψε, τὸ μὲν ἄπορον σφίσι, τὸν δὲ πολλῷ ἀξιώτερον ἐργασάμενος.

η΄. Οὐ μόνον δὲ τοὺς ἐν Βυζαντίῳ προσαιτητὰς, ἀλλὰ καὶ τῶν ἑτέρωθι ᾠκημένων τινὰς ἔδρασε ταῦτα, ὥσπερ μοι αὐτίκα λελέξεται. Ἰταλίαν γὰρ Θευδέριχος ἑλὼν, τοὺς ἐν τῷ Ῥώμης παλατίῳ στρατευομένους αὐτοὺς εἴασεν, ὅπως τι διασώζοιτο πολιτείας τῆς παλαιᾶς ἴχνος, μίαν ἀπολιπὼν σύνταξιν ἐς ἡμέραν ἑκάστῳ. Ἦσαν δὲ οὗτοι παμπληθεῖς ἄγαν. Οἵ τε γὰρ Σιλεντιάριοι καλούμενοι, καὶ Δομέστικοι καὶ Σχολάριοι ἐν αὐτοῖς ἦσαν, οἷς δὴ ἄλλο οὐδὲν ὑπελέλειπτο ἢ τὸ τῆς στρα-

COURT OF JUSTINIAN · 216

a desire for the destruction of human life, that prevented him from repairing the aqueduct, for no one, from most ancient times, had ever shown himself more eager than Justinian to amass wealth, and at the same time to spend it in a most wasteful and extravagant manner. Thus this Emperor struck at the poorest and most miserable of his subjects through two most necessary articles of food—bread and water, by making the one difficult to procure, and the other too dear for them to buy.

It was not only the poor of Byzantium, however, that he harassed in this manner, but, as I will presently mention, the inhabitants of several other cities. When Theodoric had made himself master of Italy, in order to preserve some trace of the old constitution, he permitted the praetorian guards to remain in the palace and continued their daily allowance. These soldiers were very numerous. There were the Silentiarii, the Domestici, and the Scholares, about whom there was nothing military except

ΠΡΟΚΟΠΙΟΥ ΑΝΕΚΔΟΤΑ

τείας ὄνομα μόνον, καὶ ἡ σύνταξις αὕτη ἐς τὸ
ἀποζῆν ἀποχρῶσα μόλις αὐτοῖς, ἅπερ ἔς τε
παῖδας καὶ ἀπογόνους Θευδέριχος αὐτοὺς παραπέμπειν ἐκέλευσε. Τοῖς τε προσαιτηταῖς, οἳ
παρὰ τὸν Πέτρου τοῦ ἀποστόλου νεὼν δίαιταν
εἶχον, τρισχιλίους σίτου μεδίμνους χορηγεῖν
ἀεὶ τὸ δημόσιον ἀνὰ πᾶν ἔτος διώρισεν· ἅπερ
ἅπαντες οὗτοι διαγεγόνασι κομιζόμενοι, ἕως
Ἀλέξανδρος ὁ Ψαλίδιος ἐς τὴν Ἰταλίαν ἀφίκετο.

θ'. Πάντα γὰρ εὐθὺς οὗτος ὁ ἀνὴρ
ὀκνήσει οὐδεμιᾷ περιελεῖν ἔγνω. Ταῦτα
μαθὼν Ἰουστινιανὸς Ῥωμαίων αὐτοκράτωρ,
τήν τε πρᾶξιν προσήκατο ταύτην, καὶ τὸν
Ἀλέξανδρον ἔτι μᾶλλον ἢ πρότερον διὰ τιμῆς
ἔσχεν. Ἐν ταύτῃ Ἀλέξανδρος τῇ πορείᾳ καὶ
τοὺς Ἕλληνας εἰργάσατο τάδε. Τοῦ ἐν Θερ-
μοπύλαις φυλακτηρίου οἱ τὰ ἐκείνῃ γεωργοῦντες
χωρία ἐκ παλαιοῦ ἐπεμελοῦντο, ἐκ περιτροπῆς
τε τὸ ἐνταῦθα τεῖχος ἐφύλασσον, ἡνίκα δὴ
ἔφοδος βαρβάρων τινῶν ὡς ἐπισκήψει ἐς τὴν
Πελοπόννησον ἐπίδοξος ἦν.

ι'. Ἀλλ' ἐνταῦθα γενόμενος τότε Ἀλέξανδρος οὗτος, προνοεῖν Πελοποννησίων σκηπτόμενος, οὐκ ἔφη γεωργοῖς τὸ ταύτῃ φυλακτήριον
ἐπιτρέψειν. Στρατιώτας οὖν ἐνταῦθα εἰς δισ-

COURT OF JUSTINIAN 217

the name, and their salary was hardly
sufficient to live upon. Theodoric also
ordered that their children and descendants should have the reversion of this.
To the poor, who lived near the church
of Peter the Apostle, he distributed every
year 3,000 bushels of corn out of the
public stores. All continued to receive
these donations until the arrival of Alexander Forficula[1] in Italy. He resolved to
deprive them of it immediately; and, when
the Emperor was informed of this, he
approved of his conduct, and treated Alexander with still greater honour. During
his journey, Alexander treated the Greeks
in the following manner:—The peasants
of the district near the pass of Thermopylae had long manned the fortress,
and, each in turn, mounted guard over
the wall which blocks the pass, whenever there seemed any likelihood of an
invasion of the barbarians. But Alexander, on his arrival, pretended that it
was to the interest of the Peloponnesians
not to leave the protection of the pass
to the peasants. He established a garri-

[1] Shears, scissors.

χιλίους καταστησάμενος, οὐκ ἐκ τοῦ δημοσίου
χορηγεῖσθαι σφίσι τὰς συντάξεις διώρισεν,
ἀλλὰ τῶν ἐν τῇ Ἑλλάδι πασῶν πόλεων, τά
τε πολιτικὰ καὶ θεωρητικὰ ξύμπαντα ἐς τὸ
δημόσιον ἐπὶ τῷ προσχήματι τούτῳ μετή-
νεγκεν, ἐφ' ᾧ ἐνθένδε οἱ στρατιῶται οὗτοι
σιτίζοιντο, καὶ ἀπ' αὐτοῦ ἔν τε τῇ ἄλλῃ πάσῃ
Ἑλλάδι, καὶ οὐχ ἥκιστα ἐν Ἀθήναις αὐταῖς
οὔτε τις ἐν δημοσίῳ οἰκοδομία . . . . . οὔτε
ἄλλο ἀγαθὸν γενέσθαι (ξυνέβη). Ἰουστινιανὸς
μέντοι τὰ τῇδε διῳκημένα τῷ Ψαλιδίῳ οὐδεμιᾷ
μελλήσει ἐπέρρωσε. Ταῦτα μὲν οὖν τῇδε
κεχώρηκεν.

ια'. Ἰτέον δὲ καὶ εἰς τοὺς ἐν Ἀλεξανδρείᾳ
πτωχούς. Ἥφαιστός τις ἐν τοῖς ἐνταῦθα
ῥήτορσιν ἐγεγόνει, ὅσπερ παραλαβὼν τὴν
Ἀλεξανδρέων ἀρχὴν, τὸν μὲν δῆμον τοῦ στασιάζειν κατέπαυσε, φοβερὸς τοῖς στασιώταις
φανεὶς, ἔσχατα δὲ ἐσχάτων κακὰ τοῖς τῇδε
ᾠκημένοις ἐνδέδεικται πᾶσι. Πάντα γὰρ εὐθὺς
τὰ τῆς πόλεως πωλητήρια ἐς τὸ καλούμενον
μονοπώλιον καταστησάμενος, ἄλλων μὲν
ἐμπόρων οὐδένα ταύτην δὴ τὴν ἐργασίαν
ἐργάζεσθαι εἴασε, μόνος δὲ ἁπάντων αὐτὸς

COURT OF JUSTINIAN   218

son of about 2,000 soldiers, who were
not paid out of the public funds, but by
each of the cities in Greece. On this
pretext, he transferred to the public
treasury all the revenues of these towns
which were intended for public purposes
or to cover the expenses of shows and
entertainments. He pretended that it
was to be employed for the support of
the soldiers, and in consequence, from
that time, no public buildings or other
objects of utility were erected or promoted either in Athens or throughout
Greece. Justinian, however, hastened to
give his sanction to all the acts of
Forficula.

We must now speak of the poor of
Alexandria. Amongst the lawyers of that
city was one Hephaestus, who, having
been appointed governor, suppressed popu-
lar disturbances by the terror he inspired,
but at the same time reduced the citizens
to the greatest distress. He immediately
established a monopoly of all wares, which
he forbade other merchants to sell. He
reserved everything for himself alone, sold

ΠΡΟΚΟΠΙΟΥ ΑΝΕΚΔΟΤΑ

γεγονὼς κάπηλος· παρεδίδοτο τὰ ὤνια πάντα·
δηλονότι τὰς τούτων τιμὰς τῇ τῆς ἀρχῆς
ἐξουσίᾳ σταθμώμενος. Ἀπεπνίγετό τε τῇ τῶν
ἀναγκαίων σπάνει ἡ τῶν Ἀλεξανδρέων πόλις,
οὗ δὴ καὶ τοῖς τὰ ἔσχατα πενομένοις τὰ
πρότερα εὔωνα διαρκῶς ἐγεγόνει πάντα· μάλιστα δὲ αὐτοὺς ἀμφὶ τῷ ἄρτῳ ἐπίεζε. Τὸν
γὰρ σῖτον αὐτὸς ἐξ Αἰγυπτίων ὠνεῖτο μόνος·
οὐδὲ ὅσον ἐς μέδιμνον ἕνα ἑτέρῳ διδοὺς πρίασθαι, ταύτῃ τε τοὺς ἄρτους καὶ τὰ τῶν ἄρτων
τιμήματα διετίθετο ᾗπερ ἐβούλετο. Πλοῦτον
τοίνυν (καὶ) ἀμύθητον αὐτός τε δι' ὀλίγου
περιεβάλλετο, καὶ βασιλεῖ τὴν ἀμφὶ τούτῳ
ἐπιθυμίαν ἐνεπλήσατο. Καὶ τῶν μὲν Ἀλεξανδρέων ὁ δῆμος δέει τοῦ Ἡφαίστου τὰ παρόντα
σφίσιν ἡσυχῇ ἔφερεν· ὁ δὲ αὐτοκράτωρ αἰδοῖ
τῶν οἱ ἐς ἀεὶ ἐσκομιζομένων χρημάτων ἐν τοῖς
μάλιστα ὑπερηγάπα τὸν ἄνθρωπον.

ιβ'. Βουλεύσας δὲ Ἥφαιστος οὗτος,
ὅπως τὴν βασιλέως διάνοιαν πολλῷ ἔτι μᾶλλον ἐξελεῖν δύνηται, προσεπετεχνήσατο τάδε.

COURT OF JUSTINIAN 219

everything himself, and fixed the price
by the capricious exercise of his authority.
Consequently, the city was in the greatest
distress from want of provisions; the poor
no longer had a sufficient supply of what
was formerly sold at a low rate, and
especially felt the difficulty of obtaining
bread; for the governor alone bought up
all the corn that came from Egypt, and
did not allow anyone else to purchase
even so much as a bushel; and in this
manner, he taxed the loaves and put
upon them what price he pleased. By
this means he amassed an enormous
fortune, and was likewise careful to satisfy
the greed of the Emperor. So great was
the terror inspired by Hephaestus, that
the people of Alexandria endured their
ill-treatment in silence; and the Emperor, out of gratitude for the money
which flowed into his exchequer from
that quarter, conceived a great affection
for Hephaestus. The latter, in order to
secure in a still greater degree the favour
of the Emperor, carried out the following
plan. When Diocletian became Emperor

ΠΡΟΚΟΠΙΟΥ ΑΝΕΚΔΟΤΑ

Διοκλητιανὸς Ῥωμαίων γεγονὼς αὐτοκράτωρ, σίτου μέγα τι χρῆμα δίδοσθαι παρὰ τοῦ δήμου τῶν Ἀλεξανδρέων τοῖς δεομένοις ἀνὰ πᾶν ἔτος διώρισε. Ταῦτα ὁ δῆμος τηνικάδε διαδικασάμενοι ἐν σφίσιν αὐτοῖς ἐς ἀπογόνους τοὺς μέχρι δεῦρο παρέπεμψαν. Ἀλλ' Ἥφαιστος ἐνθένδε μυριάδας ἐς διακοσίας ἐπετείους μεδίμνων τοὺς τῶν ἀναγκαίων ὑποσπανίζοντας ἀφελόμενος, τῷ δημοσίῳ ἐντέθεικε· βασιλεῖ γράψας, ὡς οὐ δικαίως, οὐδὲ ᾗ ξυμφέρει τοῖς πράγμασι, μέχρι νῦν ταῦτα οἱ ἄνδρες οὗτοι κομίζοιντο. Καὶ ἀπ' αὐτοῦ βασιλεὺς μὲν ἐμπεδώσας τὴν πρᾶξιν, διὰ σπουδῆς αὐτὸν μείζονος ἔσχεν. Ἀλεξανδρέων δὲ ὅσοι ταύτην εἶχον τοῦ βίου τὴν ἐλπίδα, ταύτης δὴ ἐν τοῖς ἀναγκαιοτάτοις τῆς ἀπανθρωπίας ἀπώναντο.

COURT OF JUSTINIAN   220

of the Romans, he ordered a yearly distribution of corn to be made to the necessitous poor of Alexandria; and the people, settling its distribution amongst themselves, transmitted the right to their descendants. Hephaestus deprived the necessitous of 2,000,000 bushels yearly, and deposited it in the imperial granaries, declaring, in his despatch to the Emperor, that this grant of corn had previously been made in a manner that was neither just nor in conformity with the interests of the state. The Emperor approved of his conduct and became more attached to him than ever. The Alexandrians, whose hopes of existence depended upon this distribution, felt the cruelty bitterly, especially at the time of their distress.

ΚΕΦΑΛΑΙΟΝ ΚΖ'.

α'. Τὰ μὲν Ἰουστινιανῷ εἰργασμένα τοσαῦτά ἐστιν, ὡς μηδὲ τὸν πάντα αἰῶνα τῷ περὶ αὐτῶν λόγῳ ἐπαρκεῖν δύνασθαι. Ὀλίγα δέ μοι ἄττα ἐκ πάντων ἀπολεξαμένῳ ἀποχρήσει εἰπεῖν, δι' ὧν αὐτοῦ ἔνδηλον καὶ τοῖς ὄπισθεν γενησομένοις τὸ ἦθος ἅπαν διαφανῶς ἔσται, καὶ ὡς εἴρων τε ἦν, καὶ οὔτε θεοῦ, οὔτε ἱερέων, οὔτε νόμων αὐτῷ ἔμελεν, οὐδὲ δήμου κατεσπουδασμένου αὐτῷ δοκοῦντος εἶναι· οὐ μὴν οὔτε τινὸς τὸ παράπαν αἰδοῦς, ἢ τοῦ τῆς πολιτείας ξυμφόρου, ἢ ὅτου τι προὔργου ἐς αὐτὴν γένοιτο· ἢ ὅπως σκήψεώς τινος τὰ πρασσόμενα τυχεῖν δύναιτο, οὔτε ἄλλο τι αὐτὸν ἐσήει, ὅτι μὴ μόνη ἀφαίρεσις τῶν ἐν πάσῃ γῇ κειμένων χρημάτων. Ἄρξομαι δὲ ἐνθένδε.

β'. Ἀρχιερέα κατεστήσατο Ἀλεξανδρεῦσιν αὐτὸς, Παῦλον ὄνομα. Ἐτύγχανε δὲ Ῥόδων τις, Φοῖνιξ γένος, ἔχων τηνικάδε τὴν Ἀλεξανδρείας ἀρχήν. Ὧι δὴ ἐπέστελλεν ἐς

CHAPTER XXVII

THE evil deeds of Justinian were so numerous, that time would fail me if I were to attempt to relate them all. It will therefore be sufficient, if I select some of those which will exhibit his whole character to posterity, and which clearly show his dissimulation, his neglect of God, the priesthood, the laws, and the people which showed itself devoted to him. He was utterly without shame; he had no care for the interests or advantage of the state, and did not trouble himself about excusing his misdeeds, or, in fact, about anything else but how he might plunder and appropriate the wealth of the whole world.

To begin with, he appointed Paul bishop of Alexandria, at the time when Rhodon, a Phoenician by birth, was governor of the city. He ordered him to

222   ΠΡΟΚΟΠΙΟΥ ΑΝΕΚΔΟΤΑ

ἄπαντα Παύλῳ ὑπηρετεῖν προθυμίᾳ τῇ πάσῃ, ὅπως δὴ ἀτελεύτητον μένοι τῶν πρὸς αὐτοῦ ἐπαγγελλομένων μηδέν. Ταύτῃ γὰρ τῶν Ἀλεξανδρέων τοὺς (ἱερεῖς) ἑταιρίζεσθαι αὐτὸν ἐς τὴν ἐν Καλχηδόνι σύνοδον ᾤετο δυνατὸν ἔσεσθαι.

γ'. Ἦν δέ τις Ἀρσένιος, Παλαιστῖνος γένος, ὅσπερ Θεοδώρᾳ βασιλίδι ἐν τοῖς μάλιστα ἀναγκαιοτάτοις ἐπιτήδειος γεγονὼς, καὶ ἀπ' αὐτοῦ δύναμίν τε πολλὴν, καὶ μεγάλα περιβαλλόμενος χρήματα, ἐς βουλῆς ἀξίωμα ἦλθε, καίπερ μιαρώτατος ὤν. Οὗτος Σαμαρείτης μὲν ἦν, τοῦ δὲ μὴ τὴν ὑπάρχουσαν προέσθαι δύναμιν, ὀνόματος ἀντιλαβέσθαι τοῦ Χριστιανῶν ἔγνω. Ὁ μέντοι πατήρ τε καὶ ἀδελφὸς, τῇ τούτου δυνάμει θαρροῦντες, διαγεγόνασι μὲν ἐν Σκυθοπόλει, περιστέλλοντες τὴν πάτριον δόξαν· γνώμῃ δὲ αὐτοῦ ἀνήκεστα τοὺς Χριστιανοὺς εἰργάζοντο πάντας. Διὸ δὴ οἱ πολῖται σφίσιν ἐπαναστάντες, ἄμφω ἔκτειναν θανάτῳ οἰκτίστῳ. Κακά τε πολλὰ ξυνηνέχθη Παλαιστίνοις ἐνθένδε γενέσθαι. Τότε μὲν οὖν αὐτὸν οὔτε Ἰουστινιανὸς οὔτε βασιλὶς κακόν τι ἔδρασαν, καίπερ αἰτιώτατον γεγονότα δυσ-

COURT OF JUSTINIAN 222

show the greatest deference to the bishop,
and to execute all his instructions; for
by this means he hoped to prevail upon
the chief persons of the city to support
the council of Chalcedon. There was
also a certain Arsenius, a native of Palestine, who had made himself most necessary to the Empress, and, in consequence
of her favour and the great wealth he had
amassed, had attained the rank of a
senator, although he was a man of most
abandoned character. He belonged to
the Samaritan sect, but, in order to preserve his authority, he assumed the name
of Christian. His father and brother,
who lived in Scythopolis, relying upon
his authority and following his advice,
bitterly persecuted the Christians in that
city. Whereupon the citizens rose up
against them, and put them to death
most cruelly, which afterwards proved
the cause of much misery to the inhabitants of Palestine. On that occasion
neither Justinian nor the Empress inflicted
any punishment upon Arsenius, although
he was the principal cause of all those

κόλων ἁπάντων· ἀπεῖπον δὲ αὐτῷ ἐς παλάτιον μηκέτι ἰέναι· ἐνδελεχέστατα γὰρ τούτου δὴ ἔνεκα πρὸς Χριστιανῶν ἠνωχλοῦντο.

δ'. Οὗτος Ἀρσένιος βασιλεῖ χαριεῖσθαι οἰόμενος, οὐ πολλῷ ὕστερον ξὺν τῷ Παύλῳ ἐς τὴν Ἀλεξάνδρειαν στέλλεται, ὡς δὴ τά τε ἄλλα ὑπηρετήσων, καὶ τὴν ἐς τοὺς Ἀλεξανδρεῖς πειθὼ συγκατεργασόμενος αὐτῷ δυνάμει τῇ πάσῃ. Ἰσχυρίζετο γὰρ ὑπὸ τὸν χρόνον τοῦτον, ἡνίκα οἱ τοῦ παλατίου ἀποκεκλεῖσθαι ξυνέπεσε, τῶν ἐν Χριστιανοῖς οὐκ ἀμελέτητον γεγονέναι δογμάτων ἁπάντων. Ὅπερ τὴν Θεοδώραν ἠνίασε· τὴν ἐναντίαν γὰρ ἐσκήπτετο τῷ βασιλεῖ ἐς τοῦτο ἰέναι, ὥς μοι ἐν τοῖς ὄπισθεν λόγοις εἴρηται.

ε'. Ἐπεὶ οὖν (ἐν) Ἀλεξανδρεῦσιν ἐγένοντο, διάκονόν τινα Ψόην ὄνομα Ῥόδωνι Παῦλος παρέδωκε τεθνηξόμενον, φάσκων δὴ αὐτὸν μόνον οἱ αὐτῷ ἐμποδὼν ἵστασθαι τοῦ μὴ τὰ βασιλεῖ δεδογμένα ὑποτελέσαι. Τοῖς δὲ βασιλέως γράμμασι Ῥόδων ἠγμένος, συχνοῖς τε οὖσι καὶ λίαν σπουδαίοις, αἰκίζεσθαι τὸν

COURT OF JUSTINIAN 223

troubles. They contented themselves with forbidding him to appear at court, in order to satisfy the continued complaints that were preferred against him by the Christians.

This Arsenius, thinking to gratify the Emperor, set out with Paul to Alexandria to assist him generally, and, above all, to do his utmost to aid him in securing the favour of the inhabitants; for, during the time of his exclusion from the palace, he affirmed that he had made himself thoroughly acquainted with all the doctrines of Christianity. This displeased Theodora, who pretended to hold a different opinion to the Emperor in religious matters, as I have already stated.

When they arrived at Alexandria, Paul delivered over the deacon Psoes to the governor to be put to death, asserting that he was the only obstacle in the way of the realisation of the Emperor's desires. The governor, urged on by despatches from the Emperor, which frequently arrived and were couched in pressing terms, ordered Psoes to be flogged, and

224 ΠΡΟΚΟΠΙΟΥ ΑΝΕΚΔΟΤΑ

ἄνθρωπον ἔγνω, ὃς, ὑπὸ τῆς βασάνου κατατεινόμενος, αὐτίκα θνήσκει.

ϛ'. Ἅπερ ἐπεὶ ἐς βασι[λέα ἦλθεν], ἐγκειμένης ἰσχυρότατα τῆς βασιλίδος, ἅπαντα ὁ
βασιλεὺς ἐπὶ Παύλῳ τε καὶ Ῥόδωνι καὶ
Ἀρσενίῳ εὐθὺς ἐκίνει, ὥσπερ τῶν πρὸς αὐτοῦ
τούτοις δὴ τοῖς ἀνθρώποις ἐπηγγελμένων
ἐπιλελησμένος ἁπάντων. Λιβέριον οὖν, τὸν
ἐκ Ῥώμης ἄνδρα πατρίκιον, καταστησάμενος
ἐπὶ τῆς Ἀλεξανδρέων ἀρχῆς, καὶ τῶν δοκίμων
ἱερέων τινὰς ἐς τὴν Ἀλεξανδρέων ἔστειλε, τὴν
τοῦ πράγματος ποιησομένους διάγνωσιν, ἐν
οἷς καὶ ὁ Ῥώμης ἀρχιδιάκονος Πελάγιος ἦν,
τὸ Βιγιλίου τοῦ ἀρχιερέως ὑποδὺς πρόσωπον,
ἐπιτεταγμένον οἱ τοῦτό γε πρὸς τοῦ Βιγιλίου.

ζ'. Τοῦ τε φόνου ἐληλεγμένου, Παῦλον
τῆς ἱερωσύνης εὐθὺς καθεῖλον· φυγόντα δὲ
Ῥόδωνα ἐς Βυζάντιον τήν τε κεφαλὴν ἀφείλετο
ὁ βασιλεὺς, καὶ τὰ χρήματα ἐς τὸ δημόσιον
ἀνάγραπτα ἐποιήσατο, καίπερ τρισκαίδεκα
ἐπιστολὰς τοῦ ἀνθρώπου ἐνδειξαμένου, ἅσπερ
αὐτῷ βασιλεὺς ἔγραψε σπουδάζων τε καὶ
διατεινόμενος ἄγαν, ἐπαγγέλλων τε ἅπαντα
τῷ Παύλῳ ὑπηρετεῖν ἐπιτάττοντι, καὶ μηδ'
ὁτιοῦν ἀντιτείνειν, ὅπως ἐπὶ τῇ δόξῃ ἐπιτελέσαι
τὰ δόξαντα δυνατὸς εἴη. Ἀρσένιόν τε Λιβέριος γνώμῃ Θεοδώρας ἀνεσκολόπισε, καὶ αὐτοῦ
τὰ χρήματα δημοσιοῦν βασιλεὺς ἔγνω, καίπερ

COURT OF JUSTINIAN   224

he died under the torture. When the
news of this reached the Emperor, at
the earnest entreaty of Theodora, he
expressed great indignation against Paul,
Rhodon, and Arsenius, as if he had forgotten the orders he himself had given
them. He appointed Liberius, a Roman
patrician, governor of Alexandria, and
sent some priests of high repute to in-
vestigate the matter. Amongst them was
Pelagius, archdeacon of Rome, who was
commissioned by Pope Vigilius to act as
his agent. Paul, being convicted of
murder, was deprived of his bishopric;
Rhodon, who had fled to Byzantium,
was executed by order of Justinian, and
his estate confiscated, although he produced thirteen despatches, in which the
Emperor expressly ordered and insisted
that he should in everything act in accordance with Paul's orders, and never oppose
him, that he might have liberty to act
as he pleased in matters of religion.
Arsenius was crucified by Liberius, in
accordance with instructions from Theodora; his estate was confiscated by the

29

ΠΡΟΚΟΠΙΟΥ ΑΝΕΚΔΟΤΑ

οὐδὲν αὐτῷ ἐπεγκαλεῖν ἔχων, ἢ ὅτι ξὺν τῷ Παύλῳ δίαιταν εἶχε. Ταῦτα μὲν οὖν εἴτε ὀρθῶς, εἴτε ἄλλῃ πῃ αὐτῷ εἴργασται, οὐκ ἔχω εἰπεῖν· ὅτου δὲ δὴ ἕνεκα ταῦτά μοι εἴρηται, αὐτίκα δηλώσω.

η'. Ὁ Παῦλος χρόνῳ τινὶ ὕστερον ἐς Βυζάντιον ἥκων, ἑπτά τε χρυσοῦ κεντηνάρια τῷ βασιλεῖ τούτῳ προέμενος, ἠξίου τὴν ἱερωσύνην ἀπολαβεῖν, ἅτε αὐτὴν οὐδενὶ νόμῳ ἀφῃρημένος. Ἰουστινιανὸς δὲ τά τε χρήματα ἐδέξατο πρᾴως, καὶ τὸν ἄνθρωπον ἐν τιμῇ ἔσχεν, ἀρχιερέα τε ὡμολόγησεν Ἀλεξανδρεῦσιν αὐτὸν καταστήσεσθαι αὐτίκα δὴ μάλα, καίπερ ἑτέρου τὴν τιμὴν ἔχοντος, ὥσπερ οὐκ εἰδὼς, ὅτι δὴ τοὺς αὐτῷ ξυνοικήσαντάς τε καὶ ὑπουργεῖν τετολμηκότας ἔκτεινέ τε αὐτὸς καὶ τὰς οὐσίας ἀφείλετο.

θ'. Ὁ μὲν οὖν Σεβαστὸς ἐς ἄγαν διατεινόμενος τὸ πρᾶγμα ἐν σπουδῇ ἐποιεῖτο· Παῦλος δὲ διαρρήδην ἐπίδοξος ἦν τὴν ἱερωσύνην ἀπολήψεσθαι μηχανῇ τῇ πάσῃ. Ἀλλὰ Βιγίλιος τηνικάδε παρὼν, εἴκειν βασιλεῖ τῷ τοιοῦτον ἐπιτάττοντι οὐδαμῇ ἔγνω. Ἔφασκε γὰρ οὐχ οἷός τε εἶναι ψῆφον τὴν οἰκείαν αὐτὸς

COURT OF JUSTINIAN 225

Emperor, although he had no cause of complaint against him except his intimacy with Paul. Whether in this he acted justly or not, I cannot say; but I will afterwards state the reason why I have mentioned this affair.

Some time afterwards Paul went to Byzantium, and, by the offer of seven centenars of gold, endeavoured to persuade the Emperor to reinstate him in his office, of which he said he had been unjustly deprived. Justinian received the money affably, treated him with respect, and promised to reinstate him as soon as possible, although another at present held the office, as if he did not know that he himself had put to death two of his best friends and supporters, and confiscated their estates. The Emperor exerted all his efforts in this direction, and there did not appear to be the least doubt that Paul would be reinstated. But Vigilius, who at the time was in Byzantium, resolved not to submit to the Emperor's orders in this matter, and declared that it was impossible for him

ΠΡΟΚΟΠΙΟΥ ΑΝΕΚΔΟΤΑ

ἀνάδικον διειργάσθαι, τὴν Πελαγίου παραδηλῶν γνῶσιν. Οὕτως ἄλλου οὐδενὸς τῷ βασιλεῖ τούτῳ, ὅτι μὴ χρημάτων ἀφαιρέσεως, ἀεὶ ἔμελεν.

ι´. Εἰρήσεται δὲ καὶ ἄλλο τοιόνδε. Φαυστῖνος ἦν τις, Παλαιστῖνος γένος, Σαμαρείτης μὲν γεγονὼς ἄνωθεν, ὀνόματος δὲ τοῦ Χριστιανῶν ἀντιλαμβανόμενος, ἀνάγκῃ τοῦ νόμου. Οὗτος ὁ Φαυστῖνος ἐς βουλῆς ἀξίωμα ἦλθε, καὶ τῆς χώρας τὴν ἀρχὴν ἔσχεν· ἧσπερ αὐτὸν παραλυθέντα οὐ πολλῷ ὕστερον, ἔς τε τὸ Βυζάντιον ἥκοντα, τῶν τινες ἱερέων διέβαλλον, ἐπενεγκάμενοι ὡς Σαμαρειτῶν νόμιμα περιστέλλει, καὶ Χριστιανοὺς δράσειε τοὺς ἐν Παλαιστίνῃ ᾠκημένους ἀνόσια ἔργα. Ἰουστινιανὸς δὲ ἀγριαίνεσθαί τε καὶ δεινὰ ποιεῖν διὰ ταῦτα ἐδόκει, ὅτι δή, αὐτοῦ τὴν Ῥωμαίων ἀρχὴν ἔχοντος, τὸ τοῦ Χριστοῦ ὄνομα ὑφ' ὁτωνοῦν διασύροιτο.

ια´. Οἱ μὲν οὖν τῆς συγκλήτου βουλῆς τὴν διάγνωσιν πεποιημένοι τοῦ πράγματος, φυγῇ τὸν Φαυστῖνον ἐζημίωσαν, βασιλέως ἐγκειμένου σφίσι. Βασιλεὺς δὲ πρὸς αὐτοῦ χρή-

COURT OF JUSTINIAN   226

to annul by his own decision a sentence which Pelagius had given in his name. So that, in everything, Justinian's only object was to get money by any means whatsoever.

The following is a similar case. There was a Samaritan by birth, a native of Palestine, who, having been compelled by the law to change his religion, had become a Christian and taken the name of Faustinus. This Faustinus became a member of the senate and governor of Palestine; and when his time of office had expired, on his return to Byzantium he was accused by certain priests of favouring the religion and customs of the Samaritans and of having been guilty of great cruelties towards the Christians in Palestine. Justinian appeared to be very angry and expressed his indignation that, during his reign, anyone should have the audacity to insult the name of Christian. The members of the senate met to examine into the matter, and, at the instance of the Emperor, Faustinus was banished. But Justinian, having received

ΠΡΟΚΟΠΙΟΥ ΑΝΕΚΔΟΤΑ

ματα ὅσα ἐβούλετο κεκομισμένος, ἀνάδικα εὐθὺς τὰ δεδικασμένα ἐποίησε. Φαυστῖνος δὲ αὖθις τὸ πρότερον ἀξίωμα ἔχων, βασιλεῖ τε ὡμίλει, ἐπίτροπός τε καταστὰς τῶν ἐκ Παλαιστίνης τε καὶ Φοινίκης βασιλικῶν χωρίων, ἀδεέστερον ἅπαντα κατειργάζετο, ὅσα οἱ αὐτῷ βουλομένῳ εἴη. Ὅντινα μὲν οὖν Ἰουστινιανὸς τρόπον τὰ Χριστιανῶν δικαιώματα περιστέλλειν ἠξίου, καίπερ οὐ πολλῶν εἰρημένων ἡμῖν, ἀλλ' ἐκ τῶνδε, βραχέων ὄντων, τεκμηριοῦν ἔστιν.

COURT OF JUSTINIAN 227

large presents of money from him, immediately annulled the sentence. Faustinus, restored to his former authority and the confidence of the Emperor, was appointed steward of the imperial domains in Palestine and Phoenicia, and was allowed to act in every respect exactly as he pleased. These few instances are sufficient to show how Justinian protected the Christian ordinances.

ΠΡΟΚΟΠΙΟΥ ΑΝΕΚΔΟΤΑ

ΚΕΦΑΛΑΙΟΝ ΚΗ΄.

α΄. Ὅπως δὲ καὶ τοὺς νόμους οὐδεμιᾷ ὀκνήσει κατέσειε χρημάτων κειμένων βραχυτάτῳ δηλωθήσεται λόγῳ.

Πρίσκος τις ἐν τῇ Ἐμεσηνῶν ἐγένετο πόλει, ὅσπερ ἀλλότρια γράμματα μιμεῖσθαι εὐφυῶς ἐξηπίστατο, τεχνίτης τε ἦν περὶ τὸ κακὸν τοῦτο δεξιὸς ἄγαν. Ἐτύγχανε δὲ ἡ τῶν Ἐμεσηνῶν ἐκκλησία τῶν τινος ἐπιφανῶν κληρονόμος γεγενημένη χρόνοις τισὶ πολλοῖς ἔμπροσθεν.

Ἦν δέ τις ἀνὴρ πατρίκιος μὲν τὸ ἀξίωμα, Μαμμιανὸς δὲ ὄνομα, γένει λαμπρὸς καὶ περιουσίᾳ χρημάτων. Ἐπὶ δὲ Ἰουστινιανοῦ βασιλεύοντος, ὁ Πρίσκος διερευνησάμενος πόλεως τῆς εἰρημένης τὰς οἰκίας πάσας, εἴ τινας εὗρέ τε πλούτῳ ἀκμαζούσας, καὶ πρὸς ζημίαν χρημάτων μεγάλων διαρκῶς ἐχούσας, τούτων διερευνησάμενος ἐς τὸ ἀκριβὲς τοὺς προπάτορας, γράμμασιν αὐτῶν παλαιοῖς ἐντυχών, βιβλίδια πολλὰ ὡς παρ' ἐκείνων γεγραμμένα πεποίηται, ὁμολογούντων πολλὰ χρήματα τῷ Μαμμιανῷ ἀποδώσειν, ἅτε παρακαταθήκης λόγῳ ταῦτα πρὸς ἐκείνου κεκομισμένων.

β΄. Τό τε ὡμολογημένον ἐν τούτοις δὴ τοῖς καταπλάστοις γραμματίοις χρυσίον ξυνῄει

CHAPTER XXVIII

I MUST now briefly relate how he unhesitatingly abolished the laws when money was in question. There was in Emesa a man named Priscus, who was an expert forger and very clever in his art. The church of Emesa, many years before, had been instituted sole heir to the property of one of the most distinguished inhabitants named Mammianus, a patrician of noble birth and of great wealth. During the reign of Justinian, Priscus made a list of all the families of the town, taking care to notice which were wealthy and able to disburse large sums. He carefully hunted up the names of their ancestors, and, having found some old documents in their handwriting, forged a number of acknowledgments, in which they confessed that they were largely indebted to Mammianus in sums of money which had been left with them by him as a deposit. The amount of these forged acknowledgments was no less than a

οὐχ ἧσσον ἢ ἐς ἑκατὸν κεντηνάρια. Καὶ ἀνδρὸς δέ τινος, ὅσπερ ἐπὶ τῆς ἀγορᾶς τηνικάδε τοῦ χρόνου καθήμενος, ἡνίκα ὁ Μαμμιανὸς περιῆν, δόξαν τε πολλὴν ἐπί τε ἀληθείᾳ καὶ τῇ ἄλλῃ ἀρετῇ ἔχων, ἅπαντα ἐπετέλει τὰ τῶν πολιτῶν γραμματεῖα, ἕκαστον οἰκείοις ἐπισφραγίζων αὐτὸς γράμμασιν, ὅπερ ταβελλίωνα καλοῦσι Ῥωμαῖοι, τὰ γράμματα δαιμονίως μιμησάμενος, τοῖς διοικουμένοις τὰ πράγματα τῆς Ἐμεσηνῶν ἐκκλησίας παρέδωκεν, ὡμολογηκόσι μοῖραν αὐτῷ τινα κεῖσθαι τῶν ἐνθένδε πορισθησομένων χρημάτων.

γ´. Ἐπεὶ δὲ ὁ νόμος ἐμποδὼν ἵστατο, τὰς μὲν ἄλλας δίκας ἁπάσας ἐς τριακοντοῦτιν παραγραφὴν ἄγων, ὀλίγας δὲ ἄττας καὶ τὰς ὑποθηκαρίας καλουμένας τεσσαράκοντα ἐνιαυτῶν μήκει ἐκκρούων, μηχανῶνται τοιάδε. Ἐς Βυζάντιον ἀφικόμενοι, καὶ χρήματα μεγάλα τῷ βασιλεῖ τούτῳ προέμενοι, ἐδέοντο σφίσι τὸν τῶν πολιτῶν ὄλεθρον οὐδὲν ὠφεληκότων ξυγκατεργάζεσθαι. Ὁ δὲ τὰ χρήματα κεκομισμένος, μελλήσει οὐδεμιᾷ νόμον ἔγραψεν, οὐ χρόνοις τὰς ἐκκλησίας τοῖς καθήκουσιν, ἀλλ᾽ ἐνιαυτῶν ἑκατὸν πλήθει δικῶν τῶν αὐταῖς προσηκουσῶν ἀποκεκλεῖσθαι· καὶ ταῦτα οὐκ

COURT OF JUSTINIAN 229

hundred centenars of gold. He also imitated in a marvellous manner the handwriting of a public notary, a man of conspicuous honesty and virtue, who during the lifetime of Mammianus used to draw up all their documents for the citizens, sealing them with his own hand, and delivered these forged documents to those who managed the ecclesiastical affairs of Emesa, on condition that he should receive part of the money which might be obtained in this manner.

But, since there was a law which limited all legal processes to a period of thirty years, except in cases of mortgage and certain others, in which the prescription extended to forty years, they resolved to go to Byzantium and, offering a large sum of money to the Emperor, to beg him to assist them in their project of ruining their fellow-citizens.

The Emperor accepted the money, and immediately published a decree which ordained that affairs relating to the Church should not be restricted to the ordinary prescription, but that anything might be recovered, if claimed within a

ΠΡΟΚΟΠΙΟΥ ΑΝΕΚΔΟΤΑ

ἐν Ἐμέσῃ μόνον κύρια εἶναι, ἀλλὰ καὶ ἀνὰ πᾶσαν τὴν Ῥωμαίων ἀρχήν.

δ'. Ἐμεσηνοῖς τε τὸ πρᾶγμα τοῦτο διαιτᾶν ἔταξε Λογγῖνόν τινα, δραστήριόν τε ἄνδρα καὶ τὸ σῶμα ἰσχυρὸν ἄγαν, ὃς καὶ τὴν τοῦ δήμου ἀρχὴν ἐν Βυζαντίῳ ὕστερον ἔσχεν. Οἱ δὲ τῆς ἐκκλησίας τὰ πράγματα διοικούμενοι, τὰ μὲν πρῶτα τῶν τινι πολιτῶν δίκην κεντηναρίοιν ἐκ βιβλίων τῶν εἰρημένων λαχόντες δυοῖν, κατεδικάσαντο τοὺς ἀνθρώπους εὐθὺς, ὅ τι καὶ ἀπολογήσαιντο οὐδαμῆ ἔχοντας, διά τε χρόνου τοσόνδε μῆκος, καὶ ἄγνοιαν τῶν τότε πεπραγμένων. Ἐν πένθει δὲ μεγάλῳ ἐκάθηντο οἵ τε ἄλλοι ξύμπαντες ἄνθρωποι, ὠμῶς τοῖς συκοφάνταις ἐκκείμενοι, καὶ πάντων μάλιστα οἱ τῶν Ἐμεσηνῶν λογιώτατοι.

ε'. Τοῦ δὲ κακοῦ ἐς τοὺς πλείστους ἤδη τῶν πολιτῶν ἐπιρρέοντος, προμήθειάν τινα τοῦ θεοῦ ξυνηνέχθη γενέσθαι τοιάνδε. Πρίσκον ὁ Λογγῖνος, τὸν τοῦτο δὴ τὸ σκαιώρημα ἐργασάμενον, ἅπαντα ὁμοῦ κομίζειν οἱ τὰ γράμματα ἐκέλευσεν, ἀναδυόμενόν τε τὴν πρᾶξιν ἐρράπισε δυνάμει τῇ πάσῃ. Ὁ δὲ ἀνδρὸς ἰσχυροῦ λίαν τὴν πληγὴν οὐδαμῆ ἐνεγκὼν, ἔπεσεν ὕπτιος, τρέμων δὲ ἤδη καὶ περιδεὴς γεγονὼς, ὅλως τε

COURT OF JUSTINIAN 230

hundred years : which regulation was to
be observed not only in Emesa, but
throughout the whole of the Roman Empire. In order to see that the new rule
was put into execution, he sent Longinus
to Emesa, a man of great vigour and
bodily strength, who was afterwards made
praefect of Byzantium. Those who had
the management of the affairs of the
church of Emesa, acting upon the forged
documents, sued some of the citizens for
two centenars of gold, which they were
condemned to pay, being unable to raise
any objection, by reason of the length
of time elapsed and their ignorance of
the facts. All the inhabitants, and
especially the principal citizens, were in
great distress and highly incensed against
their accusers. When ruin already threatened the majority of the citizens, Provi-
dence came to their assistance in a most
unexpected manner. Longinus ordered
Priscus, the contriver of this detestable
invention, to bring him all the acknowledgments; and, when he showed himself
unwilling to do so, he dealt him a violent
blow in the face. Priscus, unable to

ΠΡΟΚΟΠΙΟΥ ΑΝΕΚΔΟΤΑ

Λογγῖνον ᾐσθῆσθαι τὰ πεπραγμένα [ὑπονοῶν ἐξ]ωμολόγει, οὕτω τε τῆς σκαιωρίας ἁπάσης ἐς φῶς ἐνεχθείσης, τὴν συκοφαντίαν πεπαῦσθαι ξυνέβη. Ταῦτα δὲ οὐ μόνον ἐς τοὺς νόμους ἀεὶ καὶ καθ᾿ ἑκάστην εἰργάζετο τοὺς Ῥωμαίων,

ϛʹ. Ἀλλὰ καὶ οὓς Ἑβραῖοι τιμῶσι, καταλύειν ὅδε βασιλεὺς ἐν σπουδῇ εἶχεν. Ἦν γάρ ποτε αὐτοῖς ἐπανιὼν ὁ χρόνος τὴν πασχαλίαν ἑορτὴν πρὸ τῶν Χριστιανῶν ἀγαγὼν τύχοι, οὐκ εἴα ταύτην τοὺς Ἰουδαίους καιροῖς τοῖς καθήκουσιν ἄγειν, οὐδέ τι ἐν ταύτῃ δεξιοῦσθαι τῷ θεῷ, ἢ ἐπιτελεῖν τῶν ἐν σφίσιν αὐτοῖς νομίμων. Πολλούς τε αὐτῶν οἱ ἐπὶ τῶν ἀρχῶν τεταγμένοι, ἅτε προβατείων κρεῶν ἐν τούτῳ γευσαμένους τῷ χρόνῳ, τῆς ἐς τὴν πολιτείαν παρανομίας ὑπάγοντες, χρήμασιν ἐζημίουν πολλοῖς. Ἔργα μὲν οὖν καὶ ἄλλα τοιαῦτα Ἰουστινιανοῦ ἀνάριθμα ἐξεπιστάμενος οὐκ ἄν τι ἐνθείην, ἐπεὶ πέρας δοτέον τῷ λόγῳ. Ἀποχρήσει γὰρ καὶ δι᾿ αὐτῶν τὸ τοῦ ἀνθρώπου ἦθος σημῆναι.

COURT OF JUSTINIAN   231

resist the blow dealt by a man of such bodily strength, fell backwards upon the ground, trembling and affrighted. Believing that Longinus had discovered the whole affair, he confessed; and, the whole trick being thus brought to light, the suits were stopped.

Justinian, not content with subverting the laws of the Roman Empire every day, exerted himself in like manner to do away with those of the Jews; for, if Easter came sooner in their calendar than in that of the Christians, he did not allow them to celebrate the Passover on their own proper day or to make their offerings to God, or to perform any of their usual solemnities. The magistrates even inflicted heavy fines upon several of them, upon information that they had eaten the paschal lamb during that time, as if it were an infraction of the laws of the state. Although I could mention countless acts of this nature committed by Justinian, I will not do so, for I must draw my narrative to a close. What I have said will be sufficient to indicate the character of the man.

ΚΕΦΑΛΑΙΟΝ ΚΘ.

α΄. Ὅτι δὲ εἴρων τε καὶ κατάπλαστος ἦν, αὐτίκα δηλώσω. Τὸν Λιβέριον τοῦτον, οὗπερ ἐμνήσθην ἀρτίως, παραλύσας ἧς εἶχεν ἀρχῆς, Ἰωάννην ἀντ᾽ αὐτοῦ κατεστήσατο, Αἰγύπτιον γένος, ἐπίκλησιν Λαξαρίωνα. Ὅπερ ἐπεὶ Πελάγιος ἔγνω, Λιβερίῳ φίλος ἐς τὰ μάλιστα ὤν, τοῦ αὐτοκράτορος ἀνεπυνθάνετο, εἴπερ ὁ ἀμφὶ Λαξαρίωνα λόγος ἀληθὴς εἴη. Καὶ ὃς εὐθὺς ἀπηρνήσατο, μηδὲν πεπραγέναι τοιοῦτο ἀπισχυρισάμενος, γράμματά τε αὐτῷ πρὸς Λιβέριον ἐνεχείρισεν, ἐντελλόμενος βεβαιότατα τῆς ἀρχῆς ἔχεσθαι, καὶ μηδενὶ αὐτῆς τρόπῳ μεθίεσθαι· οὐ γὰρ ταύτης ἐθέλειν ἐν τῷ παρόντι αὐτὸν παραλῦσαι.

β΄. Ἦν δέ τις τῷ Ἰωάννῃ ἐν Βυζαντίῳ θεῖος, Εὐδαίμων ὄνομα, ἔς τε τὸ τῶν ὑπάτων ἀξίωμα ἥκων, καὶ χρήματα περιβεβλημένος πολλά, ἐπίτροπος τέως τῆς βασιλέως οὐσίας

CHAPTER XXIX

I WILL, however, mention two instances of his falsehood and hypocrisy.

After having deprived Liberius (of whom I have spoken above) of his office, he put in his place John, an Egyptian by birth, surnamed Laxarion. When Pelagius, who was a particular friend of Liberius, heard of this, he inquired of Justinian whether what he had heard was true. The Emperor immediately denied it, and protested that he had done nothing of the kind. He then gave Pelagius a letter in which Liberius was ordered to hold fast to his government and by no means to give it up, and added that he had no present intention of removing Liberius. At that time there resided in Byzantium an uncle of John named Eudaemon, a man of consular rank and great wealth, who had the management of the imperial

ΠΡΟΚΟΠΙΟΥ ΑΝΕΚΔΟΤΑ

ἰδίας. Οὗτος Εὐδαίμων, ἐπειδὴ ταῦτ' ἠκηκόει ἅπερ ἐρρήθη, καὶ αὐτὸς βασιλέως ἀνεπυνθάνετο εἰ ἐν βεβαίῳ τῷ ἀδελφιδῷ τὰ τῆς ἀρχῆς εἴη. Ὁ δὲ ὅσα οἱ πρὸς Λιβέριον ἐγέγραπτο ἀρνησάμενος, πρὸς τὸν Ἰωάννην γράμματα γράψας, ἀντιλαβέσθαι τῆς ἀρχῆς δυνάμει τῇ πάσῃ ἐπέστελλεν. Οὐδὲ γὰρ οὐδ' αὐτῷ νεώτερον ἀμφ' αὐτῇ βεβουλεῦσθαι. Οἷπερ ὁ Ἰωάννης ἀναπεισθεὶς, Λιβέριον ἀναχωρεῖν τοῦ τῆς ἀρχῆς καταγωγίου ἅτε αὐτῆς παραλελυμένον ἐκέλευεν. Λιβέριος δὲ αὐτῷ πείθεσθαι οὐδαμῇ ἔφασκεν, ἠγμένος δηλονότι τοῖς βασιλέως καὶ αὐτὸς γράμμασιν. Ὁ μὲν οὖν Ἰωάννης, τούς οἱ ἑπομένους ὁπλίσας, ἐπὶ τὸν Λιβέριον ᾔει· ὁ δὲ ξὺν τοῖς ἀμφ' αὐτὸν εἰς ἀντίστασιν εἶδε. Μάχης τε γενομένης, ἄλλοι τε πολλοὶ πίπτουσι καὶ Ἰωάννης αὐτὸς ὁ τὴν ἀρχὴν ἔχων.

γ'. Εὐδαίμονος οὖν ἰσχυρότατα ἐγκειμένου, μετάπεμπτος εὐθὺς ἐς Βυζάντιον ὁ Λιβέριος ἦν· ἥ τε σύγκλητος βουλὴ τὴν διάγνωσιν ποιουμένη τῶν πεπραγμένων, ἀπεψηφίσατο τοῦ ἀνθρώπου, ἐπεὶ αὐτοῦ οὐκ ἐλθόντος, ἀλλ' ἀμυνομένου τὸ μίασμα ξυνηνέχθη γενέσθαι. Βασιλεὺς μέντοι οὐ πρότερον ἀπέστη, ἕως αὐτὸν ἐζημίωσε χρήματα λάθρα.

COURT OF JUSTINIAN

233

estates. Having been informed of what had taken place, he also inquired of the Emperor whether his nephew was assured in his government. Justinian, saying nothing about his letter to Liberius, sent John positive orders to hold fast to his government, since his views were still the same concerning it. Trusting to this, John ordered Liberius to quit the governor's palace, as having been deprived of his office. Liberius refused, placing equal reliance in the Emperor's despatch. John, having armed his followers, marched against Liberius, who defended himself with his guards. An engagement took place, in which several were slain, and amongst them John, the new governor.

At the earnest entreaty of Eudaemon, Liberius was immediately summoned to Byzantium. The matter was investigated before the senate, and Liberius was acquitted, as being only guilty of justifiable homicide in self-defence. Justinian, however, did not let him escape, until he had forced him to give him a considerable sum of money privately. Such was the

ΠΡΟΚΟΠΙΟΥ ΑΝΕΚΔΟΤΑ

Οὕτω μὲν οὖν Ἰουστινιανὸς ἀληθίζεσθαί τε ἠπίστατο, καὶ εὐθύγλωσσος ἦν.

δ. Ἐγὼ δὲ πάρεργόν τι τοῦδε τοῦ λόγου εἰπεῖν οὐκ ἀπὸ τοῦ καιροῦ οἴομαι εἶναι. Ὁ μὲν γὰρ Εὐδαίμων οὗτος ἐτελεύτησεν οὐ πολλῷ ὕστερον, ξυγγενῶν μέν οἱ ἀπολελειμμένων πολλῶν, οὔτε διαθήκην τινὰ διαθέμενος, οὔτε τι ἄλλο τὸ παράπαν εἰπών. Ὑπὸ χρόνον τε τὸν αὐτὸν καὶ τις ἄρχων γεγονὼς τῶν ἐν παλατίῳ εὐνούχων, ὄνομα Εὐφρατᾶς, ἀπελύθη τοῦ βίου, ἀδελφιδοῦν μὲν ἀπολιπών, οὐδὲν δὲ ἐπὶ τῇ οὐσίᾳ διαθέμενος τῇ αὐτοῦ πολλῇ ἐς ἄγαν οὔσῃ. Ἄμφω δὲ βασιλεὺς τὰς οὐσίας ἀφείλετο, κληρονόμος γεγενημένος αὐτόματος, καὶ οὐδὲ τριώβολόν τινι τῶν νομίμων κληρονόμων προέμενος. Τοσαύτῃ αἰδοῖ ἔς τε τοὺς νόμους καὶ τῶν ἐπιτηδείων τοὺς ξυγγενεῖς ὁ βασιλεὺς οὗτος ἐχρᾶτο. Οὕτως καὶ τὰ Εἰρηναίου, πολλῷ ἔμπροσθεν τελευτήσαντος, δικαίωμα οὐδ' ὁτιοῦν ἐπ' αὐτοῖς ἔχων, ἀφείλετο.

ε. Τούτων δὲ τὸ ἐχόμενον ὑπὸ χρόνον τε τὸν αὐτὸν γεγονὸς οὐκ ἂν σιωπῴην. Ἀνατόλιός τις ἦν, ἐν Ἀσκαλωνιτῶν λευκώματι τὰ

COURT OF JUSTINIAN   234

great respect Justinian showed for the
truth, and such was the faithfulness with
which he kept his promises. I will here
permit myself a brief digression, which
may not be irrelevant. This Eudaemon
died shortly afterwards, leaving behind
him a large number of relatives, but no
will, either written or verbal. About the
same time, the chief eunuch of the court,
named Euphratas, also died intestate; he
left behind him a nephew, who would
naturally have succeeded to his property,
which was considerable. The Emperor
took possession of both fortunes, appointing himself sole heir, not even leaving so
much as a three-obol piece to the legal
inheritors. Such was the respect Justinian showed for the laws and the kinsmen of his intimate friends. In the same
manner, without having the least claim
to it, he seized the fortune of Irenaeus,
who had died some time before.

Another event which took place about
this time I cannot omit. There lived at
Ascalon a man named Anatolius, the most
distinguished member of the senate. His

πρωτεῖα ἔχων. Τούτου τὴν παῖδα γαμετὴν γυναῖκα τῶν τις Καισαρέων πεποίηται, Μαμιλιανὸς ὄνομα, οἰκίας ἐπιφανοῦς ἄγαν. Ἦν δὲ ἡ κόρη ἐπίκληρος, ἐπεὶ μόνης αὐτῆς Ἀνατόλιος ἐγεγόνει πατήρ. Νόμῳ δὲ ἄνωθεν διωρισμένον, ἐπειδὰν βουλευτὴς τῶν τινος πόλεων, οὐκ ἀπολελειμμένων οἱ παῖδων γόνου ἄρρενος, ἐξ ἀνθρώπων ἀφανισθείη, τῶν ἀπολελειμμένων ὑπὸ τούτου χρημάτων τὸ μὲν τεταρτημόριον δίδοσθαι τῷ τῆς πόλεως βουλευτηρίῳ, πάντων δὲ τῶν ἄλλων τοὺς κληρονόμους τοῦ τετελευτηκότος ἀπόνασθαι, γνώρισμα ἤθους τοῦ οἰκείου κἀνταῦθα ὁ αὐτοκράτωρ ἐνδεικνύμενος, νόμον ἔναγχος ἐτύγχανε γράψας, ἔμπαλιν τὰ τοῦ πράγματος διοικούμενον, ὅπως δὴ, ἐπειδὰν βουλευτὴς ἄπαις τελευτῶν γόνου ἄρρενος τῆς οὐσίας οἱ μὲν κληρονόμοι τὸ τέταρτον ἔχοιεν, τἆλλα δὲ πάντα τό τε δημόσιον καὶ τὸ τῆς πόλεως λεύκωμα φέροιντο. Καίτοι οὐδεπώποτε δημόσιον ἢ βασιλεὺς, ἀφ' οὗ γεγόνασιν ἄνθρωποι, χρημάτων βουλευτικῶν μετασχεῖν ἔσχε.

ϛʹ. Τούτου τοίνυν κειμένου τοῦ νόμου, Ἀνατολίῳ μὲν ἐπεγένετο ἡ τέλειος ἡμέρα τοῦ βίου· ἡ δὲ τούτου παῖς τὸν τούτου κλῆρον πρός τε τὸ δημόσιον καὶ τὸ τῆς πόλεως βουλευτήριον κατὰ τὸν νόμον ἐνείματο, καὶ αὐτῇ γράμματα βασιλεύς τε αὐτὸς καὶ Ἀσκαλωνιτῶν οἱ τοῦ λευκώματος ἔγραψαν, τῆς

COURT OF JUSTINIAN 235

daughter, his only child and heiress, was married to a citizen of Caesarea, named Mamilianus, a man of distinguished family. There was an ancient statute which provided that, whenever a senator died without male issue, the fourth part of his estate should go to the senate of the town, and the rest to the heirs-at-law. On this occasion Justinian gave a striking proof of his character. He had recently made a law which reversed this, —that, when a senator died without male issue, the fourth part only should go to the heirs, the three other parts being divided between the senate and the public treasury, although it had never happened before that the estate of any senator had been shared between the public treasury and the Emperor.

Anatolius died while this law was in force. His daughter was preparing to divide her inheritance with the public treasury and the senate of the town in accordance with the law, when she received letters from the senate of Ascalon and from the Emperor himself, in which

περὶ τούτου αὐτὴν ἀφιέντες ἀντιλογίας, ἄτε τὰ σφίσι προσήκοντα κεκομισμένοι ὀρθῶς καὶ δικαίως.

ζ'. Ὕστερον καὶ Μαμιλιανὸς ἀπελύθη τοῦ βίου, ὅσπερ Ἀνατολίῳ κηδεστὴς ἐγεγόνει, παιδός οἱ ἀπολελειμμένης μιᾶς, ἥπερ καὶ τὴν τοῦ πατρὸς οὐσίαν, ὡς τὸ εἰκὸς, ἔσχε. Μετὰ δὲ (καὶ) αὕτη, περιούσης ἔτι οἱ τῆς μητρὸς, ἀφίκετο ἐς τὸ μέτρον τοῦ βίου, ἀνδρὶ μὲν ξυνοικισθεῖσα τῶν λογίμων τινὶ, μήτηρ δὲ οὔτε θήλεος οὔτε ἄρσενος γενομένη γόνου. Ἀλλ' Ἰουστινιανὸς πάντων ἀνελάβετο τῶν χρημάτων εὐθὺς, ἐκεῖνο ἀποφθεγξάμενος τὸ θαυμάσιον, ὡς τὴν Ἀνατολίου παῖδα, γυναῖκα γραῦν οὖσαν, τοῖς τε τοῦ πατρὸς καὶ τοῖς τοῦ ἀνδρὸς πλουτεῖν χρήμασιν οὐχ ὅσιον εἴη. Ὅπως δὲ ἡ γυνὴ μὴ ἐν τοῖς προσαιτηταῖς τὸ ἐνθένδε τετάξεται, στατῆρα χρυσοῦν ἐς ἡμέραν ἑκάστην τὴν γυναῖκα φέρεσθαι ταύτην διώρισεν, ἕως ἂν περιῇ, τοῦτο θέμενος ἐν τοῖς γράμμασι, δι' ὧν τὰ χρήματα ἐληΐσατο ταῦτα· "ὡς τὸν "στατῆρα προεῖται τῆς εὐσεβείας ἕνεκα τοῦτον· "ἔθος γάρ μοι τά τε ὅσια καὶ εὐσεβῆ πράττειν." Ἀλλὰ περὶ τούτων ἀπόχρη λέγειν, ὅπως μὴ ὁ λόγος κατακόρως ἔχοι, ἐπεὶ οὐδὲ ἁπάντων ἀνθρώπῳ γε ὄντι δυνατὸν ἀπομνημονεῦσαι.

η'. Ὅτι δὲ οὐ Βενέτων, τῶν οἱ ἐσπουδασμένων δοκούντων εἶναι, λόγον τινὰ πεποίηται,

COURT OF JUSTINIAN   236

they resigned all claim to the money, as if
they had received their due. Afterwards
Mamilianus (the son-in-law of Anatolius)
died, leaving one daughter, the legal heiress
to his estate. The daughter soon afterwards died, during her mother's lifetime,
after having been married to a person of
distinction, by whom, however, she had
no issue, either male or female. Justinian
then immediately seized the whole estate,
giving utterance to the strange opinion,
that it would be a monstrous thing that
the daughter of Anatolius, in her old age,
should be enriched by the property of
both her husband and father. However,
to keep her from want, he ordered that
she should receive a stater of gold a day,
as long as she lived; and, in the decree
whereby he deprived her of all her property, he declared that he bestowed this
stater upon her for the sake of religion,
seeing that he was always in the habit of
acting with piety and virtue.

I will now show that he cared nothing
even for the Blue faction, which showed
itself devoted to him, when it was a

ΠΡΟΚΟΠΙΟΥ ΑΝΕΚΔΟΤΑ

χρημάτων παρόντων, ἐγὼ δηλώσω. Μαλθάνης τις ἐγεγόνει ἐν Κίλιξι, Λέοντος ἐκείνου γαμβρὸς, ὃς περιεῖπεν, ὥσπερ μοι εἴρηται, τὴν τοῦ καλουμένου ῥαιφερενδαρίου τιμήν. Τοῦτον βίας ἀναστέλλειν ἐπέστελλε τὰς ἐν Κίλιξι. Ταύτης τε τῆς σκήψεως ὁ Μαλθάνης λαβόμενος, ἀνήκεστα κακὰ Κιλίκων τοὺς πλείστους εἰργάζετο, καὶ τὰ χρήματα ληιζόμενος, τὰ μὲν τῷ τυράννῳ ἔπεμπε, τοῖς δὲ αὐτὸς ἐδικαίου πλουτεῖν.

θ'. Οἱ μὲν οὖν ἄλλοι τὰ σφισι παρόντα σιωπῇ ἔφερον· Ταρσέων δὲ ὅσοι Βένετοι ἦσαν, τῇ ἐκ βασιλίδος παρρησίᾳ θαρσοῦντες, ἐν τῷ δημοσίῳ τῆς ἀγορᾶς ἐς τὸν Μαλθάνην, οὐ παρόντα σφίσι, πολλὰ ὕβριζον. Ὅπερ ἐπεὶ ὁ Μαλθάνης ἔγνω, πλῆθος στρατιωτῶν ἐπαγόμενος, ἐς Ταρσὸν εὐθὺς ἀφίκετο νύκτωρ· περιπέμπων τε τοὺς στρατιώτας ἐς τὰς οἰκίας, ὄρθρου βαθέος καταλύειν ἐκέλευεν. Ἔφοδον δὲ οἰόμενοι ταύτην οἱ Βένετοι εἶναι, ἐκ τῶν παρόντων ἠμύνοντο. Ξυνέβη τοίνυν ἄλλα τε

COURT OF JUSTINIAN   237

question of money. There was amongst
the Cilicians a certain Malthanes, the
son-in-law of that Leo who had held the
office of "Referendary," whom Justinian
commissioned to put down seditious
movements in the country. On this pretext, Malthanes treated most of the inhabitants with great cruelty.. He robbed
them of their wealth, sent part to the
Emperor, and claimed the rest for himself. Some endured their grievances in
silence; but the inhabitants of Tarsus
who belonged to the Blue faction, con-
fident of the protection of the Empress,
assembled in the market-place and abused
Malthanes, who at the time was not
present. When he heard of it, he
immediately set out with a body of
soldiers, reached Tarsus by night, sent
his soldiers into the houses at daybreak,
and ordered them to put the inhabitants
to death. The Blues, imagining that it
was an attack from a foreign foe, defended
themselves as best they could. During
the dark, amongst other misfortunes, Da-
mianus, a member of the senate and

κακὰ ἐν σκότῳ γενέσθαι, καὶ Δαμιανὸν, ἄνδρα ἐκ βουλῆς, τοξεύματι βληθέντα πεσεῖν.

ι΄. Ἦν δὲ ὁ Δαμιανὸς οὗτος τῶν τῇδε Βενέτων προστάτης. Ὅπερ ἐπεὶ ἐς Βυζάντιον ἦλθεν, οἵ τε Βένετοι δυσφορούμενοι, θορύβῳ ἀνὰ τὴν πόλιν πολλῷ εἴχοντο, καὶ βασιλέα μὲν ἀμφὶ τῷ πράγματι ἠνώχλουν ἄγαν, Λέοντα δὲ καὶ τὸν Μαλθάνην δεινοτάταις ἀπειλαῖς πολλὰ ἐδυσφήμουν. Καὶ αὐτοκράτωρ οὐδέν τι ἧσσον ἀγριαίνεσθαι ἐπὶ τοῖς πεπραγμένοις ἐσκήπτετο. Γράμμα μὲν οὖν εὐθὺς ἔγραψε, ζήτησίν τε καὶ τίσιν τῶν τῷ Μαλθάνῃ πεπολιτευμένων κελεύων γενέσθαι. Ἀλλὰ Λέων αὐτῷ χρυσίου προέμενος πλῆθος, τοῦ τε μώμου αὐτίκα, καὶ τῆς εἰς τοὺς Βενέτους στοργῆς ἔπαυσε.

ια΄. Τοῦ τε πράγματος ἀνεξετάστου μεμενηκότος, Μαλθάνην βασιλεὺς ἐς Βυζάντιον παρ᾽ αὐτὸν ἥκοντα ξύν τε πολλῇ φιλοφροσύνῃ εἶδε καὶ ἐν τιμῇ ἔσχεν. Ἐξιόντα δὲ οἱ Βένετοι ἐκ βασιλέως τηρήσαντες, πληγὰς αὐτῷ προσετρίψαντο ἐν παλατίῳ. (Καὶ) διαχρήσασθαι ἔμελλον, εἰ μὴ τῶν τινες διεκώλυσαν, οἵ γε πρὸς Λέοντος χρήματα ἤδη κεκομισμένοι λάθρα ἐτύγχανον. Καίτοι τίς οὐκ ἂν ταύτην τὴν

COURT OF JUSTINIAN 238

president of the Blues in Tarsus, was slain by an arrow.

When the news reached Byzantium, the Blues assembled in the streets with loud murmurs of indignation, and bitterly complained to the Emperor of the affair, uttering the most violent threats against Leo and Malthanes. The Emperor pretended to be as enraged as they were, and immediately ordered an inquiry to be made into the conduct of the latter. But Leo, by the present of a considerable sum of money, appeased him, so that the process was stopped, and the Emperor ceased to show favour to the Blues. Although the affair remained uninvestigated, the Emperor received Malthanes, who came to Byzantium to pay his respects, with great kindness and treated him with honour. But, as he was leaving the Emperor's presence, the Blues, who had been on the watch, attacked him in the palace, and would certainly have slain him, had not some of their own party, bribed by Leo, prevented them. Who would not consider that state to be in

ΠΡΟΚΟΠΙΟΥ ΑΝΕΚΔΟΤΑ

πολιτείαν ἐλεεινοτάτην καλοίη, ἐν ᾗ βασιλεὺς μὲν δωροδοκήσας, ἀνεξέταστα κατέλειψε τὰ ἐγκλήματα· στασιῶται δὲ, βασιλέως ἐν παλατίῳ ὄντος, ἐπαναστῆναι τῶν τινι ἀρχόντων οὐδεμιᾷ ὀκνήσει ἐτόλμησαν, ἀδίκων τε χειρῶν ἐπ' αὐτὸν ἄρξαι; τίσις μέντοι τούτων δὴ ἕνεκα οὐδεμία οὔτε εἰς τὸν Μαλθάνην ἐγένετο, οὔτε εἰς τοὺς αὐτῷ ἐπαναστάντας. Ἐκ τούτων δὲ, εἴ τις βούλοιτο, τὸ Ἰουστινιανοῦ τοῦ βασιλέως τεκμηριούσθω ἦθος.

COURT OF JUSTINIAN 239

a most pitiable condition, in which the sovereign allows himself to be bribed to leave charges uninvestigated, and in which malcontents venture without hesitation to attack one of the magistrates within the precincts of the palace, and to lay violent hands upon him? However, no punishment was inflicted either upon Malthanes or his assailants, which is a sufficient proof of the character of Justinian.

ΚΕΦΑΛΑΙΟΝ Λ'.

α'. Εἰ δέ τινα καὶ τοῦ τῆς πολιτείας ξυμφόρου ποιεῖται λόγον, τὰ ἐς δρόμον τε αὐτῷ τὸν δημόσιον καὶ τοὺς κατασκόπους εἰργασμένα δηλώσει. Οἱ μὲν γὰρ Ῥωμαίων αὐτοκράτορες ἐν τοῖς ἄνω χρόνοις γεγενημένοι, προνοήσαντες ὅπως ἅπαντά τε σφίσιν ἐπαγγέλλοιντο τάχιστα καὶ μηδεμιᾷ διδῷτο μελλήσει, τά τε πρὸς τῶν πολεμίων ἐν χώρᾳ ἑκάστῃ ξυμπίπτοντα, καὶ ταῖς πόλεσι κατὰ στάσιν ἢ ἄλλο τι ἀπρόσπτον συμβαίνοντα πάθος, τά τε πρὸς τῶν ἀρχόντων καὶ τῶν ἄλλων ἁπάντων πανταχόθι πρασσόμενα τῆς Ῥωμαίων ἀρχῆς, ὅπως τε οἱ τοὺς φόρους παραπέμποντες τοὺς ἐπετείους· διασώζοιντο βραδυτῆτός τε καὶ κινδύνου χωρὶς, δημόσιον ὀξύν τινα πανταχόσε πεποίηνται δρόμον τρόπῳ τοιῷδε. Ἐς ἡμέρας ὁδὸν εὐζώνῳ ἀνδρὶ σταθμοὺς κατεστήσαντο, πῇ μὲν ὀκτὼ, πῇ δὲ τούτων ἐλάσσους, οὐ μέντοι ἧσσον ἐκ τοῦ ἐπὶ πλεῖστον ἢ κατὰ πέντε. Ἵπποι δὲ ἵσταντο ἐς τεσσαράκοντα ἐν σταθμῷ ἑκάστῳ. Ἱπποκόμοι δὲ κατὰ λόγον τοῦ τῶν ἵππων μέτρου ἐτετάχατο ἐν πᾶσι σταθμοῖς. Συχναῖς δὲ ἵππων δοκιμω-

CHAPTER XXX

His regulations as to the public "posts" and "spies" will show how much he cared for the interests of the state. The earlier Emperors, in order to gain the most speedy information concerning the movements of the enemy in each territory, seditions or unforeseen accidents in individual towns, and the actions of the governors and other officials in all parts of the Empire, and also in order that those who conveyed the yearly tribute might do so without danger or delay, had established a rapid service of public couriers according to the following system:—As a day's journey for an active man, they settled eight stages, sometimes fewer, but never less than five. There were forty horses in each stage and a number of grooms in proportion. The couriers who were intrusted with this

ΠΡΟΚΟΠΙΟΥ ΑΝΕΚΔΟΤΑ

τάτων ὄντων διαδοχαῖς ἐλαύνοντες ἀεὶ οἶσπερ ἐπίκειται τὸ ἔργον τοῦτο, δέκα τε, ἂν οὕτω τύχοι, ὁδὸν ἡμερῶν ἀμείβοντες ἐν ἡμέρᾳ μιᾷ ἔπρασσον ἅπαντα ὅσα μοι ἀρτίως δεδήλωται, πρὸς δὲ καὶ οἱ τῶν χωρίων πανταχῇ κύριοι, ἄλλως τε καὶ ἐν μεσογείοις τὰ χωρία ταῦτα ἐτύγχανεν, εὐδαιμονέστατοι ἐπ᾽ αὐτοῖς ἐν τοῖς μάλιστα ἦσαν. Τοὺς γὰρ ὄντας ἐκ τοῦ περιόντος σφίσι καρποὺς, ἵππων καὶ ἱπποκόμων τροφῆς ἕνεκα, τῷ δημοσίῳ ἀνὰ πᾶν ἔτος ἀποδιδόμενοι, χρήματα μεγάλα ἐφέροντο. Ξυνέβαινέ τε διὰ ταῦτα τῷ δημοσίῳ δέχεσθαι μὲν ἀεὶ τοὺς ἐγκειμένους ἑκάστῳ φόρους, ἀντιπαρέχεσθαι δὲ αὐτοὺς τοῖς ἐσκομίζουσιν αὐτίκα δὴ μάλα, καὶ προσῆν τὸ γεγενῆσθαι τῇ πολιτείᾳ τὰ δέοντα. Τὰ μὲν οὖν πρότερα ταύτῃ πῃ εἶχεν.

β΄. Ὁ δὲ αὐτοκράτωρ οὗτος πρῶτα μὲν τὸν ἐκ Καλχηδόνος ἄχρι ἐς Δακίβιζαν καθελὼν δρόμον, ἠνάγκασε πάντας ἐκ Βυζαντίου εὐθὺς ἄχρι ἐς τὴν Ἑλενούπολιν οὔτι ἐθελουσίους ναυτίλλεσθαι. Πλέοντες οὖν ἐν ἀκάτοις βραχείαις τισὶν, οἵαις διαπορθμεύεσθαι τῇδε εἰώθασι, χειμῶνος, ἂν οὕτω τύχοι, ἐπιπε-

COURT OF JUSTINIAN 241

duty, by making use of relays of excellent horses, frequently covered as much ground in one day by this means as they would otherwise have covered in ten, when carrying out the above commissions. In addition, the landed proprietors in each country, especially those whose estates were in the interior, reaped great benefit from these posts; for, by selling their surplus corn and fruit every year to the state for the support of the horses and grooms, they gained considerable revenue. By this means the state received, without interruption, the tribute due from each, and, in turn, reimbursed those who furnished it, and thus everything was to the advantage of the state. Such was the old system. But Justinian, having commenced by suppressing the post between Chalcedon and Dakibiza, compelled the couriers to carry all despatches from Byzantium to Helenopolis by sea. They unwillingly obeyed; for, being obliged to embark upon small skiffs, such as were generally used for crossing the strait, they ran great risk of being shipwrecked, if

σόντος, ἐπὶ μέγα κινδύνου χωροῦσι. Τῆς γὰρ ἀναγκαίου σπουδῆς ἐγκειμένης σφίσι, καιροφυλακεῖν τε καὶ προσδέχεσθαι μέλλουσαν τὴν γαλήνην ἀδύνατά ἐστιν. Ἔπειτα δὲ κατὰ μὲν τὴν ἐπὶ Πέρσας ὁδὸν φέρουσαν τὸν δρόμον ἐπὶ σχήματος τοῦ πρόσθεν οὕτως εἴασεν εἶναι, ἐς δὲ τὴν λοιπὴν ξύμπασαν ἕω μέχρι ἐς Αἴγυπτον ἐν ἡμέρας ὁδῷ κατάσταθμον ἕνα κατεστήσατο μόνον, οὐχ ἵππων μέντοι, ἀλλ' ὄνων ὀλίγων. Διὸ δὴ τὰ ξυμβαίνοντα ἐν χώρᾳ ἑκάστῃ μόλις τε καὶ ὀψὲ τοῦ καιροῦ καὶ ὀπίσω τῶν πραγμάτων εἰσαγγελλόμενα ἐπικουρίας οὐδεμιᾶς τυγχάνειν εἰκός, οἱ δὲ τοὺς ἀγροὺς κεκτημένοι καρπῶν τῶν σφετέρων σεσηπότων τε καὶ εἰκῇ κειμένων ἀνόνητοι ἐς ἀεὶ γίνονται.

γ'. Τὰ δὲ τῶν κατασκόπων τοιαῦτά ἐστιν. Ἄνδρες πολλοὶ ἐν δημοσίῳ τὸ ἀνέκαθεν ἐσιτίζοντο, οἳ δὴ ἐς τοὺς πολεμίους ἰόντες, ἔν τε τοῖς Περσῶν βασιλείοις γινόμενοι, ἐμπορίας ὀνόματι, ἢ τρόπῳ ἑτέρῳ, ἔς τε τὸ ἀκριβὲς διερευνώμενοι ἕκαστα, ἐπανήκοντες ἐς Ῥωμαίων

COURT OF JUSTINIAN 242

they met with stormy weather. For, since great speed was enjoined upon them, they were unable to wait for a favourable opportunity for putting out to sea, when the weather was calm. It is true that he maintained the primitive system on the road to Persia, but for the rest of the East, as far as Egypt, he reduced the number of posts to one, for a day's journey, and substituted a few asses for the horses, so that the report of what was taking place in each district only reached Byzantium with difficulty and long after the events had occurred, when it was too late to apply any remedy; and, on the other hand, the owners of estates found no benefit from their products, which were either spoilt or lay idle.

The spies were organized in the following manner :—A number of men used to be supported at the state's expense, whose business it was to visit hostile countries, especially the court of Persia, on pretence of business or some other excuse, and to observe accurately what was going on; and by this means, on

243 ΠΡΟΚΟΠΙΟΥ ΑΝΕΚΔΟΤΑ

τὴν γῆν, πάντα τοῖς ἄρχουσιν ἐπαγγέλλειν ἠδύναντο τὰ τῶν πολεμίων ἀπόρρητα. Οἱ δὲ προύμαθον ἐφύλασσόν τε καὶ ἀπρόοπτον οὐδὲν ξυνέπιπτε σφίσι. Τοῦτο δὲ τὸ χρῆμα κἄν τοῖς Μήδοις ἐκ παλαιοῦ ***. Χοσρόης μὲν οὖν μείζους, ὥσπερ φασὶ, πεποιημένος τὰς πρὸς τῶν κατασκόπων συντάξεις, προμηθείας τῆς ἐνθένδε ἀπήλαυσεν. Οὐδὲν γὰρ αὐτὸς τῶν κατασκόπων ὄνομα ἐξέτριψεν ἐκ Ῥωμαίων τῆς γῆς, ἐξ οὗ δὴ ἄλλα τε πολλὰ ἡμαρτήθη καὶ Λαζικὴ πρὸς τῶν πολεμίων ἑάλω, Ῥωμαίων οὐδαμῆ πεπυσμένων ὅποι ποτὲ γῆς ὁ Περσῶν βασιλεὺς ξὺν τῷ στρατῷ εἴη.

δ΄. Ἀλλὰ καὶ καμήλους παμπληθεῖς τὸ δημόσιον ἐκ παλαιοῦ τρέφειν εἰώθει, αἳ δὴ τῷ Ῥωμαίων στρατῷ ἐπὶ πολεμίους ἰόντι ἅπαντα φέρουσαι τὰ ἐπιτήδεια εἵποντο. Καὶ οὔτε τοῖς γεωργοῖς τότε ἀγγαροφορεῖν ἐπάναγκες ἦν, οὔτε τι ἐνδεῖν τοῖς στρατιώταις τῶν ἀναγκαίων ξυνέβαινεν, ἀλλὰ καὶ ταύτας περιεῖλεν Ἰουστινιανὸς σχεδόν τι ἀπάσας. Διὸ δὴ ἐπὶ τοὺς πολεμίους ἰόντος τὰ νῦν τοῦ Ῥωμαίων στρατοῦ γεγενῆσθαί τι τῶν δεόντων ἀδύνατον. Τὰ μὲν οὖν σπουδαιότατα τῇ πολιτείᾳ ἐπεφέρετο τῇδε.

COURT OF JUSTINIAN 243

their return, they were able to report to the Emperors all the secret plans of their enemies, and the former, being warned in advance, took precautions and were never surprised. This system had long been in vogue amongst the Medes. Chosroes, by giving larger salaries to his spies, none of whom were born Romans, reaped great benefit from this precaution. Justinian, having discontinued this practice, lost considerable territory, especially the country of the Lazes, which was taken by the enemy, since the Romans had no information where the King and his army were. The state also formerly kept a large number of camels, which carried the baggage on the occasion of an expedition into an hostile country. By this means the peasants were relieved from the necessity of carrying burdens, and the soldiers were well supplied with necessaries. Justinian, however, did away with nearly all the camels, so that, when the army is marching against an enemy, everything is in an unsatisfactory condition. Such was the care he took of

244 ΠΡΟΚΟΠΙΟΥ ΑΝΕΚΔΟΤΑ

ε΄. Οὐδὲν δὲ οἷον καί τινος αὐτοῦ τῶν γελοίων ἐπιμνησθῆναι. Τῶν ἐν Καισαρείᾳ ῥητόρων Εὐαγγέλιός τις ἦν, οὐκ ἄσημος ἀνήρ, ὅσπερ ἐπιφόρου τοῦ τῆς τύχης πνεύματος γενομένου, χρημάτων τε ἄλλων καὶ χώρας πολλῆς κύριος γέγονεν. Ὕστερον δὲ καὶ κώμην ἐπιθαλασσίαν, Πορφυρεῶνα ὄνομα, τριῶν χρυσίων κεντηναρίων ἐπρίατο. Ταῦτα μαθὼν Ἰουστινιανὸς βασιλεὺς ἀφείλετο αὐτῷ τὸ χωρίον εὐθὺς, ὀλίγην τινὰ τοῦ τιμήματος προέμενος μοῖραν, καὶ τοῦτο ἀποφθεγξάμενος, ὡς Εὐαγγελίῳ ῥήτορι ὄντι οὐ μήποτε εὐπρεπὲς εἴη κώμης τοιαύτης κυρίῳ εἶναι. Ἀλλὰ περὶ μὲν τούτων ἀμηγέπη αὐτῶν ἐπιμνησθέντες παυσόμεθα λέγειν.

ϛ΄. Τῶν δὲ πρός τε Ἰουστινιανοῦ καὶ Θεοδώρας νεοχμηθέντων καὶ ταῦτά ἐστι. Πάλαι μὲν ἡ σύγκλητος βουλὴ παρὰ βασιλεῖ ἰοῦσα τρόπῳ τοιῷδε προσκυνεῖν ἠβούλοντο. Πατρίκιος μέν τις ἀνὴρ παρὰ μαζὸν αὐτοῦ προσεκύνει τὸν δεξιόν. Βασιλεὺς δὲ αὐτοῦ καταφιλήσας τὴν κεφαλὴν, ἐξῄει· οἱ δὲ λοιποὶ ἅπαντες γόνυ κλίναντες βασιλεῖ τὸ δεξιόν, ἀπηλλάσσοντο. Βασιλίδα μέντοι προσκυνεῖν

COURT OF JUSTINIAN   244

the most important state institutions. It will not be out of place to mention one of his ridiculous acts. There was at Caesarea a lawyer named Evangelius, a person of distinction, who, by the favour of fortune, had amassed great riches and considerable landed estates. He afterwards purchased, for three centenars of gold, a village on the coast named Porphyreon. When Justinian heard of this, he immediately took it from him, only returning him a small portion of the price he had paid for it, at the same time declaring that it was unseemly that such a village should belong to Evangelius the lawyer. But enough of this. It remains to speak of certain innovations introduced by Justinian and Theodora. Formerly, when the senate had audience of the Emperor, it paid him homage in the following manner :—Every patrician kissed him on the right breast, and the Emperor, having kissed him on the head, dismissed him ; all the rest bent the right knee before the Emperor and retired. As for the Empress, it was not

245 ΠΡΟΚΟΠΙΟΥ ΑΝΕΚΔΟΤΑ

οὐδαμῆ εἴθιστο. Παρὰ δὲ Ἰουστινιανόν τε καὶ Θεοδώραν τὰς εἰσόδους ποιούμενοι, οἵ τε ἄλλοι ἅπαντες, καὶ ὅσοι τὸ πατρικίων ἀξίωμα εἶχον, ἔπιπτον μὲν εἰς τὸ ἔδαφος εὐθὺς ἐπὶ στόμα, χειρῶν δὲ καὶ ποδῶν ἐς ἄγαν τετανυσμένων, τῷ χείλει ποδὸς ἑκατέρου ἀψάμενοι, ἐξανίσταντο. Οὐδὲ γὰρ ἡ Θεοδώρα τὴν ἀξίωσιν ἀνεδύετο ταύτην· ἢ δὲ καὶ τοὺς πρέσβεις προίεσθαι Περσῶν τε καὶ τῶν ἄλλων βαρβάρων, χρήμασί τε αὐτοὺς δωρεῖσθαι, ὥσπερ ὑπ' αὐτῇ κειμένης τῆς Ῥωμαίων ἀρχῆς, οὐδαμῆ ἀπηξίου, πρᾶγμα οὐ πώποτε γεγονὸς ἐκ τοῦ παντὸς χρόνου.

ζ΄. Καὶ πάλαι μὲν οἱ τῷ βασιλεῖ ξυγγενόμενοι αὐτόν τε βασιλέα καὶ τὴν γυναῖκα βασιλίδα ἐκάλουν, ἀρχόντων δε τῶν λοιπῶν ἕκαστον, ὅπη αὐτῷ ἀξιώματος περὶ τάδε ἔχει. Ἦν δέ τις τούτων ὁποτέρῳ ἐς λόγους συμμίξας, βασιλέως ἢ βασιλίδος ἐπιμνησθείη, ἀλλ' οὐ δεσπότην τε ἀποκαλοίη καὶ δέσποιναν, ἢ καὶ μὴ δούλους τῶν τινας ἀρχόντων πειρῷτο ὀνομάζειν, τοσοῦτον ὅδε ἀμαθὴς καὶ τὴν γλῶσσαν ἀκόλαστος ἐδόκει εἶναι, καὶ ἅτε ἡμαρτηκὼς τὰ πικρότατα καὶ ὑβρίσας ἐς οὓς ἥκιστα ἐχρῆν, ἐνθένδε ἀπήει.

η΄. Καὶ τὰ πρότερα μὲν ὀλίγοι τε καὶ

COURT OF JUSTINIAN 245

customary to do homage to her. But those who were admitted to the presence of this royal pair, even those of patrician rank, were obliged to prostrate themselves upon their face, with hands and feet stretched out ; and, after having kissed both his feet, they rose up and withdrew. Nor did Theodora refuse this honour. She received the ambassadors of the Persians and other barbarian nations and (a thing which had never been done before) bestowed magnificent presents upon them, as if she had been absolute mistress of the Empire. Formerly, those who associated with the Emperor called him Imperator and the Empress Imperatrix, and the other officials according to their rank. But if anyone addressed either Justinian or Theodora without the addition of the title Sovereign Lord or Sovereign Lady, or without calling himself their slave, he was looked upon as ignorant and insolent in his language, and, as if he had committed a very grave offence and insulted those whom it least became him, he was dismissed. Formerly,

246 ΠΡΟΚΟΠΙΟΥ ΑΝΕΚΔΟΤΑ

μόλις ἐν βασιλείοις ἐγίνοντο· ἐξ ὅτου δὲ οὗτοι
τὴν βασιλείαν παρέλαβον, ἄρχοντες ὁμοῦ καὶ
λοιποὶ ξύμπαντες ἐν παλατίῳ ἐνδελεχέστατα
διατριβὴν εἶχον. Αἴτιον δέ, ὅτι πάλαι μὲν
ταῖς ἀρχαῖς τά τε δίκαια καὶ νόμιμα πράσσειν
γνώμῃ αὐτονόμῳ ἐξῆν. Οἵ τε οὖν ἄρχοντες
διοικούμενοι τὰ εἰωθότα, ἐν τοῖς καταγωγίοις
τοῖς αὑτῶν ἔμενον, οἵ τε ἀρχόμενοι βίαιον
οὐδὲν οὔτε ὁρῶντες, οὔτε ἀκούοντες, βασιλεῖ,
ὡς τὸ εἰκὸς, ὀλίγα ἠνώχλουν. Οὗτοι δὲ ἄπαντα
ἐπὶ πονηρῷ τῶν κατηκόων ἐφ᾽ ἑαυτοὺς ἐς ἀεὶ
ἕλκοντες, ἅπαντας σφίσι δουλοπρεπέστατα
προσεδρεύειν ἠνάγκαζον. Ἦν δὲ ἰδεῖν εἰς
ἡμέραν σχεδόν τι ἑκάστην τὰ μὲν δικαστήρια
πάντα ἐκ τῆς ἐπιπλεῖστον ἀνδρῶν ἔρημα, ἐν
δὲ τῇ τοῦ βασιλέως αὐλῇ ὄχλον τε καὶ ὕβριν,
καὶ ὠθισμὸν μέγαν, καὶ δουλοπρέπειαν ἐς ἀεὶ
ξύμπασαν.

θ΄. Οἵ τε αὐτοῖν ἐπιτήδειοι δοκοῦντες,
τήν τε ἡμέραν διηνεκῶς πᾶσαν καὶ τῆς νυκτὸς
ἐς ἀεὶ πολλήν τινα μοῖραν ἐνταῦθα ἑστῶτες,
ἄϋπνοί τε καὶ ἀπόσιτοι παρὰ καιροὺς τοὺς

COURT OF JUSTINIAN   246

only a few were granted admission to the palace, and that with difficulty; but, from the time of the accession of Justinian and Theodora, the magistrates and all other persons were continually in the palace. The reason was, that formerly the magistrates freely administered justice and laws independently, and executed the customary sentences at their own residences, and the subjects, seeing and hearing that no injustice would be done to them, had little reason to trouble the Emperor. But this pair, taking control of all business to themselves in order that they might ruin their subjects, forced them to humiliate themselves before them in a most servile manner. Thus the courts of justice were empty nearly every day, and hardly a person was to be seen in them, while in the palace there were crowds of men pushing and abusing one another, all endeavouring to be foremost in showing their servility. Those who were on the most intimate terms with the Imperial pair remained the whole day and a great part of the night, without food or sleep, until they

ΠΡΟΚΟΠΙΟΥ ΑΝΕΚΔΟΤΑ

εἰωθότας γενόμενοι διεφθείροντο, ἐς τοῦτό τε αὐτοῖς τὴν δοκοῦσαν εὐδαιμονίαν ἀποκεκρίσθαι ξυνέπεσε. Τούτων μέντοι ἀφειμένοι πάντων, διεμάχοντο πρὸς ἀλλήλους ἄνθρωποι, ὅποι ποτὲ Ῥωμαίων τὰ χρήματα εἴη. Οἱ μὲν γὰρ ἰσχυρίζοντο ἐν βαρβάροις ἅπαντα εἶναι· οἱ δὲ βασιλέα ἔφασκον ἐν οἰκίσκοις πολλοῖς καθείρξαντα ἔχειν. Ὁπηνίκα οὖν ἡ ἄνθρωπος ὢν Ἰουστινιανὸς ἀπέλθῃ τοῦ βίου, ἢ ἅτε τῶν δαιμόνων ἄρχων ἀπολύσῃ τὸν βίον, ὅσοι τηνικάδε περιόντες τύχωσι, τἀληθὲς εἴσονται.

COURT OF JUSTINIAN 247

were worn out, and this apparent good fortune was their only reward. Others, who were free from all these cares and anxieties, were puzzled to think what had become of the wealth and treasures of the Empire. Some declared that it had all fallen into the hands of the barbarians, while others asserted that the Emperor kept it locked up in secret hiding-places of his own. When Justinian—whether he be man or devil—shall have departed this life, those who are then living will be able to learn the truth.

Lightning Source UK Ltd.
Milton Keynes UK
UKHW011949120820
368137UK00001B/124